THE INTERNATIONA
SOCIAL IMPACT ASSESSMENT

To our children and grandchildren
so that they might live in a better world

The International Handbook of Social Impact Assessment

Conceptual and Methodological Advances

Edited by

Henk A. Becker and Frank Vanclay

Edward Elgar
Cheltenham, UK • Northampton, MA, USA

Published by
Edward Elgar Publishing Limited
Glensanda House
Montpellier Parade
Cheltenham
Glos GL50 1UA
UK

Edward Elgar Publishing, Inc.
William Pratt House
9 Dewey Court
Northampton
Massachusetts 01060
USA

Paperback edition 2006
Reprinted 2008

A catalogue record for this book
is available from the British Library

Library of Congress Cataloguing in Publication Data
The International handbook of social impact assessment: conceptual and
  methodological advances / edited by Henk A. Becker, Frank Vanclay.
      p. cm.
    Includes bibliographical references and index.
    1. Social planning – Evaluation – Handbooks, manuals, etc. 2. Social
  policy – Evaluation – Handbooks, manuals, etc. 3. Community
  development – Evaluation – Handbooks, manuals, etc. 4. Evaluation research
  (Social action programs) – Handbooks, manuals, etc. I. Title: Social impact
  assessment: conceptual and methodological advances. II. Becker, H. A.
  III. Vanclay, Frank.
HN28.I493 2003
361.2'5–dc21   2003048852

ISBN 978 1 84064 935 2 (cased)
      978 1 84720 105 8 (paperback)

Printed and bound in Great Britain by Biddles Ltd, King's Lynn, Norfolk

Contents

Figures

Tables

Boxes

Preface and acknowledgments

Social impact assessment (SIA) is a developing field of practice. However, unlike environmental impact assessment (EIA), SIA is not bound by a regulatory context which defines this practice. This is both a blessing and a curse. It is a blessing in that SIA is not limited to technical practice, but it is a curse in that it is hard to determine the boundaries to SIA. Whereas Becker defines SIA as 'the process of identifying the future consequences of a current or proposed action which are related to individuals, organizations and social macro-systems', Vanclay seeks to broaden this definition to 'the process of analysing and managing the intended and unintended consequences of planned interventions on people so as to bring about a more sustainable and equitable biophysical and human environment'. This difference in definition is typical of the debates that occur in this *International Handbook*.

The International Association for Impact Assessment (IAIA) is the home where most of the debates in this book have been nurtured. IAIA was founded in 1981 and has developed as *the* forum for discussion on impact assessment, and is the leading global authority on best practice in environmental assessment, management and policy. Its website (www.iaia.org) provides useful information and further details. We owe a considerable debt to IAIA for facilitating intellectual inspiration in the field of impact assessment.

An endeavour such as this also owes gratitude to many individuals. Most significantly, Annelies Stolp, Wieger Bakker and Alan Porter provided general guidance and a mentoring role. Fred Vanclay (Frank's father) provided an important proof-reading role and an intelligent lay-person critique of all chapters. However, not all his recommendations were necessarily accepted, as the disciplinary expectations of authors and editors sometimes outweighed the common-sense advice of an intelligent reader! Remaining errors and oddities are therefore the responsibility of the editors and authors.

As an international collaboration, Frank Vanclay made several visits to The Netherlands for discussions with Henk Becker and other contributors. The Nauta family of Woudenberg graciously provided accommodation on many of these visits to The Netherlands.

Finally, endeavours such as these tend to take longer than expected, for various reasons. We are especially grateful to our contributors who adhered to our sometimes unrealistic deadlines, and we apologize for the delays that inevitably occurred. We also thank our publishers Edward Elgar, especially Francine O'Sullivan, for their patience, understanding and support.

Henk Becker and Frank Vanclay
(Doorn, The Netherlands) (Hobart, Australia)
April 2003

Abbreviations

ADR	alternative dispute resolution
AIDS	acquired immune deficiency syndrome
CBA	cost–benefit analysis
CBO	community-based organization
CIA	cultural impact assessment
CLAM	Community Land Assessment and Monitoring Programme
CLC	community liaison committee
COMPRAM	Complex Problem Handling method
CPR	common property resource
CVA	citizen values assessment
CVP	citizen values profile
DALYs	disability-adjusted life years
DHHL	Department of Hawaiian Home Lands
EIA	environmental impact assessment
EIS	environmental impact statement
EMP	environmental management plan
EMS	environmental management system
ENGO	environmental organization
EPA	Environmental Protection Agency (usually of the USA)
ESD	ecologically sustainable development
EU	European Union
FAO	Food and Agriculture Organization (of the United Nations)
FMA	forest management areas
GDP	gross domestic product
GIS	geographic information system
GMO	genetically modified organism
GNP	gross national product
GPS	global positioning system
HIA	health impact assessment
HIV	human immunodeficiency virus
IAIA	International Association for Impact Assessment
IAPs	interested and affected parties
ICT	information and communication technology
IMF	International Monetary Fund
IP	intellectual property

ISO14000	The environmental management standard of the International Organization for Standardization
ITK	indigenous technical knowledge (or local knowledge)
IUCN	World Conservation Union (previously the International Union for the Conservation of Nature)
MCA	multi-criteria analysis
MDB	multilateral development bank
MHW	Model of Hawaiian Wellbeing
MPA	marine protected areas
NAFTA	North American Free Trade Agreement
NATO	North Atlantic Treaty Organization
NEPA	National Environmental Policy Act (of the USA)
NGO	non-governmental organization
NIMBY	not in my backyard
NNCC	Nyae Nyae Farmer's Conservancy Committee
NNFC	Nyae Nyae Farmer's Cooperative
NRM	natural resource management
OECD	Organisation for Economic Cooperation and Development
PAPs	project-affected peoples
PI	public involvement
PRA	participatory rural appraisal
PUC	Public Utilities Commission
QALYs	quality-adjusted life years
RMA	Resource Management Act
RRA	rapid rural appraisal
SEA	strategic environmental assessment
SIA	social impact assessment
SoE	state of the environment
SPA	strategic perspectives analysis
SSP	Sardar Sarovar Project
TFW	Timber–Fish–Wildlife Agreement
ToR	terms of reference
TRC-Analysis	town resource cluster analysis
UNAIDS	United Nations Programme on HIV/AIDS
UNCED	United Nations Conference on Environment and Development (or Earth Summit which was held in Rio de Janeiro in 1992)
UNDP	United Nations Development Programme
UNEP	United Nations Environment Programme
UNESCO	United Nations Educational, Scientific and Cultural Organization

WCD	World Commission on Dams
WCED	World Commission on Environment and Development (sometimes called the Brundtland Commission)
WHO	World Health Organization
WSSD	World Summit on Sustainable Development (or Rio +10, held in Johannesburg in 2002)
WTO	World Trade Organization

Editors

Henk Becker has been Professor of Sociology at Utrecht University in The Netherlands. His current work involves consulting research relating to SIA for industry, and research on the theory of generations. He is author of eight books, including *Social Impact Assessment* (1997) and several books in Dutch on the theory of generations. He is a co-editor of *What has Sociology Achieved?* (1990). In addition, he has published over 100 book chapters and scientific articles in English, German, Dutch and French. He is a former President of the International Association for Impact Assessment (IAIA) and was awarded the IAIA Rose-Hulman Award in 2001.
E-mail: h.becker@hetnet.nl

Frank Vanclay is a Professorial Fellow in Rural Sociology at the Tasmanian Institute of Agricultural Research at the University of Tasmania in Hobart, Australia. His position is partly funded by the Grains Research and Development Corporation. He is a frequent contributor of chapters on SIA and has been a consultant to the World Bank; the World Commission on Dams; The Netherlands Ministry of Transport, Public Works and Water Management; the Finnish Ministry of Social Affairs and Health; the Norwegian Agency for Development Cooperation; and the Netherlands Ministry of Foreign Affairs. He is the 2000–2004 President of the International Rural Sociology Association and has been a Director of the International Association for Impact Assessment and Chair of its Publications Committee and Awards Committee. He is co-editor of *Environmental and Social Impact Assessment* (1995) and editor or author of several books on rural sociology and social aspects of natural resource management.
E-mail: Frank.Vanclay@utas.edu.au
Website: http://www.tiar.tas.edu.au

Contributors

James Baines has been active in the field of SIA for about 15 years. While practising mainly in New Zealand, he has paid particular attention to developing methods for analysing field materials and to reporting SIAs in ways that are useful to decision makers and other potential users. In recent years he has pioneered a substantial research programme focusing on ex-post assessments of social impacts from a range of facilities, beginning with solid waste and waste-water facilities and, lately, residential facilities (prisons) and large retail facilities. Together with Nick Taylor, he is currently engaged by UNDP to assist in the institutionalizing of SIA in Malaysia.
E-mail: j-baines@chch.planet.org.nz
Website: http://www.tba.co.nz

Brigid Buckenham has been a researcher with Taylor Baines & Associates in Christchurch, New Zealand for the past eight years, contributing to the firm's research and consulting activities. Particular interests have included research on facilities siting and SIAs for large retail facilities in New Zealand.
E-mail: harakeke@ihug.co.nz
Website: www.tba.co.nz

Sheridan Coakes has a PhD in community psychology from Curtin University of Technology in Australia. She is currently Director of Coakes Consulting, a specialized social research and planning consultancy, working on applied problems in urban planning and natural resource management. Her areas of expertise and interest include SIA, the development of community involvement programmes, structural adjustment, mitigation and risk communication.
E-mail: edco@ozemail.com.au

Gijs Dekkers works at the Federal Planning Bureau in Brussels, Belgium, where he researches income inequality, poverty and social exclusion. He is a coordinator of the research on the impact of the ICT revolution on different levels of the Belgian economy. He has experience in the development of static and dynamic microsimulation models, as well as in macro-economic modelling.
E-mail: gd@plan.be
Website: http://www.plan.be

Dorien DeTombe is founder and President of the Greenhill & Waterfront International Scientific Research & Development Institute on complex societal problems. Studying social science and computer science, she established the methodology for complex societal policy problems, for which she received her doctorate. She is chair of the Euro Working Group on Complex Societal Problems of the Operational Research Society, has published many books and articles, and organizes annual conferences.
E-mail: detombe@lri.jur.uva.nl

Mark Fenton is Associate Professor in the Department of Tropical Environment Studies and Geography at James Cook University in Townsville, Australia, where he teaches courses in environmental planning and environmental impact assessment. He is also Director of EBC, an SIA and planning consultancy, which provides services to private and public sector organizations in Australia. He has undertaken social assessment research in a wide range of natural resource management and planning contexts, including those of forestry, fisheries, mining and water resources.
E-mail: ebcmark@ozemail.com.au
Website: http://www.tesag.jcu.edu.au/

Gerard Fitzgerald is the Director of Fitzgerald Applied Sociology, a private sector organization based in Christchurch, New Zealand. He undertakes research and consulting on the social and cultural aspects of environment and resources development and management. He has also worked as an SIA practitioner in Australia, Polynesia, Melanesia, Indonesia and Bangladesh, including work for the World Bank. He has published and lectured on SIA methods and participatory approaches.
E-mail: gerard@fitzgerald.co.nz

Colin Goodrich is the Dean of Arts at the University of Canterbury, Christchurch, New Zealand. He has long-standing teaching and research interests in environmental sociology and SIA.
E-mail: c.goodrich@soci.canterbury.ac.nz
Website: http://www.soci.canterbury.ac.nz

Janice Jiggins is an international consultant based in The Netherlands. She is Adjunct Professor at the University of Guelph, Canada and former Professor of Human Ecology in the Department of Rural Development Studies at the Swedish University of Agricultural Sciences, Uppsala. Her current research interests include multi-stakeholder R&D, integrated pest management, participatory plant breeding and the contribution of social learning processes to resource system management.
E-mail: Janice.Jiggins@inter.NL.net

Roy E. Kwiatkowski is in charge of the Office of Environmental Health Assessment within Health Canada and has over 25 years of practical experience in both environmental and health impact assessment. He has been the driving force behind the *Canadian Handbook on Health Impact Assessment* and has been actively involved in health impact assessment capacity building internationally.
E-mail: roy_kwiatkowski@hc-sc.gc.ca
Website: http://www.hc-sc.gc.ca/oeha/

Nadine Marshall is a researcher working in the Department of Tropical Environment Studies and Geography at James Cook University in Townsville, Australia and is affiliated with the Cooperative Research Centre for Reef Research. She has been the project manager on the social assessment of Queensland's commercial fishing industry. Her current research topic is resource dependency.
E-mail: Nadine.Marshall@jcu.edu.au
Website: http://www.tesag.jcu.edu.au/

Jon Kei Matsuoka is the Interim Dean and Professor at the School of Social Work, University of Hawai'i, Manoa. His research has focused on economic development and quality of life in rural Hawai'i and Pacific Island communities. He has also served as a consultant on numerous community building and social planning projects focusing on community-based economic development, traditional cultural and subsistence practices, indigenous rights and human service planning.
E-mail: jmatsuok@hawaii.edu
Website: http://www.hawaii.edu/sswork/

Wayne McClintock is a social scientist with Taylor Baines & Associates, Christchurch, New Zealand. His current specialities include SIA, rural sociology and the socioeconomic aspects of natural resource development. He has also worked as a development practitioner and cross-cultural researcher in Tanzania and Pakistan.
E-mail: wayne@tba.co.nz
Website: http://www.tba.co.nz

Davianna Pomaika'i McGregor is an historian of Hawai'i and the Pacific and a Professor of Ethnic Studies at the University of Hawai'i, Manoa. Her research has focused on indigenous cultural, subsistence and spiritual custom and practice in rural Hawaiian communities and sustainable management of natural resources. She has conducted cultural studies for

federal, state and county agencies, and non-profit community organizations.
E-mail: davianna@hawaii.edu
Website: http://www2.soc.hawaii.edu/css/es/

Lyla Mehta is a Research Fellow at the Institute of Development Studies, University of Sussex, UK. She is a sociologist with a doctorate in development studies. She uses the case of water to explore the social and gender impacts of development schemes and social differentiation and institutional arrangements in natural resource management. She has been a consultant to the World Commission on Dams. She is the author of many articles in English and German and is currently finalizing a book on the social and political dimensions of water scarcity in western India.
E-mail: L.Mehta@ids.ac.uk
Website: http://www.ids.ac.uk

Luciano Minerbi is a Professor in the Department of Urban and Regional Planning, University of Hawai'i, Manoa. His teaching and research includes land use planning, environmental management, cultural impact assessment, sustainable development, island planning, responsible tourism and planning with indigenous people. He has undertaken consultancies for the United Nations, island governments, federal, state and county agencies, neighbourhoods and private and community-based organizations.
E-mail: luciano@hawaii.edu
Website: http://www.durp.hawaii.edu

Paula Tanemura Morelli is an Associate Professor in the School of Social Work, University of Hawai'i, Manoa. Her teaching and research focus is on cross-cultural mental health, strengthening wellbeing among Asian Pacific Islanders, and development of culturally appropriate/relevant research methodologies. She is currently researching the nature of culturally competent practice and its contribution to treatment efficacy among individuals with chronic mental illness. She consults with several agencies, including the Office of Hawaiian Affairs, to develop policies that support the wellbeing of Native Hawaiians.
E-mail: morelli@hawaii.edu
Website: http://www.hawaii.edu/sswork/

Neil Powell is a Senior Lecturer in environmental communication at the Swedish University of Agricultural Sciences, Uppsala. He is a researcher in an EU project entitled 'Social Learning for the Integrated Management and Sustainable Use of Water at Catchment Scale'. He is active both as a

researcher and as a consultant in impact assessment in complex problem situations, particularly in non-industrialized contexts.
E-mail: Neil.Powell@lpul.slu.se
Website: http://www.lpul.slu.se/index_eng.htm

Robert Rattle is a researcher and consultant based in Canada. His current research focuses on the human dimensions of global change, sustainable consumption and social and behavioural change. He has consulted for government agencies, NGOs and industry in health, transport, environment, and the technology and resources sectors. His current consulting work includes: investigating the roles of values, behaviours and lifestyles in achieving sustainability; developing a theoretical framework for quality of life indicators; integrating health and SIA; and assessing the influences of technologies on sustainable development objectives.
E-mail: at758@ncf.ca

Richard Roberts established Praxis Inc, a consulting group with offices across Canada. Praxis provides services in public involvement programmes, socioeconomic assessment and capacity building domestically and internationally. Richard has consulted extensively internationally in countries such as Colombia, Peru, Vietnam and South Africa. Recently, he has been developing training modules for building partnerships involving industry, government and civil society in the oil, gas and mining sectors. He is Adjunct Associate Professor in the Faculty of Environmental Design, University of Calgary, and has been Vice-President of the International Association for Public Participation (IAP2) and President of the International Association for Impact Assessment (1992–3).
E-mail: roberts@praxis.ca
Website: http://www.praxis.ca

Helen Ross is Professor of Rural Community Development in the School of Natural and Rural Systems Management, the University of Queensland, Gatton, Australia. She is an interdisciplinary social scientist specializing in social aspects of sustainable development and environmental management including SIA, and uses of environmental negotiation in collaborative planning and environmental management processes. She has worked intensively with Australian indigenous communities, and in Thailand. She studied co-management negotiations in Washington State, USA, under a Fulbright Senior Award in 1996.
E-mail: hross@uqg.uq.edu.au
Website: http://www.nrsm.uq.edu.au

Marlies van Schooten is a development sociologist, with emphasis on environmental issues and public administration. She works as a consultant with Slootweg & van Schooten on the integration of social issues in impact assessment. At present she is also involved in the environmental aspects of tourism development. She has worked in South America, Africa and in The Netherlands.
E-mail: SevS@SevS.nl

Roel Slootweg is an ecologist with a PhD in environmental science. His work focuses on the integration of nature conservation, natural resource management and socioeconomic development in industrialized as well as developing countries. His experience in impact assessment includes capacity development and the development of conceptual and procedural approaches towards the integration of social aspects in EIA and to the better representation of biological diversity in EIA. He currently works at the Slootweg & van Schooten consultancy.
E-mail: SevS@SevS.nl

Bina Srinivasan is a feminist writer–researcher whose interests include development, rural and urban displacement and their impacts on women. She has been the Joint Secretary of the Indian Association of Women's Studies and a consultant to the World Commission on Dams. She is at present a Scholar of Peace, an award given by 'Women in Security and Peace Management', and is currently researching the gender impacts of displacement caused by development projects in India.
E-mail: binasr@eth.net

Annelies Stolp is a biologist with a particular interest in the social issues related to environmental science. She is the Coordinator of an Advisory Unit on project communication and SIA within the Netherlands Ministry of Transport, Public Works and Water Management (Rijkswaterstaat), and Team Leader of the Citizen Values Assessment project.
E-mail: a.stolp@bwd.rws.minvenw.nl
Website: http://www.belevingswaardenonderzoek.nl

Nick Taylor is a Principal with Taylor Baines & Associates in Christchurch, New Zealand. Apart from research and consulting in SIA and natural resource management on a wide range of issues, he has conducted training internationally in SIA and is co-author of *Social assessment: theory, process and techniques* (1990; 2nd edn., 1995).
E-mail: n.taylor@tba.co.nz
Website: http://www.tba.co.nz

1 Conceptual and methodological advances in social impact assessment

Frank Vanclay

Advancing the definition of SIA

Social impact assessment (SIA) arguably originated, as a specific concept at least, with the 1969 National Environmental Policy Act of the USA (NEPA) (see Interorganizational Committee, 1994). However, in more general terms, predicting and assessing the consequences of change on society has been part of the political landscape since the Oracle at Delphi (Becker, 1997), and has been of interest to anthropology and sociology since their inception.

Today, the objective of SIA is to ensure that the developments (or planned interventions) that do occur maximize the benefits and minimize the costs of those developments, especially those costs borne by the community. Too often, these costs (externalities) are not adequately taken into account by decision makers, regulatory authorities and developers, partly because they are not easily identifiable, quantifiable and measurable. By identifying impacts in advance, better decisions can be made about which interventions should proceed and how they should proceed. Mitigation measures can be implemented, and redesign can occur, to minimize the harm and maximize the benefits. By promoting participatory processes, better consideration can be given to what appropriate development for a community may be.

Early definitions of SIA tended to see it as being inherently linked to a regulatory context. For example, basing their definition on that of the Interorganizational Committee on Guidelines and Principles for SIA (1994), which was specifically steeped in the language of NEPA, Burdge and Vanclay (1995: 32) considered that:

> Social impact assessment can be defined as the process of assessing or estimating, in advance, the social consequences that are likely to follow from specific policy actions or project development, particularly in the context of appropriate national, state or provincial environmental policy legislation.

But such an understanding is inherently limiting, particularly in those regulatory systems that are modelled on NEPA which have been implemented in many places around the world. This understanding presumes an adversarial regulatory system. It denies that assessment might be carried out internally by a corporation or by government, or even by a community itself independent of a regulatory process. The assessment of impacts of past developments is excluded from this definition. There is also no role for the management, mitigation and monitoring of impacts, or for contribution of the SIA participants in the redesign of the project, or even in decision making about what constitutes an appropriate project. Although the definition implies that the social impacts of policy actions could be considered, the practice of SIA has tended to focus only on projects. Thus, in such an understanding, SIA has been limited only to a regulatory defined role of predicting the (negative) impacts of projects.

SIA practitioners consider that SIA as a discipline is more than the prediction of negative impacts: 'it is a philosophy about development and democracy . . . [which considers the] pathologies of development (i.e. harmful impacts), goals of development (such as poverty alleviation), and processes of development (e.g. participation, capacity building)' (Vanclay, 2002: 388). This new understanding of SIA is encapsulated in Vanclay's definition:

> SIA is the process of analyzing (predicting, evaluating and reflecting) and managing the intended and unintended consequences on the human environment of planned interventions (policies, programs, plans, projects) and any social change processes invoked by those interventions so as to bring about a more sustainable and equitable biophysical and human environment. (Ibid.)

Advancing the internationality of SIA

A criticism of earlier understandings of SIA is that they were too bound to a developed country setting. There have been various attempts to develop SIA to be applicable to developing countries. In general terms, however, it became apparent that the traditional conceptualization of SIA was not appropriate, as it was bound to a specific regulatory context, and it failed to address adequately the goals of development.

As Vanclay (2002) argues, one of the features (roles) of SIA in a developed country context was its role in protecting individual property rights, with clear statements of adverse impacts required to ensure that individual rights are not transgressed. Where these rights were violated, SIA could be seen as contributing to mitigation and compensation mechanisms. In these situations, SIA tends to concentrate on the negative impacts. In other contexts, however, particularly in developing countries, there should be less emphasis on the negative impacts on small groups of individuals or on individual property rights. Rather, there should be greater concern with maximizing social utility and development potential, at the same time ensuring that such development is generally acceptable to the community, equitable and sustainable.

SIA should also focus on reconstruction of livelihoods. The improvement of social wellbeing of the wider community should be explicitly recognized as an objective of planned interventions, and as such should be an indicator considered by any form of assessment. However, awareness of the differential distribution of impacts among different groups in society, and particularly the impact burden experienced by vulnerable groups in the community, is of prime concern.

The chapters in this *International Handbook* have appreciated the need to extend SIA to developing countries. Several chapters consider developing countries specifically. Chapter 4 provides an overview of participatory land management (or co-management) using a case study in Namibia. Chapter 11 examines gender impacts in a range of contexts, primarily from developing countries. Chapter 17 includes a discussion of the complexities of HIV–AIDS in South Africa. Chapter 8 looks at the understanding of wellbeing from the perspective of Native Hawaiians. Chapter 13 considers the applicability of geographic information systems to SIA, using two case studies involving Native Hawaiian indigenous communities.

Advancing the values of SIA
An important feature of SIA is that, as a social science discipline/practice, there is a strong view that there is a professional value system that an SIA practitioner should uphold. While all impact assessment practitioners should have a commitment to sustainability and scientific integrity, they should also uphold an ethic that advocates openness and accountability, fairness and equity, and defends human rights. The role of SIA goes far beyond the ex-ante (in advance) prediction of adverse impacts and the determination of who wins and who loses: SIA also encompasses empowerment of local people; enhancement of the position of women, minority groups and other disadvantaged members of society; development of capacity building; alleviation of all forms of dependency; increase in equity; and a focus on poverty reduction.

Over several years, using various participatory processes conducted under the auspices of the International Association for Impact Assessment (IAIA), the core values of SIA were identified as follows:

1. There are fundamental human rights that are shared equally across cultures, and by males and females alike.
2. There is a right to have those fundamental human rights protected by the rule of law, with justice applied equally and fairly to all, and available to all.
3. People have a right to live and work in an environment which is conducive

to good health and to a good quality of life and which enables the development of human and social potential.

4. Social dimensions of the environment – specifically but not exclusively peace, the quality of social relationships, freedom from fear, and belongingness – are important aspects of people's health and quality of life.
5. People have a right to be involved in the decision making about the planned interventions that will affect their lives.
6. Local knowledge and experience are valuable and can be used to enhance planned interventions. (Vanclay, 2003: 9)

These values then translate into fundamental principles about development in general:

1. Respect for human rights should underpin all actions.
2. Promoting equity and democratisation should be the major driver of development planning, and impacts on the worst-off members of society should be a major consideration in all assessment.
3. The existence of diversity between cultures, within cultures, and the diversity of stakeholder interests need to be recognised and valued.
4. Decision making should be just, fair and transparent, and decision makers should be accountable for their decisions.
5. Development projects should be broadly acceptable to the members of those communities likely to benefit from, or be affected by, the planned intervention.
6. The opinions and views of experts should not be the sole consideration in decisions about planned interventions.
7. The primary focus of all development should be positive outcomes, such as capacity building, empowerment, and the realization of human and social potential.
8. The term, 'the environment', should be defined broadly to include social and human dimensions, and in such inclusion, care must be taken to ensure that adequate attention is given to the realm of the social. (Ibid.)

The core values also translate into a set of key principles relating to the practice of SIA specifically:

1. Equity considerations should be a fundamental element of impact assessment and of development planning.
2. Many of the social impacts of planned interventions can be predicted.
3. Planned interventions can be modified to reduce their negative social impacts and enhance their positive impacts.
4. SIA should be an integral part of the development process, involved in all stages from inception to follow-up audit.
5. There should be a focus on socially sustainable development, with SIA contributing to the determination of best development alternative(s) – SIA (and environmental impact assessment (EIA)) have more to offer than just being an arbiter between economic benefit and social cost.
6. In all planned interventions and their assessments, avenues should be developed to build the social and human capital of local communities and to strengthen democratic processes.

7. In all planned interventions, but especially where there are unavoidable impacts, ways to turn impacted peoples into beneficiaries should be investigated.
8. The SIA must give due consideration to the alternatives of any planned intervention, but especially in cases when there are likely to be unavoidable impacts.
9. Full consideration should be given to the potential mitigation measures of social and environmental impacts, even where impacted communities may approve the planned intervention and where they may be regarded as beneficiaries.
10. Local knowledge and experience and acknowledgment of different local cultural values should be incorporated in any assessment.
11. There should be no use of violence, harassment, intimidation or undue force in connection with the assessment or implementation of a planned intervention.
12. Developmental processes that infringe the human rights of any section of society should not be accepted. (Ibid.)

Many established international principles also have relevance to SIA, and/or form part of the premises underpinning SIA. These include:

- **Precautionary Principle.** In order to protect the environment, a concept which includes peoples' ways of life and the integrity of their communities, the precautionary approach shall be applied. Where there are threats or potential threats of serious social impact, lack of full certainty about those threats should not be used as a reason for approving the planned intervention or not requiring the implementation of mitigation measures and stringent monitoring.
- **Uncertainty Principle**. It must be recognised that our knowledge of the social world and of social processes is incomplete and that social knowledge can never be fully complete because the social environment and the processes affecting it are changing constantly, and vary from place to place and over time.
- **Intragenerational Equity**. The benefits from the range of planned interventions should address the needs of all, and the social impacts should not fall disproportionately on certain groups of the population, in particular children and women, the disabled and the socially excluded, certain generations or certain regions.
- **Intergenerational Equity**. Development activities or planned interventions should be managed so that the needs of the present generation are met without compromising the ability of future generations to meet their own needs.
- **Recognition and Preservation of Diversity**. Communities and societies are not homogeneous. They are demographically structured (age and gender), and they comprise different groups with various value systems and different skills. Special attention is needed to appreciate the existence of the social diversity that exists within communities and to understand what the unique requirements of special groups may be. Care must be taken to ensure that planned interventions do not lead to a loss of social diversity in a community, or a diminishing of social cohesion.

- **Internalisation of Costs**. The full social and ecological costs of a planned intervention should be internalized through the use of economic and other instruments, that is, these costs should be considered as part of the costs of the intervention, and no intervention should be approved or regarded as cost-effective if it achieves this by the creation of hidden costs to current or future generations or the environment.
- **The Polluter Pays Principle**. The full costs of avoiding or compensating for social impacts should be borne by the proponent of the planned intervention.
- **The Prevention Principle**. It is generally preferable and cheaper in the long run to prevent negative social impacts and ecological damage from happening than having to restore or rectify damage after the event.
- **The Protection and Promotion of Health and Safety**. Health and safety are paramount. All planned interventions should be assessed for their health impacts and their accident risks, especially in terms of assessing and managing the risks from hazardous substances, technologies or processes, so that their harmful effects are minimized, including not bringing them into use or phasing them out as soon as possible. Health impacts cover the physical, mental and social wellbeing and safety of all people, paying particular attention to those groups of the population who are more vulnerable and more likely to be harmed, such as the economically deprived, indigenous groups, children and women, the elderly, the disabled, as well as to the population most exposed to risks arising from the planned intervention.
- **The Principle of Multisectoral Integration**. Social development requirements and the need to consider social issues should be properly integrated into all projects, policies, infrastructure programmes and other planning activities.
- **The Principle of Subsidiarity**. Decision making power should be decentralised, with accountable decisions being made as close to an individual citizen as possible. In the context of SIA, this means decisions about the approval of planned interventions or conditions under which they might operate, should be taken as close to the affected people as possible with local people having an input into the approval and management processes. (Ibid.)

These principles are part of the discipline/paradigm of SIA. They are part of the premises, sometimes explicit and sometimes implicit, of the majority of SIA practitioners. They represent an explication of the value system of SIA practitioners and are shared by the authors of the chapters of this book.

Advancing the range of consideration of the social

Those who perceive SIA as meaning only the prediction step within an environmental assessment framework tend to have a limited view of what social impacts are. They tend to see social impacts only in terms of demographic changes, job issues, financial security, impacts on family life and so on. This limited view of SIA also creates demarcation problems about what are the social impacts to be identified by SIA, versus what is considered by health impact assessment, cultural impact assessment, heritage impact assessment, aesthetic impact assessment or gender impact assessment.

The understanding of SIA being advanced in this book is that SIA is a broad umbrella or overarching framework that embodies the evaluation of all human impacts including aesthetic impacts (landscape analysis), archaeological and heritage impacts, community impacts, cultural impacts, demographic impacts, development impacts, economic and fiscal impacts, gender assessment, health impacts, indigenous rights, infrastructural impacts, institutional impacts, political impacts (human rights, governance, democratization and so on), poverty assessment, psychological impacts, resource issues (access and ownership of resources), tourism impacts and other impacts on societies. Consideration of impacts needs to extend to cumulative effects as well as an assessment of the impact history of a community.

Vanclay, building on an idea by Armour (1990), considers that a convenient way of conceptualizing social impacts is as changes to one or more of the following:

- people's way of life – that is, how they live, work, play and interact with one another on a day-to-day basis;
- their culture – that is, their shared beliefs, customs, values and language or dialect;
- their community – its cohesion, stability, character, services and facilities;
- their political systems – the extent to which people are able to participate in decisions that affect their lives, the level of democratization that is taking place, and the resources provided for this purpose;
- their environment – the quality of the air and water people use; the availability and quality of the food they eat, the level of hazard or risk, dust and noise they are exposed to; the adequacy of sanitation, their physical safety, and their access to and control over resources;
- their health and wellbeing – where 'health' is understood in a manner similar to the World Health Organization definition: 'a state of complete physical, mental, and social wellbeing and not merely the absence of disease or infirmity';
- their personal and property rights – particularly whether people are economically affected, or experience personal disadvantage which may include a violation of their civil liberties.
- their fears and aspirations – their perceptions about their safety, their fears about the future of their community, and their aspirations for their future and the future of their children. (Vanclay, 2002: 389)

While all chapters in this *International Handbook* push the boundaries about what should be included in consideration of 'the social' in terms of SIA, the topic is explicitly addressed in Chapter 6. Chapter 7 considers what the impacts of a broad understanding of SIA are for the field of health impact assessment. Chapter 5 considers how all social impacts are inherently interconnected with biophysical environmental impacts. Chapter 12 promotes an awareness of the need to consider impacts on future generations. Although the use of local knowledge has long been part of SIA, Chapter 3 gives an extra impetus to explaining why the use of local knowledge is important.

Advancing the methodology

There are a number of different models to show how SIA should be implemented, but there is no universal standard for SIA (although perhaps the US Interorganizational Committee 1994 document comes close). Nevertheless, it is appropriate to state that a good SIA does the following (Vanclay 2002: 392):

- identifies interested and affected peoples;
- facilitates and coordinates the participation of stakeholders;
- documents and analyses the local historical setting in which the project will occur so as to be able to interpret likely responses to the project, and to assess cumulative impacts;
- gives a rich picture of the local cultural context, and develops an understanding of local community values, particularly how they might relate to the planned intervention;
- identifies and describes the activities which are likely to cause impacts (scoping);
- predicts likely impacts and how different segments of the community are likely to respond;
- assists in evaluation and selection of program alternatives (including a no development option);
- assists in site selection;
- recommends mitigation measures;
- provides suggestions about compensation;
- describes potential conflicts between stakeholders and advises on resolution processes;
- develops coping strategies in the community for dealing with residual or non-mitigable impacts;
- contributes to skill development and capacity building in the community;
- advises on appropriate institutional and co-ordination arrangements for all parties;
- assists in the devising and implementation of monitoring and management programs;
- collects baseline data (profiling) to allow evaluation and audit of the impact assessment process and the project itself.

There has been only a small number of SIA-specific techniques. Generally, SIA has relied on the range of social science methods. This volume presents several new techniques that contribute to the suite of tools available to SIA practitioners. Chapter 10 provides an example of the use of computer-based qualitative research methods in SIA. Chapter 11 gives an example of gender impact assessment. Chapter 12 discusses the use of soci-oeconomic modelling, especially in relation to the assessment of intergenerational impacts. Chapter 13 looks at the role of geographic information systems (GIS) in SIA. Chapter 14 presents a method of assessing capacity for change and vulnerability or risk in relation to impacts in a new technique called 'town resource clustering'. Chapter 15 presents a new technique of incorporating citizens' perspectives about their living environment into the impact assessment process and in the decision-making process. Chapter 16 discusses new ways of involving the public. Chapter 17 describes a process to address complex societal problems. Chapter 18 discusses the potential role of environmental mediation. Chapter 3 demonstrates the use of computerized qualitative data analysis packages in incorporating local knowledge. Chapter 9 presents an overarching chapter on the theory and methodology of SIA, while Chapter 2 presents a new perspective on longitudinal research, for long the cornerstone of SIA methodology.

References

Armour, A. 1990. 'Integrating impact assessment into the planning process', *Impact Assessment Bulletin*, 8(1/2): 3–14.

Becker, H.A. 1997. *Social Impact Assessment: Method and Experience in Europe, North America and the Developing World*, London: UCL Press.

Burdge, R.J. and Vanclay, F. 1995. 'Social impact assessment', in F. Vanclay and D.A. Bronstein (eds), *Environmental and Social Impact Assessment*, Chichester: Wiley, 31–66.

Interorganizational Committee on Guidelines and Principles 1994. 'Guidelines and Principles for Social Impact Assessment', *Impact Assessment*, 12(2): 107–52.

Vanclay, F. 2002. 'Social Impact Assessment' In M. Tolba (ed.), *Responding to Global Environmental Change* (vol. 4, of *Encyclopedia of Global Environmental Change,* series ed.: Ted Munn), Chichester: Wiley, 387–93.

Vanclay, F. 2003. 'International Principles for Social Impact Assessment', *Impact Assessment and Project Appraisal*, 21(1): 5–11.

PART I

CONCEPTUAL ADVANCES IN SOCIAL IMPACT ASSESSMENT

2 Undertaking longitudinal research

Nick Taylor, Colin Goodrich, Gerard Fitzgerald and Wayne McClintock

Introduction

As an important part of the planning and implementation of projects, programmes and policies, SIA is a process that is now used worldwide (Burdge and Vanclay, 1995). It is a process that uses methods of social research and analysis, as well as monitoring and public involvement (Taylor *et al.*, 1995). Although definitions of SIA encompass social analysis, and implicitly or explicitly require research, practice is often limited by the existing research base. Little social research is conducted with the specific goal of improved SIA practice.

Comparative analysis for the projection of effects is an integral part of the social assessment process (Taylor *et al.*, 1995; Burdge, 1998), so comparative case studies using systematic social research have a key role to play in SIA. Following the early phase of development in the field, Freudenburg and Keating (1985: 583–4) made the point that 'extrapolation' from comparative cases with known impacts was a basic technique for anticipatory SIA. But they noted, 'The frequent failure to make use of the relatively straightforward technique may not be due to oversight, but to the fact that the previous knowledge is often not available. Scientists cannot extrapolate from guesses alone; they need valid, reliable, empirical data.' Their call for a stronger research base to SIA over 15 years ago seems largely to have gone unheard.

The purpose of a research base for SIA is not simply to obtain empirical or descriptive data. It is now widely accepted that social assessment should be tied to a theoretical or conceptual framework and, ideally, the theoretical perspectives that are so much a part of the academic social sciences should be informing and guiding the field. Although there have been attempts to make this relationship explicit (Rickson *et al.*, 1998; Taylor *et al.*, 1995), most past and current SIA work appears to have been produced in a theoretical vacuum. Reasons for this omission may include the relative newness of the field, its legislative and pragmatic origins and directions, and the diversity of backgrounds among practitioners. It might also reflect the lack of a research base for inductive, theory-generating work. On the other hand, it is sometimes very difficult to translate the social science literature into terms that facilitate its use or application to the SIA process.

13

In most SIA work, there is a wealth of official and other social statistics and empirical data to draw on for baseline data or social profiling. Time series of these sorts of data allow for trend analysis, which is one of the basic tools used in developing scenarios of change for social impact prediction. Where there is a sufficiently robust set of data, for example, statistics on inter-industry economic relationships, it is also possible to develop tools such as economic multipliers for prediction of direct and indirect employment and expenditure impacts.

Most SIAs tends to emphasize the use of these readily available data. This means there is often ample material to develop the social profile or baseline conditions, and carry out some trend analysis and projections, including those with the use of multipliers. It may also be possible to undertake quantitative modelling. Analysis of issues identified through consultation with interested and affected parties in the affected area is also generally good. There is often, however, much less thorough and rigorous development of scenarios of change using comparative cases, through the development of conceptual models and the analysis of likely webs and chains of effects. Estimations of the potential likelihood and magnitude of these effects are usually negligible and there appear to be few tools to guide this work. In this chapter, we examine the importance of experiential and comparative social research that develops both an empirical database and conceptual frameworks for SIA. An example of longitudinal research into community formation and change in New Zealand resource communities is presented. Models of the SIA process as both a source and a user of comparative cases are discussed.

The experiential and conceptual basis for SIA
The relationship between empirical and inductive (concept-developing) research and the SIA process was developed and illustrated by Taylor *et al.* (1995) with a discussion of the application of soft-systems approaches to SIA practice. In this process, data gathering is a dominant activity in (a) social profiling to establish the baseline conditions *before* change takes place; (b) social monitoring to obtain information on change *as* it takes place; and (c) evaluation to study change and the process of change *after* changes have taken place. Conceptual development tends to have a less important role in these three phases of SIA. The reverse tends to be true of the prediction and estimation of likely effects during the design phase of the SIA process. In this work, there may still be some gathering of social data taking place, such as information on the response of different social groups to various alternatives and their possible effects, but the predominant focus during the prediction and estimation of likely effects is conceptual. Conceptual frameworks are used explicitly, or implicitly, to develop

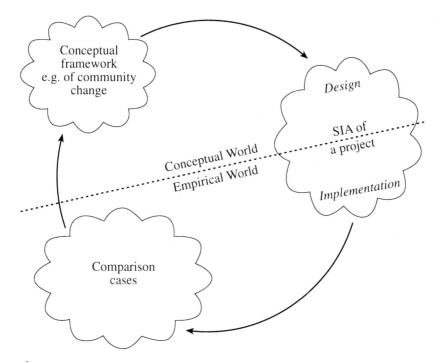

Figure 2.1   Experiential learning in SIA

models of likely effects, and chains of effects (resulting from first order effects) (see Chapter 5). These models of effects can then build into integrated scenarios of environmental change.

Ideally, there is a process of experiential learning, with iterations between the conceptual world and the empirical world, as shown in Figure 2.1. A combination of empirical data and inductive research provides the necessary road maps for SIA. But suitable comparative cases are often limited. Efforts to develop full scenarios of change can therefore be frustrated.

There are two major, potential sources of empirical data and conceptual development for SIA. The first source is formed by comparative cases generated through independent research, ideally longitudinal, as described in the example below. The second is work carried out as part of particular SIA cases, usually as part of social profiling during the design phase and monitoring during the implementation phase. Comparative cases are also available from evaluations and reviews, or ex-post studies. So SIAs themselves both use and *generate* research findings that can in turn feed into other work.

Case example: research on resource community formation and change in New Zealand

The natural resource sectors – such as agriculture, mining, energy, forestry, fishing and tourism – will experience increased global pressure for utilization in the early part of the 21st century. Resource development projects, technological change, resource conflicts and resource policy initiatives will all place heavy demands and pressures on the impact assessment process. A continuing focus for SIA, therefore, will be on the people who live and work at the interface between societies and their natural resource base.

Despite a large legacy of rural sociological and community research, particularly in the early years of SIA (Freudenburg, 1986), changes in resource communities are often poorly conceptualized for the purpose of impact assessment. There has been only limited longitudinal research or development of conceptual frameworks for understanding the processes of community formation (Tykkylainen and Neil, 1995). One example is the 'Resource Community Formation and Change' programme funded by the Foundation for Research, Science and Technology (Public Good Science Fund contracts TBA601, TBA801 and TBAX0001) over a six-year period from 1996. The focus of that research is on communities that depend on the primary production or processing of natural resources, or 'resource communities' (Taylor and Fitzgerald, 1988). The aim of the research was to provide baseline data and an understanding of community formation and change in rural and small-town New Zealand. By providing increased knowledge and understanding of the processes of social change in communities that depend directly on the primary production or processing of natural resources, the research will contribute (a) to thinking about sustainable development and the relationship between people and communities and their natural resource base, as recognized in New Zealand's Resource Management Act 1991 (RMA), the principal legislation for resource planning and environmental management; (b) to natural resources policies and plans; (c) to the assessment, monitoring and evaluation of resource consent applications as required under the RMA; (d) to planning of social services by central and local government and private sector providers; (e) to improved social assessment practice through substantive baseline information for future social assessments in the case study area; and (f) to improved social assessment practice through improved understanding of the processes of community formation and change in these types of communities.

Between 1996 and 2000, the research examined community formation and change in the six resource sectors of forestry, mining, agriculture, fishing, energy and tourism. A number of methods have been used, including:

- a review of experiences in resource communities in New Zealand and overseas, emphasizing cycles of social and economic change, technology development, labour processes and the role of the state and private sector;
- a review of the international and New Zealand contexts for community formation and change in each of the six resource sectors;
- short profiles of 58 communities in the six resource sectors using secondary data sources, including comparative census statistics;
- comparative case studies of 19 communities;
- comparative statistical analysis of 175 communities from the six resource sectors, according to social characteristics as recorded in the 1986 and 1996 Census.

The research identified substantial social and economic change in these resource-based communities over the last 20 years. Major findings of the research include the following. Populations generally have fallen, with losses of key community people, particularly through redundancy and centralization of jobs into larger centres. Changes in technology and the organization of work, including subcontracting and shift work, have increased labour productivity while reducing employment overall. People commute further to work within subregional labour markets. Substantial industry restructuring and concentration of ownership have added to job losses, coinciding with restructuring and centralization in social services and other sectors. Local oversupply has reduced the cost of housing and attracted newcomers, often characterized by low socio-economic status, higher proportions of Maori, more social and cultural diversity, and reduced community cohesion. Communities are also less clearly defined spatially, with many locales being absorbed into larger, composite communities or mosaics of communities.

Through comparisons with international experience (particularly in Australia and North America), the research has contributed to a wider conceptual framework of social change in resource communities. Previous frameworks have tended to be based on single-sector explanations of boom–bust cycles, and use levels of population and employment as primary social indicators. These frameworks can now be expanded by an understanding of external linkages and processes that influence these sorts of communities. Such external influences include shifting emphasis between the roles of the state and private sector, changes to industry ownership and investment patterns, technological changes, product markets and price cycles, environmental policy and resource management, and social policy and community development strategies.

The research has strengthened the model of resource cycles in these communities, adding an understanding of the interconnections between sectors at subregional levels. It also showed that few rural communities are dependent on a single resource sector. The model provides an understanding of changing community boundaries where there are evident clusters of economic activity and regional mosaics of resource use. Furthermore, the research found persistent periods and pockets of rural poverty that are likely to hinder creative, participatory approaches to sustainable resource and economic development and proactive approaches to impact assessment.

Application of the resource community research findings to SIA practice
A considerable amount of SIA work is being, and has been, undertaken in rural areas. So there are a number of ways by which the findings of the resource communities project can be applied to SIA practice. One example is through an improved conceptual framework based on the well-established concept of the resource community cycle (Taylor and Fitzgerald, 1988, Taylor *et al.*, 1995). Periods of rapid change in these communities have been typical trigger points for application of SIA. For instance, SIA has been utilized for planning and monitoring periods of rapid growth in a community as a result of incoming workforces. It has also been applied during periods of workforce wind-down or plant closures. Less common, but still important, are applications of SIA during periods of relative economic stability, to assess social needs or assist with economic development initiatives and strategic planning.

The concept of the resource community cycle helps the SIA practitioner to understand the process of community formation and change, as rural communities go through cycles of change with their associated social and economic benefits and costs. The concept assists social and economic planning through an increased knowledge of the importance of diversified economies, sustainable resource management practices and the potential of community-based strategies for social and economic development. Research provides the potential to move beyond the idiosyncratic case to data that enable us to develop and understand the bigger picture.

Examples of the way in which new insights from the research can be applied to the resource community cycle as formulated in previous work and the early stages of the present research programme are shown in Figure 2.2. It will also be possible to utilize these findings to revise and reformulate this framework through ongoing iterations between research (theory building) and practice. There are a number of examples of insights from the research that can be applied to the model in Figure 2.2.

First, new technology has changed the nature of the labour force, in terms of total demand for labour and the skills required. For example, the

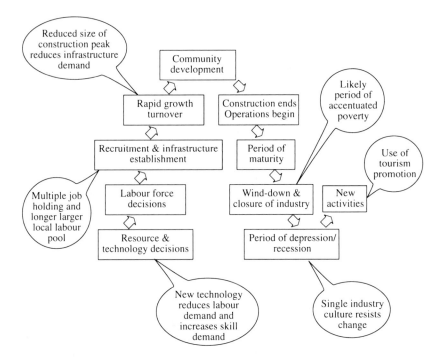

Figure 2.2   New insights into the resource community cycle

recent construction of an additional tunnel for hydroelectricity generation at Manapouri used a massive tunnel boring machine with a much smaller workforce than the original tunnel required. Fibre optic cabling has enabled the computerized operation of hydroelectricity generation stations from remote sites, with minimal on-site workforces, marking the end of the temporary construction town or workers' village.

Second, multiple job holding by individuals in the rural labour force (including farm families), better roads and a willingness to commute, have caused the rural labour market to change substantially, and to move from local to regional pools of labour.

Third, reduced demand for immigrant workers means reduced demand for infrastructure such as workforce housing and associated facilities tied to new projects. The 'new town syndrome' was last seen in New Zealand in the early 1980s.

Fourth, periods of workforce wind-down and industry closures can lead to periods of economic depression and accentuated rural poverty. Newcomers taking advantage of low housing costs do not necessarily have the skills to take part in economic diversification and instead make heavy demands on social services.

Fifth, long associations with a single resource industry in some communities develop a culture that reflects that industry and its work and social organization. It appears that this dominant culture can be inherently conservative and inflexible in relation to economic diversification and change when compared to communities with a more diversified economic base and a social composition that encourages entrepreneurship.

Finally, diverse economies are better positioned to reduce the social effects of cycles of boom and bust. They have positive attitudes to economic change and entrepreneurship, including newcomers starting and operating new types of businesses, and sustainable resource management practices.

Application and production of research in SIA

An understanding of the experiential nature of the social assessment process over the project cycle helps us to ask questions about the potential to generate research through the social assessment process itself. We need to ask *how* and *when* research is used in the SIA process. A simplified diagram of the SIA process is provided in Figure 2.3, which includes the main activities of the process: scoping, profiling, analysis of alternatives, estimation of effects, monitoring to inform mitigation and management, and evaluation (see, inter alia, Taylor *et al.*, 1995). These core SIA activities are depicted in Figure 2.3, which indicates whether they produce data that could be used to build comparative cases, or whether they are activities when there is, or should be, heavy use of comparative cases. This analysis is developed further in Table 2.1.

Of course, all activities in SIA potentially use and create social data. However, some activities are more likely to generate comparative case data, while others utilize it. In Figure 2.3, the unbroken arrows pointing outwards indicate the potential of the activity to generate data for use in other SIAs as comparative cases, that is, profiling, monitoring and evaluation. The broken arrows pointing inwards show the activities in the cycle where comparative cases are most likely to be used in an SIA: scoping, evaluating alternatives and predicting effects.

Where SIA practitioners are carrying out impact predictions (including the detailed assessment of effects and development of scenarios of change), they are likely to draw on information from one or more comparative cases, as illustrated in Figure 2.3 and Table 2.1. They should also draw on relevant, research-based, conceptual frameworks to develop models of social change, such as the application of the resource cycles model in a community that is likely to experience a resource-based project.

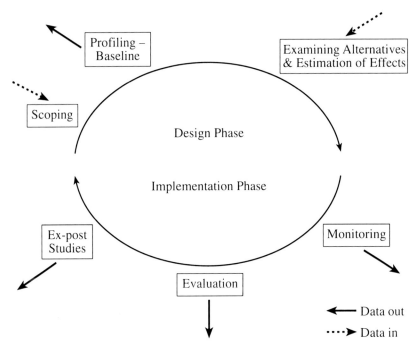

Source: After Taylor *et al.* (1995).

Figure 2.3   Application and generation of data to/from comparative cases during the SIA project cycle

A diachronic model for these uses of comparative cases in impact assessment is shown in Figure 2.4. This basic model was originally developed and published in 1977 by Burdge and Johnson and developed further by Burdge (1998). Despite its long period of availability, the model appears to have had only limited recognition and use. We have developed the model further in Figure 2.4. It can be seen from the model that an ideal type of impact assessment (a) predicting social change due to a cause (Xa) from the present state (T2a) to a possible future state (T3b) has the potential to draw on comparative case material of several types:

- monitoring and evaluation data (b) that are available when a similar impact source (Xb) has already taken place in a similar type of community, creating the change T1b to T2b. Furthermore, there is potential for ongoing monitoring and evaluation of this change as part of the implementation and management of change Xb (in the period

Table 2.1 Application and sources of comparative case data, by SIA activity

SIA activity	Description	Use and sources of comparative case data
Scoping	Identification of key issues and stakeholders, and variables to be described/measured in the profile. Early consultation, and an initial identification of impacts and likely areas of impact.	This is a key period for establishing the likely level of use of comparative case study data in the analysis. Initial analysis is often based on practical knowledge of similar cases by the practitioner. During scoping there should be a systematic search of literature for relevant cases.
Profiling	Overview and analysis of social context and trends (baseline analysis).	As host communities often experience more than one case of social impact, the profile for a new case can produce important data on how previous events have impacted the area. This information can be used in other SIAs.
Formulation of alternatives	Examination and comparison of options for change.	Comparative case material is used to help identify effects and develop scenarios of change for the options in question.
Projection and estimation of effects	Detailed examination of the webs and chains of impacts generated by one or more options, with estimates of their likelihood and magnitude.	Comparative case material is used to identify the likely webs and chains of effects based on experiences in other similar cases or social environments and to develop detailed scenarios of change.
Monitoring for mitigation and management	Collection of information about actual effects, and the application of this information to mitigate negative effects and manage change in general.	Data gathered for the purposes of managing change in a particular case provides useful comparative case data about the actual effects experienced.
Evaluation	Periodic, retrospective review of social effects.	Systematic looking back at a case using monitoring data or other additional analysis is an important source of comparative cases and experiential learning, although this opportunity often goes begging.

	Past	Present	Future	Far future
Effect of impact source x on:				
(a) impact assessment (predictive)		T2a → *Xa*	T3a	
(b) monitoring & evaluation	T1b → *Xb*	T2b →	T3b	
(c) longitudinal comparative research	T1c → *Xc*	T2c →	T3c →	T4c
(d) control research	T1d →	T2d →	T3d →	T4d

Source: After Burdge (1998:34).

Figure 2.4   Diachronic model of comparative cases for impact assessment

T2b to T3b). So ongoing monitoring and evaluation provides a series of case studies;
- comparative research (c) that is longitudinal, that is, which provides historical information (T1c to T2c) and also possibly continues into the future (T2c to T4c), on a similar impact source (*Xc*) in a similar community. Once again, a series of cases distinguished by changing historical context can be generated in this way;
- research in a similar (control) community (d) that has not experienced the source of effects *X* over the period (T1d to T4d).

There are some caveats that should be applied to this model. First, it is important to acknowledge that all social contexts are dynamic and include complex relationships between biophysical and social processes (Slootweg *et al.*, 2001). It is therefore often difficult to sort out what, specifically, is the source of social change, even when control research is available. Second, robust, longitudinal social research should provide empirical data and inductive, conceptual understanding of change, especially over multiple cases or sites. But profiling, monitoring and evaluation work undertaken as part of an applied SIA also have great potential to contribute comparative case data, certainly more than usually happens.

There seems, unfortunately, to be little incentive for SIA practitioners to get off the treadmill of applied, action-oriented work and optimize the experiential learning potential of their practice as shown by the diachronic model. Of course, it will be argued that clients of an impact study do not necessarily want to research the big picture or to contribute to the generation of research per se. In fact, this tension between research and action is a natural tension in different orientations to SIA (Taylor *et al.*, 1995). One way around this dilemma may be the development of case-specific databases by practitioner organizations such as the International Association for Impact Assessment (IAIA) and its national or regional affiliates.

Conclusion

The comparative case is a fundamental part of SIA, and longitudinal research is essential to the development of useful material on comparative cases. Longitudinal analysis that provides empirical data and a source of conceptual development can be derived both from specific research studies and from social assessment practice at various stages of the project cycle. There is no magical answer in respect to the number of cases that should be used to assess a new instance of social change. The issue facing the practitioner here is not so much about proof as about reliability and relevance. Where there are sufficient cases available for analysis, statistical comparisons might be conducted. Although this type of analysis might appear robust, the results could still vary in their relevance to any particular SIA. Equally, there will be instances where the information from one case can be regarded as sufficiently robust and relevant to provide useful information for a new impact assessment. It is possible to draw a number of conclusions in relation to the necessary production of more longitudinal research and comparative cases for SIA.

First, project SIA needs to be carried out bearing in mind the potential for developing comparative case data and experiential learning, to avoid the treadmill of case-by-case approaches. There are two key activities that generate comparative case data. The first is social profiling to provide an analysis of the social context during project design, and the second is monitoring and evaluation work during project implementation.

Second, wider social monitoring, including state of the environment monitoring and reporting by territorial authorities or central government, has the potential to provide information on comparative cases across several situations. This type of monitoring is often very general and could be focused more specifically to provide information on comparative cases as well as cumulative impacts. For example, monitoring at a regional level the social impacts of land-use change, transport systems or the location of retail facilities could provide information relevant to specific projects in these categories.

Third, government social research agencies and funding organizations can play a major role supporting research, such as the research programme described in this chapter, which was funded through the New Zealand Public Good Science Fund. It is highly unlikely that longitudinal research programmes in support of impact assessment practice will be generated without this type of government support.

Fourth, there is a need to encourage and support social science and resource management graduate students who carry out research projects that provide comparative case material. This support often requires only a low level of funding, such as assistance with living costs and field expenses. Internships for graduates to gain practical research experience should also be considered.

Fifth, there is a need to develop an international bibliography and case study database accessible on the Internet. Finally, there is a need to emphasize conceptual development, not just provide empirical case studies. Practitioners have to understand and apply frameworks for understanding the typical processes of change that are experienced.

References

Burdge, R.J. 1998. 'The social impact assessment model and the planning process', in R.J. Burdge (ed.), *A Conceptual Approach to Social Impact Assessment* (rev. edn), Middleton: Social Ecology Press, 31–9.

Burdge, R.J. and Johnson, S. 1998. 'Social impact assessment developing the basic model', in R.J. Burdge (ed.), *A Conceptual Approach to Social Impact Assessment* (rev. edn), Middleton: Social Ecology Press, 13–29.

Burdge, R.J. and Vanclay, F. 1995. 'Social impact assessment', in F. Vanclay and D. Bronstein (eds), *Environmental and Social Impact Assessment*, Chichester: Wiley, 31–66.

Freudenburg, W.R. 1986. 'Social impact assessment', *Annual Review of Sociology*, 12: 451–78.

Freudenburg, W.R. and Keating, K.M. 1985. 'Applying sociology to policy: social science and the environmental impact statement', *Rural Sociology*, 50(4): 578–605.

Rickson, R.E., Western, J.S. and Burdge, R.J. 1998. 'Social impact assessment: knowledge and development', in R.J. Burdge (ed.), *A Conceptual Approach to Social Impact Assessment*, Middleton: Social Ecology Press, 79–91.

Slootweg, R., Vanclay, F. and van Schooten, M. 2001. 'Function evaluation as a framework for the integration of social and environmental impact assessment', *Impact Assessment and Project Appraisal*, 19(1): 19–28.

Taylor, C.N. and Fitzgerald, G. 1988. 'New Zealand resource communities: Impact assessment and management in response to rapid economic change', *Impact Assessment Bulletin*, 6(2): 55–70.

Taylor, C.N., Goodrich, C.G. and Bryan, C.H. 1995. *Social Assessment: Theory, Process and Techniques* (2nd edn), Christchurch: Taylor Baines and Associates.

Tykkylainen, M. and Neil, C.C. 1995. 'Communities: evolving a comparative approach', *Community Development Journal*, 30(1): 31–47.

3   Using local knowledge

James Baines, Wayne McClintock, Nick Taylor and Brigid Buckenham

Introduction

The concept of 'local knowledge' can be used to examine the role of community consultation and participation in SIA. Local knowledge refers to information and understanding about the state of the biophysical and social environments that has been acquired by the people of a community which hosts (or will host) a particular project or programme. The origins of the term 'local knowledge' (Herrera, 1981; Mazur and Titilola, 1992) are found in the literature of rural technology transfer in Third World countries. There it has been variously referred to as traditional knowledge (Moles, 1989), traditional environmental knowledge (Morin-Labatut and Akhtar, 1992), indigenous technical knowledge (Howes and Chambers, 1979), people's knowledge (Wignaraja, 1991) and rural people's knowledge (Chambers, 1983). The local knowledge of any community has evolved over a period of time from the interaction of the people's cultural values and social organization with the physical environment in which they dwell. As such, it is a mixture of knowledge that has evolved within that community, and knowledge that has been acquired from outsiders (Morin-Labatut and Akhtar, 1992). Thus many social scientists (for example, Chambers, 1983; Richards, 1985; Gamser, 1988; Mazur and Titilola, 1992) have proposed that agricultural scientists use both local knowledge and western scientific knowledge to promote sustainable development. Taylor *et al.* (1995) present the project or programme cycle (see Figure 3.1) in order to demonstrate how the SIA process can provide an interface between the knowledge and interests of project proponents and host communities.

Realizing the full potential of SIA depends ultimately on our ability to blend together the inductive and deductive phases of theory building and application. Essential to this theory-building process is the use of comparative case knowledge and understanding derived variously from longitudinal research (see Chapter 2) and ex-post evaluatory SIAs. The full significance of the two phases described in Figure 3.1 – the design phase and the implementation phase – is to be found in their different contributions to SIA practice. Ex-ante SIA during the design phase is essentially predictive in nature. Ex-post SIA during the implementation phase is essentially evaluatory in nature. Each complements the other. Ideally, predic-

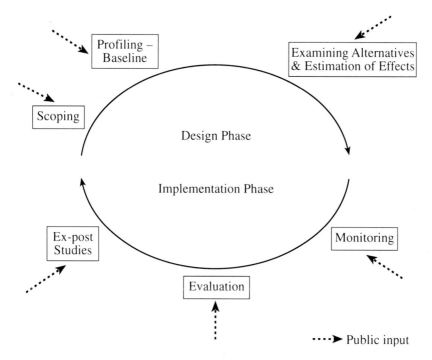

Source: After Taylor et al. (1995).

Figure 3.1   SIA project/programme cycle

tions of social impacts are formulated as a result of combining understandings from previous comparative cases with knowledge about the new circumstances of the case at hand. The corollary to this is that predictive SIAs can be very helpful in formulating and evaluating actual community experience. Local knowledge thus makes different contributions to ex-ante and ex-post assessments. For ex-ante SIA, local knowledge is necessary for a practical understanding of the new circumstances of the case at hand. Locals are unlikely to have first-hand experience of the proposal unless they have encountered something similar when living or working elsewhere, or unless the proposal being assessed is a modification of some activity which already exists locally. But they will know much about the existing patterns of activities and interests in their community and be in a position to think about potential impacts on these patterns if provided with relevant information about the proposal. By contrast, in ex-post SIA, local knowledge is essential both to describing the practical experience of locals of an existing activity, and its effects on them, and to understanding how and why patterns of impacts arise in the local community.

We take as a starting point for this chapter the observation that, to this point in the evolution of SIA, particularly in the context of public policy, the vast majority of applications have been of the predictive (ex-ante) kind. Very little attention has been paid to evaluatory SIA, despite the project cycle concept which has been articulated and advocated for many years. There is also a very practical and political context for this discussion. Members of the public, or interest group representatives engaged in community consultation around a particular project (in predictive SIA), often ask, 'What could we learn from similar situations elsewhere?' The fact that systematic, comparative case information is, more often than not, unavailable or not easily accessible merely serves to emphasize the historical bias of ex-ante applications over ex-post applications.

The perspective of many professional practitioners (of SIA) further reinforces this historical bias. Traditionally, the main focus of their efforts has been during the design phase of a project in preparing EIAs and SIAs. The potential for local knowledge to contribute to the implementation phase of the project/programme cycle has yet to be realized. Through experience, many practitioners have become convinced of the potential and real importance of using local knowledge to improve project or programme design. Community consultation at the design stage has often identified a range of mitigation initiatives that limit the extent of negative impacts and enhance the likelihood of positive impacts in a proactive way. It is often a vital factor in establishing or building community acceptance around a project, programme or policy. Despite the manifest benefits that such community consultation has brought to project or programme planning, it has taken a very long time and a great deal of argument and persuasion for project developers or programme proponents to 'buy' into this approach and back it up with the necessary skills and resources. Indeed, it has usually required a strong legislative push.

The issue of resistance to local or indigenous knowledge has been recognized in relation to different SIA paradigms. Lane *et al.* (1997) note that these have been characterized typically as technical and political approaches. The use of participatory methods to gather data for SIA involves an implicit assumption that local knowledge is valuable to the process. It requires an understanding of how local people perceive effects – not just how various technical experts understand them. From a practitioner perspective, it is still very much the norm for SIA to be dispensed with once the planning process is over. Ex-post monitoring and evaluation of any kind for major projects, programmes or policies has been slow to evolve in practice. SIA is generally not a component when it does take place.

This chapter explores the potential contribution of ex-post SIA to project and programme development and implementation, with a particular focus on the potential roles for local knowledge. It draws on research carried out in New Zealand (funded by the Foundation for Research, Science and Technology under contracts TBA602 and TBA802) which was to investigate the actual experience of host communities in the vicinity of solid waste facilities. This information is presented in order to bring real case data to the discussions. Nevertheless, our experience of SIA across a much broader range of applications convinces us that the lessons from this research are applicable generally. In the remainder of this chapter, we describe the research and its findings, and discuss the potential for using such local knowledge to improve SIA and EIA practice, the management of the solid waste facilities, and their regulatory control. As such, we hope it will contribute to achieving the vision set out in the project/programme cycle where participatory SIA becomes an integral part of both design and implementation phases.

Focus, approach and methods for ex-post SIA

The research utilized the concepts of 'host community' and 'source community' (see Figure 3.2). 'Host community' is used to refer to the community resident in the geographic area most clearly associated with a particular solid waste facility. It is not limited only to those residents who may experience direct physical effects from the operation of such a facility (such as the effects of noise, litter or odour). It extends to include members of a coherent community – perceived in a social sense – that already existed at the time the facility siting decision was taken, and which will continue to develop in ways that may or may not be affected by the presence of the solid waste facility in its locality. By contrast, the 'source community' incorporates all those who generate solid waste which requires either handling in a transfer station or disposal at a landfill. This is clearly a distinctly different set of interests, although they may indeed overlap, as is often the case with facilities located within or close to urban environments. SIA practitioners are accustomed to working in situations characterized by multiple and possibly conflicting interests.

The research employed social assessment approaches (Taylor *et al.*, 1995) to investigate the basic question, 'What effects have members of host communities actually experienced from the operation of a landfill nearby?' The approach involved drawing on a range of sources of information in order to profile the development of the solid waste facility itself, as well as its neighbouring community. Typical sources of information for profiling included planning and reporting documentation for the facility, census statistics, local histories, aerial photographs and interviews with long-time

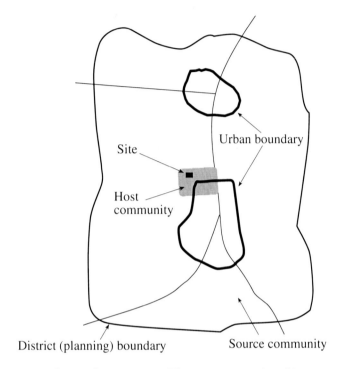

Figure 3.2   Relating the concepts of 'host community' and 'source community'

residents and with operators and administrators of the facility. Thus each case study describes the geographic location of the facility, the institutional planning context, the progressive development of the site and the facility over time, the potential effects which the facility's operations were expected to have on its neighbours (as predicted by the EIA), the current situation regarding operation of the facility (at the time of the case study field work), the nature of ongoing liaison between the facility operators and the host community, and the various roles and responsibilities in monitoring. Profiling of the host community incorporated analysis of demographic characteristics, changes in local population and the pattern of land use in the neighbourhood, and any significant developments in the local community and changes in the social character over time.

It is probably helpful to distinguish the use of the terms 'effect' and 'impact'. We use the term 'effect' to refer to the actual off-site environmental effects such as noise, odour or litter, observed by neighbours beyond the boundaries of the facility. Such effects may give rise to distinct social impacts such as varying degrees of nuisance, amenity loss, social disruption or indeed health impact experienced by those who observe the effects.

In evaluating the social impacts of the facility, as experienced within its host community, the emphasis was twofold. The main emphasis was on evaluating the day-to-day, operational impacts of the facility on its neighbouring residents and businesses. We sought to do this by making a detailed analysis of particular effects noticed by neighbouring residents and business people. We examined what these effects were attributed to (their source), the spatial distribution of these observed effects, the timing, frequency and trends in effects over time and a description of any mitigation efforts undertaken. We also undertook a detailed analysis of the severity of impacts experienced by neighbours. This led to a summary evaluation of each off-site effect as experienced in the host community. We also sought to evaluate any longer-term impacts the facility might have had on settlement patterns or community development in the locality, by virtue of its siting or its operations.

Recalling the definition of 'local knowledge' given at the beginning of the chapter, two methods were used to gain access to such local knowledge. First, a structured interview schedule was developed. This aimed to investigate the personal experience of individuals in the host community regarding effects and impacts from the landfill. Initially, respondents were asked an unprompted question to identify any effects that they had experienced. Then they were prompted from a list of effects generated from ex-ante EIA and SIA documentation for the facility. Whenever a particular effect was identified, a set of questions was then asked to elaborate on the nature, location and timing of the effect and exactly how the respondent or their household were affected. Between 40 and 100 such structured interviews were conducted for each case study, with a deliberate sampling strategy to cover all geographic directions and a range of separation distances. Those with the greatest potential exposure to off-site effects, that is, nearby residents and business people, were the main targets for interviewing, although recreational users of the locality were usually included as well. Recreational interviews sometimes became key informant interviews, since their recreational activity (such as walking, running or exercising a dog) afforded them the opportunity to experience the facility from various locations in the neighbourhood. Similarly, some interviews with local residents covered their experience of off-site effects both on their own properties and in their recreational use of the neighbourhood. Residential respondents close to the site often provided substantial, in-depth local knowledge and this was treated as 'key informant' information, additional to that provided and organized by the structured questionnaire. Key informant data were key-worded and the content analysed using software for qualitative data analysis (see Chapter 15).

The second method for gaining access to local knowledge was the use of semi-structured interviews with key informants from the local host community, the wider source community, and the facility operators, administrators and regulators. Such in-depth interviews focused on elaborating the social and community context for the solid waste facility and its operations, as well as establishing the detail of operations and mitigating measures in practice, and corroborating observations of neighbours with those of the operators and monitoring agencies. This stemmed from a deliberate strategy to triangulate observations as much as possible.

Findings of ex-post SIA

Social impact assessment is essentially about understanding the relationship between a set of activities (which occur as a result of a project, programme or policy) and people and organizations in the communities where those activities occur, whether or not they are the intended beneficiaries. It is therefore not surprising that the findings of the ex-post SIA fall logically into the following sequence which traverses this relationship: findings concerning the standard of facility operation; findings concerning host community perceptions and experience of the facilities; findings concerning the facility–host community relationship; and findings on the quality of the effects assessments.

Standard of facility operation

The adoption of impact assessment procedures in the planning arrangements of many jurisdictions over the past two decades has undoubtedly resulted in significant improvements in the way new facilities are operated. Public expectations about the standard of waste management operations are no exception. Indeed, higher public expectations have been instrumental in bringing about the improvements. Nowhere is this illustrated more clearly than in cases where current operations are on sites used previously for waste disposal. Current operations were experienced as being much improved on previous operations. This can be attributed to the higher operational standards required under the more recent planning arrangements noted above. Ex-post SIA becomes even more relevant against this backdrop of changing standards. Otherwise, the popular experience of old facilities may create inappropriate expectations of what the operational impacts of newer facilities will be like, and this in turn can feed through to inappropriate predictions of effects when consultative methods of assessment are used without up-to-date comparative case information.

Nevertheless, the ex-post assessments showed that some effects from solid waste operations were experienced off-site in all cases. We have yet to arrive at the point (in New Zealand, at least) where our waste facilities are sited

and developed with sufficient internal buffer areas, and the facilities themselves are operated to standards which will avoid all off-site impacts.
Unpleasant odours, roadside litter and heavy traffic noise were the most
common effects reported, although the impacts were not always considered
unacceptable. Other minor or less frequently reported effects included visual
and landscape effects, road safety impacts and impacts from birds attracted
to the facilities. Some recent planning decisions have in fact established a
new benchmark of 'no effects beyond the boundary'. However, this appears
at the present time to be intended as a desirable target, a measure to enable
administrative leverage, rather than an operational constraint where failure
to comply strictly would trigger permanent closure of the facility.

In a few instances (for example, with landfill gas smells), neighbours
notice effects at the margin of detection. It is to be expected also that different people will have different thresholds of observation. One person may
report no experience of bad odours or noise disturbance, while their neighbours may report significant impacts from odours or noise. Such differences
may have several possible explanations, for example a different pattern of
occupation. One neighbour may be retired and resident seven days a week,
while another may be working away from the property and therefore absent
during most of the landfill's operating hours. Other explanations include a
different sensory sensitivity, or a different threshold of tolerance.

In most cases, there are other significant sources of similar effects in the
neighbourhood. These included other sources of odour (such as piggeries,
meat processing facilities, chicken farms or sewer lines), other destinations
for heavy transport (such as quarries or forestry operations) and other
sources of industrial noise (such as quarry crushing plant, timber processing or metal foundries). The research encountered instances where landfill
neighbours either were not certain if the landfill was the source of the effect
or were inclined to blame the landfill for effects originating from other
sources, because the landfill was seen as a less desirable activity than a
quarry, a forest or a chicken farm. It was not possible to conclude from the
research whether an ex-post assessment of effects of one of these other
'sources of similar effects' would have revealed the same element of 'confusion': whether the observed 'confusion' was purely random or reflected a
bias against landfills.

Host community perceptions and experience of waste facilities
Factors such as the wind regime, topography, separation distances and
certain types of land use are critical to the distribution of the off-site effects
that are experienced. Plantation forestry, industrial land use and certain
types of agriculture or horticulture can mask off-site effects such as odour
and noise. The concept of 'buffer zones' separating landfill operations from

neighbouring activities is important to host community experience. Buffer zones can be thought of as mere space, separating one activity from another. However, intervening activities in that space can also be influential (for example, a forest plantation can provide a barrier to odour, noise, windblown litter and visual intrusion). All the landfills studied had significant elements of recreational use in the buffer zone, reflecting the fact that occasional occupation of the buffer zone is less likely than continuous occupation to lead to unpleasant experiences.

The acceptability of an impact (for example, from unpleasant odours) is generally linked not only to the magnitude of the impact, but to the likelihood of experiencing it, and also to the element of choice. Occasional or temporary, voluntary occupation of recreational space in the buffer area reduces the likelihood of experiencing unpleasant impacts, and also gives the individual the choice over whether or not to go there and, if so, how often and when to visit. Invariably, neighbours acknowledged that their actual experiences of off-site effects and impacts were less extreme than the impacts they had anticipated. Nevertheless, it was noticeable that neighbours with particular experiences of facilities (lots of effects, or peculiar effects that others do not tend to notice) were invariably very close to the facility boundary (small separation distances).

Facility–host community relationship
It is evident that many neighbours notice effects, but do not do anything about these experiences (such as making a complaint). It would be easy to conclude that in many such instances the impacts were judged to be minor or negligible. Our experience of ex-post SIA confirms that such a conclusion is only partly true. Whether or not neighbours act on their experiences is also determined by the presence or absence of appropriate communication channels and liaison mechanisms, knowledge of such arrangements, and the attitudes and organizational culture of the facility operators, administrators and consent authorities.

It remains relatively unusual for liaison mechanisms between facility developers and host communities to be set up prior to the permitting process as part of the procedure for community consultation (that is, early on in the planning process). Even if consultation has been part of the facility's planning process, participants in the planning process have generally not viewed this as a basis for contributing to future monitoring of the operations; that is to say, they have generally not sought to incorporate local knowledge into ongoing monitoring. Nor have local government agencies generally made the connection. The implication appears to be that local stakeholders' interests will be adequately addressed by initial siting decisions or initial permit conditions.

In our experience, relatively few solid waste facilities have any ongoing formalized liaison mechanism between the facility operator and members of the host community. By 'formalized liaison mechanism' we mean a mechanism which is dedicated to encouraging ongoing communications directly between the facility operators and members of the immediate host community. This might take the form of a community liaison committee in which most of the committee members are from the host community, along with facility operator representatives (possibly both staff and management). Such a committee operates proactively and meets regularly, whether or not there are complaints to be addressed. A telephone contact at the local government agency for general public enquiries would not constitute such a liaison mechanism. It is neither dedicated to the facility or the facility's host community, nor proactive. It is generally a channel for receiving complaints after the event, and is predominantly a one-way channel of communication. However, this is frequently the only point of contact for people wishing to raise issues about, or report effects from, solid waste facilities.

Part of the problem for host community members wishing to report incidents of off-site effects is the type of organizational culture they encounter when doing so. It has often been the case that operators and administrators see complaints as indications of failure or poor performance, while relatively few regard complaints as opportunities for improvement. The differences in culture influence the way complaints are received, attitudes towards the complainant and also how the organization responds. Our research indicates that sometimes the logging of complaints was not as systematic as it could be, and often appeared to be not well coordinated between various participants (operators, administrators and consent agencies).

Quality of effects assessments
Even though the statutory definition of 'environment' in New Zealand legislation clearly includes the social dimension (Resource Management Act 1991), most people who undertake EIA are not experienced in SIA. As a result, we find that EIAs generally ignore the community context in their descriptions, and generally do not discuss the social consequences of the effects (that is, they tend to ignore the social environment). Complementary EIAs and SIAs remain the exception rather than the rule. Nevertheless, our comparative case research found that in most cases very few of the off-site effects subsequently experienced were not at least identified at the planning stage, although in most EIAs the analysis was very limited. However, there were examples in several cases where some projected off-site effects identified at the planning stage were not reported as being experienced by any

members of the host community during the implementation stage (that is, they were not actual effects).

Most EIAs have been very general in their descriptions of effects, particularly as they relate to members of the host community (for example, with little discussion of severity/significance; no mention of expected frequency, or likelihood, or areas likely to be affected). Some of the more recent EIAs appear to have been more explicit and realistic in their acknowledgment and projection of effects (but still lack useful detail). Given the importance of factors such as wind regime, topography and certain types of land uses in the prospective buffer zones, it is surprising that most EIAs paid little detailed attention to analysing these aspects. For example, the prevailing wind conditions (such as patterns of speed and direction) are likely to influence the host community's experience of a range of common off-site effects (noise, dust, odour, litter and so on). We found very few EIAs which included data on the local wind regime in their assessment of effects.

Issues for interpretation

In carrying out our comparative case assessments, the assessment team had to address several issues relevant to interpreting the results and their usefulness in providing valid comparative information. These included the debate about 'perceived' or 'real' effects, the need for corroboration and the importance of timing or context as a potential influence on individual responses.

The assessments were clearly aimed at investigating people's experiences of living or working near waste management facilities. The results are therefore based on a large body of individual perceptions of effects. In some feedback discussions, the distinction was made that these effects are 'only people's perceptions; they're not necessarily real'. The question arises therefore as to what is the difference between a 'perceived' effect and a 'real' effect. Can 'perceived' effects ever become 'real' effects? In practical terms, the assessments identified clearly the proportions of those interviewed who perceived (experienced) certain types of effect. Furthermore, wherever possible, the assessment sought to investigate these effects from other respondents and from independent sources (local key informants, secondary data records and so on) or different perspectives (such as the facility operator). As researchers, it was pleasing to note how, in the great majority of cases, neighbours' perceptions and experience were strongly corroborated by the perceptions and experience of the facility operator.

We would acknowledge that a number of factors have a bearing on individual perceptions. Different people have different thresholds for noticing effects, depending, for example, on their ability to hear or to smell, or on their perception of what is 'exceptional'. Increasing the sample size addressed this factor. Different living or recreational patterns are likely to influence people's experience of effects, whether they are on the property all day, every day or working off the property. Day-time interviewing addressed this factor by increasing the likelihood of including individuals with a relatively high rate of occupancy. People get used to effects after a while – they can seem less exceptional. Following unprompted questions with prompted questions addressed this factor, by allowing interviewees 'a second chance' to respond.

Ultimately, we are forced to ask whether the distinction between 'perceived' and 'real' effects matters. The primary purpose and value of ex-post, comparative case assessment is to answer two types of question: (a) if neighbours around a facility are experiencing certain effects, and finding that they have unacceptable impacts, what can be done to reduce or eliminate the effect, or make it less likely to happen; and (b) if neighbours around Existing Facility A experienced certain effects and impacts from its operation, what is the likelihood that neighbours around Potential Facilities B, C or D will experience similar effects and impacts? In either situation, whether such effects are labelled as 'perceived' or 'real' is probably immaterial. However, we would make this observation: from a technical perspective, replication of reported effects is important to their validation, while, from a political perspective, the perceptions of just a few people affected can be sufficient to galvanize social action. We would also observe that technical experts are not necessarily in a position to offer any more than assessments of perceived effects. In the case of technical experts, the perceptions are derived with the aid of technical lenses (that is, frameworks for analysis used by the technical expert). For example, an acoustic engineer can provide measures and predictions of likely noise levels at certain distances away from the source of the noise. The acoustic engineer is not usually in a position to draw any inferences as to likely social impacts associated with these levels of noise.

The tendency for potentially affected parties to distort or exaggerate the likelihood of effects when participating in EIA activities is not an uncommon experience for SIA practitioners. Indeed, in one of the comparative case studies, background documentation from an environmental tribunal declared this point explicitly. Another set of findings which support this behaviour was noted previously: actual effects were invariably viewed as less extreme than projected effects. In comparative case assessment, this factor is addressed by ensuring that all the case studies are carried out on facilities which have no active permit applications or review processes.

Lessons for improved assessment, management and regulatory control
Although the major purpose of ex-post SIA is to document the experiences of particular host communities as a basis for improved site selection and

design of solid waste facilities in the future, these assessments provide important insights into the way local knowledge can be used during the implementation phase as well. Not only can effective use of local knowledge improve the practice of SIA, but contrasts between the experiences of different host communities make it clear that local knowledge, and the mechanisms and protocols which are established to gain access to such knowledge, can also assist with improving operating standards and regulatory oversight.

Improved impact assessment

An important aspect of social assessment theory and practice is the process of analytic induction (Taylor *et al.*, 1995). This process involves the complementary modes of deductive hypothesis testing and inductive theory building. An analogy is readily drawn between ex-ante predictive SIA and ex-post evaluatory SIA. The knowledge and understanding gained by SIA practitioners, host community members, or others involved in the planning process, from a series of comparative case studies using ex-post SIA helps us to understand and predict with greater certainty and greater usefulness the potential impacts from a new project. This applies equally to specific effect–impact combinations (such as noise–nuisance or odour–nuisance impacts) and to cumulative, longer-term social development impacts. The importance of local knowledge (from ex-post evaluations) in enhancing SIA practice derives from the demonstrable accuracy of the collective observations gathered from host community members, the ability to link environmental effects to their social consequences, and the ability to provide detail on spatial extent, likelihood of effect and severity of impact experienced.

Improved facility management

It is well established and widely acknowledged amongst SIA practitioners that members of the host community are well placed to participate in a predictive assessment of effects. Indeed, in many jurisdictions, it is their legal right to participate. Their proximity to the prospective activity, combined with their knowledge of existing physical, cultural and social conditions in the locality, enables them to assess both potential impacts and possible effective mitigation measures. In New Zealand, planning legislation acknowledges that neighbours are likely to be affected parties. Our experience with ex-post SIA confirms that indeed they are affected parties, and continue to be during the implementation phase. It seems entirely logical to us that the criteria used to justify local input during the planning phase apply with equal validity to justify local input to the ongoing monitoring of project or facility operations. Indeed, the question might well be asked:

why involve neighbours in a predictive assessment if they are not to be engaged in the subsequent monitoring and evaluation? If one purpose of SIA and EIA is to satisfy planning authorities that a certain facility will not have undue negative impacts on its host community, why not check with the host community to confirm that the predictions were correct?

However, many planning procedures produce adversarial relationships at the time of project initiation, which are not necessarily conducive to constructive collaboration later on. Using local knowledge provided by neighbours to a facility to improve its management and reduce off-site effects requires redefining the type of relationship that usually exists between facility operators and their host community. This depends on attitudes that are cultivated, where operators need to take complainants' observations seriously, neighbours need to be willing to report experience in a timely and objective manner, and both parties need to demonstrate good faith. As noted in the earlier discussion on the facility–host community relationship, effective and direct contact channels must be in place, and widely known, so that neighbours know how they can make contact quickly and their observations can be linked to the activities that cause them. While dealing with neighbours' concerns does not always occupy large amounts of time and effort – unless the facility is causing extraordinary levels of off-site nuisance and offence – it is vital that adequate staffing and resources are allocated by the facility operator to demonstrate a readiness to respond and a commitment to continuous improvement.

Another important aspect of redefining the relationship between facility operator and host community is the establishment of an ongoing dedicated liaison mechanism, such as a community liaison committee (CLC). This mechanism complements the direct one-on-one contacts that arise out of particular incidents extending beyond the facility boundary, which are reactive in nature. The CLC provides a means to (a) build personal relationships and mutual trust, (b) continuously review the operations and impacts, and (c) adopt a proactive approach to manage any issues of community or operator concern.

Improved regulatory oversight
The relationships established during the planning phase for new facilities and projects – when participatory SIAs are used in predictive mode – are not confined to the operator–host community relationship. Invariably, the planning framework of laws and procedures is administered by a public agency, whose role thereafter continues with monitoring and evaluation of matters of compliance. Once again, experience to date typically demonstrates a bias towards the relationship between the operator and consent administrator. Facility operators are usually required to carry out the

mainstream monitoring and provide periodic reports to the consent agency. The latter may conduct occasional audits of the same. There is rarely, if ever, any proactive attempt on the part of consent agencies to use host community experience as part of their compliance monitoring.

Good practice, as revealed in the minority of comparative case assessments to date, suggests that regulatory oversight could be made more effective (and more transparent and accountable) by a variety of features which connect the host community to the facility operations and regulatory agencies. It is becoming more of a standard feature, although by no means universal in practice, to have a formal incident log, which documents neighbours' calls and records the date, time, nature of the problem, cause, response, response time and outcome. This log is maintained by the facility operator as a formal requirement of the operating consent. Second, it is logical to include a representative from the consent agency on the CLC, thus institutionalizing the ongoing three-way relationship which was first established during the planning phase. Indeed, it may be appropriate to have several representatives from the consent agency, representing variously the technical and community responsibilities of the local public agency. Finally, periodic use of ex-post SIA by the consent agency – a form of periodic social monitoring – would complement the biophysical monitoring and incident reporting which is already a standard condition for resource consents on such facilities. Methods have been developed for surveying host community populations which are relatively inexpensive and quick to implement, and which provide useful information on the performance of facilities, not only for consent compliance, but also to feed back into revised standards for new consents, thus closing the institutional loop. In this way, the consent agency draws on regular input from both facility operator and host community.

Conclusion

There must be greater recognition by practitioners as well as operators and administrators that SIA is an ongoing process which occurs throughout the life cycle of a particular facility. Management of the operation, and mitigation of its off-site effects, will remain effective only if information is obtained systematically from local residents and used as an integral part of the ongoing assessment and evaluation. There will always be particular local circumstances which combine to influence the scale and distribution of effects and social impacts around any project site or programme location. We are firmly of the view that the best strategy for impact assessment is to combine the strengths of experienced SIA professionals and their understanding of comparative cases with the strengths of stakeholder groups and their detailed local knowledge.

While, in the past, planning administrators and SIA practitioners may have been convinced that the use of local knowledge is essential to good project planning, we believe that the benchmark for good practice should now be shifted. SIA methods and experience are now sufficient to do justice to the notion that the use of local knowledge is essential for effective monitoring, evaluation and continuous improvement.

References

Chambers, R. 1983. *Rural Development: Putting the Last First*, London: Longman.

Gamser, M.S. 1988. 'Innovation, technical assistance, and development: The importance of technology users', *World Development*, 16(6): 711–21.

Herrera, A.O. 1981. 'The generation of technologies in rural areas', *World Development*, 9(1): 21–35.

Howes, M. and Chambers, R. 1979. 'Indigenous technical knowledge: analysis, implications and issues', *IDS Bulletin*, 10(2): 5–11.

Lane, M.B., Ross, H. and Dale, A.P. 1997. 'Social impact research: integrating the technical, political and planning paradigms', *Human Organization*, 56(3): 302–10.

Mazur, R.E. and Titilola, S.T. 1992. 'Social and economic dimensions of local knowledge systems in African sustainable agriculture', *Sociologia Ruralis*, 32(2/3): 264–86.

Moles, J.A. 1989. 'Agricultural sustainability and traditional agriculture: learning from the past and its relevance to Sri Lanka', *Human Organization*, 48(1): 70–78.

Morin-Labatut, G. and Akhtar, S. 1992. 'Traditional environmental knowledge: A resource to manage and share', *Development*, 4: 24–30.

Richards, P. 1985. *Indigenous Agricultural Revolution: Ecology and Food Production in West Africa*. London: Hutchinson.

Taylor, C.N., Bryan, C.H. and Goodrich, C.G. 1995. *Social Assessment: theory, process & techniques*, Christchurch: Taylor Baines and Associates.

Wignaraja, P. 1991. 'The Knowledge System', in P. Wignaraja *et al.* (eds), *Participatory Development: Learning from South Asia*. Tokyo: United Nations University Press, 206–22.

4 Learning from participatory land management

Neil Powell and Janice Jiggins

Introduction

This chapter considers the perspective of development professionals faced with complex situations that are regarded by one or other stakeholder as *problematic.* They are problematic because they are complex. Complex problem situations require new approaches to the assessment of risk impacts and their management (Dorner, 1997). Such situations are characterized by irreducible uncertainty, that is, uncertainty concerning possible risk and harm which cannot be removed by more, or better, information.

Two dimensions of these new approaches that are emerging are addressed here. First, complex problem situations typically present themselves as *overdetermined* problems. Overdetermined problems are distinguished from normal hazards and risks – that is, where one thing causes another such that there is an explanatory relationship between cause and effect. Overdetermined problems are characterized by non-linear relationships. An actual cause is causative, but not explanatory: if one cause does not occur, another will. The appropriate level of explanation moves from the microscopic to the macroscopic, from the particular to the systemic.

The second dimension of complex problem situations brings into play concepts of moral reasoning as a frame for deliberating contested versions of the public good in conditions of irreducible uncertainty.

These two dimensions together challenge risk assessment professions to reconsider definitions of resilience. Measuring resilience in terms of *capacity to learn* may be the most appropriate measure in situations of uncertainty. Through an illustrative case from the Nyae Nyae, a region of Namibia, we critically reflect upon impact assessment in conditions characterized by non-linear relationships.

Impact assessment in complex problem situations

Survey evidence and other forms of empirical inquiry reveal wide divergence between scientific or expert treatment of risk and the way lay publics deal with risk and uncertainty. Scientists tend to think of risks as having objective properties (for example, evidence that harm can occur), and they assume that uncertainties can be reduced to risks, for which probabilities can be assigned. Experts assess the trade-offs between the costs and benefits of reducing the causes and mitigating the consequences (Jakobsson and Dragun, 1996). The techniques of risk communication are used to inform policy makers and the public (Lubchenko, 1998). There are difficulties in thinking about and dealing with risk in this way. The description of objective properties is presented as a true (complete) definition of the problem. The normative aspects are disguised as expertise. Underlying assumptions about the nature of reality are hidden.

The person who defines the limits of the context or the risk also determines who is being rational and, by inference, who is not. The process does not accept that a person or group can rationally oppose something judged safe (that is, no evidence harm can occur or low probability that it will occur). Expert-based risk assessment tends to exclude, if only because non-measurable, concepts such as fairness, equity or rightness. Put another way, expert-based risk assessment tends to exclude the moral structure of the domain of action.

Expert communication of risk also tends to smother or blur the crucial distinction between 'No evidence of harm' and 'Evidence that no harm can occur'. Yet ordinary people do make a distinction between the way they address these two very different issues. The guarantees of the safety of the food chain that consumers in Europe demand in the aftermath of the twin shocks of 'mad cow disease' and the 'foot and mouth' outbreaks provide examples. In addition, lay publics are seen by experts as not being able to think in terms of probabilities. This amounts to a disguised accusation of irrationality if the public opposes something to which experts assign low risk probabilities. But this view fails to take into account the evidence that the public's 'tolerance thresholds' (that is, the risk probability considered tolerable) are contextual and socially constructed. Experience leaves the lay public acutely aware that the unexpected cannot be assessed in terms of risk probabilities, even if the unexpected dominates the final risk assessment. Further, survey evidence suggests that lay publics are aware that (a) if actual experience in reality is limited, there is no valid basis for establishing estimated risk probabilities; and (b) low probability but high consequence events do not enable individuals or societies (or risk professionals) to learn easily from experience.

Increasingly, the problems facing humanity have the risk characteristics noted above (Beck, 1992; Krimsky and Golding, 1992). From the perspective presented so far, it is argued that attempts to narrow the assessment of risks beforehand, or the impacts after the fact, will not necessarily convince lay publics and hence not improve manageability. Since risk in complex problem situations, such as those addressed by ecology or social science, cannot be predicted because of the intractable qualities of their subject matter, debate, dissent and the absence of final closure (or a lack of complete information – one reasonable definition of truth) will be enduring hallmarks of SIA. SIA methodology thus needs to adjust to the dynamism of irreducible incompleteness (a reasonable definition of uncertainty).

The discussion might be taken further to consider how, in the conditions described, the public good might be identified. Over the last several decades, two related propositions have gained political standing:

1. Markets provide the most accurate definition of the public good because they are the sum total of what people want. It therefore follows that the more efficient and free the market is, the better the market can define the public good.
2. Governments provide, at best, a partial and self-serving definition of the public good, which, at worst, assimilates the public good to the perpetuation in power of the ruling class or individual. It therefore follows that the role of government in controlling and regulating should be minimized.

In this view, the very idea that risk gives rise to questions of morality, and that markets are bad at assigning value to non-monetized goods and services, is swept aside as irrelevant. Insistence that there are acute choices to be made in the face of irreducible uncertainty, and that these are fundamentally of a moral character, is dismissed as irrational. Yet all available evidence of public opinion, however diverse it is in many respects, indicates a wide public determination that the moral dimension is central to the definition of the public good as exposure to risk increases.

How then are we to understand this moral dimension? In developed economies, numerous ethics committees have been established in various sectors to puzzle this out on our behalf. The evidence from civil society, however, is that individuals are seeking, as moral actors, a more direct confrontation with the choices posed. Anthropological literature as well as the evidence of everyday experience suggests widespread compliance among lay publics with the proposition of philosophers that moral standards form complex structures in which 'boundary setting' plays an important role. Some things are perceived simply as not being on the menu of options from which a choice must be made. Further, restrictions may apply to what is considered fitting, or right to take into account, with regard to particular decisions. Five kinds of questions typically arise.

1. Can moral claims be established objectively?
2. To what extent should concern for others, and what types of concerns,

should rightfully be taken into account when we accept limitations of our own self-interest?

3. To what extent should individual rights be protected from limitation in the advancement of the public good?
4. Does the aggregation of small benefits for large numbers of people outweigh the larger cost for a smaller number of people?
5. Is the utilitarian maximization of aggregate wellbeing the dominant value (the Benthamite search for the greatest good for the greatest number)?

Scanlon (1999) explores the concept of 'co-deliberation' as an approach to considering a response to these questions. A central proposition of co-deliberation is that, as moral actors, individuals seek to justify their behaviour to others in ways which conform to principles that none could reasonably reject. Individuals therefore base their justification on a deliberation of their perception of what these principles might be (thus *co-deliberation*). When an individual knowingly transgresses these principles, then, in effect, the perpetrator is asserting that they do not care about the morality of the act, or its acceptability to others.

The co-determined judgments about what is justifiable (and the principles that bound such actions) are rooted in individual experience of what is reasonable, and not in the simple aggregation of individual values. The inadmissibility of simple aggregation as true judgment converges with recent research on the biology of cognition and the experienced world (Varela, 1999). This allows for a distinction to be made between the individual assessment of the reasonable limits to self-sacrifice in the interests of the larger whole, and the assessment of a disinterested third party. This distinction sheds light on the importance and significance of (a) the relations between moral actors in determining the reasonableness of specific actions, and (b) the more general frameworks of meaning that determine which reasons for action (principles for reasoning) are considered relevant in any particular case.

In effect, Scanlon's (1999) argument allows us to understand why cost–benefit analysis, contingent valuation, opinion polling or the deliberations of ethics committees do not take us much further with respect to the interactions between people and their environment. It helps us understand why the reduction of moral choices to the workings of the market will not satisfy. It elucidates in formal terms the everyday experience of the different moral treatment afforded (a) to the choices of disinterested third parties among competing interests; (b) to the choices of individuals to save and protect from harm the things most dear to them, even at the expense of others; and (c) to the choices of disinterested third parties in subjecting a few to harm, or loss of amenity, or additional cost, as a means of protecting many others from a greater or comparable harm.

By focusing on multi-level reasons and on reasoning as being basic to morality and conduct, Scanlon (1999) illuminates a possible way forward for citizen participation in ex-ante risk assessment and ex-post impact evaluation. His work points towards establishing new boundaries for institutional and technology design and use, and the purposeful co-evolution of futures, as well as redefinition of institutional and structural relations in context, based on a moral reasoning which is co-determined among citizens, governments, market actors and specialists.

Impact assessment and the concept of resilience
The deeper understanding of risk assessment in relation to overdetermined problem situations, and the concept of moral reasoning as an approach to the co-determination of the public good in situations of irreducible uncertainty, lead into a discussion of the concept of resilience. SIA and EIA increasingly are required to provide insight into the 'sustainability' of different courses of action. A desired characteristic of sustainability is thought to be that of resilience. There are three contrasting definitions of resilience that are in common use.

Drawing on economic theory and engineering, one definition addresses resilience as a property of systems at or near an equilibrium steady state. Thus, in this definition, resistance to disturbance and speed of return to the equilibrium can be used to measure resilience (O'Neill *et al.*, 1986; Pimm, 1984).

Another definition addresses conditions far from equilibrium. Instabilities can flip a system into another regime of behaviour, that is, to another stability domain. Measurement of resilience here is made in terms of the magnitude of disturbance that can be absorbed before the system changes its structure by changing the variables and processes that control behaviour (Walker *et al.*, 1969; Holling, 1996).

A third approach addresses the management of unstable states. Here, measurement of resilience is undertaken in terms of a coupled system's capacity to learn (evolve) co-dependently (Powell, 1998).

The first two definitions aim in management terms towards *stability*. This has been a major concern of those seeking to manage *adaptively* (Berkes and Folke, 1998). Adaptive management recognizes that uncertainty increases with complexity. It links the capacity for monitoring action outcomes to system management. It seeks to strengthen institutional capacity for responding quickly to surprises. A critique of adaptive management is presented in Jiggins and Röling (2000). Of particular relevance here is the maintenance within adaptive management of the separation of the world as a pre-given reality, distinct from our perceptions of the world. The role of institutions in this view is to *bridge* the two worlds, in order that human behaviour may be brought into conformity with the ecological dynamic of the pre-given world. The contrasting view, supported by the biology of cognition, is that the material world and the perceiver co-specify each other (Maturana and Varela, 1992). People and their environment are structurally coupled in an interactive system, in which continuing capacity to learn is the key to taking effective action (ibid., 1992: 75).

The third approach permits managing the coupled system in terms of *plasticity* of function, structure and process. It recognizes the need to acknowledge uncertainty in order for governance to function. It also notes the precautionary principle as the justification for action (rather than, as it is usually taken to be, simply a rationale for blocking action). It accepts that there will be bad decisions with serious, perhaps irreversible consequences. Thus the emphasis is on maintaining continuing capacity to *generate options and scenarios*. Shared identification of, and learning about, key variables, relationships and processes, and the opportunities for influencing these, assume particular importance (LEARN, 2000).

The justification presented for adopting the third definition of resilience in impact assessment is grounded in the work of the biological and evolution sciences (Maturana and Varela, 1992; Ceruti, 1994). These seem to demonstrate the intrinsically constructive nature of evolutionary processes. At a fundamental level, the classical values of science as a practice aspiring to establish true knowledge – omniscience, completeness and atemporality – would not seem possible in relation to evolutionary process. The spatial and temporal dynamic of non-equilibrium systems may reveal this more starkly than more stable domains of existence (Scoones, 1999; Mazzucato and Niemeijer, 2000).

The thrust of this chapter also links to recent analysis of the co-evolutionary perspective in ecological economics, which highlights systemic co-dependency between socioeconomies and their environment, and the time-indeterminancies of economy–environment change, and hence also of analysis of the institutional and ethical dimensions of human action (O'Connor, 1991).

An illustrative case: the Nyae Nyae

The case we have selected is drawn from the introduction of conservancy legislation and project support for the management of wildlife and other natural resources in the Nyae Nyae, a semi-arid area in Eastern Bushmanland in Namibia. It is a context that may be characterized as a complex system displaying vulnerability to low probability, high consequence events, and exposure to the unexpected (Powell, 1998).

The Nyae Nyae has long been perceived by outside interests as a fragile pristine wilderness increasingly threatened by the anthropogenic forces of global development and, locally, by cattle raising, burning, hunting and poaching. In parallel, the prevailing anthropological view is that the indigenous inhabitants, the Ju/'hoansi (the Nyae Nyae San), had secured, and until recently had maintained, an autonomous and stable livelihood by hunting and gathering (Lee, 1979; Yellen, 1990). The spread of cattle raising and sedentary gardening, the territorial incursion by other ethnic groups such as the Herero pastoralists, and the breakdown of the local institutions governing natural resource utilization, are seen as disturbances of an essentially equilibrium system. The characterization in both views relies on an assumption of linear causality between the anthropogenic agents and the pre-given natural system.

The Namibia Ministry of the Environment and Tourism, with the advice of the USA-based World Wildlife Fund, approved the formation of the Nyae Nyae conservancy in 1998. The conservancy institutionalizes the notion that conservation cannot be secured without the active participation and support of local communities. Compensatory mechanisms are built into the legislation to encourage communities to modify their livelihood systems, so that they do not conflict with equilibrial wildlife management principles. This has resulted (inter alia) in the transformation of the Ju/'hoansi's representative institution, the Nyae Nyae Farmers' Cooperative (NNFC), into an institution for managing the Nyae Nyae *as if* it were a common property resource subject to enforceable land-use principles agreed among a discrete user group on the basis of negotiated rules, regulation and sanctions.

In 1998, the NNFC was designated the Nyae Nyae Conservancy Committee (NNCC) and governed by the constitution laid down in the conservancy legislation. Its given purpose was to act as the community stakeholder in the 'co-management' of the conservancy. It assumed powers to enforce wildlife management principles laid out in the government's Wildlife Management Plan. The plan aimed to maintain wildlife at its maximum sustainable yield while prioritizing species considered to be of high international conservation value. Some of the rules subsequently enforced include: (a) implementation of a game harvesting quota, (b) restriction of domestic livestock to 50 animals per borehole, (c) specification of land use in accordance with the spatial restrictions identified in a land-use zoning strategy, and (d) establishment of numerous game water points. A resource-monitoring procedure has been joined to the plan. This uses the *abundance* of wildlife as an indicator of ecosystem health and provides the principal feedback information for triggering management interventions.

In numerous respects, the plan encapsulates orthodox best practice. In our view, however, the plan might be read as an example of what happens when one tries to manage a decoupled system as if it were tending towards equilibrium. For reasons set out below, the impacts are likely to stimulate 'pathological structuration'. By this we mean that the social ecology of the Ju/'hoansi is being pulled towards a relationship with a socioeconomic system that is separated from the dynamics of the context.

First, we discuss the evidence that the plan, and its impact on the structure and functions of the ecosystem and community livelihoods, has been shaped by the assumption that the Nyae Nyae is an equilibrial system that should and can be managed adaptively for stability. The sinking of boreholes to provide year-round water points, the management of the range to maximize the number and visibility of animal species favoured by tourists, and the imposition of land-use zoning, cattle quotas and market-oriented livelihood development, could be cited. As in other parts of the world where similar stabilization schemes have been introduced, technical modelling of impacts would suggest that such interventions increase riskiness, threatening to tip the system unpredictably into new states.

The contrary evidence is that the natural system is far from equilibrium and that, prior to the establishment of the conservancy, the Ju/'hoansi had evolved socioeconomic and natural resource management institutions and processes that maintained plasticity and hence resilience. Examples of such institutions and processes include the nurturing of 'cooperative knowledge' through intersubjective dialogue at intra-community, inter-community, and inter-species levels. For example, the Ju/'hoansi have established through indirect experiential dialogue with elephants in the Nyae Nyae a mechanism which serves to regulate the use of the marula fruit (*Schlerocarya caffra*). Certain fruit trees are set aside for people and other trees are left for the exclusive use of elephants (Powell, 1998). If people defect from the agreement, elephants will destroy the marula trees, so that the resource is no longer available to either people or elephants.

Other institutions and processes established include consensual processes of governance guided by the kinds of moral reasoning characterized by Scanlon (1999), as well as heterogeneous livelihood strategies, which are dynamic in time and space. Finally, hunting and other resource utilization is based on acute observation of a range of environmental trends and qualities in a temporally and spatially unbounded landscape. Thus the Ju/'hoansi consciously seek to contribute to the resilience of a coupled non-equilibrial system rather than to the stability of a system at or near equilibrium (Fairhead and Leach, 1996; Powell, 1998; Mazzucato and Niemeijer, 2000). An example is provided by the issue of burning. The Ju/'hoansi employ at the inter-community level a cooperative burning regime, which is mediated through intersubjective dialogue without recourse to any specific enforcement institutions. On the one hand, cooperative burning in the larger rangeland system is used to optimize the diversity of different successional states for wildlife and gathering needs. At another level, burning is used to bring forth an environment that protects subsystems that can be maintained nearer equilibrium, such as stands of woodland. At the intra-community level, the Ju/'hoansi cultivate reciprocal interdependence with other ethnic groups in a variety of ways which can be called into being as and when required. In brief, the Ju/'hoansi call into being a mosaic of opportunities that can be actuated in response to systemic uncertainty.

Further, the co-learning that is inherent in the processes of intersubjective dialogue and consensual governance generates the systemic memory that enables the system to endogenize and transcend stress and uncertainty. In 1993–4, an attempt was initiated to develop methods for conservation and resource management that built on the understanding of the Nyae Nyae as a resilient non-equilibrial system (Powell, 1997).

The Community Land Assessment and Monitoring Programme (CLAM) arose as it became clear that Ju/'hoansi knowledge and perspectives on their own environment and actions could not be captured readily and assimilated into the standard formalized routines and formats of rangeland management modelling and data interpretation. Neither could they be accommodated within the dominant expert analysis of what was problematic about the Nyae Nyae, or subsumed into expert advice concerning the 'solution'. The Ju/'hoansi themselves found it difficult to contribute to the deliberations of the co-management forum (that pre-dated the 1998 legislation), and the other stakeholders found it difficult to elicit Ju/'hoansi views through the standard research methods and protocols. However, with the help of a facilitator, the Makuri community resorted to the naturalistic language of metaphor as a dialogic tool for describing, explaining and analysing systemic relations, patterns and trends.

A 'crippled hand' was one metaphor the Ju/'hoansi used to explain their relationship to land and natural resources in the Nyae Nyae (see Figure 4.1). The image of a crippled hand served to characterize the structural coupling between the socioeconomic and biophysical. The notion of 'crippled' is indicative of the perception that the system is at present decoupled. For the Ju'/hoansi, the top of the hand depicted the biophysical elements of the system, and the bottom, the nurturing socioeconomic elements. Existing tensions in terms of rights and control (stop hand), reciprocal relations (a weak handshake), resource alienation (a bloody hand), knowledge and skills (the hand's dexterity) and so on disabled the system's capacity to deal with the uncertainty perpetuated by periodic systemic shocks.

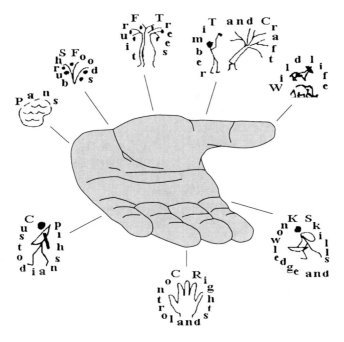

Source: Powell (1998).

Figure 4.1   The crippled hand

The crippled hand metaphor was then used to develop a community land assessment and monitoring programme intended to assist each subcommunity to generate consensual, inter-subjective statements of the status of their system:

- The strength of the hand. Strength is associated with the presence/absence of natural resources, including plant and animal species and their seasonal contribution, the nature of the land in relation to human demography, the history of residence in the area, and the skills, knowledge and means needed to subsist from the area.
- The hand's weakness. Weakness is associated with natural resource problems and constraints in relation to problems a community might have in controlling the use and management of the resource(s).
- The treatment for the hand. Treatment is associated with management strategies, and to the attitudes and aspirations of the community utilizing the land and other resources.

Each community created a map through participatory techniques of the settlement's natural resource context, identified as one level of tenure (N!/o), and of their larger hunting and gathering area (N!/ore). The elements identified on the final versions of the maps were subsequently described by community members in qualitative and quantitative terms. At the same time, subcommunities appointed members to monitor the land in the course of their normal movements, and report the information to their communities in terms of the strength, weakness and treatment of the Crippled Hand. Heated debates arose as the maps, the elements and the monitoring information became 'visible' in the emergent collective land perception. Each item was passed only after consensus had been reached as to interpretation and meaning. The land monitors became the collecting points, or the 'eyes and ears', of the whole community, with all members observing, assessing and updating information.

As the community land assessment processes developed, members of the community became more adept at articulating the community's perceptions at the co-management forum and at entering into dialogue with those presenting the formalized perceptions of western range science and conservation. They helped create the space at the forum for the development of multilayered scenarios which could be tested and interpreted against experiential and abstract understanding, and used to elucidate contested purpose. However, such clarification also sharpened the conflicts over the 'right' way to manage the Nyae Nyae, the nature of truth claims (the grounds for knowing) and the nature of the reality that was to be managed. In our view, the 1998 legislation and subsequent transformation of the NNFC into the NNCC, and the land monitors into community-based game guards appointed and paid by the conservation project would tend to undermine resilience rather than build towards stability.

Re-conceptualizing risk and impact

Table 4.1 describes how moral reasoning is acted upon in a conventional impact assessment approach and in the case of the Ju/'hoansi where the system is viewed as non-equilibrium. Reading the right-hand column, we might interpret the moral reasoning which governs the Nyae Nyae – when viewed as a non-equilibrium system – as a process of co-deliberation among actors in which both human and non-human species are seen as deliberative actors in a coupled system. What would need to be assessed would be the relations among these actors as co-determinants of reasonable action, and as the frameworks of meaning through which reasoned deliberation are mediated (Jiggins and Röling, 1999).

One might also argue that the consensual communication and decision-making processes among the Ju/'hoansi, and between them and other

Table 4.1 Comparison between conventional impact assessment and the Jul'hoansi on a range of moral reasoning issues

Moral reasoning issue	Conventional impact assessment	Jul'hoansi
Establishment of objective moral claims	Contingent valuation, concept capture tools, etc	Intersubjective dialogue – people–people – people–environment – inter–species
Concern for others, and a sacrifice of advancement of own interests	CBA, social CBA	Win–win visioning, double-loop and triple-loop learning
Protection against excessive limitation of individual rights in balance with the notion of a public good	Market assumed to equilibriate private and public interest. Within the family, patriarchy assumed to equilibriate the interests of family members. Pigovian analysis	Within Nyae Nyae: dynamic consensual process between Jul'hoansi and other stakeholders: co-management forum and new dialogic analysis
Focus on small benefits for large numbers of people; and a concern about large costs falling on small numbers of people	Market failure, institutional and gender inequities analysed by adjusted Pigovian tools, for example	Intertemporal, inter-scale relations assessed so as to sustain/induce diversity of impacts by diversity of species' actors
Utilitarian maximization as the dominant value	Yes	Balanced by inter-people, inter-species maintenance of socioeconomic and biophysical key values

species, nurture the plasticity of socioeconomic and biophysical structuration over time and space. In contrast, the Conservancy intrudes more rigid institutional and communicative relations in which 'third parties' assume coordinating roles in determining frameworks of direct dialogue and experiential feedback, and the market substitutes indirect and incomplete symbolic exchange for these. The monitoring mechanism of the community game guards replaces inter-species dialogue and co-learning with extractive knowledge appropriation. In this way, the riskiness of risk is increased. In contrast, the co-management forum, and the semi-formalized tools of participatory land assessment and computer-assisted dialogic tools, have the potential to reinstate protocols, methods and multi-level moral reasoning adapted for proactive and retrospective SIA in a non-equilibrium environment (Daniels and Walker, 1996; Jiggins and Röling, 2000).

Turning now to the concept of resilience as the continuing capacity to generate scenarios and options, we observe in the Nyae Nyae that, under Ju/'hoansi management this is a distributed capacity; that is, Ju/'hoansi interventions serve to maintain distributed capacity among species, and across time and space. The new arrangements shift the management of resilience to higher system levels, and reduce resilience to resistance to disturbance and speed of return to the presumed equilibrium. An intervention within this framework of understanding is thus liable to compound instability, by highlighting adjustments that adapt the Conservancy to the *exogenous* system. Alternatively, wildlife management that is informed by an understanding of sustaining a coupled system's capacity to learn would highlight processes that enable the Conservancy to track the plasticity of social–ecological function, structure and process.

Conclusion

This chapter develops a frame for SIA in the context of overdetermined problem situations. We argue three points which collectively imply that the institutional space for the evolution of coupled systems must also be reviewed as a key concern in systems far from equilibrium. First, conventional approaches and tools need to be stretched in order to encompass frameworks of moral reasoning necessitated by the increasing riskiness of the world we have created. Second, the shaping of sustainable futures must address more centrally the concept of resilience. We propose that this be done in terms of assessing a *structurally coupled system*'s continuing capacity to generate co-evolving scenarios and options, using methods which recognize the interplay of the human, the non-human and their environment. Third, we contend that participatory approaches, which may combine intersubjective and 'high tech' instrumentation, are well suited (perhaps uniquely so) to sustaining capacity for shared learning.

References

Beck, U. 1992. *Risk Society: Toward a New Modernity* (trans. M. Ritter), London: Sage.

Berkes, F. and Folke, C. (eds) 1998. *Linking Social and Ecological Systems*, Cambridge: Cambridge University Press.

Ceruti, M. 1994. *Constraints and Possibilities: The Evolution of Knowledge and the Knowledge of Evolution*, Lausanne: Gordon and Breach.

Daniels, S.E. and Walker, G.B. 1996. 'Collaborative learning: Improving public deliberation in ecosystem-based management', *Environmental Impact Assessment Review*, 16(2): 71–102.

Dorner, D. 1997. *The Logic of Failure: Recognizing and Avoiding Error in Complex Situations* (trans. Rita Kimber and Robert Kimber), Reading: Addison-Wesley.

Fairhead, J. and Leach, M. 1996. *Misreading the African Landscape: Society and Ecology in a Forest–Savanna Mosaic*, Cambridge: Cambridge University Press.

Holling, C.S. 1996. 'Engineering resilience versus ecological resilience', in P.C. Schultze (ed.), *Engineering within Ecological Constraints*, Washington: National Academy Press, 31–44.

Jakobsson, K.M. and Dragun, A. 1996. *Contingent Valuation and Endangered Species*, Cheltenham, UK and Brookfield, US: Edward Elgar.

Jiggins, J. and Röling, N. 1999. 'Interactive Valuation: the social construction of the value of ecological services', *International Journal of Environment and Pollution*, 12(4): 436–50.

Jiggins, J. and Röling, N. 2000. 'Adaptive Management: potential and implications for ecological governance'. *International Journal of Agricultural Resources, Governance and Ecology*, 1(1): 28–42.

Krimsky, S. and Golding, D. (eds) 1992. *Social Theories of Risk*, Westport: Praeger.

LEARN Group 2000. *Cow Up a Tree: Knowing and Learning for Change in Agriculture*, Paris: INRA Editions.

Lee, R. 1979. *The Kung San: Men, Women, and Work in a Foraging Society*, Cambridge: Cambridge University Press.

Lubchenko, J. 1998. 'Entering the Century of the Environment: A New Social Contract for Science' *Science*, 279 (23 January): 491–6.

Maturana, H.R. and Varela, F.J. 1992. *The Tree of Knowledge: The Biological Roots of Understanding* (rev. edn), Boston: Shambhala.

Mazzucato, V. and Niemeijer, D. 2000. 'Rethinking Soil and Water Conservation in a Changing Society: A case study in eastern Burkina Faso', Tropical Resource Management Papers 32, Wageningen University, Wageningen.

O'Connor, M. 1991. 'Entropy, structure, and organisational change', *Ecological Economics*, 3(2): 95–122.

O'Neill, R.V., DeAngelis, J.B., Waide, J.B. and Allen, T.F. 1986. *A Hierarchical Concept of Ecosystem*, Princeton: Princeton University Press.

Pimm, S.L. 1984. 'The Complexity and Stability of Ecosystems', *Nature*, 307: 321–6.

Powell, N. 1997. 'Co-management of Natural Resources: Method Development Incorporating the Needs and Aspirations of Nomadic Land Users in Natural Resource Management', SUM Report no. 7, Centre for Development and Environment, University of Oslo, Norway.

Powell, N. 1998. 'Co-management in Non-Equilibrium Systems: Cases from Namibian Rangelands' (Agraria 138), Swedish University of Agricultural Sciences, Uppsala.

Scanlon, T.M. 1999. *What We Owe To Each Other*, Cambridge: Cambridge University Press.

Scoones, I. 1999. 'New Ecology and the Social Sciences', *Annual Review of Anthropology*, 28: 479–507.

Varela, F. 1999. *Ethical Know-How: Action, Wisdom and Cognition*, Standford: Standford University Press.

Walker, B.G., Ludwig, D., Holling, C.S. and Peterman, R.M. 1969. 'Stability of Semi-Arid Grazing Systems', *Journal of Ecology*, 69: 471–98.

Yellen, J. 1990. 'The Transformation of the Kalahari Kung', *Scientific American*, 262(4): 72–9.

5 Integrating environmental and social impact assessment
Roel Slootweg, Frank Vanclay and Marlies van Schooten

Introduction

There is a growing concern about the environmental and social consequences of development efforts. The developed world potentially faces
enormous costs due to the need to restore and protect the environment in
order to safeguard natural resources for future generations. Developing
countries must consider how their social and economic development can be
combined with protection of the environment and preservation of their
natural resources. This should be regarded, not as a luxury, but as a necessity for sustainable development.

When applied in the earliest stages of the decision-making process, environmental impact assessment (EIA) and social impact assessment (SIA) can
become important project planning instruments. They provide information
on the consequences of specific development activities in such a way that
these consequences can be taken into account and used in the process leading
to a final decision and in designing mitigation measures. Proper application
of EIA and SIA can significantly improve the quality of project proposals and
will eventually lead to important savings on project implementation because
of reduced negative impacts and better acceptance of the project objectives.

Since the publication of the Brundtland Report (WCED, 1987) and the
United Nations Conference on Evironment and Development (UNCED), or
Earth Summit, in Rio de Janeiro in 1992, the concept of sustainable development has gained wide acceptance. The idea that environment and development are strongly interrelated is now recognized by many. Further, poverty
and gender assessments are likely to become widely used instruments of
planning in development cooperation. Since EIA is the most developed
instrument, backed by a legal framework in many countries, it is increasingly
used also to assess the social and economic impacts of planned interventions.
The obvious consequence of the desire to integrate environmental, social and
economic aspects of project assessment is the apparent need for an integrating framework. So far, the worlds of environmental impact assessment, *in the
strict sense*, social impact assessment and economic cost–benefit analysis
have operated in their separate realms.

In this chapter, an attempt is made to construct a conceptual framework which provides a harmonized and integrated way of thinking and which will assist in the identification of potential environmental, social and economic impacts of a planned intervention. The framework is designed to have broad application and to provide insight in, and understanding of, the complex cause–effect chains that may lead to desired or undesired effects. It is partially based on an approach that translates nature and natural resources into functions for human society, often referred to as *function evaluation* (R.S. de Groot, 1992). This bears some similarity to the discussion of environmental goods and services that is going on in some countries. We realize that the terminology used in this discussion can easily lead to misunderstandings, since some terms may have a different meaning in other contexts. To assist, we provide a glossary of the terms we use in a specific way in the Appendix.

The settings
The conceptual framework presented here aims to provide insight into the relations between human society and the biophysical environment. The focus of this conceptualization is the characterization and classification of the functions provided by the biophysical environment and the assessment of their value for supporting human activities. The framework is based on the so-called 'function evaluation' of nature. Leading authors in this field are, among others, R.S. de Groot (1992) and W.T. de Groot (1992). The starting point in this approach is that society utilizes products and services that are provided by the biophysical environment. In economic terms, society constitutes the demand side, and the environment constitutes the supply side (see Figure 5.1). Simply stated, sustainability deals with the equilibrium in supply and demand, now *and in the future*. Perceived imbalances in this equilibrium trigger institutions to act by managing either the supply from nature or the demand from society. Institutions can, in this sense, be national, regional or local authorities with their formal instruments and regulations. Alternatively, they can be traditional chieftains or village elders with their traditional techniques and customary laws. In a globalized world, international agencies that exert effective control over human activities could also be included, for example, the Framework Convention on Climate Change, the Biodiversity Convention or the Montreal Protocol on Substances that Deplete the Ozone Layer.

Three main settings can be identified (see Figure 5.1):

1. The natural environment (or *biophysical setting*) comprises a combination of living and non-living resources and their interactions.

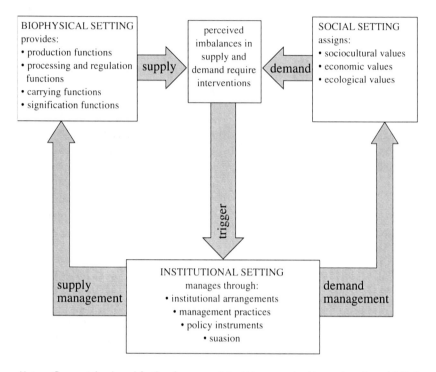

Note: Concept developed further from an original idea conceived in conjunction with Rob
Koudstaal in a study for the Wetland Group Foundation: *'Wise use of wetlands: a
methodology for the assessment of functions and values of wetlands'* (unpublished document).

Figure 5.1   Main settings in function evaluation

Resources perform functions in providing goods and services which are
used by each society.

2.   Human society (or the *social setting*) encompasses all human activities,
knowledge, beliefs and values. As a result of human activities and
social values (which are influenced by societal knowledge and beliefs,
that is, culture), environmental goods and services (that is, the functions of the biophysical environment) are valued in a social context.
These environmental values can be expressed in economic, sociocultural (including spiritual) or ecological terms. To a large extent, these
values depend on the societal context, differing between cultures, and
they also differ for different groups within a society.

3.   The *institutional setting* consists of the institutional arrangements
(authorities, legal framework, traditional laws and regulations), management practices (such as physical structures – dykes, roads and so

on), policy instruments (permits, subsidies, quotas and so on), and the use of suasion by governments or agencies in an attempt to change people's beliefs or behaviour.

Figure 5.1 depicts how the need for action is triggered by a perceived inequilibrium in the relation between supply and demand. The demand for goods and services from nature may surpass the available supply, which leads to a present or expected future *problem* (for instance, overexploitation or insufficient supply). The opposite may also occur when some of the functions of the natural environment are not exploited. To the extent that they are recognized, this represents a development *opportunity*. Both problems and opportunities may trigger an initiative from the policy or decision makers, who, through their institutional arrangements, policy instruments, management practices and suasion, will try to solve the problem or benefit from the development opportunity. This intervention either works via the side of the biophysical setting by managing the supply of environmental goods and services (such as provision of agriculture, forestry or hydraulic engineering), or via the side of the social setting by managing the demand for goods and services (through tax incentives, setting of quota, trade negotiations and so on).

The biophysical setting
The natural system comprises many environmental functions that provide goods and services that can be utilized by human society. Whether all of these functions are actually utilized is dependent on the social, economic and cultural 'behaviour' of the society concerned, its state of development and technical knowledge and so on. It is not necessary for all of the identified functions of an ecosystem to be used. Furthermore, ecosystems may possess functions that are not as yet identified – this is one of the primary arguments in support of biodiversity protection. Combining the clear but somewhat simplified classification of Rudolf de Groot (1992) and the theoretically more appropriate classification of Wouter de Groot (1992), four categories of environmental functions can be distinguished: production, processing and regulation, carrying, and signification functions.

Production functions relate to the ability of the natural environment to generate useful products for humanity. A distinction is made between natural production functions and nature-based human production functions. Natural production functions include products that the natural environment largely produces on its own, that is, without human input other than humans being harvesters (hunting and gathering). Products can be produced over a short term (for example, firewood, fruit, streamwater, ocean fisheries) or over a long time period (for example, oil, minerals, fossil groundwater). Those in the first category are often referred to as renewable resources, while those in the latter are considered non-renewable. The logging of old-growth forests for lumber or pulp would be renewable if undertaken on a sustainable yield basis, or would be arguably non-renewable if done by clear-felling operations with little or no regeneration of native forests. Nature-based human production functions relate to the production of biological (animal or plant) products by the biophysical environment in ways that involve active management and inputs by people. Examples here include most agricultural and horticultural activities, forestry plantations and managed forests, and fish ponds (aquaculture and mariculture).

Processing and regulation functions (or maintenance functions) relate to the maintenance of ecosystem support systems. The interactions between biotic and abiotic components result in complex processes that influence the conditions for maintenance of life support systems. These functions are often not recognized until they are disturbed. They refer to the ability of ecosystems to maintain or restore dynamic equilibria within the system, or in other linked ecosystems through physical, biological and chemical processes and interactions. Processing functions often undo the harm caused by human activities or reduce the risk to humans. Such functions include the sequestration of carbon dioxide, the dilution of pollutants and the active chemical transformation of harmful substances such as organic waste. Examples of regulation functions are maintenance of groundwater levels, maintenance of biological diversity, protection against natural forces (coastal protection by mangroves) and protection against harmful cosmic radiation (ozone shield). Water storage in wetlands is an example of a regulation function for river flow regulation.

Carrying functions are related to space or to a substrate that is suitable for certain activities and for which there may be a demand. The availability of space, together with a particular set of environmental conditions associated with that space, makes an area more or less suitable to perform certain functions for humans. Examples include suitability of an area for human habitation and settlement, nature conservation areas, areas for nature-based recreation (such as mountain climbing, bushwalking, skiing or beach tourism), waterways for navigation and sites for energy conversion (such as hydropower reservoirs).

Signification functions involve the social values that are ascribed to nature itself (natural heritage values) and to other features of the landscape, including the human constructed landscape (cultural heritage values). Nature provides opportunities for spiritual enrichment, aesthetic enjoyment, cognitive development (contemplation, meditation) and recreation. Different from the provision of physical space as in carrying functions, these functions refer to the meaning (significance) associated with the biophysical environment. The world's largest economic sector, tourism, is largely based on this function – that is, human appreciation of nature and landscape. Examples include aesthetic information (scenery, landscape), spiritual and religious information (religious and sacred sites), psychological information (emotional attachment, nostalgic attachment to place), historic information (historic and archaeological elements), cultural and artistic information (inspiration for folklore, music, dance, art) and educational and scientific information (natural science classes, research, environmental indicators).

The difference between the 'classical' approach to describe nature in terms of natural resources (water, soil, forest and so on) and function evaluation is that the latter provides much more insight into the multifunctionality of resources. For example, instead of just describing the resource, 'water', function evaluation provides insight into the multiple functions of water, such as production function for agriculture, carrying function for shipping and recreation, regulation function to counterbalance seawater intrusion, and signification function for science or religious groups or nature-based tourism. When the functions are recognized, the relevant units of measurement can be identified and decision making can be based on a more profound understanding of the role that the biophysical environment plays for human society. It is important to realize that many functions can occur simultaneously (see the example for water, above), but that with human intervention these functions may become mutually exclusive. The creation of a dam to enhance water storage in a river basin will block the pathway for migratory fish as well as for long river water transport. Intensive exploitation of freshwater for agricultural productivity will reduce or exclude other functions such as shipping, balancing the intrusion of seawater and maintenance of downstream wetlands.

The social setting
The social setting creates the demand for environmental goods and services. The existence of goods and services that derive from environmental functions is what determines the perceived value of those functions for humanity. This perceived value is also related to what is socially valued in that society, which in turn, is related to the culture of that society, the level of technology and so on. Three broad categories of values can be distinguished: social values, economic values and ecological values.

Social values refer to the quality of life in general and can be expressed in many different units, depending on the social context and cultural background of the situation/society. Some examples are health and safety (expressed as prevalence of diseases or number of people protected from forces of nature), housing and living conditions, space for settlement, the value of the environment as a source of food (or in-kind income) in subsistence economies, and religious and cultural values.

The *economic value* of an environmental function refers to the monetary value of the goods and services that are provided. It can be expressed as a monetary value assigned to individual economic activities (agriculture, industries, fisheries, construction), to household income (as an overall indicator on the financial conditions of the population) or to per capita gross regional or domestic product, as an overall indicator for the income of the society as a whole.

Ecological values refer to the value that society places on or derives from the maintenance of the earth's life support systems (particularly the processing and regulation functions). They come in two forms. Temporal ecological values are the potential future benefits that can be derived from biological diversity (genetic, species and ecosystem diversity) and key ecological processes that maintain the world's life support systems for future generations. The appropriate way to express these values is hotly debated. A simple, regularly used measure is the proportion of endemic species (that is, only locally occurring species) as a measure for uniqueness of the area. Other measures try to indicate the 'naturalness' of an area, that is, the level at which natural processes can still structure and maintain the environment and its functions. Spatial ecological values involve the interactions ecosystems have with other systems, and thus perform functions for the maintenance of other systems. Coastal lagoons and mangroves that serve as breeding grounds for marine fish provide a good example. The ecological value of the mangroves is the support they provide for economic activity elsewhere: without mangroves there would be fewer fish. Other examples are wintering areas for migratory birds, or flood plains that recharge groundwater aquifers for neighbouring dry lands or act as a silt trap that prevents downstream rivers and reservoirs from silting up.

These values are not mutually exclusive, since functions cannot always be unequivocally assigned an economic or a social value. For example, the suitability of a certain area for a traditional crop (production function) can be valued in economic terms (for example, income, employment, subsistence) as well as social terms (for instance, cultural preservation), or even in ecological terms (for instance, the use of a traditional and unique variety of salt-resistant rice that merits being maintained in a seed bank for future uses). It is important to realize that values differ for different (groups of) individuals in a society. Therefore the identification of values should include the views and opinions of many people.

Interventions, changes and impacts

As shown in Figure 5.1, imbalances between the supply of goods and services provided by the biophysical environment and the demand for these goods and services from society may lead to the identification of an actual or a perceived (current or future) problem or opportunity. The problem or opportunity, in its turn, will trigger a reaction from the institutional setting to undertake interventions (or activities, projects and so on) to address the issue. Interventions may be designed to have direct influence on the biophysical setting, or on the social setting.

In impact assessment, we are interested in predicting the environmental (biophysical and social) impacts of such planned interventions. There are several key questions for impact assessment:

1. How can social and biophysical impacts be integrated in one process and, more importantly, how are social and biophysical impacts interlinked?
2. What are the chains of events that lead from a proposed intervention to expected impacts?
3. Can second- and higher-order effects be identified?
4. Can off-site impacts (away from the site of the intervention) be identified?

We use the function evaluation framework as a way of understanding how impacts develop from physical interventions. Separating the concepts of a change in the biophysical setting from the impact on the environmental functions, and the impact experienced by people as a result of those biophysical impacts, is useful (see Figure 5.2). The figure shows that physical interventions (A) create changes to the characteristics of the natural resources in the biophysical setting (B). These *biophysical changes* can be measured and quantified. A change in the characteristics of a natural resource will occur under all circumstances, irrespective of the type of ecosystem or land-use type in which the intervention is carried out. For example, a project (intervention) which will divert water from one watercourse into another will change the downstream hydrology (the biophysical change), whether it be in the Amazon River, a mountain stream (natural ecosystems) or an irrigation feeder canal (an artificial land-use type). Magnitude and direction of change are determined by the combined characteristics of the intervention and the natural resource involved. This conceptual framework, however, only allows for the identification of *likely* biophysical changes. Field observations and detailed information on the proposed interventions are needed to determine the actual magnitude and the direction of the change.

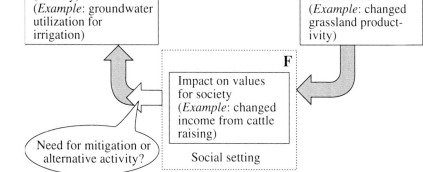

Figure 5.2   Steps in determining impacts resulting from physical interventions

The biophysical change that directly results from an intervention is a *first-order change*. This change may in turn cause *second- and higher-order* biophysical changes (C). As in the example above, a river diversion is likely to result in a change in river hydrology (first-order change); the change in hydrology may lead to a change in flooding regime in downstream flood-plains, or change the salt and other pollutant concentration along the river (second-order changes).

The example in Figure 5.2 shows that changes in the physical and biolog-ical properties of natural resources will change the functions of the natural environment (E); that is, the goods and services provided by nature. These changes are called the *biophysical impacts*. The type and quality of the bio-physical environment determine the functions affected. For example, a change in groundwater level in forested upland areas will affect functions such as wood production, and the provision of water for lowland areas. In coastal lowlands, however, the same biophysical change in groundwater level will affect functions such as the prevention of underground seawater intrusion, and productivity of meadowlands. From this framework, then, a long list of potential impacts can be derived for all imaginable environmental conditions. However, field observations are needed to confirm or reject the potential impacts.

With some knowledge of the specific location, it would be possible to improve the identification of potential impacts by using the concepts of ecosystem and land-use type. By knowing the ecosystem or land-use type in which a biophysical change occurs, it would be possible to indicate the functions that potentially will be affected. The long list of potential impacts can thus be narrowed down considerably by introducing a so-called 'landscape filter' (D). For practical reasons, the combined term 'landscape' is used, being defined as a biologically and/or geographically recognizable unit representing either a natural ecosystem (for example a lowland rainforest), a semi-natural ecosystem (such as managed forest) or a human land-use type (irrigated cropland). This landscape filter 'filters' the relevant impacts from the long list of potential impacts.

When the first- and higher-order biophysical changes that result from an intervention are known, the area of impact can be determined. Many changes will only occur in the area where the intervention is carried out and will result in on-site impacts that can be determined when the landscape type in which the intervention is carried out is identified. But some biophysical changes will have a broader geographical range of impact. For example, air pollution drifts to other areas with the wind; interventions in river hydrology may have impacts on the entire river basin (upstream and downstream); an airport or road produces noise that can be mapped in terms of noise contour lines. For each physical change, the geographical range where changes can be expected can be defined. By defining this range, the so-called 'off-site impacts' of any intervention can be determined. An example is the geographical range of a change in peak discharge of a river downstream from an intervention site. By determining the landscape types that lie downstream of the intervention site and that depend on river water, the off-site impacts can be determined. If, for example, the peak discharge will be significantly diminished, the identified downstream floodplains will suffer from reduced or total absence of flooding, and the estuary where the river empties will experience a change in the fresh–salt water balance. The impacts in each landscape type will be very different, but they result from the same intervention and the same biophysical change.

Biophysical impacts are expressed in terms of changes in the products and services provided by the environment and will consequently have impacts on the values of these functions for human society (F). Changes in the *functions* of nature will lead to changes in the *values assigned* to nature. For example, when, owing to the construction of a dam, the surface area of floodplains downstream changes (physical change), downstream fish productivity will change (biophysical impact), which in turn influences society through a change in the economic livelihoods of downstream fisherfolk. These impacts on society are considered to be *indirect human impacts.* The word 'indirect', in this case, refers to the fact that the impact on humans takes place through biophysical changes and impacts, in contrast to the direct impacts where the proposed intervention directly leads to changes and impacts in society.

The word 'human' instead of 'social' is introduced to avoid semantic discussions on what should be considered 'social' impacts. Human impacts are the real and perceived impacts experienced by humans (at individual and higher aggregation levels) as a result of biophysical and/or social change processes caused by planned interventions. We assume that human impacts encompass all final impact variables that are studied in environmental impact assessments, social impact assessments, health impact assessments and even biodiversity impacts assessments, given that the maintenance of biological diversity (a function of nature) is currently valued by society (as an ecological value) to guarantee the livelihoods of future generations.

Decision making in relation to a proposed project is (or should be) based on the assessment of all these values, and on possibilities of defining alternatives or mitigation measures in the case of undesirable impacts. Changes to the proposed intervention, or the implementation of mitigation measures, are a new intervention, making the process circular. Over time, too, the type of new projects that are proposed (A) is dependent on the experience of past interventions (F).

Social change processes and human impacts

We have presented above a framework to identify human impacts that result from physical interventions (changes to the biophysical setting). We now elaborate further the framework to address the human impacts that result from social interventions (changes in the social setting). Among SIA practitioners, there is general agreement that social impacts relate to 'all social and cultural consequences to human populations of any public or private actions that alter the ways in which people live, work, play, relate to one another, organise to meet their needs, and generally cope as members of society' (Interorganizational Committee, 1994, page 107). In contrast to biophysical impacts, human impacts can occur as soon as there are changes in social conditions, even from the time when a project is anticipated. People do not simply experience social changes, they react to them and are able to anticipate them. This makes prediction of social changes and human impacts difficult and situation-specific. As a consequence, and for many other reasons elaborated by Burdge and Vanclay (1995), too many social impact assessment studies have been inadequate, often presenting little more than demographic or economic predictions.

In the context of our approach, human impacts should be seen in the broadest sense. This means that they refer to quantifiable variables such as economic or demographic issues, as well as to changes in people's norms, values, beliefs and perceptions about the society in which they live, the gendered differentiation of impacts and all other facets of life. See Vanclay (1999) for a full discussion of the nature of human impacts.

Analogous to the distinction between biophysical changes and biophysical impacts in the biophysical setting, we argue that a distinction between *social change processes* and *human impacts* should be identified in the social setting. Policies or project interventions cause social change processes. These can be intended (for instance, conversion of economic activities) or unintended (for instance, job loss). In our opinion, social change processes take place regardless of the social context of society (groups, nations, religions or whatever). The resettlement or relocation of local people owing to the building of a dam, or the influx of new residents, whether permanent, seasonal or weekenders, are social change processes, and are not in themselves social impacts. Under certain conditions, depending on the characteristics of the existing community and the nature of mitigation measures, these social processes may cause impacts. There is, therefore, a distinction to be made between social change process and human impacts that is rather akin to the difference between biophysical changes and biophysical impacts. Conceptually, too, it is obvious that an 'impact' has to be experienced or felt in a corporeal (physical) or cognitive (perceptual) sense, whether at the level of individual, household, or society/community. An increase in population, or the presence of strangers, is not the experienced impact: the experienced impact is likely to be a changed perception about the nature of the community (communityness, community cohesion), changed perception about personal attachment to the community, and possibly annoyance and upsetness as a result of the project. The ways in which social change processes are perceived, given meaning or valued depend on the social context in which various societal groups act. Some sectors of society, or groups in society, are able to adapt quickly and make use of the opportunities of a new situation. Others (for instance, various vulnerable groups) are less able to adapt and will bear most of the negative consequences of change.

Integrating the biophysical and social settings
Figure 5.3 presents a revised version of the framework combining all elements, the biophysical setting, the social setting and interlinkages – in particular, showing that the social setting can be influenced by interventions

through two pathways: *indirect* and *direct*. Indirect human impacts result from changes in the natural resource base and the derived functions, that is, from biophysical impacts. Direct human impacts originate directly from (social) interventions (via the social change processes) and either are especially designed to influence the social setting (objectives) or are an unintended consequence of the intervention.

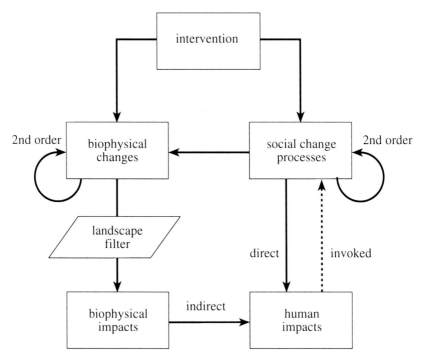

Figure 5.3   Pathways to derive biophysical and human impacts

Change has a way of creating other changes. This notion of circularity or iteration has been incorporated in the framework in several ways. Social change processes that result directly from the intervention, the so-called 'first-order changes', can lead to (several) other social change processes, the second- and higher-order change processes. For example, resettlement can lead to processes of rural to urban migration and changes in food production. In addition, the social experience of change (that is, the human impacts) can also prompt people to undertake other behaviour or further social change processes. For example, the negative human impacts (experiences) associated with unemployment can activate the social change process of rural to urban migration in search of work.

Social change processes can also provoke biophysical changes. Economic developments which increase the number of tourists in a particular area can have a serious influence on land use and water quality, which, in their turn, can have indirect human impacts through a reduction in agricultural production and subsequently on income level for smallholder farmers.

A social filter?
So far, there has been a close comparison between the biophysical setting and the social setting. Somewhat analogous to the landscape filter in the biophysical setting, we can conceive of a *social group filter*. The aim of such a filter would be that, by using information about the types of social groups present, it might be possible to narrow down the long list of potential human impacts and to identify the relevant impacts for that group. The filter would be placed between the social change processes and the human impacts and between the biophysical impacts and the human impacts (see Figure 5.3).

Conceptually, this is straightforward, especially once the logic of the framework is accepted. However, the construction of such a social filter in any practical application of this framework appears to be very compli-cated, and there is resistance amongst SIA professionals to considering the possibility. In the biophysical setting, biophysical impacts are related to ecosystems and landscape types. The classification of ecosystems or land-scapes into meaningful units is reasonably established and accepted amongst EIA professionals and within the discipline of ecology. In con-trast, there is not a generally accepted classification of social groupings for which sufficient knowledge exists to make predictions about the likely expe-rience of human impacts. Further, landscape or ecosystem units have common elements around the world, but cultural groupings tend to be unique in many respects.

It is clear that the concept of a social filter still needs further thinking. The fact that most (all?) social scientists who have worked for some time in a community can identify vulnerable groups, or can predict the likely effects of a specified intervention at least to some extent, suggests that intrinsic social filter mechanisms exist. The challenge is to articulate and operation-alize the criteria that underlie this intrinsic knowledge.

What is new about our approach?
The framework presented in this chapter is an attempt to provide a means to structure social and biophysical knowledge in impact assessment. It should be stressed that *it is not a procedural framework for impact assess-ment and that it is not a predictive model*. Rather, it is a *way of thinking*. Impact assessment has always dealt with the identification of the

cause–effect chains that may result from a planned intervention. By providing an integrating framework that combines the biophysical and the social aspects of impacts, we hope that the previously separate worlds of EIA and SIA can join forces to produce better impact assessment, better project design and, it is hoped, bring about a better livelihood for today and in the future.

We have deliberately introduced the term 'human impact', so as to avoid the sometimes difficult and unfruitful discussion about whether SIA encompasses EIA, or whether EIA should encompass both the social and the biophysical dimensions. It is our strong conviction that all impacts are human impacts, but the pathways through which these impacts arise can be complex and include both the social and the biophysical settings. It makes no sense to separate the biophysical from the social environment.

The framework forms the basis of a computerized instrument that assists in identifying (qualitatively) the potential impacts of proposed projects. For that purpose, the authors were forced to create a rigid and unequivocal framework of thinking. In doing so, it was realized that the analytical side of EIA and SIA practice could be strongly enhanced. Very often, implicit knowledge is used in both EIA and SIA without this being realized. For example, in many terms of reference for EIA studies, impacts on water quality are considered negative impacts, without any statement of the reasons why this should be the case. Implicitly, water is assumed to have functions for public water supply, irrigation or fisheries. Would water quality be an issue if the water would drain into an uninhabited area without any living organisms?

The rigid division between change processes (being tangible, objectively verifiable and measurable processes) and impacts (as subjective, context-dependent final variables of impact studies) provides considerable analytical assistance in the early identification of potential impacts. It adds something new to both EIA and SIA. EIA studies usually stop at the level of biophysical changes, such as changes in the quality or quantity of air, water or soils. The notion of functions provides a mechanism to translate these changes into explicitly identified issues that are of relevance to human society. Water quality per se does not provide insight; the functions of this water and its values for society provide the relevant information.

For SIA studies, the distinction between social change processes and the experience of (social or human) impacts is new. Many social scientists state that each situation is unique and that SIA studies are by definition context-specific. However, nobody will doubt that inundation of populated areas will cause migration, if not relocation, or that the creation of new factories will increase employment opportunities. These change processes do not give any clue as to the nature and severity of impacts that may be expected.

This depends on the context of different groups in society and should be subject to SIA studies.

We believe that the framework presented in this chapter provides a useful tool in the identification of issues that should be subject to impact studies. It also provides the means to focus on relevant issues, thus avoiding lengthy scoping processes, and it reduces the risk of overlooking important issues. Furthermore, by providing simple and clearly defined links between the biophysical and social environments, the division of tasks and the communication between members of multidisciplinary study teams can be greatly enhanced.

Acknowledgments

This chapter has been published in *Impact Assessment and Project Appraisal*, 19(1), March 2001. Permission to reprint (slightly modified) has been granted by the copyright owners (the International Association for Impact Assessment) and publishers. The theoretical framework presented in this chapter is partly based on unpublished work of Rob Koudstaal and Roel Slootweg that was commissioned by the Wetland Group Foundation. Further elaboration of the framework has been made possible by the Netherlands Ministry of Foreign Affairs, which commissioned a decision support system to assist donor organizations in determining the potential impacts of proposed projects. We would like to thank personally Anneke Wevers for her support in this innovative and challenging endeavour.

References

Burdge, R.J. and Vanclay, F. 1995. 'Social Impact Assessment', in F. Vanclay, and D. Bronstein (eds), *Environmental and Social Impact Assessment*, Chichester: Wiley, 31–65.

de Groot, R.S. 1992. *Functions of nature: Evaluation of nature in environmental planning, management and decision making*, Groningen: Wolters-Noordhoff.

de Groot, W.T. 1992. *Environmental science theory: Concepts and methods in a one-world, problem-oriented paradigm*, New York: Elsevier.

Interorganizational Committee on Guidelines and Principles for Social Impact Assessment 1994. 'Guidelines and Principles for Social Impact Assessment', *Impact Assessment*, 12(2): 107–52.

Vanclay, F. 1999. 'Social impact assessment', in J. Petts (ed.), *Handbook of Environmental Impact Assessment* (vol. 1), Oxford: Blackwell Science, 301–26.

World Commission on Environment and Development 1987. *Our Common Future*, Oxford: Oxford University Press.

Appendix: Glossary of working definitions for terminology used in the framework

The terminology in this chapter is only used to distinguish steps in the presented framework. The authors make no pretensions as to the wider meaning of the terms. In order to avoid semantic discussions on terminology, we use the following working definitions:

Physical intervention: planned human activity that physically intervenes in, and possibly alters, the biophysical environment.

Social intervention: planned human activity that intervenes in, and possibly alters, the social environment.

Biophysical change: change in the characteristics of a natural resource (including soil, water, air, flora and fauna) resulting from a physical intervention.

Biophysical impact: change in the quality (or quantity) of the goods and services that are provided by the biophysical environment; that is, a change affecting the functions of the biophysical environment.

First-order change: change that results directly from the intervention.

Second- and higher-order changes: changes that may result from the first-order change through a causal chain of events or processes.

Landscape type: a recognizable area with a consistent set of natural, semi-natural or managed resources: water, land, climate, and flora and fauna.

On-site impacts: impacts resulting from a physical (or social) intervention that occur in the area where the intervention is conducted.

Off-site impacts: impacts caused by a physical (or social) intervention, but that occur away from the location where the intervention is conducted, owing to biophysical or social changes that influence distant areas. Off-site impacts are usually, but not necessarily always, second- or higher-order impacts.

Social change process: a discrete, observable and describable process which changes the characteristics of (parts of) a society, taking place regardless of the societal context (that is, independent of specific groups, nations, religions and so on). These change processes may, in certain circumstances and depending on the context, lead to the experience of human impacts.

Human impact: the effect resulting from social change processes or biophysical impacts, as experienced (felt) by an individual, family or household, community or society, whether in corporeal (physical) or perceptual (psychological) terms.

Direct human impacts: human impacts that result directly from an intervention through social change processes. They may be the intention of specially designed interventions to influence the social setting (intended impacts, project goals, objectives) or may unintentionally result from the interventions (unintended consequences).

Indirect human impacts: these result from changes to the biophysical environment, affecting the functions with which the environment provides people.

Invoked social change processes: because of the ability of people to act in response to perceived or real impacts, human impacts may in their turn cause other social change processes to occur.

6 Conceptualizing social change processes and social impacts

Marlies van Schooten, Frank Vanclay and Roel Slootweg

Introduction

The authors were involved in the development of a decision support system (DSS) to help development agency staff determine when impact assessment was required in development cooperation projects. They were required to specify a comprehensive listing of social impacts for inclusion in the DSS. Initially, a set of variables was to be compiled through a meta-analysis of previously published lists of social impact variables. However, a high degree of inconsistency between such lists, and internal inconsistency in many of the lists, meant that a systematic reconsideration of the nature of social impacts was called for.

This chapter, which builds on Chapter 5, discusses a new understanding of social change processes and social impacts, as well as a listing of processes and impacts which were developed using the function evaluation framework for integrating social (SIA) and environmental (EIA) impact assessment as elaborated by Slootweg *et al.* (2001). It is our view that, while there has been an attempt at completeness, the impacts listed are quite likely to exhibit our prejudices and biases. Colleagues from other cultures and economic settings may well classify impacts differently.

Existing social impact variable lists

Many publications provide a generic classification of the types of social issues that should be considered in SIA. A small number of publications include lists of social impacts. In these publications, social impacts can refer to quantifiable variables such as numbers of immigrants (newcomers), but can also refer to qualitative indicators such as cultural impacts involving changes to people's norms, values, beliefs and perceptions about the society in which they live.

Most social impact specialists stress that it is impossible to detail all dimensions of social impact – social change has a way of creating other changes. Further, most of the changes are seen as situation-specific and are therefore dependent on the social, cultural, political, economic and historic context of the community in question, as well as the characteristics of the proposed project and of any mitigation measures put in place.

This ambiguity associated with impacts, the lack of operational definitions for many constructs, as well as an asocietal mentality (Burdge and Vanclay, 1995), has led to a focus on investigation of measurable variables (for example, economic and demographic) and/or politically convenient indicators such as population change, job creation or use of services (Gramling and Freudenburg, 1992). At the other extreme, Cernea (1994) complains that there have been some in-depth social analyses which have a tendency to become lengthy social overviews without any focus on the likely future social impacts.

Attempts have been made by various social scientists to develop classifications of types of social impacts, but few have developed lists of specific social impacts, and fewer still have provided operational definitions of their variables. Amongst the classifications are those by Vanclay (2002: 389) (building on Armour, 1990) who identified the following as important:

- people's way of life – that is, how they live, work, play and interact with one another on a day-to-day basis;
- their culture – that is, their shared beliefs, customs, values and language or dialect;
- their community – its cohesion, stability, character, services and facilities;
- their political systems – the extent to which people are able to participate in decisions that affect their lives, the level of democratization that is taking place, and the resources provided for this purpose;
- their environment – the quality of the air and water people use; the availability and quality of the food they eat; the level of hazard or risk, dust and noise they are exposed to; the adequacy of sanitation, their physical safety, and their access to and control over resources;
- their health and wellbeing – where 'health' is understood in a manner similar to the World Health Organization (WHO) definition: 'a state of complete physical, mental, and social wellbeing and not merely the absence of disease or infirmity';
- their personal and property rights – particularly whether people are economically affected, or experience personal disadvantage which may include a violation of their civil liberties.
- their fears and aspirations – their perceptions about their safety, their fears about the future of their community, and their aspirations for their future and the future of their children.

Juslén (1995) made an analysis of the social impacts identified in several studies. He determined that a universal list of social impacts that would suit every case was not possible, but he argued that a checklist would be useful, especially in scoping. He identified several general impact categories:

- 'standard' social impacts concerning noise level, pollution, and so on;
- psychosocial impacts (such as community cohesion, disruption of social networks);
- anticipatory fear;
- impacts of carrying out the assessment;
- impacts on state and private services;
- impacts on mobility (such as transport, safety, obstacles).

In more general typologies, Taylor *et al.* (1995) identified lifestyles, attitudes, beliefs and values, and social organization. Branch *et al.* (1984) highlighted community resources, community social organization, and indicators of individual and community wellbeing. Gramling and Freudenburg (1992) distinguished between six systems of the human environment: biophysical and health systems, cultural systems, social systems, political/legal systems, economic systems and psychological systems.

The Interorganizational Committee (1994) included a list of social impact variables. These variables point to measurable change in human population, communities and social relationships resulting from a development project or policy change. The Committee suggests a list under the headings of: (i) population characteristics, (ii) community and institutional structures, (iii) political and social resources, (iv) individual and family changes, and (v) community resources. Burdge (1994), a member of the Interorganizational Committee, uses a largely similar list of 26 variables.

The first observation in our search for lists of social impacts is that there is a strong reluctance by SIA researchers to provide them. It is argued that impacts are context-dependent and therefore should not be listed and predicted in advance. The second observation has to do with the contents of the lists: there are substantial differences among SIA researchers about which variables are included, and even the way that social impacts should be categorized or grouped. Wide discrepancies exist about what constitutes social impacts. Besides, many impacts are missing from the lists. Impacts that are described tend to be focused on negative impacts only and tend to be biased towards a western cultural setting.

In most lists there appears to be an emphasis on empirical measures. It could also be argued that many of the variables are not social impacts in themselves. For example, taking the first grouping of variables, 'population characteristics', from the Interorganizational Committee's list, none of the 'variables' listed constitutes an 'impact' where an impact is an actual expe-rience of an individual or community. Social impact variables such as increase in population, increase in ethnic or racial diversity, relocation, presence of temporary workers and/or seasonal residents are not, in them-selves, impacts. Under certain circumstances they may result in social impacts such as loss of community cohesion, fear and uncertainty amongst residents, fluctuating real estate (property) values, shortage of housing and so on, but, if properly managed, these demographic changes may not create impacts. Whether impacts are caused will depend on the characteristics and history of the host community, and the extent of mitigation measures that are put in place. Thus there is confusion in the literature between social change *process* and social *impact.*

Important social impacts are missing from the lists. Occupational health and safety issues provide a good example. Disease, death and injury are social impacts that can be the direct or indirect result of a project, for example increased traffic in a neighbourhood or increased exposure to vector-borne diseases in irrigation schemes. Another example of social impacts that have been absent from previous consideration is changes in human rights situations: social impacts in the form of violation of human rights can occur when governments use force to implement a project, or when public opposition to the project is suppressed.

There is a western orientation to the lists that have been developed, for example the focus on individual property rights. Broader social objectives and goals of development are given less consideration. It is clear that the lists of social impacts that have been produced and the variables considered in most SIA studies relate mostly to the negative social impacts of projects. Positive impacts, the impacts of policies and programmes, and the benefits, goals or objectives of planned interventions are not considered seriously, despite rhetorical statements that they should be.

The conceptual framework
The integration framework of Slootweg *et al.* (see the previous chapter) identifies the pathways by which environmental and social impacts may result from proposed projects. Figure 6.1 assists in thinking about a full range of social impacts. The distinction between a change process and impact in the physical environment encouraged us to think about social impacts in much the same way.

Social change processes can be measured objectively, independent of the local context. If 'social impact' refers to the impacts actually experienced by humans (at individual and higher aggregation levels) in either a corpo-real (physical) or cognitive (perceptual) sense, then many impact variables commonly measured in SIA studies – for example, population growth or

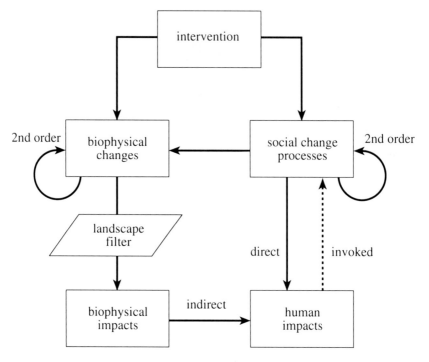

Source: Slootweg, Vanclay and van Schooten (2001).

Figure 6.1   Framework to integrate environmental and social impact assessment

presence of construction workers – are not impacts, but social change processes that may lead to social impacts.

The ways in which the social change processes are perceived, given meaning or valued depend on the social context in which various societal groups act. Some sectors of society, or groups in society, are able to adapt quickly and exploit the opportunities of a new situation. Others (for example, various vulnerable groups) are less able to adapt and will bear most of the negative consequences of change. Social impacts, therefore, are implicitly context-dependent.

To complete the interpretation of Figure 6.1, some explanation of the iterations and feedback mechanisms is required. Social change processes that result directly from the intervention, the so-called 'first-order changes', can lead to (several) other social change processes, the second- and higher-order change processes. For example, resettlement can lead to processes of rural to urban migration and changes in food production. In addition, the social experience of change (that is, the human impacts) can also prompt people to undertake other behaviour that leads to further social change processes. For example, the negative human impacts (experiences) associated with unemployment can activate the social change process of rural to urban migration in search of work. Social change processes can also provoke biophysical changes. Economic developments which increase the number of tourists in a particular area can have a serious influence on land use and water quality. This, in turn, can have indirect human impacts through a reduction in agricultural production and subsequently on income level for smallholder farmers.

'Social change processes' are set in motion by project activities or policies. They take place independently of the local social context. Resettlement, for example, is a social change process, set in motion by, inter alia, the activity of land clearing (for a road or an agricultural project) or inundation of an area by dam construction. As mentioned above, and explained in Chapter 5, social change processes can lead to several other processes. Depending on the characteristics of the local social setting and mitigation processes that are put in place, social change processes can lead to social impacts.

'Direct social impacts' result directly from the social change processes that are invoked by a project. These impacts may be the intention of specially designed activities to influence the social setting (intended impacts), or may unintentionally result from these activities. 'Indirect social impacts' are a result of changes in the biophysical environment. 'Biophysical changes' can affect the functions with which the environment provides people. For example, if an activity causes land degradation, one of the biophysical impacts can be that the productive capacity of the land will decrease. The resulting reduction of income from farming activities is an indirect social impact. Biophysical changes can also have effects on disease organisms or disease vectors that can lead to health impacts. An example here is the introduction of irrigated agriculture. This leads to social change processes such as the creation of jobs and an increase in food supply. A direct social impact resulting from these social change processes is the raising of social wellbeing. However, the same activity leads to biophysical changes such as the creation of breeding sites for mosquitoes and snails, resulting in biophysical impacts such as increased transmission of malaria and schistosomiasis and consequently in the impairment of health (indirect social impact).

The framework presented by Slootweg *et al.* (2001) presents a useful way of thinking about the integration of social and environmental impacts, and for conceptualizing the full range of social impacts that are likely to occur from a given intervention. By following impact pathways, or causal chains, and specifically by thinking about the iterations that are likely to be caused, the full range of impacts can be identified. This makes the model a useful scoping mechanism and a heuristic aid.

Social change processes
Below we outline some of the social change processes that are important in social impact assessment. It is an indicative listing of examples of social change processes and is not intended to be comprehensive. In fact, it is likely that no list could ever be complete. New technologies and new social phenomena are occurring all the time, and it would be impossible to predict them or their likely social influence (the rapid expansion of new communication technology is a good example).

Processes are not uniquely definable, conceptually clear and mutually exclusive phenomena. The types of identified processes are linked to the purposes, objectives or interests of the observer. When the topic of interest is different, it is likely that the processes will also be defined differently. For example, the terms an economist would use differ from the terms used by a sociologist. In any case, processes can be described at different levels. Some processes tend to be very specific and singular, whereas others, such as globalization, may involve a wide range of different processes.

Demographic processes
Demographic processes are those that relate to the movement and/or composition of people in the region(s) affected by the project.

- **Processes related to natural birth and death rate (including fertility, distribution among age and sex):** very few projects will directly affect natural birth or death rates or fertility rates, although some activities may be specifically designed to influence these parameters.
- **In-migration.** Population growth due to permanent settlement of people from other areas. This complex process can be further subdivided into
  - **Presence of newcomers.** The social impacts of in-migration are exacerbated when the newcomers (new settlers) are different from, or perceived as being different from, 'old-timers'.
  - **Presence of (temporary) construction workers.** Newcomers who are resident in the project area on a short term (or commuting/fly in, fly out) basis.
  - **Presence of seasonal residents.** People who live for only some part of the year (perhaps summer or winter) in a particular region. In one sense they may have legal rights as citizens to participate in

decisions about the community, but they may also be profoundly different from permanent (year-round) residents.
- **Presence of weekenders.** Similar to seasonal residents is the phenomenon of weekenders. This refers to the influx of people who do not live permanently in the community, but who regularly visit, say, at weekends, and who may own property in the community.
- **Presence of tourists and day-trippers.**

- **Out-migration.** Decline in population due to the movement of people out of a region, for example because the area affected by a project becomes less desirable as a place to live, or because a project at some distance lures people in search of work.
- **Resettlement.** Resettlement refers to a coopted or coerced process by which local people surrender land for a project (such as a dam) and are relocated elsewhere as part of a compensation package.
- **Displacement/dispossession.** Displacement and dispossession refer to the processes by which development projects and policies cause people to lose land and/or other assets and/or access to resources, but for which they are not (adequately) compensated. The land lost may be their homes or their agricultural lands, or other areas on which they depend for resources.
- **Rural to urban migration.** Many projects accelerate the rate of rural to urban migration as jobs or social services become increasingly only available in the cities, or because of a growing perception of the attractiveness (lure) of life in the city (cultural hegemony).
- **Urban to rural migration.** In many European countries, with improved transport and communication networks, many previously urban people are now choosing to live in rural environments, significantly altering the demographic and cultural characteristics of those areas.

Economic processes
Economic processes are those that affect the economic activity in a region, including the way people make a living as well as macroeconomic factors that affect the society as a whole.

- **Waged labour.** Change in the number of available jobs.
- **Conversion and diversification of economic activities.** Change in the nature of economic activities from one type of production to other types of production. At the macro level this might be from agricultural to industrial forms of production. At lower levels, it might be from subsistence farming to cash cropping, or from grazing stock to cropping or to horticulture.

- **Impoverishment.** The process by which (groups in) a society experience a downward spiral of poverty.
- **Inflation.** The process of escalating prices. It can occur at the national level as a result of macroeconomic factors, or it can occur at local levels caused by the spending power of increasing numbers of high-income people.
- **Currency exchange fluctuation (devaluation).** Changes in the exchange rates of local currency.
- **Concentration of economic activity.** At the sectoral level, concentration of economic activity refers to the lack of diversification in the country as a whole; it refers to concentration of activity in a single industry. This makes the society and nation vulnerable to the fortunes of that commodity. On a geographical scale, it refers to concentration of economic activity in a small number of places.
- **Economic globalization (conversion to global market-oriented production).** Globalization, the incorporation of the local into the global, of the local economy means that the focus of local production changes towards international markets instead of local or regional markets, for example the transition from traditional mixed agriculture to mono-cropping of cash crops, and the shift from payment in kind to payment in cash.

Geographic processes
Geographic processes are those that affect the land-use patterns of a society.

- **Conversion and diversification of land use.** Change in the way land is utilized, both in terms of the area of land appropriated for a particular activity, the intensity of utilization of the land and whether there are areas of land not utilized for production, and in terms of the type of land-use activities and the pattern or mix of those activities.
- **Urban sprawl** is the expansion of urban areas into previously rural or peri-urban areas with associated land-use changes.
- **Urbanization** is both the process that promotes rural-to-urban migration and the process of transforming smaller centres (towns) into more densely populated cities.
- **Gentrification** is the process whereby (usually) inner city suburbs become converted from lower-class areas to middle- or upper-class suburbs.
- **Enhanced transport and rural accessibility.** Improvements in transport facilities results in increased accessibility, which results in various demographic changes.
- **Physical splintering.** Infrastructure projects like highways, railways,

transmission corridors, irrigation canals and the impoundment of water can lead to the physical division or splintering of communities.

Institutional and legal processes

Institutional and legal processes are those processes that affect the efficiency and effectiveness of various organizations that are responsible for the supply (and security of supply) of the goods and services on which people depend. These organizations include government agencies, non-government organizations and the commercial sector. This category definitely needs further elaboration.

- **Institutional globalization and centralization.** The incorporation of the local into the global in terms of institutions relates to the loss of autonomy of decision making at the local level.
- **Decentralization.** Something of a counter-force to institutional globalization is the process of decentralization, that is, a change from a centralized to a decentralized public administration system.
- **Privatization** refers to the process of transfer of responsibilities from the public to the private sector. It is often associated with the sale of government-owned enterprises.

Emancipatory and empowerment processes

Emancipatory and empowerment processes are those that lead to an increase in the ability of local people to affect (contribute to) the decision making that affects their lives.

- **Democratization** is the process by which people are granted increased influence in political decision making.
- **Marginalization and exclusion** are the processes by which various groups in society are denied access to services or to participation.
- **Capacity building** refers to increasing knowledge, networking capacity and increasing skill base amongst local people.

Sociocultural processes

Sociocultural processes are those that affect the culture of a society, that is, all aspects of the way that people live together, including the following.

- **Social globalization.** The incorporation of the local into the global at the sociocultural level refers to the change in the nature of the local culture, particularly as a result of the cultural hegemony of western cultural expression (often described as 'McDonaldization' or 'Coca-Cola development').

- **Segregation** refers to the process of creation of social difference within a community.
- **Social disintegration** refers to the falling apart of existing social and cultural networks.
- **Cultural differentiation.** Increase in the differences between various groups in a community based on cultural values, traditions, rituals, language, traditional skills and so on.
- **Deviant social behaviour.** Types of social behaviours that might be considered deviant or antisocial, such as excessive alcohol consumption, illegal drugs use, various types of risk-taking behaviours and vandalism.

Social impacts

We emphasize the need for a reconceptualization of social impacts. In this chapter, we have differentiated social change processes from social impacts, arguing that impacts need to be experienced or felt in corporeal or perceptual terms. We have argued that the SIA literature has confused impacts and social change processes. A listing of social impacts follows, which has been developed with considerable thought. However, there is no guarantee that it is exhaustive. It may contain a western bias and may not adequately represent economic and institutional impacts. The list was developed by a review of the literature and our accumulated practical experience as SIA and EIA consultants. The dimensions vary in their specificity. Some are macro concepts that may be difficult to measure, while others may lend themselves to operational definition, variable creation and measurement.

Social impacts must be experienced or felt. Ideally, the list of impacts should be capable of addressing positive benefits as well as negative consequences. And because social impacts (that is, *all* impacts on humans) cover a wide variety of issues, the list must be broad-ranging. Some impacts are experienced at the level of an individual, others are experienced at the level of a family or household unit, and others again are experienced by social organizations, institutions, or a community or society as a whole. Some impacts are corporeal – that is, felt by the body as physical reality – other impacts are perceptual or emotional.

The list presented recognizes seven categories of impacts. This categorization assists in thinking about the range of impacts. We accept that impacts may be categorized in different ways. Therefore they are defined here, as much as possible, in neutral terms and should be understood as being prefixed by '*a change in* . . .'. The impacts can be interpreted in a positive or negative direction. However, not all impacts can be phrased (bidirectionally) in such neutral terminology, as is illustrated by the impact, death – there is no opposite direction to dying.

Health and social wellbeing
Health is an essential category of social impacts. Health impact assessment (see Birley, 1995; Birley and Peralta, 1995) serves as a process to identify the health impacts, and health impact assessment professionals may have an extended range of health indicators that they consider. Here we have included health aspects from a social perspective expressed in non-medical terminology.

- **Death of self or a family member** – personal loss; has major conse-quences for other members of the family or household (grieving and economic impacts).
- **Death in the community** – loss of human capital.
- **Nutrition** – adequacy, security and quality of individual and house-hold food supply.
- **Actual physical health and fertility.**
- **Perceived health**.
- **Mental health** – feelings of stress, anxiety, apathy, depression, nostal-gic melancholy, changed self-image, general self-esteem (psychoso-cial factors).
- **Aspirations** for the future for self and children.
- **Autonomy** – an individual's independence or self-reliance.
- **Stigmatization or deviance labelling** – the feeling of being 'different' or of being excluded or socially marginalized.
- **Feelings in relation to the project** (positive or negative) which may result in the formation of interest groups. Projects often generate uncertainty or fear and sometimes the impacts perceived in anticipa-tion of the planned intervention can be greater than the impacts that ultimately result from the intervention (Burdge and Vanclay, 1995). Impacts here include uncertainty, annoyance (a feeling/experience such as that due to disruption to life, but which is not necessarily directed at the intervention itself), dissatisfaction due to failure of a project to deliver promised benefits, and experience of moral outrage (such as when a project leads to violation of deeply held moral or religious beliefs).

Quality of the living environment (liveability)
Here we deal with the liveability of the neighbourhood and workplace. This category contains many of the variables traditionally considered in SIA and EIA studies. Some of these variables relate directly to the biophysical environment and come through the pathway of biophysical impacts (see Figure 6.1). This concept has both a perceptual dimension and an actual dimension.

- **Quality of the living environment (actual and perceived)**, that is, physical environment or neighbourhood at home or at work – in terms of exposure to dust, noise, risk, odour, vibration, artificial light and so on.
- **Leisure and recreation opportunities and facilities.**
- **Environmental amenity value/aesthetic quality** – the non-market, non-consumptive aesthetic and moral value ascribed to a location (impacts on outlook, vistas, shadowing and so on).
- **Availability of housing facilities.**
- **Physical quality of housing (actual and perceived).**
- **Social quality of housing** (homeliness) – the degree to which inhabitants feel that their house is their 'home'.
- **Adequacy of physical infrastructure** – water supply, sewage, land, roads and so on.
- **Adequacy of and access to social infrastructure** – change in the demands for and supply of basic social services and facilities, such as education, police, libraries and welfare services.
- **Personal safety and hazard exposure (actual and perceived).**
- **Crime and violence (actual and perceived).**

Economic impacts and material wellbeing
This relates to the wealth and prosperity of individuals and the community as a whole.

- **Workload** – amount of work necessary in order to survive and/or live reasonably.
- **Standard of living**, level of affluence – a composite measure of material wellbeing referring to how well off a household or individual is in terms of their ability to obtain goods and services. It is also related to the cost of living, and is affected by changes in local prices and so on.
- **Economic prosperity and resilience** – the level of economic affluence of a community and the extent of diversity of economic opportunities.
- **Income** – both cash and in kind income.
- **Property values.**
- **Employment** – includes actual level of (un)employment, employment options and status of employment.
- **Replacement costs of environmental functions** – the cost of replacing a product or service that was formerly provided by the environment, such as clean water, firewood and flood protection.
- **Economic dependency** – the extent to which an individual or house-

hold (or higher entity) has control over economic activities, the degree of incorporation into larger production systems.

- **Burden of national debt** – such as the intergenerational transfer of debt.

Cultural impacts
This includes all impacts on the culture or cultures in an affected region, including loss of language, loss of cultural heritage or a change in the integrity of a culture (affecting ability of the culture to persist).

- **Change in cultural values** – such as moral rules, beliefs, ritual systems, language and dress.
- **Cultural affrontage** – violation of sacred sites, breaking taboos and other cultural mores.
- **Cultural integrity** – the degree to which local culture such as traditions, rites and so on are respected and likely to persist.
- **Experience of being culturally marginalized** – the structural exclusion of certain groups because of their cultural characteristics, thus creating a feeling of being a second class citizen.
- **Profanization of culture** – the commercial exploitation or commodification of cultural heritage (such as traditional handicrafts, artefacts) and the associated loss of meaning.
- **Loss of local language or dialect**.
- **Natural and cultural heritage** – violation, damage to, or destruction of cultural, historical, archaeological or natural resources, including burial grounds, historic sites and places of religious, cultural and aesthetic value.

Family and community impacts
Impacts may be related to the family, social networks and the community generally.

- **Alterations in family structure** – such as family stability, divorce, number of children at home, presence of extended families.
- **Obligations to living family members and ancestors**.
- **Family violence** – physical or verbal abuse.
- **Social networks** – impacts on the social interaction of household members with other people in the community.
- **Community identification and connection** – sense of belonging, attachment to place.
- **Community cohesion (actual and perceived)**.
- **Social differentiation and inequity** – creation of differences between

various groups in a community or differentiation in level of access to certain resources (actual and perceived).
- **Social tension and violence** – conflict or serious divisions within the community.

Institutional, legal, political and equity impacts
A range of impacts on institutions are included here, most notably those that affect the capacity of organizations, regulatory authorities and institutions to cope with the workload generated by proposed interventions.

- **Functioning of government agencies** – capacity of the formal institutions to handle additional workload generated by the project.
- **Integrity of government and government agencies** – absence of corruption, competence in which they perform their tasks.
- **Tenure or legal rights**.
- **Subsidiarity** – the principle that decisions should be taken as close to the people as possible.
- **Human rights** – any abuse of the human rights, arrest, imprisonment, torture, intimidation, harassment and so on, actual or fear or censorship and loss of free speech.
- **Participation in decision making.**
- **Access to legal procedures and to legal advice.**
- **Impact equity** – notions about fairness in the distribution of impacts across the community.

Gender relations
According to the World Bank (2001), 'gender discrimination remains pervasive in many dimensions of life – worldwide. . . . In no region of the developing world are women equal to men in legal, social, and economic rights. Gender gaps are widespread in access to and control of resources, in economic opportunities, in power and political voice'. Women tend to bear the largest and most direct social impacts. For these reasons, gender is a core social impact issue, and a development objective in its own right, requiring explicit consideration in the form of gender assessments (DGIS, 1994; Feldstein and Jiggins, 1994; Gianotten *et al.*, 1994; Guijt and Shah, 1998).

- **Women's physical integrity** – refers to the right of women to be able to make informed decisions about their own body, health and sexual activity, having control over fertility and childbearing and childrearing practices, and having the resources to implement those decisions safely and effectively, and to be free from coercion, violence and discrimination in the exercise of those decisions.

- **Personal autonomy of women** – the level of independence, self-reliance and self-respect in physical, economic, political and socio-cultural aspects.
- **Gendered division of production-oriented labour** – refers to the unequal distribution of workload between men and women in relation to production, in terms of cash cropping, subsistence food production, wage labour and other household (cash) income strategies.
- **Gendered division of household labour** – refers to the gendered and uneven distribution of workload in relation to the maintenance of the household.
- **Gendered division of reproductive labour** – refers to the gendered and uneven distribution of workload in relation to the care and maintenance of household members, that is the personal burden of child-bearing and childrearing.
- **Gender-based control over, and access to, resources** – including land, water, capital, equipment, knowledge, skills, employment opportunities and income, and services such as health facilities, education and agricultural extension services.
- **Political emancipation of women** – women's influence on decision making at household, community and society level.

Conclusion

In this chapter we have argued that a differentiation should be made between the concepts of social change processes and social impacts. This important conceptual distinction, based on the framework presented by Slootweg *et al.* (2001), has not been previously made in the SIA literature. Many previously measured SIA variables are not in themselves social impacts, but rather are social change processes which might lead to social impacts under certain conditions, depending on the characteristics of the impacted community and of mitigation measures.

The lists of social change processes and social impacts are broad and represent most of the issues relevant to social impact assessment. However, depending on the conditions under which any assessment is being carried out, the change processes as well as the impacts can be and may need to be redefined in more appropriate language and/or in more detail. Furthermore, the involvement of various disciplines in a specific assessment may result in a need for more discipline-oriented concepts and terminology. A further field of research would be the identification of the conditions under which certain social change processes would lead to social impacts. Documentation on success or failure of development activities provides a wealth of baseline information from which such conditions may be distilled (see the previous chapter for a discussion on the use of a 'social filter').

The list of potential social impacts is described in terms of issues that can be changed in a positive or negative direction. This provides room to define positive as well as negative impacts, and to consider intended as well as unintended impacts. The existing SIA literature strongly emphasizes the negative, unintended impacts of projects. By providing a neutrally defined list of issues of importance to impact studies, it becomes possible to assess also the goals of projects, programmes and policies and weigh these against the unintended impacts.

The listings are useful for expanding awareness of the full range of social impacts, but should not be used as a checklist. Because of the existence of second- and higher-order impacts, the complex iterative processes by which impacts are caused, and the complex impact pathways and causal chains, we advocate a thorough analysis using the conceptual framework of Slootweg *et al.* (2001).

By analysing the pathways leading to social impacts, we believe that greater awareness will arise of the processes by which impacts are caused. Acceptance of the potentially greater range of impacts will then occur. Further, through utilization of the conceptual framework, better scoping of SIA studies will be possible. Together, this will lead to better impact predictions. In turn, these will lead to improved SIA and EIA studies, and potentially to better projects and improved quality of life of affected communities.

Acknowledgments

This chapter, which is a further development of the ideas presented in Chapter 5, is a result of collaboration made possible by the Netherlands Ministry of Foreign Affairs. We thank Anneke Wevers for her support and vision in this innovative and challenging endeavour. We also thank Annelies Stolp for encouragement, perspective, balance and for being a sounding board. A revised version of this chapter has been published in *Environmental Impact Assessment Review*, 22(3).

References

Armour, A. 1990. 'Integrating impact assessment into the planning process', *Impact Assessment Bulletin*, 8(1/2): 3–14.

Birley, M.H. 1995. *The Health Impact Assessment of Development Projects*, Norwich: Her Majesty's Stationery Office.

Birley, M.H. and Peralta, G. 1995. 'Health impact assessment', in F. Vanclay and D. Bronstein (eds), *Environmental and Social Impact Assessment*, Chichester: Wiley, 153–70.

Branch, K., Hooper, D.A., Thompson, J. and Creighton, J.C. 1984. *Guide to Social Assessment*, Boulder, CO: Westview Press.

Burdge, R. 1994. *A Community Guide to Social Impact Assessment*, Wisconsin: Social Ecology Press.

Burdge, R. and Vanclay, F. 1995. 'Social impact assessment', F. Vanclay and D. Bronstein (eds), *Environmental and Social Impact Assessment*, Chichester: Wiley, 31–65.

Cernea, M.M. 1994. 'Using knowledge from social sciences in development projects', *Project Appraisal*, 9(2): 83–94.

DGIS 1994. 'Gender Assessment Study; A guide for policy staff'. Special Programme Women and Development, Directorate General for International Co-Operation, Netherlands Ministry of Foreign Affairs, The Hague.

Feldstein, H. and Jiggins, J. (eds) 1994. *Tools for the field: Gender analysis in farming systems research and extension*, West Hartford: Kumarian Press.

Gianotten, V., Gorverman, V., van Walsum, E. and Zuidberg, L. 1994. *Assessing the gender impact of development projects*, London: Intermediate Technology Publications.

Gramling, R. and Freudenburg, W.R. 1992. 'Opportunity-threat, development, and adaption', *Rural Sociology*, 57(2): 216–34.

Guijt, I. and Shah, M. (eds) 1998. *The Myth of Community: Gender Issues in Participatory Development*, London: Intermediate Technology Publications.

Interorganizational Committee on Guidelines and Principles for Social Impact Assessment 1994. 'Guidelines and Principles for Social Impact Assessment', *Impact Assessment*, 12(2): 107–52.

Juslén, J. 1995. 'Social impact assessment: a look at Finnish experiences', *Project Appraisal*, 10(3): 163–70.

Slootweg, R., Vanclay, F. and van Schooten, M. 2001. 'Function evaluation as a framework for the integration of social and environmental impact assessment', *Impact Assessment and Project Appraisal*, 19(1): 27–36.

Taylor, C.N., Goodrich, C. and Bryan, C.H. 1995. 'Issues-oriented approach to social assessment and project appraisal', *Project Appraisal*, 10(3): 142–54.

Vanclay, F. 2002. 'Social Impact Assessment', in M. Tolba (ed.), *Responding to Global Environmental Change* (vol. 4 of *Encyclopedia of Global Environmental Change*, series ed.: Ted Munn), Chichester: Wiley, 387–93.

World Bank 2001. *Engendering Development: Through Gender Equality in Rights, Resources, and Voice*, New York: Oxford University Press.

7 Integrating health and social impact assessment

Robert Rattle and Roy E. Kwiatkowski

Introduction

Human activity continues to exert increasing environmental pressures, and this has produced widespread undesirable consequences for many individuals and groups. Every effort must be made to ensure that development activities meet the needs of the present generation without harming people or compromising the needs of future generations. Only if this is achieved can we be certain that development activities are sustainable.

Many different definitions and interpretations of sustainable development have materialized in recent years. Often these focus on specific elements rather than the varied and complex relationships that describe quality of life and wellbeing. One simple process cannot express the complexities of quality of life and sustainable development and their interrelationships. A holistic or multidisciplinary approach is necessary.

Thirty years or so ago, environmental impact assessment (EIA) did not exist. Today, it is a formal process used in many countries and organizations to help decision makers consider the environmental consequences of proposed actions. It is considered a valuable tool to meeting sustainable development objectives. The results of an EIA may suggest important, indeed essential, interventions which may mitigate, reduce or prevent undesirable consequences and enhance the beneficial effects of development activities. Once the results are applied, they may improve the quality of specific proposals and help achieve sustainable development.

An International Study of the Effectiveness of Environmental Assessment (Sadler, 1996) identified social impact assessment (SIA) and health impact assessment (HIA) as areas that are insufficiently considered or are inadequately treated in EIA. In this chapter, an effort is made to identify both the essential and the desirable features of a conceptual framework for integration of SIA and HIA into an EIA. It will begin by reviewing the basis for integrating SIA and HIA. This will consider the common features, goals and complementary elements, and the advantages which may be achieved from a holistic or multidisciplinary assessment. The chapter will also review some challenges to integration. Important features for a conceptual framework will be identified. Finally, the ultimate desirability of integrating SIA and HIA, and next steps, will be discussed.

Common features reviewed

The World Health Organization (WHO) has defined health as 'a state of complete physical, mental and social wellbeing and not merely the absence of disease or infirmity' (WHO, 1967). This includes 'the extent to which an individual or group is able, on the one hand, to realize aspirations and to satisfy needs, and, on the other, to change or cope with the environment' (WHO, 1984). This definition suggests a holistic interpretation of health linking the complex interrelationships between social, economic, political and cultural health determinants with the natural environment. Given such a comprehensive definition, it is evident that proposed development activities have the potential to create significant human health impacts. They may arise directly and indirectly, and result in cumulative and synergistic impacts, characterized by complex cause–effect relationships. If these activities are to be sustainable, the potential human health impacts must be assessed, along with other potential consequences, and appropriate actions must be taken.

It has also been recognized that sustainable management and a holistic understanding of the complex interrelationships between the human and natural environments are crucial to human health. 'Health depends on our ability to understand and manage the interaction between human activities and the physical and biological environment' (WHO, 1991).

This definition incorporates many concepts and linkages among other human activities which may, initially, seem unrelated to health. Income, income distribution, jobs and employment, demographics, lifestyles, literacy, social order and cultural elements all influence health to one degree or another. These latter elements often better describe social wellbeing, but can actually have an impact on the rates of disease/health outcomes and quality of life (CPHA, 1997).

Health, therefore, combines social, economic, cultural and psychological wellbeing, as well as the physical, biological and geochemical environments, and includes the ability to adapt to daily stresses and changes. FPTACPH (1994) examined what makes and keeps people healthy and identified 11 determinants of health. Each of them is important to health, yet they are all intricately interrelated.

1. Relative income and socioeconomic status: evidence suggests that relative income and socioeconomic status are significant health determinants. People are progressively healthier the higher they are on the income scale. This seems counter-intuitive in countries which provide universal or virtually equal access to the health care system. As wealth distribution becomes more equitable, the population becomes healthier, regardless of the amount spent on health care.

2. Education: since increased education may improve employment opportunities, income, job security and satisfaction, and enhance knowledge and skills for solving problems, health status tends to improve with increasing levels of education.
3. Employment and working conditions: employment and unemployment contribute significantly to health status. Unemployed individuals may experience increased psychological distress, anxiety and other health problems. Stressful jobs and unsafe working conditions may increase health problems.
4. Physical environment: our basic physical necessities are derived from the natural environment: air, water, food and shelter. Therefore human health is fundamentally dependent on the natural environment.
5. Biology and genetic endowment: obviously, biological systems and human bodies, development and aging play key roles in human health. Similarly, genetic predispositions may expose certain individuals to particular diseases and health risks.
6. Social support networks: social support networks contribute coping, management and problem-solving skills and opportunities. These diminish the effects of and prevent health problems.
7. Health practices and skills: healthy lifestyle and behaviour choices increase opportunities for improved health. Personal responses to stress and daily challenges determine resilience to unhealthy situations.
8. Healthy child development: early life experiences seem strongly to influence one's ability to manage and cope later in life. Prenatal conditions help determine future risks, including neurological, congenital and retarded development and even premature deaths.
9. Health services: health care services are most effective when they prevent disease and health problems and maintain or promote healthy lifestyles and behaviours. Educational services to do with health risks are vital to promoting better health. Similarly, the promotion of lifestyles and behaviours which recognize the relationship of human health and the environment can significantly improve the effectiveness of health care services by reducing remedial health costs.
10. Culture: certain established socioeconomic environments, largely determined by dominant cultural values, may contribute to the perpetuation of health risks such as marginalization, stigmatization, loss or devaluation of language and culture and lack of access to culturally appropriate health care and services.
11. Gender: differing norms which are a function of gender-based social status or roles influence the health system's practices and priorities.

> Gender refers to the array of society-determined roles, personality traits, attitudes, behaviours, values, relative power and influence that society ascribes to the two sexes on a differential basis.

Clearly, the health and social wellbeing of people, families and communities are subject to many factors, and their influence on the human environment defies simple relationships. Factors such as the above are intricately related, and include many, often intangible, factors which, when integrated, define the health and wellbeing of people and communities. The significant overlap and linkages between these factors must be reflected in development practices, particularly EIA (FPTCEOHTF, 1997).

On the basis of these definitions and influences on health, a HIA must include the estimation in advance of the health consequences which may result from specific policy actions or development projects. These include the health consequences to a human population of any public or private actions that alter 'the extent to which an individual or group is able, on the one hand to realize aspirations and to satisfy needs, and on the other to change or cope with the environment' (WHO, 1984). Health impacts include any changes to the determinants of health.

Of course, this partial description is remarkably similar to the elements of SIA which estimate in advance social consequences which may result from specific policy actions or development projects. Social impacts include the 'social and cultural consequences to human population of any public or private actions that alter the ways in which people live, work, play, relate to one another, organize to meet their needs, and generally cope as members of society' (ICGP, 1994). The elements of cultural impacts include 'changes to the norms, values, and beliefs that guide and rationalize people's cognition of themselves and society'. Vanclay (2002: 387) defined SIA as 'the process of analysing and managing the intended and unintended consequences of planned interventions on people so as to bring about a more sustainable and equitable biophysical and human environment'.

The Interorganizational Committee on Guidelines and Principles for SIA (1994) identified several general social variable headings for SIA:

1. Population characteristics: these address the present and expected changes in population, cultural diversity and movement of transient residents, including seasonal and leisure residents.
2. Community and institutional structures: these are the size, structure and level of organization of local government. They also include current employment and industrial patterns and history, characteristics of the voluntary sector, and religious and interest groups and their inter- and intra-community relationships.

3. Political and social resources: these include the distribution of power and authority, stakeholders and affected public, and community or regional leadership properties.
4. Individual and family changes: these factors comprise the individual and family attitudes, perceptions, characteristics and social networks which influence daily life. 'These changes range from attitudes toward the policy to an alteration in family and friendship networks to perceptions of risk, health, and safety' (ibid.).
5. Community resources: these include natural resource and land use patterns, housing and community services including health, police and fire protection and sanitation. Historical and cultural resources are also included here, as well as consequences for indigenous peoples and religious subcultures.

These variables have strong links to health determinants and quality of life. Comparing them to the determinants of health (FPTACPH, 1994), we see that there is significant similarity and complementarity between SIA and HIA. Health and social consequences of development activities contribute valuable information to each other and draw extensively on comparable and closely interrelated data. How people and communities are affected, together with knowledge about the social and economic consequences of development, provide critical information for HIA. Similarly, knowledge of the impacts on the quality of life and health of people and communities is vital to SIA. Both HIA and SIA can be seen to address public concerns; integrate the human dimensions into an EIA; minimize adverse and maximize beneficial impacts; enhance cost-effectiveness; balance development and community goals; and embrace sustainable development.

First, as regards public concerns, they examine qualitative and quantitative concerns voiced by the public which may otherwise be neglected or omitted by EIA practitioners and managers. These are frequently of a health, wellbeing or quality of life nature. Unless these concerns are explicitly addressed and a method to accommodate them is available, they may easily be overlooked, dismissed or discounted.

Second, the values generating development goals are nourished by our need to maintain or improve our wellbeing, quality of life and health. Clearly, human dimensions are vital to ensure development goals are sustainable. Health and social impact assessments incorporate the human aspects of the motivations for, and the effects and consequences of, development activities. They ensure that the health and social factors are explicitly confronted. This can also prevent expensive mitigative costs and often insufficient actions.

Third, both HIA and SIA provide advice to ensure that development activities contribute a maximum of benefits and a minimum of impacts to people and communities. These recommendations can have a significant influence on the success of development activities. Identifying barriers to or opportunities for development activities at an early stage may also enhance the mitigation and monitoring of adverse impacts and strengthen the potential of beneficial impacts.

Fourth, in pursuit of cost-effectiveness, by assessing the human dimensions, costly mitigation, remediation and compensation expenses may be avoided. This is accomplished by employing a more holistic approach to assessing potential problems related to development activities. By effectively soliciting and addressing public concerns and examining and evaluating potential changes to the human environments, the consequences of development activities may be thoroughly determined. The costs of conducting this work through either a health or a social impact assessment are likely considerably less than the costs to remediate health and social impacts in the event that they were to occur unexpectedly. It is also likely that mitigation and compensation would be insufficient under such circumstances. Therefore early identification of potential problems is both cost-effective and preferable to confronting the longer-term costs associated with the impacts. Similarly, identifying opportunities to enhance proposed development activities early in the development process may produce financial gains otherwise unforeseen.

Fifth, both HIA and SIA balance the goals of conventional development with those of people and communities by ensuring participation of the community. In this sense, development activities may match the goals of the community more closely. Rather than explaining to people and communities what will happen, SIA and HIA listen to and encourage full participation from the community, the better to identify how their quality of life and wellbeing are characterized and determined. In fact, techniques, such as collaborative and participatory approaches, applied by both health and social practitioners function to diversify the expectations and realizations of community members and development proponents.

Finally, HIA and SIA both evaluate how well the human elements of development activities meet sustainable development objectives. They permit meeting community needs without compromising those of future generations. The human dimensions of environmental change are vital.

Both SIA and HIA capture crucial elements of the human environment and generate important information about proposed development activities and sustainable development objectives. Yet with the obvious overlap of interests, goals and objectives of SIA and HIA, there remains a conspicuous absence of collaboration and integration between these assessments.

Furthermore, the distinctively human elements addressed by social and health assessments convey a crucial message to EIA decision makers: human factors determine the activities undertaken which will in turn influence our relationships with the natural environment and its impact upon us. It is the human elements which embody the values and beliefs guiding our lifestyles and behaviours and shaping our social institutions and decisions. Improved identification and characterization of these factors within an EIA will more effectively drive sustainable human activities. By uniting SIA and HIA, their expanded and strengthened role can provide a stronger voice for sustainability and sustainable development practices.

The links between health impacts and social and cultural changes have been observed by Burdge and Vanclay (1995). They note that often 'the greatest social impact of many projects or policies, particularly those planned for community benefit . . . is the stress that results from the uncertainty associated with it – for example, living near a major development and being uncertain about the impacts that the project may have'.

Benefits of greater integration

Many quality of life concepts, such as spirituality, social cohesion, a sense of community and sacred places, are central to the health and social wellbeing of communities and peoples. Yet, because they are difficult to quantify and communicate, they are typically discounted or rejected in the EIA process. The bounded beliefs and social practices incorporated in conventional development activities advocate specific, and often conflicting, values and interpretations. SIA and HIA must identify these concepts and sensitize development activities to the importance of, and differences between, them. Both HIA and SIA play key roles in capturing and conveying communities' quality of life and wellbeing. Opportunities to diminish the costs of development and enhance their success may hinge on these more elusive properties of quality of life and wellbeing.

Carrying out separate SIA and HIA will waste resources through duplication and lose the value of a holistic or multidisciplinary integration. However, integrating SIA and HIA will clarify the many potential direct and indirect impacts, and capture synergistic and cumulative impacts often hidden during either an SIA or a HIA. As well, linking SIA/HIA results in a more holistic analysis of the human dimensions of development projects would likely enhance the estimates and their validity in the EIA process. Second- and third-order impacts (such as the consequences compensation may create) may also be better defined and clarified by integrating SIA and HIA.

Expanding and uniting SIA with HIA will undoubtedly lead to a more holistic assessment of the human impacts and benefits, and encourage development practices which are more broad, inclusive and sustainable. Integrating the two assessments will also help enhance the legitimacy and significance of the human dimensions of development activities. This may help reconcile the often conflicting views of decision makers and their conclusions with those of impacted communities.

A properly designed SIA/HIA would (a) generate a holistic or multidisciplinary assessment, (b) reduce duplication of data and information resources, (c) enhance financial efficiency, (d) avoid potential inconsistencies, (e) enhance strengths and complementaries, (f) enhance the value of social and health sciences in proposed development activity decision making, and (g) balance mechanistic reductionism.

First, health and social variables are vital elements of quality of life and wellbeing. The diverse relationships and linkages are intrinsic to our quality of life. The complex nature of human wellbeing does not readily permit the separation of these variables. Uniting HIA and SIA would capture these relationships and linkages. A properly designed human impact assessment would effectively characterize the human consequences of proposed development activity or policy changes.

Second, significant overlaps between SIA and HIA exist. Furthermore, they address common goals and objectives, utilize similar methodologies and techniques and employ many common data sets and information resources. Both HIA and SIA characterize complementary and integral elements of the human dimensions of proposed development activities. Uniting them would minimize the duplication of data and information resources during the collection and assessment phases of an EIA.

Third, by minimizing duplication when assessing the human dimensions in an EIA, significant savings can be achieved. Uniting health and social impact assessments would also permit the design of data collection techniques, and data collection and assessment, to be more efficient. Reducing the duplication of methodologies and techniques would ensure costs and time expenditures are not unnecessarily reproduced. At the same time, the complex nature of the human dimensions of proposed development activities may be holistically captured.

Fourth, focusing attention and analyses on one set of factors or variables while neglecting others may lead to erroneous or irrelevant results and conclusions. Benefits or opportunities, for example, in the social (or health) context may not respectively translate into benefits in the health (or social) context. Uniting HIA and SIA within an inclusive and holistic framework would avoid such potential inconsistencies.

Fifth, SIA and HIA describe many elements of the human factors in EIA. Sharing methodologies, techniques, tools and experiences would enhance their effectiveness. Uniting SIA and HIA would strengthen the design of data collection methodologies, techniques and practices. An integrated and holistic assessment of the human dimensions and consequences of proposed development activities would build on the strengths and complementarities of separate health and social impact assessments. Combined, a human impact assessment would provide the tools, experiences and opportunities to enhance the ability to address public concerns, integrate the human elements into an EIA, minimize adverse and maximize beneficial impacts, improve cost-effectiveness, balance development and community goals and advance sustainable development.

Sixth, uniting HIA and SIA would comprehensively identify the human factors influencing the success or failure of proposed development activities. How these factors may be respectively enhanced or diminished may also be identified. Similarly, a human impact assessment would identify the human consequences of proposed development activities and to what degree these may improve or deteriorate the quality of life. Taken together, this knowledge would provide a powerful tool to advance the merits of the human dimensions of an environmental impact assessment.

Finally, introducing a multidisciplinary human impact assessment into the EIA framework will balance the historical trend towards reductionist assessments and the powerful motivation to apply them to biophysical and human realities. It would permit abstract thought to be enhanced by recognizing its inherent limitations and properly situating this within biophysical and human realities. Furthermore, restrictive, counter-productive, unhealthy or harmful definitions of progress and development would be revealed through broad, inclusive approaches and understandings. Often the prevailing emphasis on economic, demographic, employment and similar variables reflects values and beliefs established from narrowly defined assumptions, which are then erroneously applied to biophysical and human realities. Although the assumptions may be judicious, they only remain so within given limits. Although economic and similar variables are important, they only represent a segment of overall wellbeing and quality of life. Additional variables are necessary to describe biophysical and human realities effectively. The inclusion of all variables in assessing the consequences of proposed development activities is essential both to balance conventional development practices and to help achieve sustainable development. The prevailing emphasis on economic, demographic, employment and similar variables would be lifted as implicit values were articulated.

To realize these enrichments, integration of HIA and SIA is required. If HIA/SIA integration is to proceed, the barriers and challenges to integration must be identified and overcome. In the next section we will consider these challenges.

Challenges to an integrated assessment
Five general categories of challenges which will be encountered as an integrated health and social impact assessment proceeds are disciplinary, institutional, organizational, resources/capacity and conceptual.

Disciplinary
The powerful predictive success of physics has functioned to establish numerous branches of study – chemistry, biology, sociology and so on – as the dominant form of enquiry. Each of these fields has evolved in relative autonomy and the deductive appeal of this approach continues to guide theoretical work.

It is this very organization of knowledge which is a barrier to integration. The process of defining a discipline necessitates the articulation of a method most appropriate to the subject matter. Although this process distinguishes each discipline from the others, it selects the features of the subject matter that will be considered and studied and, perhaps more important, limits those who may be associated with the discipline (Daly and Cobb, 1994). Thus the discipline is shaped often to neglect its relationship to the broader human and biophysical environment realities.

The rigid boundary delineation of past academic thought is yielding to more interdisciplinary and cross-disciplinary efforts, as awareness that reductionist efforts are too confining to describe real world phenomena grows. Indeed, transdisciplinary thought is emerging as a more powerful, deductive, predictive and holistic form of enquiry. Nevertheless, society, institutions and social organization predominantly remain fixated on reductionist mechanization.

Scientific reductionism, disciplinary worldviews and similar institutional barriers will need to be confronted. An appropriate framework for integrating SIA and HIA will need to address these challenges. Therefore an appropriate framework will need to introduce and conceptualize a fundamentally different way of thinking.

Institutional
Closely linked with disciplinary barriers are the institutional barriers. As disciplinary thought became specialized and abstracted, each discipline and its practitioners became ever more committed to and dependent on its specific ideologies and methodologies. As a result, thought within each disciplinary field was effectively biased by its abstractions and assumptions. Practitioners established vested interests in maintaining their worldviews. Relationships grew more out of disciplinary need than out of human or biophysical realities. Funding, income, prevailing theories, models and assumptions became the basis of fiercely competitive efforts to emphasize

particular worldviews, often to the exclusion of others. This process continues at an escalating rate today. This response is largely, and perhaps con-
testably, a consequence of its own process – the emergence of dominant
economic beliefs has produced a critical inversion of priorities which guide
social thought and human activity with specific biases rather than predict
the behaviour of complex systems (Glasser and Craig, 1999).

Practitioners and students of a particular discipline who do raise fundamental questions or challenge or criticize established abstractions typically
encounter obvious problems. New ideas can be difficult to accept, and
introducing them into established forms of thought can be virtually impossible. New subdisciplines may be established, but fundamental transformations of established disciplines are extremely rare. This contributes to the
confusion over SIA and HIA boundaries. Worldviews have been shaped by
a multiplicity of social inputs. For this reason, many social assessment
practitioners feel health is a part of the social environment (indeed, this
may be, in part, why HIA was a recent, yet distinct, introduction to the
EIA). Similarly, many HIA practitioners perceive social impacts as only a
part of a broader health framework. In either case, the whole becomes lost
within a particular set of abstractions. Changing the semantics, a human
impact assessment (an integration of SIA and HIA) would manifest more
than a mere combination of both these worldviews. Part of the reason for
integration will be to dissolve these barriers to achieve a holistic assessment
of human impacts.

These very real and often deeply divisive barriers will need to be confronted by any conceptual framework linking SIA and HIA. Therefore an
appropriate framework will need to accommodate these differing worldviews, needs, practices and models.

Organizational
As a result of disciplinary and institutional barriers, the challenge of oper-
ationalizing and implementing a new way of thinking will lead to organizational barriers. Legal and regulatory frameworks, existing authorities and
agencies, and established practices and norms have all emerged from the
reductionist mechanization of disciplinary thought and the segregation of
differing worldviews, purposes and needs. To overcome this may prove the
greatest challenge of all. It may appear as if we are suggesting the rejection
of years of knowledge, understanding and practice to achieve a holistic
understanding of potential human impacts. This is not the case, and a
human impact assessment will have to reflect this reality.

Yet this is only the tip of the proverbial iceberg. Predominant beliefs,
social institutions and values have established their organizational regimes.
Although these have served us to this point and permitted the evolution of

EIA, they may now become an impediment. Economic assumptions, models and theories, social and cultural beliefs, and valuation techniques are but a few which have advanced particular belief structures largely reflected in current development goals. Although not all these practices exhibit shortcomings, those which do must be assessed and modified.

Financial and legal frameworks, existing authorities and agencies, and established practices and norms reflect these beliefs and therefore function to advance conventional development goals. These frameworks, agencies and practices form an essential foundation. In practice, they will need to recognize these serious shortcomings and incorporate new understandings into their operation. This may be partially achieved if separate, disaggregated health and social impact assessments shift their focus to an integrated human impact assessment. For a truly holistic human impact assessment to succeed, however, it will also have to challenge and assess the very beliefs, assumptions and practices upon which proposed development activities and prevailing definitions of sustainable development are founded. Human assessments will need to identify, articulate, assert and apply understandings which are consistent with current knowledge from many disciplines. The inclusive, or holistic, nature of a human impact assessment will therefore be essential. A human impact assessment will estimate in advance the human consequences which may result from specific policy actions or development projects. This will include many features, such as economic, social, cultural and health. It will be inclusive and holistic.

One way to achieve this integration without discarding the valuable knowledge, understandings and practices already established would be to articulate and value disciplinary abstractions while recognizing their inherent limitations. Any framework linking SIA and HIA will require greater communication and appreciation across and beyond disciplinary boundaries. These will also be essential features of an integrating framework.

Resources/capacity

A greater shared understanding between policy and decision makers in all sectors is a necessary starting point for ensuring actions are more supportive of the SIA/HIA framework. The vertical organization of governments, industry and academia often hinders the collaborative approach that is needed to address the broader components of a SIA/HIA framework.

Methods, indicators, time and resources are needed to ensure the integration of SIA and HIA into a simple, rational, equitable and consistent framework. But who should develop these and, more importantly, who should pay for their development?

As additional resources are always difficult to find, there is a need to work smarter. Professionals must learn 'how to do more with less' through the sharing of resources and expertise, promoting secondments, strengthening coordination and collaboration between social and health professionals, and promoting national SIA/HIA consistency in application. There are great benefits to be gained if partners from the health, social services, economic, business, labour, education and other sectors can work together. Having a common framework for action would mean concerted efforts could be made by all partners to address the factors known to have the most significant influences and deliver the greatest beneficial outcomes. This would enable partners to see more clearly what their potential contribution could be, to pool their resources and expertise when appropriate, reduce duplication and get the best return on their investment.

There is a significant need to build capacity in an integrated SIA/HIA, not only in developing countries, but also in developed countries. Partnerships within and among countries are needed to generate a lasting improvement in the ability to obtain baseline community information, commonly accepted indicators, methods for measuring effects on sociocultural health, and improved methods for assessing these in small populations. Universities and government organizations need to promote capacity building to build stronger bridges between SIA and HIA.

Conceptual

The appropriate framework and methodology for integration will additionally present obvious conceptual challenges. As already mentioned, there will be numerous features an appropriate framework must exhibit. In addition, it will need to incorporate flexibility and inclusiveness and reflect holism. The precise procedures and methodologies for bringing about integration will also lead to numerous challenges. It is hoped this section will have introduced some of these challenges, and in this sense will contribute to the process of identifying an appropriate framework for integrating HIA and SIA.

Abstract thought is an important and very valuable tool. However, we must recognize its limitations. If this can be achieved, the limits to conceptual thought can be overcome. If the trend towards increased professional specialization can be overcome, the tendency for professionals to observe a particular worldview and set of abstractions, *to the exclusion of others*, will be avoided. This will introduce a much-needed element of balance. Consequently, the functional barriers to integration will become less obstructive. The value of existing financial and legal frameworks, existing agencies and established practices and the expected demands from a new conceptual framework linking health and social impact assessments will need to be merged. Predominant beliefs guiding development activities will need to be articulated and evaluated through broad public discourse. The identification of roles and responsibilities for capacity building and resources distribution will be essential. Effective coordination to ensure actions are supportive of the SIA/HIA framework, national consistency in application, and partnerships and sharing of knowledge and experiences internationally will all be needed. Finally, the actual framework selected and the methodology to apply it will need to incorporate many essential features.

A conceptual framework will ensure that the human elements of an impact assessment, essential if development activities are to be sustainable, are included. In addition, other valuable and important information dependent on the specific circumstances of any given proposal will be collected and acted upon in the eventual assessment.

Conclusion

A human impact assessment will be an attempt to bridge the disciplinary specialization and distinct worldviews currently reflected in HIA and SIA. Although the precise procedures and methodologies for bringing about integration will lead to numerous challenges, we can now identify several features a conceptual framework will need to exhibit.

It will need to accommodate differing needs, practices and models. At the same time, it will need to incorporate knowledge from diverse disciplines. This will be used to assess existing practices, and identify and apply practices consistent with current understandings. Generating communication across and beyond disciplines will also be essential. Clearly, a great deal of flexibility and inclusiveness will be central to the framework. It will be both holistic and inherently transdisciplinary in nature. To achieve this, a human impact assessment will need to overcome diverse and often rigid disciplinary barriers. Moreover, guiding beliefs and values will need to be articulated and, if necessary, modified to conform with current understandings. This may require transformations in current practices and norms, financial and legal frameworks, and established authorities and agencies. A human impact assessment will contribute to these transformations. The selected framework should facilitate this.

The objective for undertaking development activities should be to improve human health, quality of life and wellbeing. In this context, human impacts are essential to determining whether proposed development activities will ultimately achieve that improvement. Altruistic appeals may be avoided through a properly structured and applied conceptual framework for a human impact assessment. This would contribute a powerful tool to encourage sustainable development practices, assess potential consequences of proposed development activities and help to generate the required institutional and organizational changes necessary to achieve these goals. Such an extended framework would equip decision makers and professional practitioners with the required techniques to apply and integrate appropriately what is known within disciplinary abstractions to the broader biophysical and human realities.

It has been observed that integration 'sounds good in theory, but could it work in practice?' There are several responses to this question. First, it needs to work, based principally on the arguments made above. The enormous resources currently duplicated in many situations where separate HIAs and SIAs are undertaken are out of step with the common visions of either of these, the impact assessment process as a whole and today's fiscal realities. The common elements of HIAs and SIAs compel a closer working relationship.

Second, the essential importance of the human dimensions to the assessment of proposed development activities, and, indeed, the human dimensions of sustainable development, need a stronger platform from which they may be articulated. Uniting HIA and SIA is a logical step to achieve this.

Furthermore, SIA has been applied to assess potential health impacts and, conversely, health has been observed as a primary consequence of potential social changes. These activities establish that integration can and does work. They also exemplify the pervasive bonds between society, human activities, quality of life and human health. All that remains is the formalization of this process.

We realize that this chapter does not describe a specific framework or detail potential candidates. Although there are several frameworks which could be applied, elaboration and discussion of these, as well as the details of how they might be selected and applied, is beyond the scope of this present chapter.

The primary purpose of this chapter was to show that the concepts and activities carried out in both HIA and SIA have undergone considerable evolution and have very similar objectives. The social impact assessment process has been applied much longer than the HIA process. SIA has developed extensive experiences and well established methodologies and practices. HIA, on the other hand, is in an early and rapid growth and development phase. Yet, as with any relationship, there is much to be learned and gained from each other. In this context, SIA is likely to furnish effective and valuable tools, methods, experiences and techniques, while HIA might offer a rich conceptual framework from which to integrate the two practices into an effective human impact assessment. It is our belief that the next step in the evolutionary process is the integration of SIA and HIA within an EIA process. This chapter has articulated some challenges and benefits facing the integration of HIA and SIA, along with some essential features a framework for integration might exhibit.

In this regard, we hope we have succeeded. In particular, we hope to have presented an argument favouring the desirability of structured HIA/SIA integration. At the very least, we hope to have further stimulated the dialogue on HIA/SIA integration.

References

Burdge, R.J. and Vanclay, F. 1995. 'Social Impact Assessment', in F. Vanclay and D. Bronstein (eds), *Environmental and Social Impact Assessment*, Chichester: Wiley, 31–65.

Canadian Public Health Association (CPHA) 1997. *Health Impacts of Social and Economic Conditions: Implications for Public Policy*, Ottawa: Canadian Public Health Association.

Daly, H.E. and Cobb, J.B. 1994. *For the Common Good*, Boston: Beacon Press.

Federal, Provincial, Territorial Advisory Committee on Population Health (FPTACPH) 1994. 'Strategies for Population Health: Investing in the Health of Canadians' (notes for the Meeting of Ministers, Halifax, Nova Scotia, 14–15 September 1994).

Federal, Provincial, Territorial Committee on Environmental and Occupational Health Task Force (FPTCEOHTF) 1997. 'Draft Canadian Health Impact Assessment Guide Volume 1: The Beginners' Guide'.

Glasser, H. and Craig, P.P. 1999. 'All of Keynes' Horses: The need for end-goal driven assessment of ecosystem services', *Ecological Economics*, 29(3): 321–7.

Interorganizational Committee on Guidelines and Principles (ICGP) 1994. 'Guidelines and Principles for Social Impact Assessment', *Impact Assessment*, 12(2): 107–52.

Sadler, B. 1996. *Environmental assessment in a changing world: evaluating practice to improve performance*, final report of the International Study of the Effectiveness of Environmental Assessment, Ottawa: Ministry of Supply and Services.

Vanclay, F. 2002. 'Social Impact Assessment', in M. Tolba (ed.), *Responding to Global Environmental Change* (vol. 4 of *Encyclopedia of Global Environmental Change*, series ed.: Ted Munn), Chichester: Wiley, 387–93.

World Health Organization (WHO) 1967. 'The Constitution of the World Health Organization', *World Health Organization Chronicles*, 1: 29.

World Health Organization (WHO) 1984. *Health Promotion: A Discussion Paper on the Concept and Principles*. Copenhagen: World Health Organization Regional Office for Europe.

World Health Organization (WHO) 1991. 'Commission on Health and Environment'.

8 An ecological model of wellbeing

Davianna Pomaika'i McGregor, Paula Tanemura Morelli, Jon Kei Matsuoka and Luciano Minerbi

Introduction

'Wellbeing' is a multifaceted concept drawing on both environmental and intrapsychic factors. An ecological model of wellbeing assumes that a healthy ecological system is the foundation for a functional economy and social system that can sustain a high quality of life for its residents. In western societies, wellbeing is measured using indicators such as asset income, poverty rates, residential stability, and disease and mortality rates (Office of the Assistant Secretary for Planning and Evaluation, 1997). In non-western cultures, including those of indigenous Pacific Islanders, human wellbeing is often synonymous with the health and vitality of natural resources in addition to the perpetuation of cultural traditions and a communal identity (McGregor *et al.*, 1998; Papa Ola Lokahi, 1992).

A number of theorists have proposed ecological systems models that explain the effects of environment on personal identity and predispositions, family structure and roles, and communal networks and patterns (for example, Bronfenbrenner, 1977, 1995; Bronfenbrenner and Ceci, 1994). Bronfenbrenner (1995) asserted that human development and wellbeing were established through a series of reciprocal interactions between bio-psychological human beings and their social and physical environments. This proximal process occurs between individuals and their families and within peer, learning and recreational activities. The significance and impact of features within the proximal realm are apt to vary across cultures.

Social impact assessments (SIAs) conducted in the context of non-western cultures, indigenous cultures, or subcultures within a predominant western one, should consider the culturally distinct properties associated with wellbeing. SIAs are a critical means of determining the anticipated impacts of land development on people in the context of social systems. They provide planners and decision makers with a basis for deciding whether to approve development proposals and ways to mitigate negative social impacts. In the past, SIAs have generally omitted variables that are critical to an analysis of impacts affecting indigenous peoples. Factors including spirituality, subsistence practices and indigenous economies, collective and mutual social patterns, sense of place and 'ways of knowing' have been missing from conventional approaches to impact assessment. Yet, as development encroaches closer to pristine ecological and cultural areas, it poses greater threats to the lifeways of indigenous people who draw their existence from the elements of nature.

As SIAs evolve in scope and method, a myriad of new cultural phenomena need to be considered as potential receptors of impacts related to proposed development. The purpose of this chapter is to conceptualize an ecological model of indigenous wellbeing that can be used to identify cultural receptors and potential types of impacts which should be assessed through SIAs. The conceptualization of person-in-environment not only represents a marked departure from western social constructions, it also serves to explain the etiology of social pathos resulting from disruptions to customary and traditional land-use patterns in indigenous rural communities.

Native Hawaiians are a prime example of a population that has been severely impacted by western development. Nevertheless, throughout the islands of Hawai'i, there are distinct rural Hawaiian communities where the concept of wellbeing is deeply embedded in an interdependence between people and nature, in beliefs in the sacredness of the animate and inanimate world, in collective gathering and sharing, and in the centrality of the *'ohana* or organic family system. Thus the authors conceptualize an ecological model of wellbeing for indigenous peoples using the phenomena and experience related to rural Native Hawaiian communities.

An ecological context to Hawaiian wellbeing
In traditional Hawaiian genealogies and origin myths, all life springs from the *'āina* or land and nature. *Aloha 'āina* or love of land and nature is a pervasive cultural theme that refers to having a deep appreciation of nature's abundant offerings and a spiritual rootedness to the land. A legacy connected to ancestral lands, sacred sites and nature deities is transmitted to each successive generation. A unique set of place-based competencies are instilled in developing children and leads to the formation of the community's local character. Hawaiian psyche and identity is partly derived from belonging to the land itself (see Robillard and Marsella, 1987).

Owing to the centrality given to the *'āina* or sacred land and nature, changes in land and natural resources ultimately have an impact on the lives of the people at various levels of the social system. Western notions that suggest social systems can remain intact, or that sociocultural impacts can be mitigated in the face of land transformations, imply a degree of separation of people from the land. For Hawaiians and indigenous peoples generally, wellbeing is synonymous with people–environment kinship and an organic relationship that bonds humans to the land. A human ecological

Ho'oulu Lāhui Aloha
'Raising a Beloved Nation'

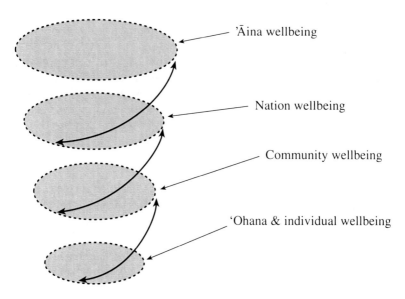

'Āina wellbeing

Nation wellbeing

Community wellbeing

'Ohana & individual wellbeing

Figure 8.1   An ecological model of Hawaiian wellbeing

analysis is a way to understand how human systems – ranging from the national to community and family levels – interact with the environment and lead to social outcomes. In the case of Native Hawaiian rural communities, the health of all social systems is inherently tied to the *'aina*. Knowing the dynamic process of interaction of the *'ohana* and community with natural resources is critical in terms of predicting outcomes spurred by changes to those resources.

The ecological model (see Figure 8.1) is a visual aid in conceptualizing how human systems interact within the context of the *'āina*. The model also assumes that individuals, families and their communities have reciprocal effects on each other. What happens to an individual affects the family. This, in turn, affects the community, and vice versa. Thus cohesive, healthy, functional families generally produce healthy individuals, who ultimately contribute to healthy communities. Cohesive, healthy communities reinforce the positive behaviours of young people. When families fall short of their responsibilities, the community may serve as a surrogate source of support and, thereby, save children from neglect or delinquency. The ecological model of wellbeing, therefore, serves as a tool when conducting an

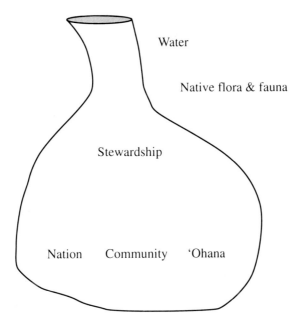

Figure 8.2   'Āina wellbeing

SIA. The model aids in understanding the systematic relationships that contribute to Hawaiian wellbeing at various levels, and in assessing potential impacts on Native wellbeing.

'Āina wellbeing

The *'āina* (land and natural resources) are the foundation of traditional Native Hawaiian cultural and spiritual custom, belief and practice (see Figure 8.2). Land and all of nature are alive, respected, treasured, praised and honoured. Throughout the islands, many Native Hawaiian *'ohana* in rural communities continue to practise subsistence cultivation, gathering, fishing and hunting as part of their livelihoods. Rural Hawaiians conduct subsistence activities in accordance with the cultural and spiritual values and responsibilities they were taught by their ancestors, who nurtured both physical and spiritual relationships with the ancestral lands. *'Āina* is *'one hānau*, sands of birth, and *Kula iwi*, resting place of ancestral bones.

At the core of traditional Native Hawaiian spirituality is the belief that the land lives as do the *'uhane*, or spirits of family ancestors, who cared for the ancestral lands in their lifetime. The land has provided for generations of Hawaiians, and will provide for those yet to come. In communities where

Native Hawaiians live on and work the land, they become knowledgeable about the life of the land. In daily activities, they develop a partnership with the land so as to know when to plant, fish or heal the mind and body according to the ever-changing weather, seasons and moons. Native Hawaiian subsistence practitioners speak of their cultural and spiritual relation to the lands of their ancestors, and their commitment to take care of it and protect it for future generations. Hawaiians acknowledge the *'aumakua* and *akua*, the ancestral spirits and gods of special areas. They even make offerings to them. They learn the many personalities of the land, its form, character and resources. They name its features as they do their own children. The land is not viewed as a commodity; it is the foundation of their cultural and spiritual identity as Hawaiians. They trace their lineage to the lands in the region as being originally settled by their ancestors. The land is a part of their *'ohana* and they care for it the same as they care for the other members of their families.

The quality and abundance of the natural resources in many rural Hawaiian communities has preserved community wellbeing in those communities. However, an inherent aspect of the *'ohana* values is the practice of conservation to ensure availability of natural resources for present and future generations. The ancestral knowledge about the land and its resources is reinforced through continued subsistence practices. While travelling to the various locations where these traditional cultural practices take place – along dirt roads and trails, by spring-fed streams and the shore – villagers continually renew their cultural knowledge and understanding of the landscape, the place names, traditional names of the winds and the rains, traditional legends, historical cultural sites and the location of various native plants and animals. The villagers stay alert to the condition of the landscape and the resources, and they observe the changes due to seasonal and lifecycle transformations. This orientation is critical to the preservation of the natural and cultural landscape.

There are five basic principles of Hawaiian stewardship and use of natural and cultural resources, which are relevant to sustaining Native Hawaiian wellbeing. These principles identify the principal elements which must be protected in order to sustain the wellbeing of the *'āina*.

First, the *ahupua'a* is the basic unit of Hawaiian cultural resource management. An *ahupua'a* runs from the sea to the mountains and contains a sea fishery and beach, a stretch of *kula* or open cultivable land and, higher up, the forest. The court of the Hawaiian Kingdom described the *ahupua'a* principle of land use in the case *In Re Boundaries of Pulehunui,* 4 Haw. 239, 241 (1879) as follows:

A principle very largely obtaining in these divisions of territory [ahupua'a] was that a land should run from the sea to the mountains, thus affording to the chief and his people a fishery residence at the warm seaside, together with products of the high lands, such as fuel, canoe timber, mountain birds, and the right of way to the same, and all the varied products of the intermediate land as might be suitable to the soil and climate of the different altitudes from sea soil to mountainside or top.

Second, the natural elements – land, air, water, ocean – are interconnected and interdependent. The atmosphere affects the land which, in turn, affects running streams, the watertable and the beaches and ocean. Cultural land management must take all aspects of the natural environment into account. Hawaiians consider the land and ocean to be integrally united, and that these land sections also include the shoreline as well as inshore and offshore ocean areas such as fishponds, reefs, channels and deep sea fishing grounds. Coastal shrines called fishing *ko'a* were constructed and maintained as markers for the offshore fishing grounds that were part of that *ahupua'a*.

Third, of all the natural elements, fresh water is the most important for life and needs to be considered in every aspect of land use and planning. The Hawaiian word for water is *wai* and the Hawaiian word for wealth is *waiwai*, indicating that water is the source of wellbeing and wealth.

Fourth, Hawaiians ancestors studied the natural elements and the land and became very familiar with its features and assets. Ancestral knowledge of the land was recorded and passed down through place names. Chants name the winds, rains, features of particular districts and legends. Hawaiians applied their expert knowledge of the natural environment in constructing their homes, temples and cultivation and irrigation networks. Hawaiian place names, chants and legends inform Hawaiians (and others who know the traditions) about the natural and cultural resources of a particular district. Insights about the natural and cultural resources inform those who use the land about how to locate and construct structures and infrastructure so as to have the least negative impact on the land. This ancestral knowledge about the land and its resources is reinforced through continued subsistence practices.

Fifth, an inherent aspect of Hawaiian stewardship and use of cultural and natural resources is the practice of *mālama 'āina*, or conservation, to ensure the sustainability of natural resources for present and future generations. These rules of behaviour are tied to cultural beliefs and values regarding (a) respect for the *'āina*, (b) the virtue of sharing and not taking too much, and (c) a holistic perspective of organisms and ecosystems that emphasize balance and coexistence. The Hawaiian outlook which shapes these customs and practices is *lōkāhi*, or maintaining spiritual, cultural and natural balance with the elemental life forces of nature. Hawaiian families who rely upon subsistence for a primary part of their diet respect and care for their surrounding natural resources. They only use and take what is needed in order to allow the natural resources to reproduce. They share what is gathered with family and neighbours. Through understanding the cycles of the various natural resources, and how changes in the moon phase and the seasons affect the abundance and distribution of the resources, the subsistence practitioners are able to plan and adjust their activities to keep the resources healthy. Such knowledge has been passed down from generation to generation, through working alongside their *kūpuna*, or elders.

Throughout the islands of Hawai'i, wellbeing and subsistence livelihoods thrive in particular rural communities (Matsuoka *et al.*, 1997). Surrounding these communities are pristine and abundant natural resources in the ocean, the streams and the forest. This is largely due to the continued practices of *aloha 'āina/kai* (cherish the land and ocean) and *mālama 'āina/kai* (care for the land and ocean). These rural communities were bypassed by mainstream economic, political and social development (ibid., 1997). Hawaiians living in these communities continued, as their ancestors before them, to practise subsistence cultivation, gathering, fishing and hunting for survival. Thus we find in these areas that the natural resources sustained a subsistence lifestyle, and that this subsistence lifestyle, in return, sustained the natural resources.

A comprehensive SIA would assess impacts on natural and cultural resources utilized by indigenous peoples for subsistence, cultural and spiritual purposes. Impacts to assess include changes in the condition, integrity, use, access to and boundaries, ownership and quality of experience with natural and cultural resources.

Nation wellbeing

Native Hawaiian *'ohana* and communities all function within the framework of a sovereign nation. A nation is a historically constituted stable community with a shared unique language; culture and spirituality; ancestral national lands; economic life and governance structure (see Figure 8.3). Native Hawaiian language, which was on the verge of extinction in the 1980s, has made a remarkable recovery with the establishment of *Pūnana Leo* Hawaiian language immersion pre-schools, the *Kula Kaiapuni*/Native Hawaiian Language Immersion Public Schools and various Hawaiian language charter schools. In the 1999–2000 school year, for example, some 1750 students were enrolled in 18 Hawaiian language immersion public schools.

Beginning in the 1970s, Native Hawaiians engaged in a cultural renaissance which reaffirmed the consciousness, pride and practice of Hawaiian

Ho'oulu Lāhui Aloha
'Raising a Beloved nation'

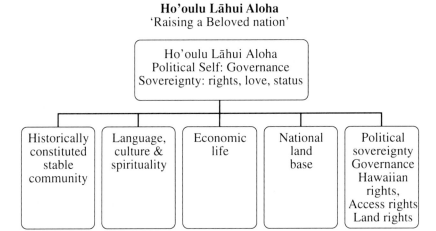

Figure 8.3   Nation wellbeing

cultural and spiritual customs and beliefs. In rallying around protection of the island of *Kaho'olawe* from bombing by the United States military, the traditional practice of *aloha 'āina* gained prominence and Hawaiian religious practices, such as the *Makahiki*, or annual harvest ceremonies, were revived on the island. Traditional navigational arts and skills were revived with the transpacific voyages of the Polynesian Voyaging Society in the traditional voyaging canoes, *Hōkūle'a*, the *Hawai'i Loa*, and the *Makali'i*. The schools that teach traditional Hawaiian dance and chant, *Hālau hula*, increased and flourished. *Lā'au Lapa'u*, traditional herbal and spiritual healing practices, were recognized as valid holistic medicinal practices. Hawaiian studies, from the elementary to university level, were established as part of the regular curricula. Hawaiian music evolved into new forms of expression and gained greater popularity.

Rural Hawaiian communities which were threatened with development organized themselves to protect their subsistence livelihoods, ancestral landholdings and natural resources in their districts from the assault of proposed tourist, commercial and industrial development. For example, on the island of Hawai'i, *Ka'ū* Hawaiians formed the *Ka 'Ohana O KaLae* to protect the natural and cultural resources of their district from a planned spaceport to launch missiles. The Pele Defense Fund was formed to protect the volcano deity, *Pele*, from the development of geothermal energy to fuel electric plants. On the island of Moloka'i, community groups (such as *Hui Ala Loa, Ka Leo O Mana'e* and *Hui Ho'opakela 'Āina*) were formed to protect the natural and cultural resources from tourist resort development.

Native Hawaiians have not had their own distinct governance structure since the Hawaiian monarchy was overthrown by United States naval forces on 17 January 1893. One hundred years later, in November 1993, the United States Congress passed an Apology Resolution (Public Law 103–150, 107 Stat. 1510) which explicitly acknowledged that the inherent sovereignty of the Native Hawaiian people at the time of the overthrow of the Hawaiian Kingdom was never relinquished. The unique and distinct status of Native Hawaiians was also recognized. The Resolution stated, 'the Native Hawaiian people are determined to preserve, develop and transmit to future generations their ancestral territory, and their cultural identity in accordance with their own spiritual and traditional beliefs, customs, practices, language, and social institutions'.

At one level, nation wellbeing is reflected in the exercise of indigenous rights. These would include rights customarily and traditionally exercised for subsistence, cultural and religious purposes, such as access rights, fishing rights and water rights. Impacts on Hawaiian rights would include any change which would affect the exercise of the Hawaiian rights and responsibilities outlined above. Changes that would affect the quality, integrity, use of and access to the natural and cultural resources would constitute an impact upon the rights of Native Hawaiians. Development projects and infrastructure can affect the present and future access to, and the condition and the use of natural resources.

The national land base of the Native Hawaiian people include lands now under US federal and state governments which were originally the Crown and Government lands of the Kingdom of Hawai'i. It also includes lands which are part of charitable trusts endowed by the Hawaiian chiefs for their people, including the trust lands of The Kamehameha Schools, the Queen Emma Foundation, the Queen Lili'uokalani Children's Center, and the Lunalilo Home. Development projects can affect future uses and value of the lands, and revenues generated from the leases, rents, royalties and use fees.

Community wellbeing

Traditional Hawaiian communities can be conceptualized as aggregates of family or *'ohana* systems which have a long history of residing in one locality. The term *wahi noholike I ka po'e* is a Hawaiian term for community that translates into 'the place where people live together' (Figure 8.4). The term suggests that social and environmental factors have shaped the character and values of residents over a long evolutionary course. Further, communal and cultural identity is formed by lengthy exposure to a set of physical attributes and by the transmission of place-based behaviours and mores. A *sense of place*, which has spiritual and psychological meaning, is derived over time from a reliance on the natural resources within a prescribed

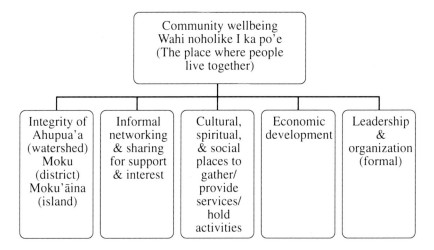

Figure 8.4   Community wellbeing

locale. Social structures and systems emerged from the local economy, and cultural beliefs and spirituality support and promote human wellbeing. Communities are habitats that have critical effects on human behaviour. Hawaiian communities are not merely places for coexistence, they are places for social interaction and organizational activity, and the development of a collective identity.

Hawaiians and other Pacific peoples place a premium on gathering places where formal and informal social, cultural and political activities take place. Today's gathering places may be of historic and spiritual importance where forebears engaged in similar events in earlier times. The *mana* or spiritual energy from these places bolsters current practice and connects people with their past. The significance of gathering places that have historic meaning comes from a continuity that brings together ancestral legacies and modern, often restorative, activities.

Physical settings are critical in shaping and guiding human behaviour. Qualities emitted from the environment condition behaviour and act as determinants of future behaviour. Some gathering places serve to elicit formal behavioural protocols associated with traditional events and spiritual beliefs. They may be places of worship where chants, prayers and gift-giving are a way to pay homage to deities. Ceremonies carry with them prescriptive and proscriptive norms related to social hierarchies, styles of dress and inappropriate behaviours. In Hawaiian culture, there is also the notion of *pu'uhonua*, or places of refuge. These are historic places where individuals under threat can find respite and safety.

Gathering places, such as recreational facilities and community centres, and places, such as schools and churches associated with certain activities, promote pro-social behaviours. The opportunity to engage regularly in structured activities is inversely related to involvement in anti-social activities that are often attributed to a lack of structure and adult supervision. Physical facilities are the focal point, or node of activity, for community and family events and youth activities. Social functions such as *lū'au* that celebrate the first anniversary of the birth of a child, or a high school graduation, are often held at community centres and social halls. They bring together residents in celebrations which enhance social bonds and community cohesiveness.

Communities that have places for social gathering are able to offer programmes and services to meet the desires and needs of residents, to influence the socialization of children and to support senior citizens. Community gathering places also include less formal and physically nondescript settings. They may be at the beach, the park, a playground, or in restaurants and shopping areas. They are places where people, drawn together by common interests and schedules, gather to converse and find mutual social support. Informal gathering places are especially critical to more vulnerable age cohorts such as the elderly and youth.

Opportunities to engage in pro-social cultural activities, however, are not always associated with a community centre or physical structure. Hawaiian youth are often mentored in various cultural activities that occur in natural environs. The development or restoration of a *lo'i kalo* (taro patch) and fishponds, the gathering of medicinal plants and learning of their uses, learning traditional fishing and gathering methods, canoe paddling and the maintenance of sacred areas are examples of traditional activities that are the basis for a cultural resurgence.

Traditionally, Hawaiians were the caretakers of resources and ecosystems that lie within or are adjacent to their communities. They practised a system referred to as *kapu*, which carried highly proscriptive norms related to resource management. For example, fish and *limu* (seaweed) were harvested seasonally and not during spawning season. When it was deemed that resource levels were declining, areas were designated off-limits to fishers and harvesters. Violators were severely punished. Many of the historic sentiments and practices related to resource management and *kapu* remain today. The long-time residents of an area assume caretaking responsibility for resource management within their geographic domain and dissuade outsiders from coming in – especially those who are inclined to misuse or over-harvest resources for commercial purposes.

In some communities, critical habitats have the designation of Community Management Areas. That is, community residents are authorized to manage and patrol particular resource areas. There are strict controls placed on times, amounts, species/types and methods used in acquiring resources. Many communities have been involved in initiatives to empower themselves through community-based planning processes. They have engaged multiple constituencies in a dialogue to develop a vision for their community. Mapping techniques are often used to identify the services, resources and other qualities that lie within the community. They are a means to assess deficits and strengths as a basis for developing a strategic plan. Community Development Corporations are also becoming a common approach to promoting a range of community-based activities related to programmes and services, economic and technical innovations, resource protection and sustainability, and cultural preservation.

Many Hawaiian communities have been economically deprived and marginalized by a western market economy. Economic development and formal jobs are not analogous to human wellbeing. In fact, they often detract from traditional and customary practices by diminishing vital natural resources and denying access to traditional grounds, and lead to environmental and cultural degradation. Conversely, many community-based economic initiatives in Hawaiian communities reflect a set of values and principles that emphasize empowerment and self-sufficiency, cultural preservation and resource conservation and protection.

Subsistence economies in rural Hawaiian communities need to be recognized as viable alternatives to western economic models. The protection of natural resources and habitats, access routes and associated customs and practices will ensure the continuation of indigenous economies that are the foundation to Hawaiian culture and wellbeing. When assessing economic vitality related to Hawaiians and other indigenous communities, it is critical to redress notions and biases related to formalized work, employment rates, gross domestic product and other economic indicators. The benefits derived from subsistence economies are not adequately valued because they cannot be enumerated. Subsistence provides a regimen of physical activity that binds practitioners to the *'āina*, enhances a nature-based spirituality, produces healthy food products for family consumption, cultivates social cohesion in the community through the sharing and exchange of resources, and promotes social welfare as younger practitioners share resources with older, less mobile residents. A regimen of subsistence-related activities reduces the likelihood of less healthy behaviours (such as listlessness leading to obesity or substance abuse) that are often associated with having too much idle time.

An economic system that is based on sharing and exchange involves other activities beyond the transfer of goods. For instance, childcare, adult care and a variety of other service exchanges (such as hula lessons or rock wall building) represent aspects of an indigenous economic system where skills are a commodity. Small, community-based businesses that serve to keep money in the community, and employ family members and local residents, can be encouraged through business development programmes and low-interest start-up loans. Job training programmes teach skills to youth and young adults and help to orient the previously unemployed or unemployable to work roles.

Community-based strategic planning is a community-wide process involving the major constituent or stakeholder groups. The process involves creating a vision for the future of the community and then developing strategies on how to implement the vision. Enhancing social capital is a critical precursor to community building. This involves stimulating resident interest in community affairs and higher levels of civic participation. This facilitates the building of social bonds in order to form collaborative non-political associations.

The community-building process focuses on building organizational capacity through participation and leadership development. The process begins with support for those recognized community leaders who are able to garner the support and participation of residents as they move towards developing and implementing a set of community-based goals and objectives. Building capacity requires an organizational structure and process, resources, training and staff development, and people qualified to perform specialized activities. Leadership development is critical to the longevity of an organization as leaders retire from civic duty and young leaders are needed to continue the mission.

The following are types of impacts that might be considered when examining Native Hawaiian and indigenous communities in the conduct of an SIA:

- change in multicultural balance/percentage, leading to greater cultural homogeneity and decreased diversity;
- alteration or loss of social/cultural activity nodes/interchange;
- change in adequacy of social/cultural infrastructure to accommodate community needs related to quality;
- change in population size, distribution/nodes, in relation to multiculturalism;
- change in demographic characteristics of a community which correlates with changing values;
- disruption in the natural course of community development, continuity and family permanence;
- change in activities and attributes that constitute lifestyle/lifeways; the persistence of indigenous economies;

- increase in rate, type and severity of crimes with indigenous perpetrators;
- increase in rate of substance abuse and type of substance; its influence on behaviour and related problems (such as crime);
- change in rate, patterns and severity of domestic violence; family and community response;
- change in educational achievement and aptitude; delinquency (for example, substance abuse, crime, status offences); socioemotional issues/family supports; educational, employment and recreational opportunities;
- change in social cohesion; degree of social/racial integration or conflict; changes in community leadership;
- change in number and types of events/activities, participation rates, relevance to traditional and contemporary conditions, decision-making power;
- change in levels of community/cultural identity, personal sense of connection and pride tied to a locale; related to genealogical and intergenerational ties.

'Ohana wellbeing

Native Hawaiians, like other indigenous peoples, sustain extended family relationships that are multigenerational. In Hawai'i, the *'ohana* or family, extends beyond the immediate family to include distant cousins and *keiki hänai* (adopted children). *'Ohana* ties were closest to but not limited to the living or to those born into blood relationship' (Pukui *et al.*, 1972: 167). This deep sense of relatedness is at the core of Hawaiian values, beliefs, ways of knowing and being, and Hawaiians' relationship with the *'äina* (earth, land). A culturally appropriate and relevant SIA, therefore, requires an understanding of Hawaiian ways: the nature of relationships, values, beliefs, interactions, processes and traditions that form the foundation of harmonious *'ohana* life.

As members of various *'ohana*, Native Hawaiians are linked to a long line of progenitors, descendants and unborn future generations in a manner that transcends time. This connection between past, present and future (see Figure 8.5) is embodied in the concept of triple *piko*, which refers to shared spiritual and emotional bonds (*piko* has many meanings: umbilical cord, genital organs, crown of the head, or relationship with one's ancestors, living relatives and descendants) (ibid.: 182). To begin with, Native Hawaiians are symbolically connected to their ancestors via the *po'o* (head), where the family *aumäkua* (ancestor gods, the god spirits of those who were in life forebears of those now living) hover and his own *'uhane* (spirit) resides (ibid.: 35, 188). In the 'Ohana Wellbeing (see Figure 8.5)

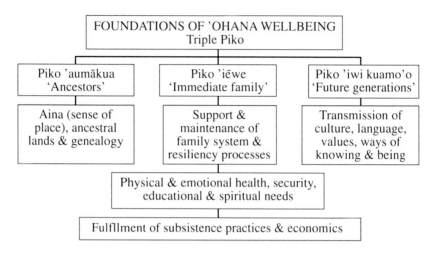

Figure 8.5   Family wellbeing

segment of the Model of Hawaiian Wellbeing (MHW), we refer to this connection as the *piko aumākua,* the link to one's ancestors or heritage. Second, a Native Hawaiian's connection to her/his immediate family and the present is represented by *piko 'iëwe* (placenta), as in the bond between mother and infant. Finally, the connection to future generations is represented by *piko'iwi kuamo'o* (genitals).

This traditional understanding of the connection between Native Hawaiians and *piko amumäkua, piko 'iëwe* and *piko'iwi kuamo'o,* ancestral heritage, the immediate family and future generations, is a central concept in revitalizing, sustaining and fostering *'ohana* wellbeing. Figure 8.5 depicts the key elements of the triple *piko* concept: values, beliefs, processes, knowledge, resources and practices that support *'ohana* wellbeing. Equally important, the *lokahi* (balance or harmony) of the triple *piko* processes in relation to the individual and his *'ohana* must be examined in the assessment of wellbeing among Native Hawaiians (Blaisdell and Mokuau, 1991).

The model hypothesizes that *'ohana* wellbeing is enhanced when (a) Hawaiians *mālama 'āina* (care for the land, earth) reaffirming their sense of place and their relationship to the ancestral lands and genealogy, the *piko aūmākua;* (b) the activities, processes and resources that support and enhance the immediate or present family which includes the extended family (*piko 'iëwe*) are maintained; and (c) the transmission of culture, language, values and Hawaiian ways of knowing and being are sustained and carried forward for future generations (*piko 'iwi kuamo'o*).

The triple *piko* conceptualization of *'ohana* wellbeing finds support in systems-based research on healthy family processes (Walsh, 1998), which has identified key processes that contribute to family resilience and well-being:

- family belief systems: utilizing relationally based strengths, making meaning of adversity, positive outlook, transcendence and spirituality;
- organizational patterns: flexibility, connectedness, mutual support and social and economic resources;
- communication processes: clarity, open emotional expression, collaborative problem solving.

Another essential element in understanding the nature of wellbeing among Native Hawaiians is the distinction between the relational and linear worldviews. The relational perspective recognizes the intuitive, spiritual, non-temporal, fluid nature of collective cultures in their search for balance and harmony in all relationships between humans, nature, earth and the universe as well as the events of life (Cross, 1998). In contrast, the linear worldview, the dominant perspective of western science, holds that cause always precedes effect. This temporal view has enabled the development of narrowly defined, sophisticated measurement techniques, which have facilitated new knowledge, theories and interventions (ibid.) to be performed by sanctioned experts. However, the linear perspective may obscure our view of people's processes within their cultural, geopolitical and historic contexts. For example, the focus of treatment for mental illness among indigenous people living in a western society is most often the individual, not adjustments to the social systems or environmental circumstances. Nor do treatments take into account the indigenous group's worldview. This limits the potential for healing that could include cultural practices and family support networks.

The distinction between relational and linear worldviews is a critical prerequisite to developing funding policies that support the wellbeing of indigenous people such as Hawaiians. For example, an indigenous family seeking help for issues to do with emotional wellbeing utilizing the public health system or medical insurance is usually limited to western psychiatric treatment services. The culturally based practice such as *ho'oponopono* – a well-defined healing process in Hawaiian culture – is not a recognized treatment option.

The relational–linear distinction can also serve as an aid in recognizing the limitations of conducting SIAs that exclusively utilize quantitative indicators and methods. For example, the effectiveness of a social policy designed to get Hawaiian families off welfare and back to work with the help of a time-limited structure of resources cannot be measured simply by the number of individuals that find employment. A realistic evaluation will need to examine the suitability of job options for the individual and appropriate training methods that accommodate cultural nuances, and to consider the family's beliefs regarding employment: for example, gender appropriate work, and sociocultural norms about productivity and work.

Changes that cause disruption and imbalance may affect 'ohana stability and wellbeing in multiple ways. The family's structure, its ability to maintain its economic means of survival, its organizational patterns, communication processes and belief system may be impacted by the following:

- change in the 'ohana family system (for example, increase in nuclear families rather than the traditional extended family and single-parent families);
- change in marital status (for example, increase in divorce, widowhood and isolation of individuals);
- household composition, change in the number of families per household;
- imbalance of age distribution (for example, more children under 18 or more adults per household, isolation of the elderly);
- increased employment, unemployment or underemployment;
- change in employment status (for example, increased dependency on public assistance, decline in subsistence resources);
- change in amount of gross family income and/or subsistence resources;
- change in types and levels of socioemotional support: food, resource sharing, advice sharing, child-care/rearing, elderly care, *kōkua* labour (shared labour), *hānai* children (family adoption);
- change in number of relatives living within close proximity and kinship patterns;
- intergenerational conflicts (such as differential acculturation), change in quality of relational exchange between children, parents and grandparents;
- departure/retention of youth, increased retention or out-migration of youth;
- housing situation, increased home ownership, renting or homelessness;
- increased rates of domestic violence, incest/child sexual abuse;
- change in teenage pregnancy rate;
- youth psychosocial problems, change in rate of mental health and delinquency among youth;
- change in general patterns and practices related to child-rearing

which ultimately lead to changing values and personality, land dis-possession and loss of burial family grounds/sites;

- Change from a collective/family orientation to an individualistic identity.

Unfortunately, within the context of western society, Native Hawaiian practices and family processes that maintain *lōkāhi*, or harmony and balance, within the *'ohana* may be a source of conflict to the individual and therefore not always serve Native Hawaiians' survival in the mainstream society. For example, when the transmission of culture (or lack of culture transmission which is critical to Hawaiians' sense of self) contributes to discord with the mainstream society, it may affect the individual's outlook on life, be a source of stress, and contribute to depression or loss of mean-ingfulness in life. Depression in one *'ohana* member may affect other members, leaving them physically, emotionally, economically and spiritu-ally vulnerable (Crabbe, 1998). Therefore an SIA of indigenous families requires multifaceted efforts. In order to capture important processes and complexities, SIA's need to examine family systems, resiliency processes, maintenance of belief systems, spirituality, organizational patterns and communication, as well as the historic geopolitical context of their survi-val.

Conclusion
The model of Hawaiian wellbeing presented here is based on a structural adaptation of an ecological paradigm. It can be used to assess critically changes in the lifeways of Hawaiians and other indigenous peoples. We have emphasized the significance of cultural systems and their distinct components. The ecological paradigm provides us with a basis for under-standing the dynamic relationship between people and their environments. Special emphasis was placed on the organic relationship Hawaiians have with the land and sea.

The conceptualization calls for novel and culturally appropriate approaches to designing SIAs. Cultural impact assessments (CIA) have become a major legal requirement in the approval process for development in Hawaii. Within the United States, numerous laws at the federal, state and county levels impinge on the legal compliance and defensibility of CIAs (Federal Clean Water Act, National Register Bulletin, Hawaii Revised Statute 343). Despite such legal requirements, CIA guidelines continue to be amorphous and they vary in terms of the way they are conducted. The framework presented in this chapter provides a scope of analysis and study that is intended to promote consistency, uniformity, integrity and higher levels of impact predictability.

We have promoted a conceptual model that represents cultural issues and meanings that are drawn from within Hawaiian culture. We have paired these elements with a human ecological approach that is highly consistent with Hawaiian phenomenology. We believe that these are critical first steps towards developing culturally appropriate approaches to assessing the sociocultural impacts of development. The social wellbeing of Hawaiians and other indigenous groups is at stake when development encroaches on their traditional domains. New approaches to social and cultural assessment must reflect the complexities and subtleties, as well as the tangible and intangible aspects, of their life experiences to preserve the wellbeing of indigenous groups.

References

Blaisdell, K. and Mokuau, N. 1991. 'Kanaka Maoli: Indigenous Hawaiians', in N. Mokuau (ed.), *Handbook of Social Services for Asian and Pacific Islanders,* New York: Greenwood Press, 131–54.

Bronfenbrenner, U. 1977. 'Toward an experimental ecology of human development', *American Psychologist*, 32(7): 513–31.

Bronfenbrenner, U. 1995. 'Developmental ecology through space and time: A future perspective', in P. Moen, G. Elder and K. Luscher (eds), *Examining lives in context: Perspective on the ecology of human development*, Washington: American Psychological Association, 619–47.

Bronfenbrenner, U. and Ceci, S.J. 1994. 'Nature–nurture reconceptualized in developmental perspective', *Psychological Review*, 101(4): 568–586.

Crabbe, K. 1998. 'Etiology of Depression Among Native Hawaiians', *Pacific Health Dialog*, 5(2): 341–5.

Cross, T. 1998. 'Understanding Family Resiliency From a Relational World View', in H. McCubbin, E. Thompson, A. Thompson and J. Fromer (eds), *Resiliency in Native American and Immigrant Families*, Thousand Oaks: Sage, 143–58.

Matsuoka, J., McGregor, D. and Minerbi, L. 1997. 'Native Hawaiian ethnographic study for the Hawai'i Geothermal Project proposed for Puna and Southeast Maui', Oak Ridge National Laboratory, Oak Ridge, TN.

McGregor, D., Minerbi, L. and Matsuoka, J. 1998. 'A holistic assessment method of health and well-being for Native Hawaiian Communities', *Pacific Health Dialogue*, 5(2): 361–9.

Office of the Assistant Secretary for Planning and Evaluation, 1997. United States Department of Health and Human Services (website: *aspe.os.dhhs.gov/hsp/97trends/intro-web.htm*).

Papa Ola Lokahi 1992. *Native Hawaiian Health Data Book*, Honolulu: Papa Ola Lokahi.

Pukui, M., Haertig, E. and Lee, C. 1972. *Nana I Ke Kumu* (vol. 1), Honolulu: Queen Liliuokalani Children's Center.

Robillard, A. and Marsella, A. (eds) 1987. *Contemporary Issues in Mental Health Research in the Pacific Islands*, Honolulu: Social Sciences Research Institute, University of Hawai'i.

Walsh, F. 1998. *Strengthening Family Resilience*, New York: Guilford.

PART II

METHODOLOGICAL APPROACHES FOR BEST PRACTICE

9 Theory formation and application in social impact assessment

Henk Becker

Introduction

While substantial progress has been made in discipline-oriented research in most disciplines in recent years, few of these advances have been integrated in social impact assessment (SIA) practice. The reason for this mismatch is not difficult to guess. Most members of the SIA community have been trained at university in the applied sciences and in technology rather than the social sciences. In their professional careers, they have further qualified in the application and utilization of scientific knowledge and in methods related primarily to practical problems.

Typically, SIA practitioners have had neither the time nor the inclination to study subjects like epistemology, methodology or theory formation. They have carried on in their daily work without much knowledge regarding matters they might consider esoteric or academic. For a long time, this neglect has been of no consequence. However, SIA is changing. More and more, it has to reflect upon its scientific foundations. In this chapter, we want to facilitate this process of change. This requires a number of preliminary remarks. First, we will elaborate upon the application of theory in SIA. Second, we will link the application of theory to models of the project cycle.

In SIA, but also in environmental impact assessment (EIA) and other forms of assessment, the formation and application of theory is, in the first place, important, if we are dealing with theories which present summaries of knowledge that are already available. As an example, we mention the book *Diffusion of Innovations* by Rogers, the fourth edition being published in 1995. Rogers analysed and summarized more than 2000 evaluation reports on innovation processes. He presented generalizations of research findings. He also presented methods for innovation processes related to those generalizations. Many diffusion processes are related to the environment. As an example, we mention organic farming. Other diffusion processes deal with social and economic change.

In the second place, theories that present a basis for an informed guess about future behaviour, of individual actors, and of corporate actors (like organizations and social networks) are important. When we use theories for exploring future behaviour, we look at (a) the past behaviour of actors, (b) their preferences, (c) their resources, (d) the constraints that confront them, (e) the options they have for their behaviour, and (f) their future behaviour. With regard to past behaviour, we analyse which preferences are revealed in this behaviour. We analyse the preferences of actors by interviewing them, studying documents and observing them. Their resources can be described, but we have to make allowances for hidden resources. The constraints have to be analysed by looking at the social setting of the actors, making an informed guess about changes in the social setting in the time to come. Options for choice can be analysed by interviewing the actors, analysing their documents and observing their behaviour. Future behaviour has to be studied for a long series of phases, each time making an informed guess of behaviour in period $x + 1$, taking behaviour in period x, $x - 1$, and so on into account. The theory about social behaviour sketched above is a 'meta-theory'. It is 'empty', because it does not refer to any specific kind of behaviour. In the course of this chapter, we will present an application of an empty theory that is related to specific social processes. Other examples of the application of this theory are also found in environmental policy, economic policy and social policy in relation to racial discrimination.

Next we have to take a look at models for project cycles. In Table 9.1, the first column reproduces a well-known example of the project cycle in EIA, while the second column reproduces an example of the project cycle in SIA (Becker, 1997). These preliminary remarks have paved the way for the presentation of a conceptual framework. Next, an example of the application of this framework will be described. Finally, the application of the conceptual framework in SIA will be discussed and the future of this kind of framework will be explored.

A conceptual framework
SIA usually deals with 'single case, multi-stage studies'. The single case may be an assessment of the future social consequences of an action like building a new large dam or reservoir, introducing a new national pension scheme or launching a new technology. In such single cases, a number of phases can be identified. For instance, the construction of a large dam entails a phase of political and technical preparation, a phase of construction and a phase of maintenance. Each phase requires impact assessments, including SIAs. Social impact assessors can use the first phase, inter alia, for exploring social impacts in the second and the third phase. They can also use the second phase to explore social impacts in the third phase.

If more than one case is available, these cases can be compared and the knowledge gained in each of them can be combined. We can develop hypotheses about social impacts of constructing and operating large dams,

Table 9.1 Models of project cycles in environmental and social impact assessment

EIA	SIA
1. Site selection, environmental screening, scoping of essential issues	1. Problem analysis and communication strategy
	2. Systems analysis
	3. Baseline analysis
	4. Trend analysis and design monitoring
2. Detailed assessment of significant impacts, identification of mitigation needs, input to cost–benefit analysis	5. Project design
	6. Scenario design
	7. Design of strategies
	8. Assessment of impacts
	9. Ranking of strategies
3. Detailed design of mitigation measures	10. Mitigating of negative impacts
	11. Reporting
	12. Stimulating implementation
4. Implementation of mitigation measures and environmental strategy	13. Decision making
	14. Implementation of policy
5. Monitoring, impact management, post-evaluation and lessons for future projects	15. Monitoring
	16. Impact management
	17. Auditing and ex-post evaluation

for example. If the hypotheses can be linked in a causal way, we have a theory at our disposal. This theory can be used to explore future social consequences of new large dam projects. We assume that the future social consequences of the new dam project will be an analogue to the social consequences of prior dam projects. 'Analogue' means 'partly the same, partly different'.

By now, we have sufficiently cleared the ground for introducing the core of a conceptual framework of an interpretive–explanatory social science analysis. This analysis is summarized in Figure 9.1 and will be elaborated later. The concept of 'situation' in this framework is related to systems analysis. We are referring to the central (or focal) system the social impact assessor is dealing with, plus the surrounding systems (Becker, 1997: 62).

Next, the concept of 'actor' demands our attention. We have to identify the central (or focal) actor that initiates the action that might have future consequences. We also have to identify further actors related to the action, either as co-initiators, or as objectives of the action. We can encounter individual actors and collective actors, as we have seen. This component of the conceptual framework also requires an identification of the problem that

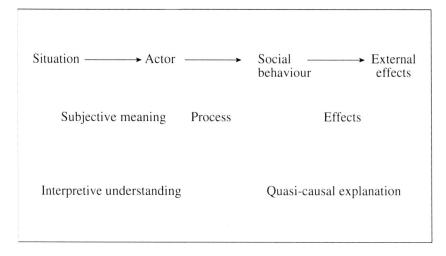

Source: Esser (1993).

Figure 9.1 *The three steps in interpretive–explanatory social science analysis*

the actor wants to eliminate or reduce. Furthermore, this component requires a specification of the cooperation between the actors. Will there be a participatory approach to the problem, or will the central actor deal with the problem in an authoritarian way?

In SIA we are interested in social behaviour that actually leads, or could lead, to the acquisition or change of values and value orientations. Values are defined as what people consider to be important: for instance, liberty, equality and fraternity, or social justice. Value orientations reflect the attitude that the actor shows with regard to a specific value. An actor may consider social justice to be important, but may be willing to permit a certain degree of social injustice in times of an economic crisis. Values are assumed to be relatively stable as soon as they are acquired, value orientations may vary considerably over time. Values are part of our preferences.

The term 'external effects' is used (by economists) for the past, current or future consequences of an action. Effects are called 'external' if they are not intended by the central actor. In SIA, this part of the terminology of economists is adopted.

The second and third line in the conceptual framework refer to concepts that come from different traditions in social science research. For a long time, 'subjective meaning' has been associated with the interpretive tradition. The concept of 'quasi-causal explanation' originates from the analytical tradition (formerly the neo-positivist tradition). For a long time, these two traditions were treated as opposites, but, since the 1990s, they have been treated more and more as complementary. According to the advocates of a cooperation between the two traditions, problems in social research increasingly require both interpretation and explanation. We will discuss both traditions and their relationship now, very briefly. Elsewhere more elaborate discussions can be found (for example, Becker, 1990; Esser, 1993; Bryant, 1995).

Key concepts in the interpretive tradition

Some social scientists claim that only understanding is possible and that a causal analysis is never possible. A classical example of the interpretive tradition is *Awareness of Dying*, by Barney Glaser and Anselm Strauss (1965). Glaser and Strauss were interested in the quality of dying of terminal patients in a cancer ward. Which interventions in the care of these patients would have a positive effect on the quality of dying? Who should tell the patient that he or she is in the terminal stage of the illness – a doctor, a nurse or a member of the family? What would be the effect of a straightforward answer to the question of the patient: 'Am I in the terminal stage?' The data gathering in this research project was done by participant observation by researchers, disguised as members of the hospital staff. Note that the research model closely resembles the research model used in SIA. The researcher looks at the consequences of a current or future action.

Later contributions to this tradition include, inter alia, Giddens' theory of structuration. According to Giddens (1984; 1987) the structuring, or 'structuration' of social interaction, or social relations, across time and space always involves three elements: the communication of meaning, the exercise of power and the evaluative judgment of conduct. Structure as signification involves semantic rules; as domination, unequally distributed resources; and as legitimation, moral or evaluative rules. 'Interpretive schemes' are the modes of typification incorporated within actors' stocks of knowledge, applied reflexively in the sustaining of communication (Giddens, 1984).

In the research setting of Glaser and Strauss (1965), the doctors, nurses, members of the family of the patient and the patient used structured social interaction. They used interpretation and interpretive schemes. Each actor took the role of the other in order to interpret the meaning of the action of other actors. In a hospital ward with terminal patients, participant observation is the most adequate way of gathering data, as it would be impossible to apply precise measuring instruments like structured questionnaires.

Key concepts in the analytical tradition
In the analytical tradition, explanation has long been approached by way of the 'covering law model', as presented by Hempel (1942) in his essay 'The function of general laws in history. D'Andrade (1986: 19) describes this model as follows:

> The covering law model of science seems close to the way people think about science: on the surface, the model seems unexceptional. Its main outline goes as follows: (a) science consists of a search for 'general laws' to explain events; (b) the statement of a general law can have different logical forms, but it typically makes a universal generalization across some domain of events; (c) the main function of general laws is to connect events in patterns, which are usually referred to as 'explanation' and 'prediction'.

Major debates about the covering law model have involved whether it corresponds to what historians do, or could do, and whether it can be used more generally in explanation of human behaviour. There has also been an extended and inconclusive discussion of the necessary and sufficient characteristics a statement must have to be a general law.

Since the mid-1970s, most social scientists treat the covering law model and the methodological prescriptions of testing hypotheses by predictions as metaphors only and not as rigorous requirements. Social scientists deal with systems that contain a lot of 'disorder' (also called 'chaos' and 'noise'). As a consequence, the best they can do is to search for 'underlying mechanisms' capable of explaining the emergence of phenomena. Any predictions they make will not provide decisive tests of their theories.

The most convincing contemporary approach to explanation in social research comes from Boudon (1984). With regard to social change, Boudon distinguishes relatively closed and relatively open situations and social systems. Open situations show a relatively large degree of 'disorder'. He sees two categories of generalizations, matching these types of situations. In the first place, there are laws and theories 'stricto sensu'. Laws and theories belonging to this category, which might be falsified according to the requirements formulated by Popper, are rare in the social sciences, and presumably they will remain rare, because the subject matter of the social sciences shows a lot of disorder. Boudon's second category contains formal theories. These theories he sees as not in themselves directly applicable to reality, but offering a mode of discussion or describing ideal examples which may be useful in the analysis of certain process.

Boudon has little faith in the search for general theories 'stricto sensu'. But if partial or local theories are aimed for, some situations might be sufficiently 'closed' to make success feasible. He states that 'the only scientific theories of social change are partial and local ones' (Boudon, 1984: 220; 1986: 208).

Towards cooperation between the two traditions

Max Weber (1968) tried to formulate rules for the cooperation between the two antagonistic traditions. He argued that an understanding of human behaviour based on interpretation presents at first a certain qualitative self-evidence. That an interpretation shows this self-evidence to a high degree does not provide proof of its empirical validity, because processes of behaviour showing the same development and results can occur under highly differing constellations of motives. What seems the most evident motive is not always the motive that really guides the behaviour. For this reason, the 'understanding' of relationships has to be checked with customary methods of causal analysis before any seemingly self-evident 'understanding' becomes an intellectual explanation.

Durkheim (1952) contributed an example of a causal analysis applying the covering law approach that has become a classic: his book, *Suicide*. A modern advocate of combining elements of both traditions in the analysis of social behaviour and institutions is Esser (1993). His approach requires an iteration of interpretive understanding and quasi-causal explanation.

An example: assessing strategic decisions

We will present now an illustration of theory formation and application in SIA applying a conceptual framework from both the interpretive and the analytic tradition. The example we want to discuss focuses on ex-ante evaluation of strategic intervention in collective decision making. Stokman *et al.* (2000) use an approach that is based on (a) a decomposition of the problem into a few main controversial issues; (b) systematic interviews of subject area specialists to obtain a specification of the decision setting, consisting of a list of stakeholders with their capabilities, positions and salience on each of the issues; and (c) computer simulation. The approach provides insights into the likely outcomes of the process, that is, it provides a SIA. Furthermore, the approach informs us about the amount of conflict involved, and the stability of the outcomes. The interviews held with subject area specialists provide the kind of interpretive schemes advocated by Giddens. Computer simulation provides the kind of explanation by modes of discussion advocated by Boudon.

First, we will take a look at the main components of the approach: the decomposition of the problem; next, the analysis of positions, capabilities and salience will demand our attention; following this, the processes and strategies involved will be discussed; finally, examples of outcomes will be presented.

The decomposition of the problem

We first have to specify the problem at stake in terms of a limited number of issues on which decisions have to be made. Each issue represents a major controversy requiring a decision. Decisions of the stakeholders on the specified set of issues reveal the contours of the chosen solution. In most cases, one to five issues are sufficient. In complicated situations, up to 20 issues will have to be used. 'Misspecification of the issues is the main cause of the failure in model predictions' (Stokman *et al.*, 2000: 133).

It is good practice to specify at least the two extreme positions on each issue. Intermediate positions indicate more moderate positions. They also suggest possible compromises. The decomposition of the problem also requires a specification of the main stakeholders. Such a specification is required in order to identify extreme and intermediate positions. In practice, both individuals and organizations can act as stakeholders. Individuals can represent organizations.

Positions, capabilities and salience
Next, a strategic decision analysis is required. Stokman *et al.* (2000) advocate interviews with one or two experts who make estimates relating to all stakeholders. The experts should be able to provide a good overview of the whole decision-making setting.

The second element is an analysis of the capabilities of the stakeholders to determine or codetermine the outcomes. We are dealing with the potential mobilization of the capabilities. The actual mobilization enters the scene at a later time. We are confronted with formal discretionary or voting power. But not only power but also influence plays an important role. People with authority who would frequently overrule the interests of others would quickly provoke societal and political opposition.

Third, the salience of the issues for the stakeholder has to be taken into consideration. The salience represents the willingness of the stakeholder to push his position in the decision making. If the issue does not touch essential interests of a stakeholder, hardly any fight will arise. In that case the stakeholder will not put his weight into the struggle and he is to be expected to compromise quickly. Salience does not operate in isolation. Combinations of position and salience determine the behaviour of stakeholders (ibid.: 135). Capabilities and salience together determine the effective power of stakeholders. Salience represents the extent of capabilities that stakeholders are willing to mobilize to enhance their position in the outcome of the decision (ibid.: 136–7).

Processes and strategies
A stakeholder may change his position through three main processes: first, by receiving convincing information implying that another position better reflects his incentive structure (management of meaning); second, by feeling more or less forced to change his position because others challenge

his position; third, by being prepared to take another position in exchange for a (for him) favourable move by another stakeholder on another issue (Stokman *et al.*, 2000: 137).

In management of meaning processes convincing information has an important impact. Stokman *et al.* (ibid.: 138) present a theory to strengthen this argument:

> The more directly an issue is connected to the central higher ordered objectives of a stakeholder and the more an issue is seen as an important condition for their realization, the more salient the issue is to him. His position on the issue corresponds to the outcome of the decision that he sees as optimal for the realization of his objectives.

New information can drastically change the perception of salience of the best position of a stakeholder only if the new information is seen as reliable and is accepted as relevant. The likelihood that this will happen may be enhanced substantially by the following conditions (stated as theories):

> Convincing new information is generally more easily accepted in earlier stages of the decision making than in the later ones. During the decision-making process, positions taken by the stakeholder tend to freeze. In the beginning, stakeholders often do not have very crystallized ideas about the connection between the issue and theory objectives. They are relatively open to information that clarifies that connection. (Ibid.: 138)

> A substantial amount of trust in the provider of the information increases the likelihood that information is accepted as relevant and reliable. Trust will be greater if the provider has proven to be reliable in the past and if the provider can be expected to experience future negative consequences of providing distorted or incomplete information. (Ibid.: 138)

A stakeholder can also change his position by applying challenge strategies. In that case at least three elements have to be considered. The first involves the choice of one's own position at the beginning of the decision-making process. Sometimes a more extreme position will result in a better outcome. In other situations, it is better to choose a more moderate position. Sometimes it is better to push with all available clout. Sometimes a less involved stance leads to better results. There are theories enlightening the consequences of challenge strategies:

> In loss situations individuals are more willing to accept risks, whereas they tend to be more risk averse in gain situations. If a stakeholder confronts his adversaries with a strong loss situation by taking an extreme position and showing a high leverage, his adversaries tend to become more risk seeking and resisting. The consequence may well be that he loses support for his position and that he has to accept a worse outcome. (Ibid.: 140)

Impact assessors will notice that at this point concern for the consequences of current or proposed actions enters the argumentation of Stokman *et al.* SIA is a logical next step in the analysis of challenge strategies. Stokman *et al.* (ibid.: 141) formulate this as follows:

> In addition to an explicit reflection on one's own position and leverage, an explicit evaluation of the likelihood of success of challenges is recommended. If a stakeholder takes an extreme minority position, his own chances of successful challenges are likely underestimated (resulting in no or less challenges).

Another approach a stakeholder can follow is applying exchange processes. While management of meaning strategies are most effective among like-minded stakeholders, exchanges of positions are most profitable between stakeholders who have either opposing positions on the issues, or very different patterns of salience.

Evidently, these strategies can be combined. We also have to keep in mind that the power distribution between stakeholders is related to institutional arrangements. For instance, long-lasting deprivation of certain stakeholders often results in a demand for institutional change, for example through changes in the composition of advisory committees, changes in competencies between bodies or extension of possibilities for appeal. Changes in institutional arrangements and customs are the most important ways to change the power distribution among stakeholders. Also other, more informal, capabilities can be increased or diminished. As examples we mention alliances, takeovers and mergers that can shift the power balance considerably (ibid.: 148).

Applications

The approach presented above has passed the experimental phase. The team around Stokman and an American team around Bueno de Mesquita have analysed more than 6000 issues. In the United States, the first applications were related to American foreign policy. Gradually, the emphasis has switched towards business applications. In The Netherlands, the method has been applied for several ministries, large municipalities and large companies for the analysis of complicated and important issues.

A good illustration of the accuracy of the models was given in 1996. At the start of the labour negotiations in the Dutch metal industry (July 1996), Rojer and Stokman collected data on 16 controversial issues and publicly announced that they had given their predictions in a sealed envelope to a notary. At the end of the negotiations in September, the envelope was opened at a press conference. Of the 16 issues, it was clear immediately that the authors had predicted 13 correctly. A further one issue was subsequently validated. Among these 13 were exact predictions of the salary increase and the changes in the retirement arrangements, two of the most controversial issues (Stokman *et al.*, 2000: 150).

Applications of the conceptual framework now and in the future
We now have the major components of the conceptual framework and the three steps in interpretive–explanatory social science analysis discussed earlier at our disposal. We can elaborate them to make them applicable in SIA. The first step is a problem analysis, focusing on the major issues to be dealt with. In this phase of the SIA project, interpretive understanding and quasi-causal explanation go hand in hand. The formulation of the SIA problem acquires the format of the definition of SIA: what are the most likely consequences of a current or proposed action?

The second step is dominated by interpretive understanding. The major sources of information are individuals that are knowledgable about the problem situation. Stokman *et al.* (2000), for instance, asked subject area specialists to provide information. In this phase of the SIA project, hypotheses are developed. Some hypotheses are derived from observations in the problem area, yielding grounded theories. Other hypotheses are derived from theories used in more general problem areas, like the diffusion of innovations. In this way, both induction and deduction are applied.

The third step is dominated by quasi-causal explanation. Stokman *et al.* (ibid.), for instance, used computer simulation. Designing a computer simulation is as a rule preceded by a simulation with human players of individual roles and system roles. As an example, we take playing the role of a policy maker. This is an individual role. Playing the role of the organization of the policy maker is a system role, however. Besides computer simulations, other approaches can be used, for instance linear models.

The three-step model discussed above is a simplified representation of the approach used in theory-driven SIA. In practice, iteration is also applied. The three steps are repeated many times. The iteration is terminated by the social impact assessor as soon as the analysis is 'saturated'. A rule of thumb for determining 'saturation' is that, when three times in succession no new elements have emerged in the analysis, the analysis can be terminated.

The case of Stokman *et al.* (2000) presents an example of designing and using hypotheses that are 'down to earth', related to the formation of grounded theory. The evaluation of their project illustrates that this approach has important capabilities for the future.

Theory formation and application in SIA in a broader perspective
At the beginning of this chapter, we advocated that social impact assessors pay more attention to the scientific foundations of their discipline. Now we

want to draw attention to a number of changes taking place in the scientific foundations themselves.

Max Weber, early in the 20th century, elaborated a complex scheme known as 'singular causal analysis'. In this type of analysis, particular historical events are traced to their causally relevant antecedents. In Weber's perspective, singular causal analysis is performed by means of probabilistic and counterfactual reasoning, and not by using deductions from causal laws. He views history as a complex network of causal relations among particulars, as a scene of alternate processes and possible outcomes that are more or less probable, more or less strongly favoured by relevant causes. The historian's paradigmatic causal question is not whether a particular event necessarily followed one or more antecedent conditions, but why a certain historical path or outcome was what it was, and not something else. A cause is not a sufficient condition for the occurrence of the effect, according to Weber, but rather a factor that, in conjunction with other background conditions, is comparatively likely to bring about one outcome rather than alternatives. We can explain aspects of the world by means of probabilistic and counterfactual comparisons between what has actually happened and what would have happened in the absence of appropriate causes (McAllister, 2002: 29).

The scheme of the singular causal analysis was taken up again in the 1990s. Philosophers and sociologists of science have pointed out that, in the natural sciences, the humanities (inter alia historiography) and social sciences, analyses have more in common than was admitted in the past. The interplay between the consequences of systematic constraints and regularities on the one hand, and the results of historical events and contingencies on the other, can be witnessed in many disciplines. The natural historical sciences routinely give accounts of events – the extinction of a species or the formation of a volcano, for instance – accounts which involve no laws but constitute intuitively successful explanations (ibid.: 42).

These developments will have particular consequences for the demarcation of the natural sciences, humanities and social sciences. The future of every science depends on the ability to use all instruments from the toolbox, whatever their origin. The extent to which 'laws' may be formulated, that is, the extent to which a 'structural element' is introduced, will vary between physics, biology and the social sciences. One must be wary of oversimplification (ibid.: 42).

For scientific disciplines cooperating in SIA, such as sociology, social psychology, environmental sciences and economics, the changes in the demarcation of the sciences will have substantial consequences. These disciplines will increasingly share methods and theories. More cooperation will also develop between the two traditions discussed earlier in this chapter. The third tradition, treating interpretation and explanation as complementary, will gain in importance. This does not imply that each and every publication in SIA will demonstrate the characteristics of both interpretation and explanation, but it does imply that both interpretation and explanation will contribute to research programmes dealing with problem areas in SIA, sometimes in separate publications.

The changes in the scientific foundations of SIA also require that two types of definitions be used. First, there are descriptive definitions. For example, we defined SIA as 'the process of identifying the future consequences of a current or proposed action which are related to individuals, organisations and social macro-systems' (Becker, 1997: 2). This descriptive definition treats SIA as a subfield of impact assessment. The latter is defined by the International Association of Impact Assessment as 'the process of identifying the future consequences of a current or proposed action'.

Descriptive definitions have to obey the requirements for definitions formulated in logic, in use since Plato and Pascal. For instance, a definition may not be circular. It must be possible to falsify the definition and the definition must not be creative (von Kutschera and Breitkopf, 1971: 131).

If scientists want to issue mission statements, they can add these statements to the descriptive definition as comments. For example, if social impact assessors want to advocate that the identification of future consequences of current or proposed actions be combined with other components of the policy cycle, they can state this as a comment to the definition. Combining ex-post evaluation and ex-ante evaluation is to be advocated, but only if there has already been a current action. To give another example: if a proposed action does not take place because the ex-ante evaluation has identified disastrous side effects, the ex-ante evaluation cannot be combined with further elements of the policy cycle. This does not mean that this particular ex-ante evaluation has to be excluded from the category of ex-ante evaluations called 'social impact assessment'.

Second, normative and evaluative definitions will be required. In these types of definitions, mission statements and value judgments have become part of the definition. As a classical example we take the definition 'ownership is theft'. Another example is the definition of sociology as 'the science of promoting the emancipation of the disadvantaged'. Radical students advocated this definition in The Netherlands in the 1960s and early 1970s. Nowadays, groups of research methods like SIA have been defined as methods to promote sustainability. The promotion of sustainability is a mission statement, just like advocating the promotion of sustainable growth or advocating justice between generations. It is a noble endeavour to advocate justice between generations. It is also a noble endeavour to require that each generation solve its own problems, because redistribution between generations would create problems worse than 'laissez faire'. Normative definitions can advocate innovations, to give an example (von Kutschera and Breitkopf, 1971: 131). In this sense, they can play an important role in innovating SIA.

In summary, social impact assessors will have to participate in reflecting on the foundations of science. But not every social impact assessor will have the time and inclination to do so, which means we will need a division of labour. Have a number of experts in SIA follow these changes closely and report to the community of social impact assessors at large, and discussions will surely follow.

References

d' Andrade, R. 1986. 'Three scientific world views and the covering law model', in D.W. Fiske and R.A. Shweder (eds), *Metatheory in Social Science*, Chicago: University of Chicago Press, 19–41.

Becker, H. 1990. 'Achievement in the analytical tradition in sociology', in C. Bryant and H. Becker (eds), *What has Sociology Achieved?*, London: Macmillan, 8–30.

Becker, H. 1997. *Social Impact Assessment: Method and Experience in Europe, North America and the Developing World*, London: Routledge.

Boudon, R. 1984. *La Place du Désordre*, Paris: Presses Universitaires de France.

Boudon, R. 1986. *Theories of Social Change*, London: Polity Press.

Bryant, C. 1995. *Practical Sociology, Post-Empiricism and the Reconstruction of Theory and Application*, London: Polity Press.

Durkheim, E. 1952. *Suicide* (in French, 1897), London: Routledge.

Esser, H. 1993. *Soziologie*, Frankfurt: Campus.

Giddens, A. 1984. *The Constitution of Society*, Cambridge: Polity Press.

Giddens, A. 1987. *Social Theory and Modern Sociology*, Cambridge: Polity Press.

Glaser, B. and Strauss, A. 1965. *Awareness of Dying*, New York: Aldine.

von Kutschera, K. and Breitkopf, A. 1971. *Einführung in die Moderne Logik*, Freiburg: Verlag Karl Alber.

McAllister, J.W. 2002. 'Historical and structural approaches in the natural and human sciences', in P. Tindemans, A. Verrijn-Stuart and R. Visser (eds), *The Future of the Sciences and Humanities*, Amsterdam: Amsterdam University Press, 19–54.

Rogers, E. 1995. *Diffusion of Innovations* (4th edn), New York: The Free Press.

Stokman, F., van Assen, M., van der Knoop, J. and van Oosten, R. 2000. 'Strategic decision making', *Advances in Group Processes*, 17: 131–53.

Weber, M. 1968. *Methodologische Schriften*, Frankfurt am Main: Fischer.

10 Computer-based qualitative data methods
Gerard Fitzgerald

Introduction

Assessing the social impacts of projects, programmes or polices is a data-gathering or research-intensive activity. Social research is therefore part of social impact assessment (SIA) practice, along with action to manage impacts. SIA practitioners, as analysts and managers of social change, typically make use of a range of methods for gathering information about the people, communities and organizations associated with some past or future intervention or event. They do so in order to describe and explain what intended and unintended changes have occurred or, more often, what changes might occur in the future.

As noted by Taylor *et al.* in Chapter 2 of the present volume, social research is integral to SIA. But in SIA, research is generally 'a means of collecting and using data for an immediate social objective', rather than for testing sociological concepts or to refine existing knowledge, as might be expected of academics (Taylor *et al.*, 1995: 35). Data gathering, along with analysis, takes place iteratively throughout the SIA process. It is particularly marked in the scoping, profiling, estimation of effects and monitoring phases of an assessment. Most SIA practitioners recognize the value of having available a range of data drawn from a variety of sources and covering different aspects of the social situation being analysed. The data may be new and collected especially for the purpose at hand (primary data), or it might be pre-existing, perhaps gathered for some previous purpose by another party (secondary data). Data may come in a range of forms, from databases and tables of numbers to pages of handwritten or printed text, sound recordings and still or moving images. And they may be voluminous. The handling and processing of research data, especially when non-numerical, can, however, be a particular challenge for the practitioner when working under the time pressures typical of SIA projects. This chapter addresses the challenges of dealing with non-numerical data, and, using examples from recent research in New Zealand, outlines how computers may be of assistance.

Types and sources of data

A distinction is often made in social research between quantitative and qualitative data; that is, between data that are immediately amenable to statistical analysis, and data that are not. In the social sciences, the apparent distinction between quantitative and qualitative research and data – in particular the efficacy of the methods used to gather information to help describe and understand social phenomena – is the outward face of the competing positivist and interpretative research paradigms (Neuman, 1997). The positivist paradigm holds that the social world, like the physical world, exhibits regularity and structure, and therefore neutral and objective hypotheses or generalizations about the social world can be deduced from empirical observation of many individuals. The common method for enabling deductive generalizations to be made is through conducting tightly controlled, standardized probability-based sample surveys or experiments. In the interpretative paradigm, understandings of social phenomena are arrived at inductively by reference to the subjective states or meanings of the particular actors in socially natural situations. The methods employed to understand the meanings of people's and groups' social actions in these situations include various forms of case study conducted by engaging with those in the situation (referred to as doing fieldwork, typically involving participant observation and unstructured interviews with key individuals or groups), and analysis of documents (Tolich and Davidson, 1999).

However, the paradigmatic difference is neither as strong as might appear, nor is it particularly helpful when it comes to doing applied social research such as in SIA (Hammersley and Atkinson, 1983; Fielding and Fielding, 1986). For example, individuals experience their worlds and interpret their experiences in terms of what they perceive to be the commonalities and regularities of the wider society of which they are part. At the same time, not all social phenomena and experience can be understood by reference to regularity described in terms of statistical relationships between predefined 'variables'. Also the distinction between quantitative and qualitative data gathering methods is not always clear in practice. Qualitative data can be, and frequently are, gathered in sample surveys (by using open-ended questions). Qualitative methods can produce data which can be summarized or described statistically (by coding, counting, and comparing occurrences of themes, views or issues reported in unstructured interviews). With the increasing use of computers in social science, especially for processing textual data, as described below, the quantitative/qualitative distinction is becoming even more blurred.

To understand potential social changes arising from a proposal, SIA practitioners make use of a range of data and data-gathering techniques, depending on the time available for their research, the availability of existing information and the impact situation under assessment. Surveys, including secondary sources (such as the official census of population), are generally used where the relative occurrence of some relevant social char-

Table 10.1   Examples of data sources for SIA

	Quantitative data	Qualitative data
Secondary sources	previous surveys census data official statistics monitoring studies maps	local histories/accounts previous studies/SIAs other literature newspapers photos, video, film maps
Primary sources	sample surveys observations	interviews discussion/focus groups workshops participant observation photos, video, film

acteristic or behaviour of the people of an area can be meaningfully quantified, and where a statistical summary is useful. Qualitative methods and
fieldwork tend to be used to learn about life in a community or area and the
potential impacts of a proposal, as perceived and spoken about by those
living there. Table 10.1 provides examples of commonly used sources of
data in SIA.

In the often time-pressured world of the SIA practitioner, secondary
data sources can be especially valuable for scoping, profiling and estimations of effects. Useful documentary or non-numeric data sources include
written histories of the area or community or of similar communities or
districts, reports of previous social research or social assessments in the
area, official documents and local newspapers (Taylor *et al.*, 1995). These
can be analysed using qualitative techniques such as content analysis, her-
meneutics and archival analysis, but SIA also requires the doing of fieldwork, both as a means of gathering data directly from those affected and
as a way of involving people and communities in the decisions about the
particular project or programme being proposed. Fieldwork methods that
are commonly employed in SIA, and tend to generate qualitative data,
include (a) semi-structured face to face or telephone interviews with 'key'
people (those that are likely to have a special knowledge of some aspect of
local life), (b) group interviews and focus groups, (c) workshops, and (d)
participant observation.

As implied by the label, qualitative data expresses the quality of something,
rather than the quantity of it. Kirk and Miller (1986: 5) see the kind of
methods mentioned above as 'blatantly interpretative' and exploratory.
However, it would be wrong to assume that using such methods means a

commitment to innumeracy, or that they lack rigour. Consistent with enabling, community-based SIA, qualitative research implies 'a commitment to field activities' (ibid.: 10) and to engaging the world on its own terms (Dick, 1990). It therefore requires interaction between those affected by a proposal and the SIA practitioner–researcher. In fieldwork, the practitioner–researcher places themself in the context of the person and community being studied, and those being researched become participants in the impact assessment. This is evident in semi-structured or unstructured interviewing, where the researcher shares information (about the project or programme being assessed), poses questions and explores the person's responses in detail in a natural process of discussion (almost a conversation), while attempting to make an accurate record of what happened and what is said. In contrast, in structured questionnaire surveys, the interviewer (if there is one) puts a series of tightly formulated, predetermined and consistent questions to a much larger number of subjects, and the answers are recorded as numbers or symbols according to predetermined and pre-coded answers, all the while deliberately minimizing personal interaction and extraneous conversation with the subject. The direct engagement of a participant–informant in an open interview/discussion invariably requires more time and interpersonal skills than a structured questionnaire survey, but tends to produce a richer picture of the community or social issue being studied.

Qualitative data are typically available to the SIA practitioner in the following forms:

- memories of interviews, discussions and observations;
- hand-written fieldnotes, which can follow a variety of styles of recording, including use of a structured style such as the ethnographic convention;
- audio recordings of interviews and discussion groups/focus groups;
- still and moving pictures, graphics and so on;
- transcripts (typed notes) of fieldnotes, and audio recordings;
- other documents;
- notes on, or summaries of, secondary sources.

Commonly, SIA practitioners use qualitative methods in conjunction with quantitative methods to enable a more complete picture of a social situation or community to be constructed, rather than for strict theoretical paradigm reasons. More simply, some find that such methods afford a greater degree of flexibility, timeliness and convenience in their fieldwork. In summary, qualitative methods are often used in SIA for the following reasons:

- they enable local people to speak for themselves – in their own words and in terms of their own circumstances;
- they enable the researcher to tap into local knowledge, expertise and experience directly;
- they are consistent with a consultative or enabling approach, in which information is exchanged between the researcher and the participant–informant in real time;
- they are flexible, dynamic and immediate, and therefore enable in-depth exploration of unexpected issues and unanticipated impacts, and identification of appropriate action responses to these issues;
- they allow for generalizations, explanations and conclusions to emerge from the data itself – what Glaser and Strauss (1967) refer to as 'grounded theory';
- they offer a range of data-gathering techniques and thus enable triangulation of method as well as sources/perspectives;
- they assist in the design of quantitative surveys and the interpretation of quantitative data;
- they are cost effective.

Challenges and problems

Like any approach, the use of qualitative social research methods presents a number of challenges to the SIA practitioner. Some of the more common challenges and possible responses are summarized in Table 10.2. While it is only one of a number of interlinked challenges, one of the most common is the handling and analysis of the considerable volume of text-based information often generated in the course of an SIA. The difficulties can be appreciated from the experiences of SIA practitioners and social researchers outlined below:

- fieldnotes of interviews, interactions and observation can be scrappy, partial, unsystematic, or even non-existent;
- fieldnotes are usually linear records of interviews, whereas semi-structured and open-ended interviews, like conversations, are not usually linear in terms of the topics or issues covered;
- there is a common feeling of being overwhelmed by the amount of material that needs to be analysed and reported on in a limited time frame;
- key observations or conclusions tend to be derived from the most impressive, articulate and memorable interviewees or groups;
- the process of data analysis tends to be idiosyncratic and not particularly systematic or replicable; and
- fieldnotes are not fully utilized, and are seldom archived for use in subsequent studies.

Table 10.2   Challenges of qualitative research in SIA

Challenge	Response
Deciding on research 'participants' or informants, and the focus of the interviews and discussions	Systematic selection should be informed by scoping work and by the conceptual framework – which should identify the 'key' people and perspectives. The flexibility and adaptability of the methods also allows 'discovery' to occur.
Participant–informants may have highly idiosyncratic or divergent views or experience, be dishonest, and/or exaggerate or underestimate likely impacts	Triangulation of data 'sources, informants, methods and researchers in the field' should be used for cross-checking and verifying views and claims. Field data should also be weighed up by the analyst against previous incidences of change in the area and similar impact situations elsewhere.
Handling the 'screeds' of variable text/ data that are collected (and making it accessible for assessments and studies)	The method adopted (manual or electronic) needs to be as systematic and transparent as possible, with data stored in a secure, technically accessible, flexible and open-ended form.
Analysing and interpreting the data	The approach must be methodical in ordering, filtering and comparing data, while maintaining its integrity and letting it 'speak'. The need for replicability has to be balanced with the need to remain open to 'discovery' of new understandings.
Ensuring validity, reliability and rigour throughout	The approach must be systematic, triangulate data collection, types of data and (possibly) interpretation, and be iterative.

Such difficulties can have direct consequences. The apparent lack of rigour can easily undermine validity of social data and findings, and the assessment process itself. The practitioner using qualitative (rather than quantitative) methods can be exposed to methodological criticism in formal settings such as environmental courts. As experienced in New Zealand, this can lead to social impact findings receiving less consideration than technical (natural science) studies. Finally, the gathered data become unavailable for use in future SIA cases and for theoretical development.

A common issue raised by those who work within a traditional positivist science perspective is that the data collection, data analysis and findings from qualitative research lack 'rigour', 'reliability' or 'validity' (Tolich and Davidson, 1999). However, such criticisms tend to reflect a poor under-standing of epistemology and of the methods themselves. Kirk and Miller (1986: 20) take reliability to be 'the degree to which the finding is independent of accidental circumstances of the research (or the extent to which the same observational procedure in the same context yields the same information)'. Validity is 'the degree to which the finding is interpreted in a correct way (or the quality of fit between an observation and the basis on which it is made)'. Objectivity is the outcome of the simultaneous maximizing of reliability and validity.

One of the basic means of achieving reliability and validity that has been adopted in qualitative research is the use of triangulation, the examination of some issue or phenomenon from a variety of positions. Generally, the more systematic the triangulation, the better cross-referencing of findings there will be, and the better the check on reliability and validity. Denzin (1970) described four types of triangulation: (a) of data, including in time (giving time series data), space (giving comparative cases) and person/group triangulation (giving data from different individuals and groups in the situation); (b) of investigator, where more than one researcher examines the same situation, as in team fieldwork; (c) of theory, where a situation is examined from different theoretical perspectives; and (d) of methodology, typically 'between-method' where different methods are used to examine the same situation, and 'within-method', where the same method is used to examine a situation at different times.

Such multiple triangulation is mainly achieved during fieldwork and other data-gathering activities. But as Coffey and Atkinson (1996: 4) suggest, triangulation can also be applied in the analysis of the data gathered: researchers should 'explore their data from a variety of perspectives, or at least be able to make informed decisions about the analytic strategy adopted for a particular project'. This implies that, as well as sound practice, research has to be informed by a clear schema or conceptual framework.

Data analysis
Various writers, such as Miles and Huberman (1994), Dey (1993), Walcott (1994) and Dick (1990), have offered strategies for the handling and analysis of qualitative data, especially text derived from interviews and discussions. Tesch (1990), who identified at least 26 published analytic strategies

for dealing with textual data, observed (a) that such data analysis is a cyclical and reflexive (iterative) process; (b) that it should be comprehensive and systematic, but not rigid; (c) that data generally need to be segmented and divided into meaningful units while maintaining connections to the whole data set; (d) that data are best organized according to a system derived from the data themselves; and (e) that, overall, data analysis is an inductive, data-led activity.

In addition to collecting the data, and making it available in an accessible form for processing (for example, transcription of audio tapes or hand-written fieldnotes into legible text), Miles and Huberman (1994) indicate it consists of (a) data reduction by summarising, coding, theme-ing, clustering, or categorizing; (b) displaying and compressing the data, and indicating connections or interrelations within it (by diagramming, outlining and so on) in order to show what the data implies; and (c) drawing conclusions and verification through comparing and contrasting cases, noting and exploring themes/patterns and so on, and using metaphors.

Assuming the SIA practitioner–researcher has a dataset which has a degree of consistency of focus (that is, it is grounded by a clear impact assessment problem or case, and has a conceptual framework which provides a schema for data analysis), doing such analysis typically involves repeated reading of the fieldnotes or transcriptions, developing a topic-code scheme, coding the notes, chopping up and sorting the notes by topic, and summarizing the content into key predetermined or evident themes. Having done this work, the researcher begins the job of interpretation and drawing conclusions about the likely impacts that will occur.

In practice, much of the analysis effort and time tends to go into reading and understanding the content of the notes/text/pictures, developing a coding or classification schema which reflects both the particular social impact situation and what the data are telling the researcher, and physically organizing (and iteratively reorganizing) the material so that summary observations and conclusions can be drawn.

For large datasets, traditional manual methods for doing these tasks can hinder the repetitive reorganization of the data that is necessary for exploring or discovering the impact issues, themes or associations (that is, tapping into the richness of the data). They make it difficult to make the most of the triangulation done during data gathering.

With the development of increasingly powerful personal computers, new methods and accompanying software have become available which can assist in the intelligent management and analysis of large amounts of qualitative data. In so doing, computer-assisted qualitative data management and analysis can help resolve issues of reliability and enhance the validity of derived findings (Kelle and Laurie, 1995; also see Weitzman and Miles, 1995; Fisher, 1997; and Burgess, 1995, for a discussion of computer-based methods and software developments). Such technology was put to work in a large social impact research exercise in New Zealand, which, along with the use of quantitative methods, involved large numbers of community fieldwork interviews, discussions and observations, and the analysis of secondary sources. In the following section, the process of data recording and analysis used in that study is outlined in order to illustrate how computer technologies might improve the use of qualitative methods, data processing and analysis in SIA.

A case example: background
The illustration presented here is drawn from an ongoing study examining social and economic changes over the last 20 years in a series of New Zealand resource-dependent communities. The study sought to understand the process of community formation and change in relation to the natural resource base, and the relevant resource industries. At the same time, it sought to provide (among other things) a body of empirical data and cases which could be used to inform impact assessment practice, especially the formulation of conceptual frameworks to assess effects, development of scenarios for the estimation of effects, and the management and mitigation of social impacts. The study involved the use of a range of research methods, including (a) longitudinal and comparative statistical analysis of census data; (b) detailed social and economic profiling of selected communities, including review of previous social and historical studies; (c) statistical and descriptive profiling of resource sector industries, and identification of key trends; (d) a series of 19 community case studies, each involving fieldwork and the use of semi-structured interviews of at least 30 key community contacts, participant observation and supporting statistical profiling; and (e) community workshops and team discussions on preliminary findings.

The approach to data collection and analysis used in the Resource Communities Study flowed out of conceptual development of the process and nature of resource community formation and change. It drew on experience with previous SIA studies and community research. The approach was further refined, as noted in Figure 10.1, through additional scoping studies. As can be seen, the overall approach sought to combine the use of qualitative and quantitative data. Methods to enable theoretical ideas about change in particular types of communities emerged from the data and were tested across various case studies. Glaser and Strauss (1967) refer to ideas and theories that emerge from the data and fieldwork as 'grounded theory'.

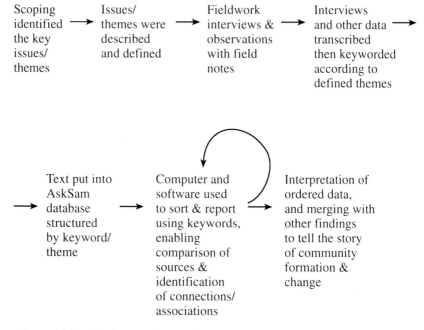

Figure 10.1   Qualitative data collection and processing for the Resource Communities Study

Key components of the data collection and analysis process
The choice of data collection, including selection of informants and methods, and subsequent approach to data handling were guided by the conceptual framework, and preceded the fieldwork. This also involved identifying and defining the key themes (covering aspects of social life, changes and issues) and likely cross-linkages between the themes and issues. Some 29 keywords were adopted and defined. The list of keywords and theme definitions was assembled in a fieldwork guide, along with rules and suggestions for carrying out the fieldwork. The keywords are listed in Figure 10.2a, and, by way of illustration, two of the keywords and their associated themes are also presented (Figure 10.2b).

To assist in notetaking in the field, and subsequent keywording, the research team produced a specially designed notebook, which had separate spaces for interview content, background information, observations, comments on the interview and follow-up contacts and information sources. The researchers were encouraged to review their notes while in the field and annotate the hand-written text using the keywords. A snapshot of one page of one of the author's notebooks is provided as an example in Figure 10.3.

This relates to an interview with a resident of 'ATown', a settlement associated with the hydroelectricity industry. In the examples provided, names and locations have been changed to maintain confidentiality.

Following the fieldwork in each community, the hand-written notes were transcribed using a wordprocessor. The keywording was then reviewed and, where individual pieces of text related to more than one theme, additional keywords were applied. (This time-consuming job of transcribing handwriting could have been reduced, and possibly eliminated, with the use in the field of a digital recorder and voice recognition software, or by using a palm-top computer and handwriting recognition software, as discussed below.) The data preparation was completed with the addition of the special codes demanded by the particular database program, AskSam, being used for the study. Such codes are only required when the program is being used in 'fixed field' mode, in order to separate individual documents (in our case each interview, observation or notes on documentary material) and to recognize different pieces of data within a document, though the software can also handle unstructured or uncoded data. The prepared data, prior to processing by AskSam, are illustrated (for the same example data as above), in Figure 10.4. As with similar computer programs such as NVivo, summaries of quantitative data, literature notes and other materials (such as the contents of video tape, digital photographs and audio recordings) can be handled alongside textual information.

Using the AskSam software, all the prepared text was sorted and merged according to the predefined themes, with one output file per theme keyword. A section of one file (for the keyword 'industry') covering the example data provided in Figures 10.3 and 10.4 is illustrated in Figure 10.5. As can been seen, data from different interviews are brought together in this

---

Standard keywords

Interviewee, date, organisation, contact, date, place, background, process, followup.

Keywords that address content and theme

Agency, business, class, community, consent, council, culture, economy, elderly, employment, environment, health, housing, income, industry, infrastructure, labour, maori, problem, profile, school, state, strategy, technology, training, trend, women, work, youth.

Figure 10.2a   Keywords used for the Resource Communities Study data processing and analysis

---

Keyword: 'council'
Theme:
The role of territorial local authorities and regional councils in promoting the development of the resource industry, including any assistance with establishing or modifying the settlement patterns in the district.

Data:
- Where is the HQ of the local authority; is there a service centre in the town?
- How have local government services changed – any loss of employment?
- Any issues in access to services?
- Role of local and regional government in economic development.

Link:
- Role of local and regional government in planning and resource consents – see 'consent'.

Keyword: 'industry'
Themes:
- The changing ownership and organisational structure of the resource industry.
- The role of the industry in local body affairs and as a corporate citizen in developing the infrastructure of a region and community, and in promoting public participation in the administration of the town.

Data:
- The background to the industry and resource sector in the area, particularly its development over time.
- The ownership structure of the industry, foreign ownership and any significant changes in these, such as amalgamations.
- The relationship between the industry and the community, such as liaison mechanisms.
- The role of the industry in town administration.

Figure 10.2b   Examples of the definitions of keywords used to address content and themes

step, enabling triangulation and comparison of different data sources to be carried out. Other types of data in the dataset also appear in the relevant output files. With the multiple keywording of sections of the data, the output also enabled the researchers to examine linked themes easily. Having the data in this form also facilitated the identification of subthemes or issues. With relatively little effort, a dataset or parts of it could be reprocessed using new keywords to reveal new associations. Programs such as NUD.IST (Non-numerical Unstructured Data – Interactive Searching and Theorising) and NVivo provide for hierarchical coding, thus giving 'trees' of horizontal and vertical connections between themes and underlying

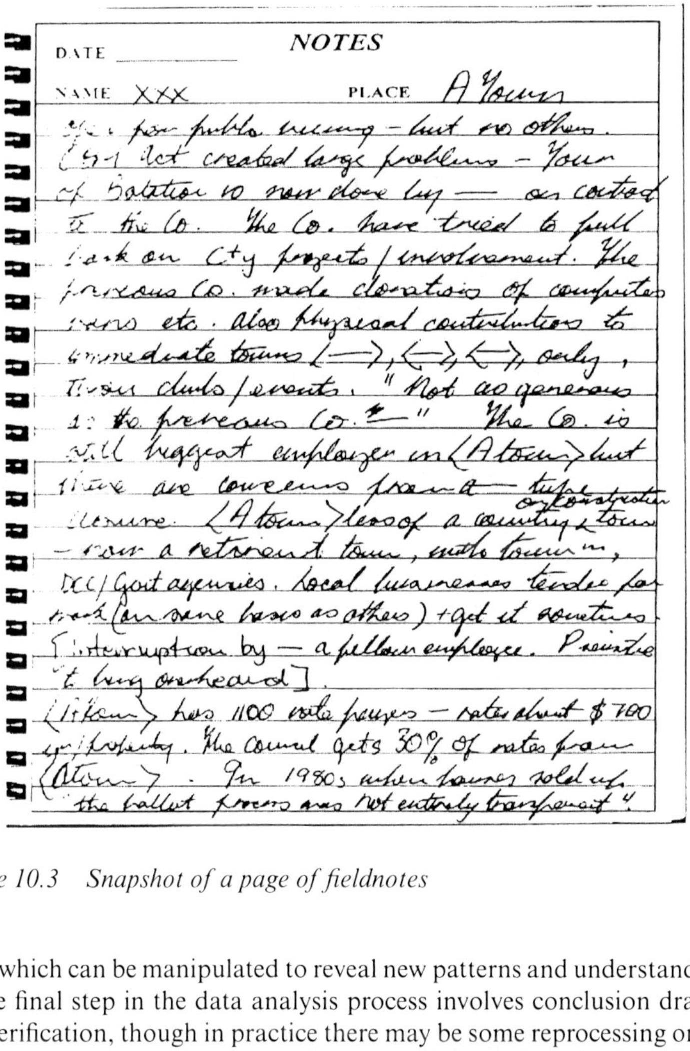

Figure 10.3   Snapshot of a page of fieldnotes

data, which can be manipulated to reveal new patterns and understandings.

The final step in the data analysis process involves conclusion drawing and verification, though in practice there may be some reprocessing or iteration, as suggested above. In the Resource Communities Study, this final stage focused on testing models of community formation and change. However, in an SIA of a project development, for example, it would involve the drawing of a series of conclusions about the likely impacts.

The computer-based approach
This example of qualitative data processing and analysis is based on the use of the AskSam computer program. A variety of other programs, such as NUD.IST, NVivo, ATLAS.ti, the Ethnograph and others, provide similar

$$
interviewee[xxxx]
organisation[xxx, Company X]
place[ATown]
contact[xxx, xxx, e-mail address provided]
Background[photos of housing and town centre shops]
Labour[The company has around 50–60 staff in the Atown area and more on contract]

Technology[Machinery maintenance etc. used to be programmed, regardless of need/technology tolerances. Now it's determined through risk analysis. Physical efficiencies in the system plus financial savings – especially unnecessary maintenance.]

Industry[No necessity at moment for additional hydro stations. Tourism and hydro – lot of interest in the power stations. 'BStation is the only station open for public viewing' – but no others. 'OSH Act created large problems'. Tour of BStation is done by another company on contract to the power company. The Company have tried to pull back on community projects/involvement. The previous company made donations of computers, vans, etc. Physical contributions to immediate towns – Btown, Ctown and Dtown only – thru clubs/events. Present Company is 'not as generous as the former company'. The Company is still biggest employer in ATown, but there are concerns from the town to the closure. 'ATown less of a country or construction town – now a retirement town with tourism, Government agency etc.' Local businesses tender for the Company work on same bases as others and get it sometimes.]

Council[ATown has 1100 ratepayers. Rates are about $700 per year per property. The District Council now gets about 30% of its rates from ATown. In 1980s 'when houses put up to ballot, process was not entirely transparent'. There was a system for keeping houses reserved. Former government department got some for its workers. The Council was given the town – and sold it up to house buyers. 'ATown will survive – especially if the Company etc. facility is retained locally.']

State[The Company is an SOE – generally feeling is that the Company would be retained by new government.]

Tourism[Tourism future looks 'very bright'.]

Economy['The downward indicator on property values is a worry to the negative few.' Some are speaking now negatively about the future. This affects morale. The gift shop is closing.]

Housing['Property values crumbled overnight' 5 years ago when the ski-field proposal came up. Now the values are adjusting down, rather than reflecting any big impact of the Company personnel transfers and redundancies.]

Figure 10.4   Example of transcribed, keyworded and encoded interview text

---

ATOWN – Keyword: industry

The Company and the Government Agency are not contributing much to the community overall – especially in terms of social contribution and membership of societies etc.

Mr YYYY
ZZZ Business.

. . . No necessity at moment for additional hydro stations. Tourism and hydro – lot of interest in the power stations. Bstation is the only station open for public viewing – but no others. 'OSH Act created large problems'. Tour of Bstation is done by another company on contract to the Company. The Company have tried to pull back on community projects/involvement. The previous company made donations of computers, vans, etc. Physical contributions to immediate towns – Btown, Ctown, Dtown only – thru clubs/events. Present company is 'not as generous as the former company'. The Company still biggest employer in ATown, but there are concerns from the town to the closure. 'ATown is less of a country or construction town – now a retirement town with tourism, Government agency etc.' Local businesses tender for the Company work on same bases as others and get it sometimes.

XXXX.
XXX, & Company X.

The former company donated a mini van to the school in the past. The Company sponsor particular events – e.g. launch of 'the College' but they are generally contributing little to the community now. They have also withdrawn from sponsoring X-sport.

Ms ZZZZ.
Organisation Z, Institution X

Figure 10.5   Example of a section of AskSam output for some text coded with keyword 'industry'

and sometimes more powerful capabilities (Richards, 1999, 2000). The three main capabilities of interest to social researchers and SIA practitioners are as follows. First, such computer programs provide for the storage of large amounts of data in almost any form, including numerical data, text, graphics, pictures and sound. In the AskSam software, for example, one file can be a very large database, with up to 4 gigabytes of data, made up of related documents or items, all of which can be searched. This helps eliminate many of the qualitative data handling difficulties discussed earlier.

Second, they can rapidly search for and retrieve any word, phrase or other data item, along with its context and source, and match it with similar data. In AskSam, this can be achieved whether the data is in structured form (for example, keyword-coded) or free form. A log of search and sort strategies can also be kept, reviewed, modified and repeated as necessary.

Third, such programs enable the linking of words, phrases and other data within the same document or file, or from different documents and files. Such flexibility allows for new views of data to be created easily, and makes cumulative data from different studies or impacts assessments available and searchable in the future. As mentioned, in some programs, the logical structure of the linkages can be displayed and manipulated graphically.

Complementary technologies include digital audio recorders that can be linked with voice recognition software, and scanners linked with optical character recognition. Multimedia handheld computers which can serve as digital cameras or audio recorders, and can recognize hand-written input, enable researchers to get their field observations and interview notes into a text format for processing by such programs as AskSam, NUD.IST or NVivo and so on. They also allow associated video or still images to be linked with the text. New developments in software such as intelligent (self-learning) and flexible search engines can also add to the power of computer-based qualitative data processing. Such technology can also assist in the building of archives of data for use in future SIA work and for the generation of comparative cases. Furthermore, with increasingly powerful laptop computers, much of the work of establishing electronic datasets, data exploration and analysis can be done while in the field. This enables the rapid formulation of ideas and conclusions which can be tested immediately through subsequent interviews, discussions and observations.

Conclusion
The use of computer-based data processing, as illustrated above, can help eliminate a number of the practical difficulties experienced by SIA practitioners and researchers when using qualitative research methods. They can assist in neutralizing potential accusations of unreliability of their data collection and processing methods and lack of validity in their findings. To gain the benefits of computer-based qualitative data analysis, SIA practitioner–researchers will inevitably be challenged to review, justify and strengthen their research methodologies, orientations to practice, and field-work procedures. Meeting this challenge can be particularly beneficial to the practitioner.

On the practical side, the use of computers can substantially reduce the inevitable repeated and tedious handling and organizing of large amounts of paper-based information. They also provide compact storage and rapid retrieval of raw primary data and secondary information in a variety of forms. In terms of the analysis of qualitative data, the use of specialist software allows the SIA practitioner (a) to restructure non-linear interview data at will; (b) to treat the data from a number of interviewees even-handedly; (c) to utilize fully the various data gathered; and (d) to systematize and replicate the analysis procedure.

Importantly, triangulation can be maximized easily by juxtaposing different types of data, and data derived from different informants and sources, and by different methods. Crucially, for any particular study or impact assessment, the technology enables the practitioner–researcher to explore a dataset more freely and deeply. This enables them to better understand the key social impact issues, to test hypotheses about social change, to draw more valid conclusions and, perhaps, to hear better what members of a community are trying to say about themselves and their current and future situation.

References

Burgess, R. (ed.) 1995. *Computing and Qualitative Research* (Studies in Qualitative Methods, vol. 5), Greenwich: JAI Press.

Coffey, A. and Atkinson, P. 1996. *Making Sense of Qualitative Data*, Thousand Oaks: Sage.

Denzin, N. 1970. *The Research Act: A Theoretical Introduction to Sociological Methods*, Chicago: Aldine.

Dey, I. 1993. *Qualitative Data Analysis: A User-Friendly Guide for Social Scientists*, London: Routledge.

Dick, B. 1990. *Rigour Without Numbers: The Potential of Dialectical Processes as Qualitative Research Tools*, Brisbane: Interchange.

Fielding, N. and Fielding, J. 1986. *Linking Data* (Qualitative Research Methods Series, vol. 4), Beverley Hills: Sage.

Fisher, M. 1997. *Qualitative Computing: Using Software for Qualitative Data Analysis*, Aldershot: Ashgate.

Glaser, B. and Strauss, A. 1967. *The Discovery of Grounded Theory*, Chicago: Aldine.

Hammersley, M. and Atkinson, P. 1983. *Ethnography: Principles in Practice*, London: Tavistock.

Kelle, U. and Laurie, H. 1995. 'Computer use in qualitative research and issues of validity', in E. Kelle (ed.), *Computer-Aided Qualitative Data Analysis: Theory, Methods and Practice*, London: Sage, 19–28.

Kirk, J. and Miller, M. 1986. *Reliability and Validity in Qualitative Research*, Beverly Hills: Sage.

Miles, A.M. and Huberman, M.B. 1994. *Qualitative Data Analysis: An Expanded Sourcebook*, Thousand Oaks: Sage.

Neuman, W.L. 1997. *Social Research Methods: Qualitative and Quantitative Approaches*, Boston: Allyn and Bacon.

Richards, L. 1999. *Introducing NVivo: A Workshop Handbook*, Bundoora: Qualitative Solutions and Research.

Richards, L. 2000. *Introducing N5: A Workshop Handbook*, Bundoora: QSR International.

Taylor, C.N., Goodrich, C. and Bryan, H. 1995. *Social Assessment: Theory, Process and Techniques* (2nd edn), Christchurch: Taylor Baines and Associates.

Tesch, R. 1990. *Qualitative Research: Analysis Types and Software Tools*, New York: Falmer.

Tolich, M. and Davidson, C. (eds) 1999. *Social Science Research in New Zealand: Many Pathways to Understanding*, Auckland: Longman/Pearson.

Walcott, H. 1994. *Transforming Qualitative Data: Description, Analysis, and Interpretation*, Thousand Oaks: Sage.
Weitzman, E. and Miles, M. 1995. *Computer Programs for Qualitative Data Analysis*, Thousand Oaks: Sage.

For more information on software for computer-assisted qualitative data analysis see the following:
AskSam Systems website (for AskSam software) (*http://www.asksam.com*).
QSR website (for NUD.IST and NVivo software) (*http://www.qsr.com.au*).
ATLAS.ti software (website: *http://www.atlasti.de*).
Qualis Research website (for The Ethnograph software: *http://www.QualisResearch.com*).
ResearchWare Inc website (for HyperRESEARCH software: *http://www.researchware.com*).
Banxia Software website (for Decision Explorer software tools: *http://www.banxia.com*).
GESIS/ZUMA website (for TEXTPACK software:
http://www.gesis.org/en/software/textpack/index.htm).

11 Assessing gender impacts
Bina Srinivasan and Lyla Mehta

Introduction

Infrastructure projects have multiple and differential impacts on women, men and children. An evaluation of social impacts, especially on vulnerable groups, such as poor women and children, has to go beyond an assessment of monetary loss (Colson, 1999; Thukral, 1996; Parasuraman, 1993, 1997; Srinivasan, 1997, 1999). In this context, the intangible nature of social impacts, the tendency to emphasize the quantifiable impacts, the relatively poor integration of a qualitative perspective in evaluative exercises and reductionist assumptions of cost–benefit analyses are some of the issues that require discussion. Superimposing itself on all these factors is the central issue of gender.

Assessment of social impacts is clearly a complex process that involves in-depth understanding of the multiplicity of contexts in which affected communities are situated. This process is rendered even more complex when gender is integrated in evaluation exercises. One of the major reasons for this complexity stems from the need to prise out the often hidden dimensions of the way gender is organized and has become manifest. Compounding the issue is the inevitable social transition that affected communities go through in the course of the planning, execution and implementation of development projects. Such transitions imposed upon a community, or even initiated by it, have many implications for its gender organization.

Gender imbalances exist in every society (World Bank, 2001). There are high levels of inequality in terms of access to, and control over, resources, gender roles and relationships. Our review of the available literature suggests that development has often tended to aggravate existing inequalities and increase rather than close gender gaps. These problems arise from existing patriarchal structures. However, technological interventions interact with the existing sociocultural system to produce new forms of social organization which entail both opportunities and constraints for women and men. Thus, from a social point of view, development projects need to be evaluated in terms of their contribution to reducing gender gaps and improving the conditions under which women and men lead their lives.

Owing to its cross-cutting nature, no social, equity or distributional analysis can proceed without a discussion of gender. Thus a growing constituency of policy makers, social advisers and gender scholars talk of gender mainstreaming and engendering activities. They use gender conceptually and practically to approach a whole array of issues ranging from forced migration (for example, Indra, 1999) to development cooperation and health. This chapter essentially looks at social impacts and their evaluation through a gendered perspective. We believe that such an approach is indispensable because an assessment that overlooks gender remains a truncated process as it ignores the very basis of social, economic, cultural and political organization of a society or community. We begin by looking at what the term 'gender' means and why gender impact assessment is essential. The next section looks at some experiences of the gendered impacts of displacement due to large dams, using the Sardar Sarovar Project, a multi-purpose irrigation project on the Narmada River in Gujarat, India, as an example. The analysis of the gendered impacts of displacement helps us formulate a general framework for gender evaluation of social impacts of development projects. As a basic framework, it would need to be adapted to specific projects in ways that take into account the full range of factors that impinge on communities affected by development. Finally, recommendations for integrating gender perspectives into policy and planning are provided.

What is gender?
Gender constitutes the entire ambit of relations that govern the social, cultural and economic exchanges between women and men in different arenas, from the household to the community, state and multilateral agencies (Jackson and Pearson, 1998). It also constitutes the very axis of power relationships that determine the social, familial and institutional locations of women and men. Gender is central to the way societies assign roles, responsibilities, resources and rights between women and men. Allocation, distribution, utilization and control of resources are thus incumbent upon gender relations embedded in both ideology and practice.

Gender is a dynamic concept: it changes and is changed by a variety of interrelated factors including geographical and historical contexts. Gender does not exist in a vacuum: caste, class and ethnicity impinge on gender and form a complex matrix. Gendered positionings are crucial in the multidimensional meanings that are attached to, and formulated in, the processes and outcomes of developmental projects.

Women and men are not homogeneous units but are differentiated within and amongst each other according to their varied social, economic and cultural locations. The household and the community therefore need to be seen as gendered units in which women and men have different sets of interests. They have demonstrated that the household is not a unit of congruent interests where resources are shared equitably by all its members (Agarwal, 1996). Thus gender scholars have argued that economic growth does not affect men and women equally. Genderless categorization of the community, the state and its institutions tends to conceal the complexities that underpin exchanges between women and men (Elson, 1998; Boserup, 1970; Kabeer, 1994). Hence women's needs and interests require a specific priority focus in practice and policy for development to be truly gender-just.

Displacement and gender impacts

Displacement is often a concomitant of development projects. It is usually forced upon communities already victims of systemic injustice, such as indigenous communities, as has been well documented in the case of large dams (Thukral, 1992). Women as marginalized entities within marginalized communities are often forced to suffer the ordeal of displacement far more intensely than do men. Additionally, displacement is often accompanied by the covert or overt use of force. This entails repression of dissenting voices and large-scale violation of democratic rights (Thukral, 1996).

Resettlement is a traumatic experience for most communities (Cernea, 1999; Morse and Berger, 1992). 'Resettlement involves a re-ordering of gender relations across a wide spectrum, but that re-ordering emerges from previous assumptions about gender and the gendered experience of those involved' (Colson, 1999: 26). Efforts towards resettlement and rehabilitation may be flawed in terms of their understanding of gender, and of how gender roles are changed by displacement. Gender-blind policies, gender assumptions and roles embedded in social and cultural practices in affected communities also work to the disadvantage of women. Both men and women experience disempowerment as a result of being uprooted. However, women are often at the receiving end of the transitions wrought upon communities, especially in relation to the domestic sphere and the market.

The rigidities of gender assumptions are internalized by both women and men in project-affected communities. These gender assumptions are often reinforced by policy. They play a key role in discouraging women from availing themselves of the increased opportunities that development projects may offer (Colson, 1999). Besides, the household is usually seen as an undifferentiated unit with men presumed to be the 'head'. So, while 'the settler, his wife and children' make up the displaced community, the settler is primarily assumed to be male. Such assumptions embedded in policy and implementation exacerbate the inequalities already present in the social organization of communities.

The Sardar Sarovar Project (SSP), described as 'one of the most flawed projects' (Cernea, 1999), will displace mainly adivasi (tribal) communities in the Narmada Valley in three Indian states, Madhya Pradesh, Maharashtra and Gujarat. Resettlement proceeded at an uneven pace, subject to many pressures in the face of widespread protest against the dam. In 1985, the people from 19 villages in Gujarat were relocated to 175 different locations (TISS, 1997: 184–214). The main gender impacts emerging from displacement and resettlement in the case of SSP are as follows.

The fragmentation of the communities in the valley has led to a disruption of social cohesion. Isolation from kinship structures because of increased transport costs has led to increased insecurity and fear amongst women (Thukral, 1996; Srinivasan, 1997; Mehta, 2000). Some studies have pointed out that displaced women's central anxieties concern inability to visit their married daughters (Thukral, 1996; Hakim, 1997).

Women's access to, and control over, resources have been severely curtailed by resettlement. Women do not have landrights in adivasi communities (most adivasi communities in the Narmada Valley are classified as 'encroachers': Morse and Berger, 1992). However, they have usufructuary rights and control over common property resources (Mehta, 2000). Their forest-based work gives them an independent income which is lost upon resettlement. Their role in the forest economy is not recognized. Married or adult daughters and widowed women with land records in the original villages have not been compensated (Bhatia, 1997). Women's interests are seen as linked to the household and thus only men and married sons are being given land according to the Gujarat Resettlement and Rehabilitation policy. Additionally, loss of forests, river, forest produce, fuel, fodder and common property resources affect women in the resettlement sites (Mehta, 2000; Srinivasan, 1997; Parasuraman, 1993).

Skills such as basket weaving, pottery and knowledge of herbal remedies are being made redundant at resettlement sites (CSS, 1997). Additionally, while the Gujarat government has introduced training programmes such as soap making and sewing, the women (especially older women) of Parveta, a resettlement site, are resisting them (CSS, 1997). This is because these activities are far removed from the lives and realities of adivasi women. They also reinforce notions of women performing typical female tasks, thus undermining the role of adivasi women in the forest economy.

There has been a decrease in women's mobility as a result of increased intensity of certain kinds of agricultural work at the resettlement compared to original villages (Parasuraman, 1993; Mehta, 2000) and owing to the unfamiliarity of the surroundings (Srinivasan, 1997). The gendered organization of public space at the resettlement sites has led to increased insecurity and fear for women. In the absence of kinship support, this has social and domestic repercussions. Tensions between the host community and the resettled communities, usually arising out of poor resettlement implementation (Dreze *et al.*, 1997), have often resulted in violence. Increased availability of alcohol has led to an erosion of household income and domestic security (Thukral, 1996).

In adivasi villages, women were involved in decision-making processes related to the household and the farm (CSS, 1997). However, the monetized economy has marginalized women from these spheres of autonomous control on the farm and the household. Women are being forced into wage labour and to accept lower wages for equal work at the sites. Agricultural production has become more mechanized (Parasuraman, 1997) and thus women are pushed to the periphery of agricultural production.

Domestic drudgery seems to have decreased in some locations owing to the availability of hand-pumps, flour mills and so on (Parasuraman, 1997; Hakim, 1997). However, in some places, the water is saline, and women complain that lentils take longer to cook and that their skin breaks out in rashes. They also prefer to have access to clean, free-flowing water – in other words, to the river. Lack of availability of fuel and fodder has also led to an increase in drudgery (Bhatia, 1997; Mehta, 2000; Srinivasan, 1997).

Health seems to have been severely affected because of changes in cropping patterns and the lack of availability of adequate nutrition and water (Parasuraman, 1993). The sex ratio in some of the adivasi villages was higher than the Gujarat level (CSS, 1997). However, at some sites, infant mortality rates seem to have increased, with some 30 per cent of the children born in the first six years of resettlement in Parveta dying. At least five women lost all children born during those years (Parasuraman, 1993: 17). Life in resettlement sites is characterized by the lack of primary health care facilities.

Perhaps this is why some women from Madhya Pradesh resettled in Gujarat told the Morse Committee that 'none of them would give birth [at the resettlement site in Gujarat], but would, if at all possible, have their babies at [original village]' (Morse and Berger, 1992: 197). The same group of people also reported to the Morse Committee that they had to walk two kilometres to get medical help. The report says that the people did not seem to have much confidence in this help. After resettlement, when employment has been made available, it is men who have benefited (Parasuraman, 1993).

Thus we see that, as gender relations in most communities exclude women from interaction with outside forces before resettlement, state action further reinforces and exacerbates this exclusion as the state tends to negotiate only with men. The social and gender organization of the community often vests greater powers in the hands of men. This is particularly true in the case of women's ownership of land. In some cases, women do have some use-rights over land. To that extent, they have autonomy and control over resources. With displacement and resettlement, it is often found that women lose this control to men, for a combination of reasons. In principle, resettlement sites can offer, and sometimes have offered, better access to these resources. However, in the absence of gender-sensitive institutional support systems, these resources remain out of reach for women.

The other serious consequence of gender imbalances is the increase in domestic violence. Resettlement can have grim repercussions for the physical and emotional health of women. A community in transition tends to victimize its least powerful constituents, violating their fundamental rights to a life of dignity and security. Policies tend to overlook such instances of human rights violation and the potentially harmful situation that can develop in resettlement sites. There are virtually no safeguards for women in such situations, especially when they are combined with the erosion of social support structures to negotiate on their behalf.

Women's position in decision-making hierarchies change with development projects owing to the reorganization of social and gender relations. In some cases, women are ousted from previously held autonomous positions within these hierarchies. In others, with the enhancement of economic choices and the subsequent increase in social mobility, women may be in a better position in community and domestic decision-making processes. Gender blindness in policy – whereby only men are regarded as the heads of the households or community leaders – leads to a loss of social status for women. When several factors work together, as with erosion of social support structures and control/access over resources, along with economic marginalization, they lead to an increasing loss of autonomy for women.

The case for gender impact assessment

Gender influences the spread of resources. Development processes, such as economic growth, are not gender-neutral. There is a significant gap in the ways in which the fruits of development are distributed and calculated. Either women's unpaid labour has not been calculated, or benefits have disproportionately been enjoyed by men (cf. Agarwal, 1996; Elson, 1998). This gender gap still exists in both policy and practice. Despite good policy intentions, cultural biases and gender stereotypes have exacerbated gender inequalities.

Development is often equated with economic growth. It is argued that the wellbeing of all humans will be assured with economic growth. However, feminists have challenged this assumption. They assert that the drive towards growth should not distract attention from attempts at redistribution to meet the basic requirements of all (Kabeer, 1994). Thus growth or development which proceeds in an unequal way cannot lead to social and economic justice for all women and men. This necessarily entails a process of redistribution where the costs and benefits are equally borne by women and men; by the powerful and the powerless.

The 'project-affected person' – often reduced to just an acronym, PAP – is usually described as a genderless entity rather than as a woman or man with different interests and aspirations. Similarly, the household is rarely seen as a site where women and men both cooperate and are in conflict with each other (cf. Sen, 1990). Finally, the community earmarked for either compensation or benefits is usually viewed as homogeneous, with male members exclusively being the recipients. Thus the impacts of infrastructure projects, be they positive or negative, have been analysed in a gender-blind way as though differences between women and men in the household, community or nation simply do not exist.

For a realistic impact assessment, gender needs to be placed squarely on the agenda. The costs and benefits of development projects have to take into account the social, cultural and political. This perspective is in opposition to a narrow, ungendered economic analysis. Large projects, especially those that involve displacement of people, have a lasting impact upon kinship structures and community identities (Dreze *et al.*, 1998). Kinship structures are social resources that determine individual wellbeing and cannot be ignored in impact assessment studies. Other resources include forests, land, rivers and environment – all of which are inextricably part of the cultural and social matrix of the affected communities.

Gender impact assessment makes inevitable taking into account the tangible and intangible costs and benefits of any project. The exercise is both qualitative and quantitative. There is no denying the importance of some quantitative parameters to measure standard of living in terms of assets like land, cattle, common property resources, nutritional intake and so on. However, it is important also to focus on what cannot be measured, such as cultural identity, social structures, wellbeing and political power. These do not fall into the ambit of economic yardsticks which are reductionist and narrow in their approach. Additionally, economic indicators do not cover those activities that do not fit within a monetized economy. These activities are often central to the way a community, household or individual organizes, accumulates and uses resources.

Social differentiation between women and men demarcates specific spaces and roles for them. An examination of these roles reveals that women's labour within, and outside, the household is often unaccounted for. As social practice often excludes women from public spaces like markets or political institutions, they are rendered invisible. This invisibility of women in statistics, and the policies that ensue from these data, render women's labour as an intangible. For example, how would we cost women's roles in nurturing and providing for the family? How would we account for the amount of time women usually spend in collecting fuel, fodder or water? Equally, it is important to consider production of goods outside the market. The provision of goods and services to the household has to be included in a measurement of costs or benefits. Changes in time allocation for different activities within the household as direct or indirect effects of development projects should be looked into. Similarly, in the case of displacement due to development projects, loss of cultural identity is an intangible loss. Likewise, knowledge systems that are rendered redundant because of loss of forests or other familiar terrain are usually not accounted for. These and other comparable losses are social losses and have long-term implications for the communities that are affected adversely by development projects. As these social and familial losses manifest themselves differentially across gender, their implications are also different for women and men.

In terms of the benefits, increased social mobility and leisure time, and enhancement of life choices, are intangibles that need to be taken into account. Development brings about a possibility of increase in the cultural capital of beneficiaries in the context of increased access to information and so on. These benefits are not spread evenly in society and their implications for gender assessment are complex. For example, women may find that their economic mobility has increased as a result of development, but this may not necessarily translate into an increase in social status. Gendered locations determine consumption patterns within the household and in all communities that are affected by development projects. Thus costs and benefits have to be seen within a broader framework that acknowledges the gendered heterogeneity of communities and the multilayered nature of the social impacts.

A holistic picture of costs or benefits will not emerge unless the hitherto unaccounted for cultural, social and political dimensions are included. Thus a non-economic framework for evaluation of costs and benefits is unavoidable for the formulation of principles that would have any bearing on the realities of the communities affected by development projects. A gender perspective can help to throw up the invisible and intangible impacts of the development process.

Principles of gender impact assessment
In the formulation of gender-sensitive principles of evaluation, it is important to go back to policy and see how policy understands gender. It is not enough to include gender as a means of facilitating development objectives. It has to be seen as a means in itself (Jackson and Pearson, 1998). There has to be a clear commitment to the inclusion of gender as a means of addressing inequalities between women and men in the development process. Programme, policy and outcome cannot be directly linked. Through collective or individual agency, women have used programmes to extend far beyond their intended goals. These kinds of potentially empowering avenues are inherent to participation in development programmes. Communities, and constituents, interact with them in complex ways. The

consequences can have both positive as well as negative outcomes for gender equity. The important issue here is that development projects should recognize and anticipate such agency.

Gender is one of the most basic aspects of a realistic impact assessment. As gender cuts across all communities, neither benefits nor costs can be determined without examining impacts on gender. This is not only because women and men enjoy different kinds of rights within the household, community or kinship structures. It is also because perceptions of wellbeing, power and powerlessness are all predicated on subjective as well as social and cultural contexts. Thus benefits and losses can have entirely different meanings for women and men. All of these perceptions and realities interact with other overarching social structures such as caste, ethnicity and so on. Thus the inclusion of gender entails the use of a framework that is far more nuanced than conventional parameters would allow. It also means the unpacking of several assumptions to do with the household, the community and the social, political and economic matrix that informs use of and access to resources.

A gender impact evaluation would require an examination of the following:

- gender and policy,
- gender and rights,
- gender, community and household,
- the gendered nature of participation in development planning,
- the gendered impacts of adverse outcomes such as displacement, compensation, resettlement and rehabilitation,
- the gendered spread of benefits such as irrigation, electricity and access to information,
- the gendered nature of institutions that represent all the various communities involved in and affected by the development process.

Rights

Assertions on the part of vulnerable communities and social groupings have led to the creation, enhancement and acknowledgment of various kinds of rights. Participation, consultation and representation are instrumental in the institution of rights, and these are gendered processes. In the context of development projects, a discussion on rights should include all the constituents of communities that benefit or suffer losses.

Rights have to be seen at various levels: the regional, the national, the local. Rights also need to be seen in various locations and at different points in time. They have to include individual as well as collective rights. Gender equity should encompass the rights of the community as well as those of its constituents. Rights include (a) the right to property and common property resources, to use, plan and manage local resources; (b) the right to participation in decision-making processes; (c) the right to information and redress; (d) the right to fair and just compensation; and (e) the right to employment and equal wages for equal work.

Gender is an important aspect of the rights discourse. We find that women and men in any community or grouping have different kinds of access to rights. Development policy has in some measure attempted to act upon the gender gap in terms of rights. The invisibility of women's work or needs in official data, the gender biases of implementors, the limitations of the institutions meant to oversee the implementation of these rights, the underrepresentation of women in these institutions, and the use of reductionistic frameworks of evaluation of gender roles are some of the factors that undermine such attempts. This is a simplified list of factors that influence the gendered institution and implementation of rights. It is a complex interaction of social norms, gender biases and cultural contexts that determines how and when women can enjoy certain rights. Examining the gender content of these rights, it is obvious that each of them has differential implications for women and men. While neither women nor men are to be seen as homogeneous, given that gender discrimination is an indisputable fact, it is clear that these rights would be manifested differently for women and men, all other things being equal.

None of these rights should be seen in isolation. For example, the right to property in resettlement schemes is linked to the right to fair and just compensation. As we have seen, women's property rights are often eroded by large projects (Agarwal, 1996). Sometimes, where women are not granted property rights at all, large development projects exacerbate existing inequalities. Also property rights such as land and water rights are marked by sharp gender asymmetries in most parts of the world.

Development can enhance women's rights to property in the form of compensation, but institutional support may be required to maintain these. The erosion of existing rights is possible because of national laws or because of gender inequalities intrinsic to the community. Gender-sensitive principles would take this into consideration. Similarly, right to employment as compensation for loss of land should be equally applicable to women and men. Equal wages for equal work is yet another right that is theoretically agreed upon, but often overlooked. Women routinely get paid less for the same work.

The right to planning and use of resources is fundamental to gender equity. Participation at all levels is crucial for any meaningful implementation of this right. Here it is important to recognize that women are, in many contexts, historically excluded from public fora. Equally, women's articulation is often dependent on various interlinked factors like culture, exposure, experience and so on (Jackson and Pearson, 1998). If equity is to be maintained, it is important to provide women with the tools to negotiate with authorities and institutions within and outside the community to enable true participation. However, this cannot be done without political will.

The right to participation in planning processes and use of resources has to be seen in conjunction with the right to redress, and free and informed prior consent. Only if gender differences are acknowledged will there be any attempt to facilitate women's interaction and participation in the planning process. Thus, if women are burdened by domestic chores during the day, it is preferable to have meetings at a more convenient time. These are a few practical issues that impinge on women's participation and have to be taken into account. It must be remembered that women's participation in consultative processes could face some resistance from within the community. This is another issue that planners would have to address.

Equal participation needs to apply to beneficiary communities too. It can have implications for a gender-just distribution of the benefits. For example, employment opportunities need to extend equally to women and men. As is often the case, enhanced economic status implies greater access to resources. As women are often excluded from the market, if they have to benefit on an equal basis with men, it is important to dismantle the structural inequality that prevents them from doing so.

As is often the case, women's labour within the household and outside is often overlooked or devalued. Gender-sensitive indicators are indispensable if women's contributions to farm and non-farm activities are to be included. Equitable distribution of compensation includes the household as well as the farm. It also presumes the recognition of the various roles that women and men perform towards the sustenance of the household economy. Thus work would have to include household chores and labour expended on collection of water, fuel or fodder, to give just a few examples.

Institutions
The term 'institutions' usually refers to regularized social practices that may be formal or informal in nature. Often formal and informal institutions overlap and coexist, as with, for example, the coexistence of customary law with formal institutional arrangements. Women and men have different institutional positions. Institutions usually reflect prevailing gender and power relations. They may not necessarily address gender inequities embedded in the communities they govern. Not all institutions can be painted with the same brush. Informal institutions within communities can provide women with scope for negotiation, though this may not be generalized. The most basic institution at the community level is the household, which exhibits a

range of interests and biases, as already outlined. Within the household, allocation of resources, expenditure of labour and consumption patterns are all determined by gender. The context in which these are operationalized is specific to cultural and social norms.

In terms of planning and construction, informal institutions existing at the community level can be used to facilitate local participation. Other informal or semi-formal institutions are caste groups, kinship networks and other local mechanisms that oversee the arrangement and distribution of resources, or the dispensation of justice. Where informal institutions exclude women, it is necessary to facilitate change that is more gender-inclusive.

Both formal and informal institutions may display gender discrimination in their policies or composition. Legal regimes are often blatantly patriarchal in their assumptions about women's roles and identities. Law often designates for women a secondary, dependant status. Thus structural inequalities get further formalized through laws and legal instruments. Customary laws may also designate similar discriminatory locations for women. But some customary legal arrangements may contain fewer gender biases than formal legal law. For example, in some tribal societies in India, women and men have equal use rights over forest resources. By contrast, formal forest user groups initially tended to exclude women. Gender-sensitive assessment would seek to look at the imbalances in such institutions and move beyond them. As these institutions (both formal and informal) are important in decision-making processes, it is important to ensure that gender representation is even. The creation of new institutions as a result of development projects can either replicate or exacerbate existing gender inequalities or seek to move beyond them in the creation of greater spaces, whereby women and men can participate in equal measure.

As institutions play a key role in the conceptualizing and implementation of rights, gender will again be crucial. There are many kinds of inequalities that institutions need to be working on. Institutions, both informal and formal, can also be made to act upon social, cultural and gender inequalities. This is possible in the case of forward-looking visions. Such a process necessarily entails acting upon existing inequalities that are born of, and consolidated in, a historical sense. It also means dismantling the assumptions that create such inequalities in the first place, whereby historically disadvantaged communities and social groupings will be given priority over others in the decision-making process.

Thus institutions are important media through which equity considerations can be implemented. This requires a thorough and careful investigation of existing biases against different sets of people in the various stages of project planning and implementation.

Allocation, appropriation and consumption of resources

Development creates large-scale transformations in terms of existing resources and those that are made available to communities. This transformatory potential has clear implications for gender-sensitive impact assessment. Increased consumption of energy, enhanced food production and greater food security have many positive implications for large sections of urban and rural populations. However, the distribution of the resources generated by these benefits is predicated on existing social and gender relations. It is important to look at these imbalances. For those sections of a community that enjoy privileges at social, economic and political levels, the benefits will accrue as a natural corollary of their locations.

Inevitably, those sections or social groupings that do not enjoy the same privileges will get a minuscule share of the benefits, and at a higher price. Increased sources of water in urban settings may not translate into a direct benefit for the urban poor. Gender organization of communities is an added component in the intricate social matrix where these benefits accrue. It may only add to the domestic burden that women shoulder in a situation where resources are scarce to begin with. Thus the appropriation of the resources can reinforce inequity in absolute terms. Likewise, access to markets, and the benefits that follow from this, are dispersed along many different lines. As the market exhibits all the gender biases existing in the social context, it is not surprising that women are often excluded from it. This is not to say that the market always discriminates against women, but, as a means of increasing access to resources and consumption, the market is not always equitable.

Development often brings about a transformation of common property resources into private resources. These are then slated for consumption and appropriation by only a certain section of people. These resources include land, water, forests, common property resources, cultural identities, knowledge systems, economic resources like minor forest produce, social spaces, social support structures, formal and informal institutions, and cultural institutions.

Knowledge systems and skills that are lost in the process of displacement due to development projects often increase the vulnerability of women. While men are also affected, because most agencies and policies see men as the representatives of the community, women are pushed to the periphery in the process of negotiation. The intangible and unaccounted nature of women's contribution and participation in these knowledge systems requires gender-sensitive parameters for a realistic mapping.

All constituents of the entire range of communities affected and benefiting from development projects should have equal participation in decision-making processes. It is true that decision-making structures at all the various levels of the project planning process would be characterized by all the social and gender contradictions in the larger society. It is important, therefore, to set up mechanisms that would facilitate greater participation. The creation of such structures, backed up by institutional commitment, would in the long run initiate and sustain democratic and gender-sensitive practices in the allocation, appropriation and distribution of resources.

Recommendations

Compromising on gender justice and equality underscores the existing invisibility of gender and goes against international processes committed to enhancing and promoting gender equality. We list below a set of recommendations that could make development a more gender-friendly process and could balance the deleterious impacts of large-scale projects.

- There is a greater need for more gender-aware and gender-sensitive policies concerning the planning, implementation and monitoring of development projects.
- The notion of the 'project-affected-person' needs to be gender-inclusive. With respect to resettlement, this means that women and men should be co-beneficiaries of any compensation packages awarded to households. Single and widowed women should receive individual compensation.
- Developmental processes that infringe upon the human rights of any section of society are inimical to the long-term goals of progress. It is important to set up human rights monitoring institutions and ensure the protection of the human rights of the affected population.
- Women's networks and interest groups should be given priority in consultative processes involving the affected communities. If local male leaders resist the formation of women's groups, additional time and effort will have to be invested in dealing with on-the-ground gender biases and stereotypes. Extension workers should be gender-aware.
- Policy formulation should take into account the varied roles that women play in the domestic sphere and should be flexible enough to accommodate this in the consultation process.
- Commitment to gender justice will ensure that women do not have to bear a disproportionate cost in developmental processes. Thus there is a need for greater awareness of existing gender roles, relations and biases in the project areas. Existing inequalities in gendered access to, and control over, resources should be minimized. Projects should not exacerbate existing gender inequalities. Project appraisal should be sensitive to, and take account of, the gender division of labour in the

household and community. It should include gender impacts on social practices like shared labour and the consequences of fragmentation of kinship support systems.

- Gender mainstreaming is indispensable as a means of integrating gender into policy, planning and implementation. For this it is important to generate gender-specific indicators that take into account the varied locations of men and women at all levels of society.
- It is essential to generate detailed gender-specific data of affected communities in all project impact areas. Lack of information can nullify the most well-meaning intentions and policies.
- Gender equity should be an explicit concern in planning and executing development projects.
- Gender empowering goals should be built into policy. Women's land and water rights should be part of the discourse. Where existing national and international legal provisions militate against women's autonomy and control, they should be amended to rectify the damages caused to women.
- Project planners need to be sensitive to local understandings of equity. Often ignorance of customary law and local use understandings of access to, and control over, resources can undermine the existing rights that women or indigenous peoples have over resources, in particular common property resources.
- Cost–benefit analysis should be reconsidered as a tool in informing decisions concerning development projects. While such analyses might be useful in informing and stimulating debate, it is questionable whether they are useful in decision-making processes or as tools for negotiations. This is because they fail to capture the intangible social and cultural impacts. Consequently, cost–benefit analysis mirrors the interests of the powerful and masks the losses faced by constituencies that lack voice and political clout. Analyses should have a broader understanding of the multifaceted nature of losses incurred by project-affected communities. More participatory forms of planning involving all the actors in the project areas should be employed, where all have a say in determining and assessing the nature of the costs and benefits and their effects on their lives, livelihoods and environment.

Conclusion

Gender impact assessment calls into question the notion that all development projects are icons of progress. Instead, the goals of justice, equity, sustainability and fair economic growth need to be placed up-front. We have attempted to link gender and development projects at conceptual and empirical levels. One major concern is the ways in which benefits and costs are distributed across various social groups. We acknowledge that development projects can potentially lead to benefits for many women and men in project areas. However, the examples around displacement indicate that many projects have been problematic. This is because technology has largely been perceived as neutral and divorced from the sociocultural system. We have argued that all projects are embedded in, and interact with, social practices and relations. Thus, within a gender or power relations framework, we see that many projects are problematic.

Moreover, the planning, implementation, evaluation and monitoring of development projects have proceeded in a gender-blind way. Even when the benefits from projects have trickled down to project-affected families, in many cases it is men and male interests that have been both served and targeted. Prevailing gender biases in both policy and practice can lead to the exclusion of women from the benefits of development projects. This can be attributed to a number of factors. First, there is the exclusion of gender considerations in the planning and implementation. Technical issues have been given more importance than sociocultural and socioeconomic considerations. Second, it has been fallaciously assumed that all benefits are shared equally by a community or society, without analysing the relational aspects of projects and how these are linked with issues concerning a wider political economy. Third, development projects are not apolitical or gender-neutral interventions. They build on, or feed into, existing social and power relations. Unless these are addressed, the goals of equity and fair and just distribution of resources will not be addressed. Fourth, policy and planning are often ignorant of local organizational and institutional arrangements to govern natural resources and local notions of justice and equity. Thus, in some circumstances there might be an erosion of existing rights that women have over land and water which are enshrined in customary arrangements.

Finally, cost–benefit analyses have failed to take intangibles into account. As women's labour and roles in social organization are often invisible, existing measures of costs and benefits tend to reflect gender biases. They also lack social components as economic interests of powerful stakeholders are often prioritized over the non-economic interests of the less powerful. It is unlikely that the interests of the poor or landless will be favoured when compared with the interests of a powerful constituency. Participation of women has been negligible.

With respect to the costs of development projects, women have clearly been very disadvantaged. Marginalized entities and groups like women and indigenous peoples have been adversely impacted in many ways. These include the following:

- being declined access to, and control over, resources such as land, water and the commons. Women's existing rights to resources in forest-based economies are often ignored by planners;
- an overemphasis on economic yardsticks such as cash compensation and land, and a neglect of vital life-sustaining issues such as water, fuel-wood and food. This increases women's chores and has implications for the health and sense of wellbeing of the entire family;
- changing gender relations have not always been favourable for women. The market economy and its gender biases can sometimes work against women's interests. For example, when a community is forced to depend on wage labour at resettlement sites, women are at a disadvantage. Changed social environments at project sites have often led to increased domestic tensions;
- fragmentation of community structures leads to social isolation for displaced communities, often increasing the vulnerability of women to internal and external pressures;
- policy often fails to see women as autonomous entities. It has disregarded underlying social and cultural processes that shape women's lives in affected communities.

It will take considerable political will and a reorientation of policy and practice to bring about changes that will enable infrastructure projects to live up to the promises of development and growth. Conscious strategies that centre on the twin goals of equity and gender-just distribution could change the picture somewhat. However, given the disparities and resource constraints that face affected communities, and women in particular, only careful and judicious planning will ensure fair representations of marginalized communities. Pursuing this strategy might also mean taking more seriously the need to investigate more gender-just and equitable ways and alternatives to harness water and power.

The past few decades have witnessed an impressive body of work by academics, activists and non-governmental organizations (NGOs) arguing for the need to recognize the social and economic fallibility of large-scale development projects. This evidence needs to be absorbed in policy, programme and implementation if the negative effects of such projects are to be mitigated. There is a need to overhaul the old assumptions concerning prosperity and growth, and notions concerning the good of all. These issues cannot be overlooked simply because more and more people the world over have been asserting their right to some of the benefits proposed by such developmental processes. Falling short of a just and equitable spread of benefits does not strengthen the case for large-scale projects. When costs are disproportionately borne by certain sections, large-scale projects can come to mean a greater infringement of people's rights to basic and life-sustaining resources.

Acknowledgments

This chapter is based on a paper commissioned by the World Commission on Dams.

References

Agarwal, B. 1996. *A Field of One's Own: Gender and Land Rights in South Asia*, Cambridge: Cambridge University Press.

Bhatia, B. 1997. 'Forced evictions in the Narmada Valley', in J. Dreze, M. Samson and S. Singh (eds), *The Dam and the Nation*, Delhi: Oxford University Press, 267–321.

Boserup, E. 1970. *Women's Role in Economic Development*, New York: St Martin's Press.

Centre for Social Studies 1997. 'Resettlement and rehabilitation in Gujarat', in J. Dreze, M. Samson and S. Singh (eds), *The Dam and the Nation*, Delhi: Oxford University Press, 215–35.

Cernea, M. 1999. 'Why economic analysis is essential to resettlement. A sociologist's view', in M. Cernea (ed.), *The Economics of Involuntary Resettlement*, Washington, DC: World Bank, 5–49.

Colson, E. 1999. 'Engendering those uprooted by development', in D. Indra (ed.), *Engendering Forced Migration*, Oxford: Refugee Studies Programme, 23–39.

Dreze, J., Samson, M. and Singh, S. (eds) 1997. *The Dam and the Nation*, Delhi: Oxford University Press.

Elson, D. 1998. 'Talking to the boys: gender and economic growth models', in C. Jackson and R. Pearson (eds), *Feminist Visions of Development*, London: Routledge, 189–214.

Hakim, R. 1997. 'Resettlement and Rehabilitation in the context of "Vasava" culture', in J. Dreze, M. Samson and S. Singh (eds), *The Dam and the Nation*, Delhi: Oxford University Press, 136–67.

Indra, D. 1999. 'Not a room of one's own', in D. Indra (ed.), *Engendering Forced Migration*, Oxford: Refuge Studies Programme, 1–21.

Jackson, C. and Pearson, R. (eds) 1998. *Feminist Visions of Development: Gender Analysis and Policy*, London: Routledge.

Kabeer, N. 1994. *Reversed Realities: Gender Hierarchies in Development Thought*, London: Verso.

Mehta, L. 2000. 'Women Facing Submergence: Displacement and Resistance in the Narmada', in V. Damadoran and M. Unnithan (eds), *Postcolonial India: History, Politics and Culture*, New Delhi: Manohar, 267–87.

Morse, B. and Berger, T.R. 1992. *Sardar Sarovar: Report of the Independent Review*, Ottawa: Resource Futures International Inc.

Parasuraman, S. 1993. 'Impact of Displacement by Development Projects on Women in India' (Working Paper Series no. 159), Institute of Social Studies, The Hague.

Parasuraman, S. 1997. 'The anti-dam movement and rehabilitation policy', in J. Dreze, M. Samson and S. Singh (eds), *The Dam and the Nation*, Delhi: Oxford University Press, 26–65.

Sen, A. 1990. 'Gender and cooperative conflicts', in I. Tinker (ed.), *Persistent Inequalities*, Oxford: Oxford University Press, 123–49.

Srinivasan, B. 1997. *In Defence of the Future*, Mumbai: Vikas Adhyayan Kendra.

Srinivasan, B. 1999. *Trespassers will be Prosecuted*, Mumbai: Vikas Adhyayan Kendra.

Tata Institute of Social Sciences 1997. 'Experiences with resettlement and rehabilitation in Maharashtra', in J. Dreze, M. Samson and S. Singh (eds), *The Dam and the Nation*, Delhi: Oxford University Press, 184–214.

Thukral, E. 1992. *Big Dams, Displaced Peoples: Rivers of Sorrow, Rivers of Joy*, Delhi: Sage.

Thukral, E. 1996. 'Development, displacement and rehabilitation: Locating gender', *Economic and Political Weekly*, 31(24): 1500–1503.

World Bank 2001. *Engendering Development: Through Gender Equality in Rights, Resources and Voice*, New York: Oxford University Press.

12 Socioeconomic modelling for estimating intergenerational impacts
Gijs Dekkers

Introduction
The use of empirical models to evaluate potential economic, fiscal or social policy is widely accepted. The best known models of this type are macro-economic models, which simulate the effect of intended policy measures (including changes to existing policy) or possible exogenous changes (such as a change in the price of oil) on aggregated variables such as gross domestic product (GDP), inflation, the budget deficit, external debt, tax benefits or social security payments. The effects of potential policy changes are expressed in terms of how they change the aggregate variables over time. For example, a decision by the Minister for Social Affairs to increase the minimum pension benefit, with the intention of decreasing poverty among retirees, will result in an increase in pension expenditure by government.

Macroeconomic models are also often used in the field of social policy. For example, government agencies in almost every developed country have models that evaluate the effects of demographic changes (notably aging), in combination with social and fiscal policy, on the financial viability of the social security scheme and specifically the pension scheme. This long-term financial viability of a scheme is often referred to as its 'sustainability' (that is, financial sustainability) and is defined in terms of the (dis)equilibrium of future costs and revenues. If the financial sustainability of a scheme was considered, the cost-increasing effect of linking the average pension benefit to wages – or the cost-decreasing effect of setting a maximum pension benefit – would be made obvious.

A macroeconomic figure, such as the total pension benefit paid in a year, however, is a compound rather than a singular entity. It is, by definition, the aggregate of a large number of individual figures, such as the individual pension benefits paid to individual retirees. Every macroeconomic figure, therefore, includes many figures from individuals or households; and the change in a macroeconomic variable as a result of a certain policy measure is therefore, by definition, the result of changes in a related variable at the individual level. These individual figures can be arranged in ascending or descending order and transformed into the distribution of this variable. A certain policy measure affects the macroeconomic variable if the sum of the new individual values changes. By contrast, this measure can have a distributional effect if the values of individual variables change *relative to each other*. Almost every policy change has a macroeconomic effect and also a distributional effect.

Macroeconomic models tend not to consider that policy measures have not only an effect at the aggregate level, but also a distributional effect. Therefore, questions like 'Who gains and loses from a particular policy measure?' or 'What will be the effect of a particular policy on income inequality or poverty?' cannot be answered using these models, even though these questions are very important in the evaluation of (potential) social policy measures. For example, a reduction in (future) pension benefits may be desirable to increase the financial sustainability of the public pension system. However, it is unlikely to be desirable in welfare terms, since it will result in a deterioration of the financial position of the elderly relative to the young, potentially resulting in poverty amongst the elderly and an increasing income inequality within society. Thus the evaluation of a policy measure needs to consider whether or not it is 'just', whether or not it increases welfare, and not only in financial terms. Moreover, the impact of policy measures can no longer be expressed solely in terms of time series. It requires a specification of the effects of potential policy measures on different groups within the population in a comparative way. In other words, we need to analyse the redistributive effects of a policy measure at a particular point in time (income inequality and poverty) and over time (differences between generations).

This chapter begins by extending financial sustainability to include poverty and income inequality. Next, three recent techniques of socioeconomic modelling will be presented and an application of each will be discussed. Lastly, conclusions will be drawn.

Financial sustainability and social considerations
Financial sustainability is based upon the (in)equality of the perceived costs and benefits of a certain policy measure. However, this is an insufficient means by which to evaluate policy, and therefore additional criteria need to be considered. The goal of these additional criteria is to take the distributional effects of policy measures into account: for example, poverty reduction and equity. A situation with lower poverty is considered more desirable than one with higher poverty. Equity is conceived of as intragenerational equity and intergenerational equity. In terms of intragenerational equity, more egalitarian distributions are preferred to less egalitarian ones. Intragenerational equity and poverty reduction can be conceived as the 'inequality dimension of sustainability'. Intergenerational equity will be discussed later.

There is a need for models that show the redistributive effects of potential social and fiscal policy measures. As a result, this kind of modelling is becoming increasingly popular, although relatively new to the field of economic modelling. If social impact assessment (SIA) is defined as 'the process of identifying the future consequences of a current or proposed action for individuals . . . and society as a whole' (Becker, 1997: 123), it is clear that these models are part of SIA.

Two techniques of empirical economic modelling that belong to SIA are microsimulation (MSM) and Generational Accounting (GA). In this chapter, these techniques will be presented, emphasizing not so much their methodological pros and cons, but rather their links with the dimensions of sustainability as identified above.

It is necessary to reflect on the concept of generation. First, generation can be interpreted longitudinally as well as laterally (WRR, 1999). Laterally, age or stage of life is the discerning factor. Thus, at a certain moment in time, 'youth', 'young adults', 'the elderly' and so on are groupings that form different lateral generations. When interpreted longitudinally, the emphasis is not age, but the year or period in which one is born. In this sense, individuals do not shift from one generation to another as they get older, but remain in the same generation throughout their life. In this longitudinal definition, two important definitions of generation are possible. In numerous econometric models, generation is defined as one or more contiguous cohorts (usually five). This is the definition of generation which will most often be used in this chapter. However, another discourse of generation, stemming from generational theory (Becker, 1995; Inglehart, 1977), considers that generations are formed by individuals whose life courses are marked by common major events (such as wars, recessions or cultural shifts) during their formative period. In this chapter, either the lateral understanding of generation is used, or the former understanding relating to longitudinal understanding.

Microsimulation

Microsimulation models (MSMs) differ from other types of models used in empirical economics in that they take groups of individuals as the starting point, rather than one or more countries or industries as is the case with macroeconomic or inter-industry models. Reflecting on Figure 12.1, suppose we have a cross-sectional dataset of the population today (time t). This dataset can be used, for example, to calculate income inequality or poverty, or to analyse who are net recipients or contributors to the social security scheme. A typical question is how this representative dataset will change in the future (that is, for $t + 1$, $t + 2$ and so on).

Two main groups of MSMs can be distinguished. First, there are static

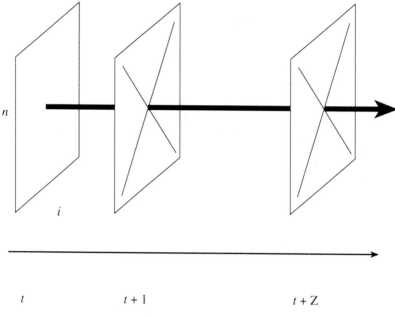

Source: Dekkers (2000c).

Figure 12.1   The basis of microsimulation

microsimulation models. Most cross-sectional datasets contain a weighting variable which gives the individual more or less importance (that is, a greater or smaller weight) in the sample in order to make the sample more representative for the population at large, thereby, for example, to control for the effect of selective non-response or a biased sample. The technique of static microsimulation involves adjusting these individual weights to let the dataset in the base year (time t) meet descriptions of the future population, which are exogenous from the point of view of the model. Suppose, for example, that a 1992 dataset consists of a certain percentage of female individuals aged between 15 and 19, and that we know from demographic projections that this proportion will decrease by 8.5 per cent between 1992 and 2020. The '2020 proportion' of women can be formed by multiplying the weighted variable of the women in this age group by 0.915 (that is, 1.0 minus 0.085). Note that the weighting factors of other categories must be adjusted upwards to neutralize the effect of this decreasing proportion of young women on the weighted size of the dataset as a whole.

   A problem with static microsimulation is that the range of applications is not very broad. In fact, reweighting is often limited to capturing demographic changes. So these classic, static microsimulation models assume that the macroeconomic world is 'frozen'. To overcome this, reweighting is accompanied by a second technique, called 'uprating'. Uprating is a technique 'where attempts are made to adjust monetary variables to account for movements since the time of the survey or future anticipated movements' (Harding, 1993: 19). Static MSMs are routinely used in industrialized countries, such as in Australia and New Zealand, North America and most European countries.

The second category is dynamic MSM. Taking a representative cross-sectional dataset at the current time, individuals face certain probabilities of a change in each of their n attributes (variables). In the modelling process, this is simulated by chance. Consider an individual of a particular age. Given this age, there is a known risk of mortality denoted by d. For the test case individual, a random number is selected. If the resulting number is below the mortality risk d (which is a function of other variables) then the individual is considered to be dead in the next period, and their partner widowed. If not, the individual remains alive, and their age is incremented. In a similar fashion, our living individual faces a known probability of becoming married, of having a child, of finding or losing a job, and so forth. The number of variables that can be modelled this way depends entirely on the availability of computer power and how much information on transition probabilities or risks is available.

Even though both static and dynamic models are microsimulation models, they are very different (Caldwell, 1996). Static MSMs are technically simple (relative to dynamic models) and therefore require less time to develop, and less maintenance. Moreover, by using the simulated weights, other researchers can use the results of a static model in other empirical research without requiring technical knowledge about the model itself. By contrast, dynamic MSMs are much more flexible. The most important advantage of dynamic microsimulation, however, is that it is possible to sum individual variables over time. For example, the lifetime income of an individual can be calculated by summing past annual values of income (adjusted to today's dollars) over the entire lifetime of the individual. As a result, the effect of socioeconomic policy measures can be expressed in terms of lifetime income instead of annual income of various groups and generations of individuals. In static MSMs, this is not possible or meaningful, since the individual variables do not change, only their weights do. The advantage of using lifetime income is that annual income figures are biased, in that the redistributive effect of a certain measure is generally overestimated when expressed in terms of annual income (Nelissen, 1994, 1998; Harding, 1993). Moreover, by analysing the impact of a certain social security scheme on lifetime income of various subsequent generations, intergenerational redistribution of income via that scheme is highlighted. This will become clear below, when examples of research using static or dynamic MSM will be discussed, taking pensions in the context of demographic aging as an example. More details are available elsewhere (see Dekkers 2000a, 2000b, 2000c).

Static microsimulation

Most developed countries are in a period of demographic aging. This causes concern about the financial sustainability of public pension systems, because most are based on a system where the benefits paid out to retirees today are financed by the current contributions of the active population. The pension benefit that a retiree receives is based, among other things, on the wages earned in the past. However, there may be a lower and upper limit to the pension benefit. If so, this introduces solidarity between participants, since high-earners will receive a lower pension (relative to their wage) whereas very low earners will receive a relatively higher pension benefit.

Because aging of the population means that the proportion of elderly increases, the cost of such a pension scheme could increase drastically. It is for this reason that the Federal Planning Bureau of Belgium developed a model, PENSION (Festjens, 1997), in order to analyse the future development of the cost of the public pension system in Belgium. In general terms, its main conclusion was that the system would remain financially sustainable. However, this conclusion was based on certain assumptions. First, it was assumed that the pension benefit would increase by 1.0 per cent (or 1.25 per cent in another scenario) per year in real terms (that is, above the annual inflation rate), whereas real wages would increase by 2.25 per cent per year. It also presumed that the maximum pension benefit (i.e. the 'ceiling') would also increase by 1.0 per cent per year.

The effect of these assumptions on financial sustainability was well considered by PENSION, so it is not the conclusions that should be criticized. However, the effect of the assumptions on the inequality dimension of sustainability remains unclear. What is the effect of these assumptions on the income of (lateral) generations, relative to each other? If pension benefits are allowed to lag behind wage increases, the scheme becomes less expensive, since this lag is equivalent to a decrease of the pension benefit (in relative terms). If there is a benefit ceiling which lags behind wages, the costs of the pension scheme decreases as well, since the pension benefits of the richest participants are limited. Moreover, the effect of this ceiling becomes stronger over time, since ceiling increases are less than wages growth. But what would be the effect of these assumptions on the levels of poverty among the elderly and income inequality in general? Or, put differently, what would happen if pension benefits only increased at the same rate as inflation and/or if there was no pension ceiling?

The model of the Federal Planning Bureau could not answer these questions because it simulates time series (for various groups within society). It is for this reason that the static microsimulation model, STATION, was developed. Four variants were simulated, controlling for the effect of indexing the pension benefit on wages, and the existence of the lagging of the pension ceiling (see Table 12.1). Across the four variants, pension benefits are either not indexed, or partially indexed to wages. In addition, a ceiling on pension growth is either fixed or is partially indexed. Other combinations were possible, but would have violated the conclusion of the Federal Planning Bureau with regard to the financial sustainability of the pension scheme. The significant question then becomes: which of these four simulation variants leads to the most optimal solution, minimizing both poverty among elderly and income inequality in general?

Table 12.1   Simulation variants

Variant	Wage growth 2.25%	Indexing pension benefit to wages	Existence of a partially indexed pension ceiling (1%)
Base variant	yes	no	no
Second variant	yes	partially (1%)	no
Third variant	yes	no	yes
Fourth variant	yes	partially (1%)	yes

To answer this question, we consider poverty among households where the head belongs to one of four age categories (see Figure 12.2). Here, the pension benefits of the retirees are indexed only to the inflation rate. The working generations do not share welfare increases (wage growth minus inflation) with the retired generations. This results in a strong increase in poverty among the elderly from the current 10 per cent to about 25 per cent in 2025. In the case of this base variant, the increase in poverty among the elderly up to 2010 is caused by the divergence of the pension benefits from the increasing wages. Moreover, because a large number of the elderly have an income slightly above the poverty line, even a small divergence between pensions and incomes has a strong increasing effect on poverty. After 2010, the diverging effect is neutralized by the increase in pension contributions that non-retired generations have to pay as a result of aging. As a consequence, the incomes of the retired and non-retired generations converge, and this causes the (relative) poverty of the retired generations to decrease after 2010.

Figure 12.3 shows the effect of the four simulation variants on poverty among households where the head is retired. It is likely that the implementation of a partially linked pension ceiling (a cap or maximum benefit) will

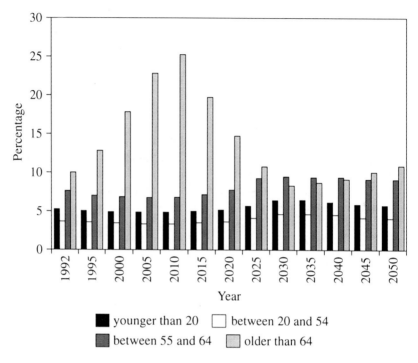

Figure 12.2   Development of poverty in the base variant: no ceiling and no indexation

not have a strong effect on poverty. This is confirmed by comparing the poverty rates in the base variant with the third variant, and by comparing the second variant with the fourth variant in Figure 12.3. In contrast to the effect of a ceiling, even partially indexing the pension benefit of the currently retired to wages results in a very strong decrease in poverty among the elderly. Thus, in terms of the inequality dimension of sustainability, partially indexing pension benefits to wages is highly desirable.

The effect of the two potential policy measures on the inequality of income can be represented by the Theil coefficient, which ranges from zero (in the case of complete income equality) to the log of the sample size (see Cowell, 1995). Figure 12.4 shows the effect of the potential policy measures on overall income inequality. In all cases, income inequality increases over time. The reason for this is that income inequality among retired households is higher than income inequality among non-retired households. As national demographic aging means that the proportion of non-retired households decreases relative to retired households, overall income inequal-

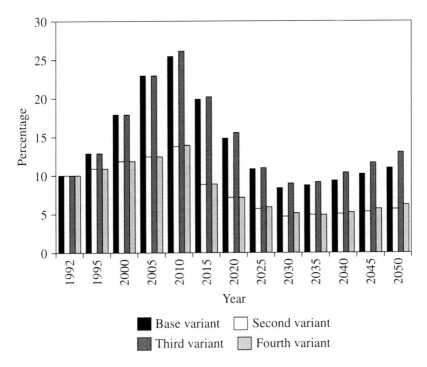

*Figure 12.3   Development of poverty among retired households: effect of
the ceiling and indexation*

ity increases. It can be seen that both policy measures result in a decrease in
income inequality. There are several reasons for this. First, if the pension
benefits of those already retired are not indexed to wages, as in the case of
the base variant, pensions lag behind wages. If pension benefits are partially
indexed, this lagging is partially countered, thereby decreasing income
inequality. If a pension ceiling is implemented and not fully indexed, then
the highest pension benefit grows more slowly than other pension benefits,
consequently income inequality amongst beneficiaries decreases, but overall
income inequality increases (in the total population). The conclusion from
the inequality dimension of sustainability is that the combination of both
policy measures is preferred.

Dynamic microsimulation
In order to discuss an application of dynamic microsimulation, it is necessary to (re)define some important notions. First, the word 'generation',
which was interpreted laterally when dealing with static microsimulation

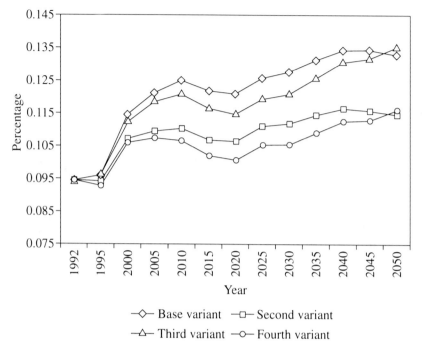

Figure 12.4   Development of income inequality in the population: effect of the ceiling and indexation

models, will now be interpreted longitudinally. The generational dimension of sustainability also needs to be defined. The situation becomes more complex as the effect of a certain measure on the generational dimension of sustainability can be further divided into the effect on intergenerational risk sharing and the effect on the implicit intergenerational contract.

Consider a country with a pension system financed from current contributors (usually called Pay-As-You-Go, or PAYG), as is the case for most European countries. Such a pension scheme increases intergenerational risk sharing, and therefore is optimal for risk-averse individuals (Ponds, 1995), since the retirees know that sudden and unexpected shocks (such as inflation), which might jeopardize their pension incomes, will be covered by the generations which are not yet retired. From this point of view, such a pension scheme improves sustainability. However, the current contributors to the pension system will only contribute if they believe that they will receive a pension benefit when they retire. In other words, every longitudinal generation will only support the previous generations if it is confident that the pension scheme will be supported by future generations as well.

This means that every generation arguably has a moral obligation not to put the PAYG-financed pension system in jeopardy, for example, by letting the cost burden on the contributing generation increase excessively at a particular point in time. This 'generational dimension of sustainability' is similar to the Brundtland concept of development that meets the needs of the present without compromising the ability of future generations to meet their own needs. Two types of models can deal with this kind of analysis: dynamic microsimulation and generational accounting (which is discussed in the next section).

Dynamic microsimulation models are used for questions related to the generational dimension of sustainability (see Dekkers *et al.*, 1995). Consider several generations in an aging population. In the Netherlands, the case that will be discussed here, demographic aging is caused by one generation (the babyboom generation) being much larger than surrounding generations. The public pension system provides every retiree of this large generation with a base entitlement, which is financed through PAYG. The babyboom generation paid for pension benefits of the preceding smaller generations, but expects other, much smaller, generations to pay for their pension benefits. So, for benefits and contributions being measured over the entire lifetime of generations, the summed benefits paid to the babyboom generation as a whole exceed the contributions made by that generation, whereas the smaller generations which follow have the opposite experience. This puts tension on the implicit intergenerational contract and could therefore decrease sustainability.

The hypothesis is, therefore, that, even though a PAYG-financed pension scheme can be optimal for risk-averse generations, it also incorporates a risk, in that a generation can jeopardize the entire system by transferring large costs to future generations to pay. But is this situation actually the case in the Netherlands? Are there generations that gain from the pension scheme, in terms of lifetime income, whereas other generations lose? This is where dynamic microsimulation models are useful, since they are designed to simulate lifetime income, the effect of various social and fiscal measures on income and whether or not some generations cover the costs generated by other generations.

In an earlier study, Dekkers *et al.* (1995) simulated the Dutch pension system in order to model the patterns described. Table 12.2 shows the lifetime income adjusted to 1992 levels of four subsequent generations. The second row of data provides the average net benefit of the pension scheme: that is, lifetime benefit received, less contributions made to the pension scheme. The research showed that the older cohorts profit from the public pension scheme, while the younger cohorts make a loss. For the 1930 cohort, the value of the pension scheme is equal to 6.8 per cent of their

Table 12.2   Effect of lagging the pension benefit (thousands of guilders)

Cohort	1930	1940	1950	1960
Wages	2119	2494	2804	2908
Net benefit	144	74	−11	−72
Benefit as a % of wages	6.8	3.0	−0.4	−2.5

Source: Dekkers *et al.* (1995).

lifetime income, while, for the 1940 cohort, the profit is 3.0 per cent of income. The younger two cohorts face losses of 0.4 per cent and 2.5 per cent, respectively. Whether or not this makes the Dutch pension system unsustainable is unclear, but it certainly imposes a risk since the young generations might not want to cover for the pension benefit of the large generation preceding them.

Generational accounting
The generational dimension of sustainability was shown to be related to the implicit intergenerational contract using the pension system as an example. Here, the same issue will be approached more broadly by considering, not just the pension schemes, but all the social and fiscal relations between the population of a country and its government. The social and fiscal system of a country is defined as being less sustainable if current generations transfer costs (or responsibility for mitigation/restoration) to future generations.

In most traditional macroeconomic models, the effect of macroeconomic (fiscal) policy on the budget deficit, and therefore on the public debt, is used to get an idea of whether or not the government is shifting the costs of planned or implemented fiscal policy from the present to the future (Rosevaere *et al.*, 1996). There are various reasons why, in practice, the budget deficit is not very useful for this kind of analysis. One will be discussed. A budget deficit is a cash-flow indicator which ignores any implicit commitments a government has accepted (Dellis and Lüth, 1999). For example, whether or not future pension income will be financed by future generations through a public pension system (as in the case of the pension schemes in most West European countries) or whether it is mostly financed by present private savings (as in the case of the Capital Funding pension schemes in the USA, the UK and Australia), does not affect the budget deficit at the present time. Nevertheless, it is clear that countries with an unfunded pension system have an implicit public debt, since they have transferred pension costs to future generations to bear.

Generational Accounting (GA) was popularized by Kotlikoff (1992).

'Generational accounts indicate, in present value, what the typical member of each generation can expect to pay, now and in the future, in net taxes (taxes paid net of transfer payments received). Generational accounting indicates not only what existing generations will pay, but also what future generations must pay, given current policy and the government's intertemporal budget constraint' (Auerbach *et al.*, 1994: 75). This last notion means that all implicitly and explicitly promised expenditures of the government, as well as the current debt, must be serviced through payment by existing and future generations. Given the payments of the existing generations to the government, the higher these costs are, the more unsustainable the situation of a country.

The relationship between GA and dynamic MSM has been discussed by Dekkers (2000d). GA sums all future social security benefits, subtracting future social security and tax payments for the generations currently living. These figures are aggregated over all generations living today. If the result is positive, it means that the currently living generations (will) receive more from the government than they (will) contribute. So this is the amount of money (minus current net wealth of the government) which has to be paid for by all future generations. These future generations, therefore, not only have to cover their own social security benefits and other government expenditures, but also costs which the generations before them incurred. Stated differently, the difference between current and future generations is that the former are not limited by the intertemporal budget constraint of the government, unlike future generations. So current generations are free to determine how much of the costs of current and past social and fiscal policy are shifted to the future generations, and these future generations are obliged to pay the bill.

A way in which this can be visualized is by comparing the net lifetime benefit of the youngest generation currently alive (and which is the last generation not subject to the intertemporal budget constraint) with the net lifetime contribution that future generations will face. This is illustrated by the 'absolute generational imbalance' (that is, the sum of the GAs of the future generations minus the GA of the current newborn generations) (see Table 12.3). The table shows, for a range of countries, the difference in generational accounts between the current generation and a future generation. The number represents the cost that is being transferred to future generations. For example, apart from having to finance their own benefits, future generations in the USA will have to pay an extra bill of $45 300 (in adjusted terms) per individual, to cover the unpaid benefits of the current newborn generation.

The conclusion to be drawn from Table 12.3 is clear and is the same for virtually every study on GA – there are intergenerational imbalances. In

Table 12.3   Absolute generational difference for various countries

Country	Imbalance US$000s	Country	Imbalance US$000s
Japan	246.4	Portugal	29.7
Germany	151.7	Australia	24.0
Italy	145.1	Brazil	11.9
The Netherlands	87.6	Argentina	10.4
France	79.2	Canada	2.7
Norway	55.9	New Zealand	−2.0
Belgium	46.3	Thailand	−7.4
USA	45.3	Sweden	−38.0
Denmark	44.0		

Source: Kotlikoff and Leibfritz (1998).

most countries, current generations pass on an important proportion of the costs of their benefit schemes to future generations. The situation is especially gloomy in Japan, Germany and Italy. Canada, however, is more or less in generational balance, while New Zealand, Sweden and Thailand are favouring future generations. 'Their policies, if maintained, would leave future generations facing lower lifetime net tax rates than current newborns. The main reason is that in these countries the ageing of populations is less rapid and also their governments are currently following a strict course of fiscal consolidation' (Kotlikoff and Leibfritz, 1998: 10). In the case of Thailand, part of the reason is that there is no pension scheme, so the implicit debt such a scheme creates is avoided. GA therefore shows us to what extent current social and fiscal policy is 'generational-unsustainable'. Kotlikoff and Leibfritz (1998) have modelled the effect of the two main determinants of intergenerational imbalances, namely demographic aging and public debt. Their conclusion was that, in general, the effect of public debt on generational imbalance is smaller than controlling for demographic change.

Conclusion

Important changes in the evaluation of socioeconomic policy have occurred. It has gradually been acknowledged that such policy should not be evaluated solely on macroeconomic results, but that this evaluation should also take distributional effects into account. In this chapter, the concept of sustainability in socioeconomic modelling was extended from its narrow understanding of financial sustainability to include consideration of poverty and equity. Following a brief introduction to MSM, a distinction between static and dynamic MSM was made. It was argued that the choice between these models should be based, among other things, on the kind of redistribution one wants to make visible. Static MSMs are designed for the simulation of redistributive patterns between individuals at a certain point in time. In this, dynamic and static MSMs are similar, but also allow for the modelling of redistribution of income between longitudinal generations via PAYG-financed pension systems. Moreover, they simulate the redistribution of lifetime income of generations.

Generational accounting models the development of financial relations between the population, grouped in longitudinal generations, and the government, over time. Using GA, the financial burden that current generations impose on future generations can be estimated. Most developed countries are in a more or less unsustainable situation.

The main advantage of these socioeconomic models is that they allow policy makers to take the redistributive consequences of social and fiscal policy into account. It becomes possible to compare the welfare effects of policy alternatives by considering the effects of these measures on (lifetime or annual) income inequality, poverty and the intergenerational redistribution of income. This allows policy makers to have access to more and better information which – one might hope – should help in making better policy decisions.

REFERENCES

Auerbach, A., Gokhale, J. and Kotlikoff, L. 1994. 'Generational accounting: a meaningful way to evaluate fiscal policy', *Journal of Economic Perspectives*, 8(1): 73–94.

Becker, H. 1997. *Social Impact Assessment*, London: Routledge.

Becker, H.A. 1995. 'Demographic impact assessment', in F. Vanclay and D.A. Bronstein (eds), *Environmental and Social Impact Assessment*, Chichester: Wiley, 141–52.

Caldwell, S. 1996. 'Health, wealth, pensions and life paths: the CORSIM dynamic microsimulation model', in A. Harding (ed.), *Microsimulation and Public Policy*, Amsterdam: North-Holland, 504–22.

Cowell, F. 1995. *Measuring Inequality* (2nd edn), London: Prentice Hall.

Dekkers, G. 2000a. 'De toekomstige welvaart van de gepensioneerden in België: een toepassing van het statische microsimulatiemodel STATION', in P. Pestieau *et al.* (eds), *De Toekomst van onze Pensioenen*, Leuven: Garant, 33–53.

Dekkers, G. 2000b. 'L'évolution du pouvoir d'achat des retraités: Une application du modèle de microsimulation statique STATION', in P. Pestieau *et al.* (eds), *Réflexions sur l'avenir de nos retraités*, Leuven: Garant, 37–58.

Dekkers, G., 2000c. 'Intergenerational Redistribution of Income through Capital Funding Pension Schemes: simulating the Dutch civil servants' pension fund ABP', PhD thesis, Tilburg University.

Dekkers, G. 2000d. 'Het Effect van het Overheidsbeleid op het Inkomen van Generaties: Generational Accounting versus Microsimulatie', *Economisch en Sociaal Tijdschrift*, 54(3): 359–80.

Dekkers, G., Nelissen, J. and Verbon, H. 1995. 'Intergenerational Equity and Pension Reform: the case of the Netherlands', *Public Finance*, 50(2): 224–45.

Dellis, A. and Lüth, E. 1999. 'Belgium: can fiscal policy cope with debt and ageing?', in European Commission Directorate-General for Economic and Financial Affairs (ed.),

Generational Accounting in Europe (European Economy Number 6), Brussels: European Commission Directorate-General for Economic and Financial Affairs, 29–41.

Festjens, M.J. 1997. 'De Pensioenhervorming', Federaal Planbureau Planning Paper 82.

Harding, A. 1993. *Lifetime Income Distribution and Redistribution* (Contributions to Economic Analysis 221), Amsterdam: North-Holland.

Inglehart, R. 1977. *The Silent Revolution, Changing Values and Political Styles Among Western Publics*, Princeton: Princeton University Press.

Kotlikoff, L. 1992. *Generational Accounting: knowing who pays, and when, for what we spend*, New York: Free Press.

Kotlikoff, L. and Leibfritz, W. 1998. 'An International Comparison of Generational Accounts', NBER-working paper 6447, National Bureau of Economic Research, Cambridge, MA.

Nelissen, J. 1994. *Income Redistribution and Social Security*, New York: Chapman and Hall.

Nelissen, J. 1998. 'Annual versus Lifetime Income Redistribution by Social Security', *Journal of Public Economics*, 68(2): 223–49.

Ponds, E. 1995. 'Supplementary Pensions, Intergenerational Risk-Sharing and Welfare', dissertation, Tilburg University.

Rosevaere, D., Leibfritz, W., Fore, D. and Wurzel, E. 1996. 'Ageing Populations, Pension Systems and Government Budgets: Simulations for 20 OECD Countries' (OECD-Economics Department Working Papers no. 168), Organisation for Economic Cooperation and Development, Paris.

Wetenschappelijke Raad voor het Regeringsbeleid (WRR) 1999. *Generatiebewust Beleid* (Rapporten aan de Regering 55), The Hague: Sdu Uitgevers.

13 Using geographic information systems for cultural impact assessment

Luciano Minerbi, Davianna Pomaika'i McGregor and Jon Kei Matsuoka

Introduction

Geographic information systems (GIS) are technologies encompassing telecommunication, information processing and spatial imaging (Pickles, 1995). Potentially this technology can benefit indigenous and rural communities by facilitating access to existing data and by generating new data which can be used for social impact assessments (SIAs). In contrast, there is a discussion about whether GIS increases the information monopoly of those already in power. As with most innovations, especially in the field of information and social accounting, both potentials may occur. With GIS being rapidly adopted throughout the world, a movement to increase community participation in planning can democratize the use of GIS and make it relevant to SIA.

There are a number of applications of GIS within SIA. Conventional geo-coded data can be layered over population data to study interdependence, proximity, ranges and access to resources. The data can also be associated with social indicators for a given community. GIS mapping can also be linked to SIA data in the study of changes over time. The cumulative impact on indigenous people, and the resources they need for their livelihoods, can be shown by overlaying maps depicting resources at different points in time. For this purpose, maps showing population, land ownership, land use, carrying capacity and vegetative cover can be generated by participatory methods such as resource mapping, transect walks and calendars of seasonal activity patterns, and by collecting local histories (Harris and Weiner, 1998).

There have been efforts to incorporate local knowledge into GIS mapping for public policy and land reform decisions. GIS has been used to delineate indigenous territories, assess development impacts on resource uses and codify indigenous rights and traditional practices (Sieber, 2000; Kyem, 2001; Harris and Weiner, 1998). Remapping an area from an indigenous perspective provides the basis for improved assessment. For example, the traditional hunting and fishing sites of indigenous peoples can be mapped with

GIS and overlaid on maps showing the location of contaminant sources. Such an overlay can reveal, for example, how native peoples who consume large amounts of wild meat and fish will have a greater risk of exposure to contaminants in a particular environment than non-indigenous people (Bird, 1995).

GIS mapping can also be used to arrive at a consensus regarding weighting and ranking criteria in resource management planning. For example, foresters and representatives of forest-dwelling communities in Ghana worked together to map fire hazards. The process of jointly mapping the data helped participants focus on issues, thereby lessening interpersonal conflicts and facilitating trust. The GIS map was then used to design a fire-monitoring plan for protecting the forest (Kyem, 2001).

This chapter presents two applications, one at the regional level and one at the local level for the island of Hawai'i. They illustrate the links between GIS and SIA. Although these two cases focus on Native Hawaiian indigenous communities, the methodology can be of value to other local, especially indigenous, communities. Both cases stem from the need to incorporate cultural impacts in the planning process. A human ecological model of development planning that attempts to integrate sociocultural and environmental assessment guides them (see Chapter 8).

Case 1: regional level analysis
Background
The Public Utilities Commission (PUC) mandated the electric companies of the state of Hawai'i to consider the impact of generating and distributing electricity upon communities, the economy and the environment in the design of a 20-year integrated resource management plan for energy development in the Hawaiian islands. The project called for the quantification and monetization of both direct and indirect (external) costs and benefits. The Hawaiian Electric Company commissioned an 'externality study' to assess the impact of power generation on the islands of Hawai'i, O'ahu, Maui, Moloka'i, and Lāna'i, using only existing data and focusing on the monetization of impacts. In particular, the PUC mandated the electric companies to examine the potential impacts on Native Hawaiian people as an externality.

The authors of this chapter were contracted to develop a method to identify and quantify the impacts of generating electricity on Native Hawaiian people. It was decided to use GIS mapping in a regional scoping of each island to develop a human ecology model which could illustrate potential impacts on Native Hawaiian communities, ancestral lands, cultural and natural resources and traditional and customary practices.

The human ecological framework, which emphasizes person–environment congruity, is discussed in Chapter 8 (see also Matsuoka *et al.*, 1998; McGregor *et al.*, 1998). Historically, Native Hawaiians settled in areas where natural resources were abundant. They developed a system of regulations called *kapu* which defined user responsibilities and rights and incorporated conservation measures. From generation to generation, Native Hawaiian *'ohana* (or families) developed an identity based on a sense of spiritual and ancestral attachment to the place where they were born and raised (McGregor, 1995, 1999). This place is a management district called the *ahupua'a.* An *ahupua'a* is a cultural use area, usually coinciding with a water-shed which offers resources extending from *makai* (the sea) to *mauka* (uplands) (Minerbi, 1999). Although Native Hawaiian communities have undergone varying degrees of change resulting from economic development and westernization, cultural wellbeing is still contingent upon the sustain-ability of traditional economies, institutions, practices and beliefs, particu-larly in rural areas.

A critical assumption was that the relationship to *'āina* (land and natural resources) is fundamental to the cultural identity and wellbeing of Native Hawaiians. A corollary of this assumption is that residential continuity is seen as a measure of cultural continuity and that the persistence of tradi-tional customs and practices is associated with a sense of place. The *'āina* serves as a basis for traditional economics, good diet and health, spiritu-ality, traditional and customary practices, the continuity and cohesion of family and community, and indigenous rights (Minerbi *et al.*, 1993; Minerbi, 1994). Thus the integrity of terrestrial and aquatic ecosystems is the primary determinant of quality of life for Native Hawaiian commu-nities. Terrestrial and aquatic ecosystems, mapped according to the diver-sity and abundance of native flora and fauna, could be overlaid on maps showing land ownership, zoning, historic cultural sites and the location of Hawaiian communities. This would illustrate the relationship of Native Hawaiians to the *'āina.*

Seven indicators of Native Hawaiian wellbeing were selected to serve as criteria for developing the individual maps which would be overlaid to iden-tify and assess the areas of critical significance to Native Hawaiian culture. Then the overlay-screening model was used to derive a cumulative impact analysis of Native Hawaiian wellbeing (Kaiser *et al.*, 1995; McHarg, 1969). The GIS software utilized was ArcInfo.

Mapping process
Step 1 Base maps for those Hawaiian Islands needing Integrated Resource Plans were developed. Topographical maps with main roads and place names were used as a base. See Table 13.1.

Table 13.1   Overview of GIS mapping process

Hawaiian cultural impacts/externalities
   Family
   Community
   Customs & practices
   Lands & community economy
   Human wellbeing & spirituality
   Hawaiian rights

Maps
   Hawaiian population ratio
   Known historic sites
   State conservation zones
   Rare and endangered species
   Government lands

Overlays
   Cultural/natural area layers
   Simplified overlay of all layers

Findings and characterization
   Sensitive areas of critical importance
   Areas requiring site-specific analysis

Demonstrate overlay of a proposed site
   Assess impact of site relative to Native Hawaiian externalities

---

Step 2   Map elements, which can be used as proxies to render the Native Hawaiian wellbeing indicators, were identified. A summary of these is provided in Table 13.2. To expand slightly, *family and community* are rendered in maps showing the Native Hawaiian population ratio distributed across each island. An underlying assumption is that population distribution reveals aggregates of extended families and areas where Native Hawaiian households are concentrated, and therefore comprise communities.

Subsistence, cultural and religious beliefs, customs and practice areas and natural and cultural resources are rendered through the maps of known historic sites, state conservation zones and habitats of rare and endangered species. The underlying assumption is that subsistence, cultural and religious practices rely on, and are carried out in, areas where the natural and cultural resources are abundant, and of good quality.

Native Hawaiian lands and community economy are rendered in the map which shows government lands. The government lands are inclusive of Hawaiian homelands, state lands and federal lands. Most of these lands were originally the Crown and government lands of the Kingdom of

Table 13.2   Indicators and map elements

Wellbeing indicator	Map elements
Family & community	Hawaiian population ratio
Subsistence, cultural & religious customs & practices	Known historic sites
	State conservation zones
	Habitats of rare and endangered species
Hawaiian lands & community economy	Government lands
Human wellbeing & spirituality	Cultural/natural area layers
Hawaiian rights	Simplified overlay of all layers

Hawai'i and are today called the 'ceded public lands'. The Native Hawaiian people consider these their national lands and seek to re-establish sovereign control over them. In addition to being sensitive to development, these areas are encumbered by Native Hawaiian claims and have implications for management, lease arrangements, permits and revenues.

Human wellbeing and spirituality are not explicitly rendered in maps as there are no pre-existing variables that measure these concepts. However, an underlying assumption is that mental, physical and spiritual health is related to cultural integrity and this is dependent on pristine environments. Implicitly, then, human wellbeing and spirituality will be reflected in the overlay of all layers.

Native Hawaiian rights are not explicitly rendered in the maps, again because no existing data directly measure this concept. An underlying assumption is that Native Hawaiian rights apply in areas where the cultural and natural resources are available and where Native Hawaiian lands are situated. Implicitly, therefore, Native Hawaiian rights are reflected in the maps indicating the location of cultural and natural resources and the Native Hawaiian lands now under the state and federal governments.

Step 3   Appropriate map categories and legends were developed.

Step 4   Ordinal class intervals reflecting a balanced frequency distribution of observations were created with different shading intensities used to distinguish the ordinal class intervals.

Step 5   The Native Hawaiian population ratio map was selected as the base map upon which the other map elements were placed.

Step 6   Maps for each of the above elements were generated for each island.

Step 7   The Native Hawaiian population ratio, the known historic sites, the state conservation zones and the rare and endangered species habitats were overlaid to create the cultural/natural area layers map.

Step 8   All of the map elements, including state, Department of Hawaiian Home Lands (DHHL), and federal lands were overlaid.

Step 9   Map readability was facilitated by merging the state, DHHL and federal land symbols into one shaded category representing government lands and merging the cultural and natural resource elements. This results in the simplified overlay all layers maps.

Step 10   Each map was analysed and interpreted and findings and conclusions were drawn.

Step 11   Native Hawaiian externalities as indicated by the GIS maps were characterized.

Step 12   We demonstrated how to characterize the impact of a proposed site for the generation of electricity by overlaying a proposed future generating unit area and reporting the potential impacts in a table.

Interpretation
Native Hawaiian population ratio map   The Native Hawaiian population ratio map shows where Native Hawaiians are concentrated on each island in relation to places and roads. The Native Hawaiian population ratio map overlaid on geographic areas became the basic map on which to overlay the other impact elements. In this way, each impact element is assessed relative to its potential effect on the Native Hawaiian community. According to the 1990 US Census, Native Hawaiians comprise 12 per cent of the overall population in Hawai'i. Therefore it was decided to shade only the census blocks where Native Hawaiians comprise more than 12 per cent of the population. The darker the shade, the greater the concentration of Native Hawaiians who utilize the cultural and natural resources which overlap, or are in close proximity to, the community. Unshaded areas on the map are not necessarily unimportant, but they would require site specific assessments to determine the impact of their use upon Native Hawaiian custom, belief and practice.

Comparison with 1853 population census map   The 1990 Native Hawaiian population ratio maps were also compared to 1853 population census maps of the Hawaiian islands (Coulter, 1931). A concentration of Native

Hawaiians in the same locations over time is an excellent indicator of continuity. Areas with continuity have great significance and importance. In many cases, these areas would also have family burial grounds in the vicinity, and regularly used cultural and natural resources. Continuity of residence in these areas would indicate the persistence of Native Hawaiian subsistence, cultural and religious beliefs, customs and practices. Dislocations of Native Hawaiians from these areas would have great impacts upon those families and the traditional connection they have maintained to their ancestral lands. They would also impair future Native Hawaiian practice. Because Native Hawaiian families are interconnected in an extended *'ohana* family system, dislocation of rural Hawaiians would also affect their urban kin by depriving them of the link to ancestral lands.

Overlay of Native Hawaiian population and known historic sites The overlap of points, lines and areas depicting known historic sites with the Native Hawaiian community may indicate an ongoing relationship between the community and the site. Similarly, sites that are in close proximity to the community might indicate an ongoing relationship with that place through, for example, guardianship and caretaking responsibilities. Change in areas of overlap, and in those areas which are in close proximity to the community, would result in serious impacts on the surrounding communities. These maps, therefore, provide a guide to areas where development would seriously impact Native Hawaiian customs, beliefs and practices. The maps do not represent a complete inventory of historic cultural use areas that deserve protection. This is because only known historic sites are depicted. Most archaeological surveys and excavations have been limited to areas under pressure for development. Also there is a delay in the entry of data in the known sites database. Other areas would need to be assessed on a site-specific basis to determine the presence or absence of important cultural use areas.

Native Hawaiian population and rare and endangered species Native Hawaiians do not hunt or gather rare and endangered species, but the presence of such species in an area indicates pristine, sensitive and significant natural ecosystems. The presence or absence of rare and endangered native species is an indicator of the overall health of the human ecosystem. The areas in which these species are located are usually dominated by native species of plants and animals utilized by Native Hawaiians for subsistence, cultural and religious purposes. It is the pristine condition of the natural environment that allows Native Hawaiians to experience *ho'ailona*, or spiritual natural phenomena. The site points and areas indicate the localities which have an abundance of natural resources in excellent condition. The map showing the location of the Native Hawaiian population in relation to the endangered species indicates that the range for subsistence hunting and gathering varies from island to island. Trails and access corridors to these resources are not accounted for on these maps, but should be taken into consideration when assessing impacts. The large majority of Hawai'i's native plants and animals occur nowhere else in the world, and, by conservative estimates, nearly 1000 species are threatened with extinction. Changes to their habitats would also have a serious impact on Native Hawaiian customs, beliefs and practices.

Native Hawaiian population and conservation lands   These maps, like that of rare and endangered species, indicate areas of importance for Native Hawaiian subsistence, religious and cultural purposes. Conservation lands indicate the presence of an abundance of high-quality natural resources and ecosystems which have the benefit of being protected from development. These are the principal lands used, and cared for, by Native Hawaiians in their exercise of gathering and hunting customs and practices. Development should avoid the areas indicated on these maps because their status signals the presence of sensitive and significant natural resources. Among these lands, those that overlap with, or are in close proximity to, the Native Hawaiian population would have greater significance for subsistence, cultural and religious practices.

Native Hawaiian population and government-controlled lands   The purpose of the government land and Native Hawaiian population maps is to assess the spatial relationship (proximity, continuity and overlap) between the lands encumbered by trust obligations towards Native Hawaiians and the lands where they live. This overlay also allows the depiction of those communities located in non-government lands (private lands) from those located in government lands. It is important to note that all lands, both private and public, are subject to custom and practice rights of *hoa'aina* or the tenants of the *ahupua'a* (McGregor, 1995). Integrity and congruence of uses of all these government lands with the trust obligations are important regardless of whether Native Hawaiians live there or not. The shading indicates that certain Native Hawaiian communities actually reside on, or use, many of the government lands. The lands where the two variables (government lands and Native Hawaiians) overlap are very important to Native Hawaiians, particularly the DHHL lands, because they are the lands where Native Hawaiians reside or are expected to be settled some time in the future, even if they are not living there now. Government lands are encumbered by claims which have implications for management, lease arrangements, permits and revenues. These lands have multiple layers of management jurisdiction and therefore the process for attaining use permits is more complicated and involved.

Simplified overlay of all layers These maps overlay government lands onto the cultural/natural area maps. This overlay delimits the potential areas for the siting of energy generating technologies. The overlay of one or more elements in any section of this map indicates integrated human ecosystems or cultural *kipuka* areas, which are most significant to subsistence, cultural and religious beliefs, customs and practices. Given Native Hawaiian entitlements and outstanding claims to the federal, state and DHHL lands, this map also reflects impacts which would be related to Native Hawaiian rights. The lands where cultural and natural resources overlap would have the highest demand for access by Native Hawaiians for subsistence, religious and cultural purposes. Where these cultural and natural resources occur on government lands, the right of access for subsistence, religious and cultural purposes would be presumed. Development in these areas would result in impacts which should be avoided. The more elements present, the greater the likely levels of impact. Areas of greatest sensitivity would be large contiguous shaded areas. Siting in any of the shaded areas, particularly those with more than one layer of shading, would have implications for Native Hawaiian subsistence, cultural and religious customs and practices and would incur greater external costs. Areas which have no indicators would therefore be candidates for siting of energy generation. However, they would still require site-specific assessment in order to determine how suitable or appropriate development would actually be in that area.

Simplified overlay of all layers for the island of Hawai'i The simplified overlay map of all layers for the Island of Hawai'i is shown in Figure 13.1. The overlap of government lands with cultural and natural resource areas appears as a double grid on the map. As government lands, most of these areas have a protected status as forest reserves or national parks. The double grid area covers a large contiguous area at the centre and in eastern portions of the island of Hawai'i. The lands that overlap in east Hawai'i were converted to private lands after the study. This area was examined at the local level in the cultural impact assessment of the impact of generating electricity from geothermal energy, as discussed in the next case study, and is rendered in greater detail in Figure 13.2. Of the double grid areas, those which overlap, or are in close proximity to, the Native Hawaiian population would be the most significant areas for Native Hawaiian custom and practice. Cultural and natural resource areas located on private lands appear as a single grid. Many of these areas do not have a protected status and are vulnerable to projected development. Again, the single grid areas which overlap with, or are in close proximity to, the Native Hawaiian population would be the most significant areas for Native Hawaiian custom and practice. The single grid areas are located on North and South Kona,

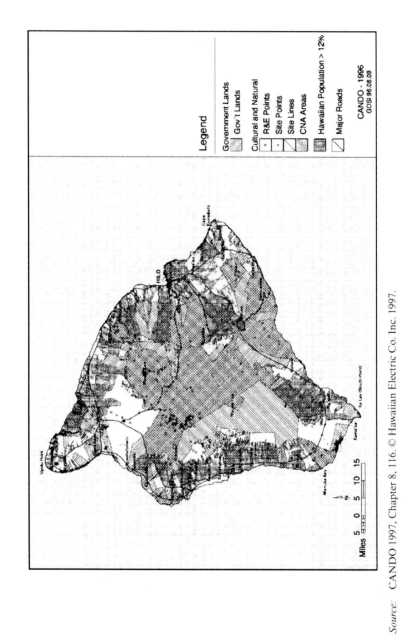

Legend

Government Lands
Gov't Lands
Cultural and Natural
R&E Points
Site Points
Site Lines
CNA Areas
Hawaiian Population > 12%
Major Roads

CANDO - 1996
GDSI 95.08.09

Source: CANDO 1997, Chapter 8, 116. © Hawaiian Electric Co. Inc. 1997.

Figure 13.1   Hawai'i simplified overlay, all layers

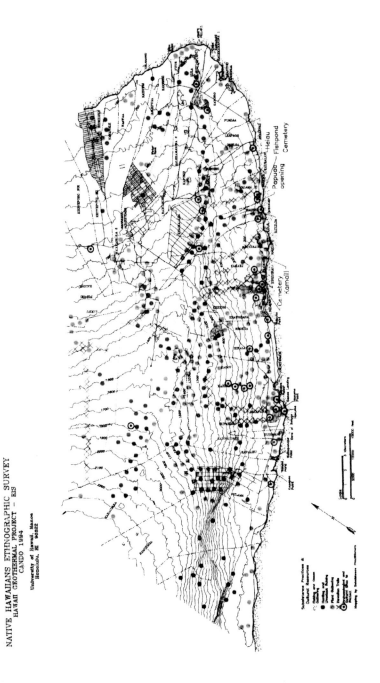

Figure 13.2   Map of Puna, island of Hawai'i

in Kohala and at Hakalau, along the Hamakua Coast. Unshaded areas of the map would require site-specific analysis to determine their suitability for use.

Case 2: local level analysis

A GIS/SIA project at the local level was the ethnographic study to assess the impact of generating electricity from geothermal energy in Puna and South-East Maui (Matsuoka *et al.*, 1996). Puna is a region in the eastern portion of the Island of Hawai'i. This project was prompted by a federal environmental impact assessment and was designed to identify Native Hawaiian cultural resources, particularly significant sites and traditional cultural properties, with regard to potential impacts of the generation and transmission of electricity from geothermal energy in the proposed project areas.

The major tasks included (a) archival research of ethnohistorical and ethnographic information; (b) review of Native Hawaiian chants to identify significant sites and cultural and religious use areas; (c) extraction of place names from historical maps for interpretation of cultural meaning by traditional bearers and practitioners; (d) in-depth interviews and focus group discussions; and (e) creation of a map of subsistence use areas by informants. The GIS component of the project was the participatory mapping by the informants of the cultural and natural resources important for their cultural practices and the routes used to gain access to the resources in the geothermal resource zone and along the electric transmission routes.

In the interviews and focus group discussions, informants were encouraged to describe and share their relationship to the study area; their knowledge of significant sites and natural resources used for traditional practices; pertinent legends, traditions, chants and deities; the meaning of place names; and information on historical persons and events.

The map of Puna represents the general location of trails, ancient sites and subsistence activities, including fishing and ocean gathering; hunting and livestock raising; plant gathering; trails and boat/canoe landing; archaeological sites; areas to protect from overharvesting and overdevelopment; and native Hawaiian plants. Each dot or symbol represents a location identified by an informant during their interview. They do not reflect rates of subsistence. The dots were intentionally large relative to the size of the map in order not to reveal specific locations where subsistence occurred. The map is useful for determining important economic and cultural areas that require protection and to document Native Hawaiian use patterns throughout the lower Puna District.

As indicated on the map, fishing occurs along the district's entire coastline. Hunting is done primarily in the mountain forested areas, although some informants reported that pigs came down to the coastline. The gathering of plants takes place throughout the district; some plants and trees were common in coastal areas, others were found in the forested mountain regions. Ancient trails were still in use by subsistence practitioners. Most of them connected mountain and coastal areas. A variety of archaeological sites, fishing shrines, rock walls and natural features were referred to in chants, folklore and *'ōlelo no'eau* (Hawaiian proverbs).

The GIS map developed by Native Hawaiian practitioners in the Puna District proved significant in assessing the impact of geothermal energy development. This is because, before the study was conducted, representatives of the Department of Business and Economic Development and Tourism and the Hawaiian Electric Company maintained that the geothermal resource zone was not utilized by the Puna residents for subsistence and cultural practices, and that therefore development of the zone would have minimal impact upon the surrounding community. The GIS map illustrated that the area was, in fact, used extensively by the Native Hawaiian community of Puna for subsistence and cultural practices.

Conclusion

The two cases show how GIS methodology was used on the island of Hawai'i to assess the impacts of development of electricity at the regional and local level. GIS mapping was an alternative to the pseudo-quantification of sociocultural data. The regional and local GIS maps provided a planning tool for cultural impact analysis and for assessing the costs of electric generation in general, and the impact on specific geographic areas, without actually assigning a numeric or monetary valuation.

In the regional case, assessing the appropriateness of energy development with regard to Native Hawaiian lifeways requires an understanding of an organic sociocultural process that would pay attention to the unity, capability for response and adaptive qualities of people acting as a community. It refers to a composite living structure whose energies are directed towards attaining a common purpose. The overlay method provided information regarding the coexistence of cultural and natural elements within a prescribed area that are the ingredients of an organic relationship, as in the case of an ecology. The coexistence of elements does not always imply a dynamic relationship; however, when multiple elements exist simultaneously, there is a high probability that such a relationship occurs. This is especially true in pristine locales where families have strong genealogical ties, and cultural practices were likely to be transmitted intergenerationally. Locales with a high degree of cultural continuity exist in rural areas that have been bypassed by commercialization and social change.

The GIS methodology at both levels takes into account how Native Hawaiian enclaves are at the root of an organic sociocultural process. Elements may coexist (for example, rare and endangered species with protected or conservation lands), but may have little relevance to Native Hawaiians unless they are embraced in an integral and reciprocal ecology within which humans and natural elements thrive. This type of ecology is sustainable, at least in part, because of an indigenous perspective on land use that promotes a balance between rates of resource utilization and replenishment, and a worldview reflecting a sense of gratitude and piety towards the deities providing the resources.

The GIS maps allow for the examination of this dynamic ecological process involving person-in-environment. Assessing cultural externalities in this manner avoids the problem of pseudo-quantification inherent in attempts to apply numeric valuations to cultural elements. Attempts to assign values or weights to elements, or any combination of elements, are dubious. For one thing, the various elements offer a mixture of ordinal data (such as the Native Hawaiian population ratio) and nominal data (for example, government lands). Assigning weights or values to nominal data (for example, state versus federal lands) is difficult unless these classifications have differential significance to Native Hawaiians. For other elements, such as historic sites, frequency of occurrence (within a given area) does not necessarily relate to level of importance. Sites are qualitatively evaluated in terms of where they are situated, their uniqueness, their relation to other sites, pristineness and so on. The mixing of quantitative and qualitative aspects does not lend itself to numeric valuation.

It is useful to conceptualize elements in terms of a continuum representing levels of cultural pristineness. At one end of the continuum lie the 'cultural *kipuka*' or the most integrated and traditional Native Hawaiian communities (McGregor, 1995). At the other end are white areas signifying the absence of critical cultural elements. The difficulty with using a continuum to reflect various community typologies or levels of integrity has to do with the points in between. Assigning values or weights to elements or any combination thereof that occur simultaneously is an arbitrary and reductionist approach to assessment. For example, ranking the overlay of historic sites, and rare and endangered species, on a continuum with regard to other elements that overlap and form combinations is very precarious, because the occurrence of elements does not automatically suggest a relationship.

The GIS maps also provide vital information concerning the spatial or proximal relations between elements. Assessing spatial or proximal relations is consistent with the *ahupua'a* context within which Native Hawaiians residing in traditional rural areas continue to function. The resources that are needed do not necessarily concur or overlap with where Native Hawaiians live, but are generally within close proximity. Assigning higher values to overlapping elements would overlook the importance of proximal relations between cultural elements that do not overlap. A narrative of the relational meaning of physical elements and their properties to humans and to each other comes in place of numeric representations of degrees of importance. This is based on the belief that GIS maps are a viable assessment tool at this regional level of planning.

The expanded use of SIA in research and analysis for policy decisions increases the opportunity to integrate the use of GIS methodology within SIA. Data and information routinely collected by line agencies are now becoming available with geographic coordinates. New SIA data can also be collected on site and the locations pinpointed with global positioning systems (GPS). Computer-generated maps using GIS can be overlaid to analyse the spatial association between relevant variables. The GIS format enables the researcher to analyse landscapes from the macro level to the micro level, and from the regional scale to the local scale.

References

Bird, B.W. 1995. 'The Eagle Project: Re-mapping Canada from an indigenous perspective', *Cultural Survival Quarterly*, 18(4): 23–4.

CANDO, 1997. 'Native Hawaiian impacts', in Energy Research Group, Inc (eds), *Hawaii Externalities Workbook* (Consultancy Report for Hawaii Electric Company), Waltham, MA: Energy Research Group, Chapter 8, 1–151.

Coulter, J.W. 1931. 'Population and Utilization of Land and Sea in Hawaii 1853', Bishop Museum Bulletin no. 88, Honolulu.

Harris, T.M. and Weiner, D. 1998. 'Empowerment, marginalization, and community integrated GIS', *Cartography and Geographic Information Systems*, 25(2): 67–76.

Kaiser, E., Godschalk, D. and Chapin, S. 1995. *Urban Land Use and Planning* (4th edn), Urbana: University of Illinois Press.

Kyem, P. 2001. 'Embedding GIS applications into resource management and planning activities of local and indigenous communities', *Journal of Planning Education and Research*, 20(1): 176–86.

Matsuoka, J., McGregor, D. and Minerbi, L. 1996. 'Native Hawaiian Ethnographic Study for the Hawai'i Geothermal Project Proposed for Puna and South-East Maui', Oak Ridge National Laboratory.

Matsuoka, J., McGregor, D. and Minerbi, L. 1998. 'Moloka'i: A study of Hawaiian subsistence and community sustainability', in M. Hoff (ed.), *Sustainable Community Development: Case Studies in Economic, Environmental and Cultural Revitalization*, New York: CRC Press, 25–43.

McGregor, D. 1995. 'Waipio Valley: a cultural Kipuka in the early 20th Century Hawai'i', *The Journal of Pacific History*, 30(2): 194–209.

McGregor, D. 1999. 'Research in action: Ethnohistory of Puna,' *Social Process in Hawai'i*, 39: 181–207.

McGregor, D., Minerbi, L. and Matsuoka, J. 1998. 'A holistic assessment method of health and well-being for Native Hawaiian communities', *Pacific Health Dialog: Journal of Community Health and Clinical Medicine for the Pacific*, 5(1): 361–9.

McHarg, I. 1969. *Design with Nature*, Garden City (NY): Doubleday Press..

Minerbi, L. 1994. 'Hawaiian sanctuaries, places of refuge and indigenous knowledge in

Hawai'i', in J. Morrison, P. Geraghty and L. Crowl (eds), *Land Use and Agriculture: Science of the Pacific Island Peoples* (vol. 2), Suva: University of the South Pacific Institute of Pacific Studies, 89–129.

Minerbi, L. 1999. 'Indigenous management models and the protection of the Ahupua'a', *Social Process in Hawai'i*, 39: 208–25.

Minerbi, L., McGregor, D. and Matsuoka, J. 1993. *Native Hawaiian and Local Cultural Assessment*, Honolulu: University of Hawai'i.

Pickles, J. (ed.) 1995. *Ground Truth: the Social Implications of Geographic Information Systems*, New York: Guilford.

Sieber, R.E. 2000. 'GIS implementation in the grassroots', *Journal of Urban and Regional Information Systems Association*, 12(1): 15–29.

14 Vulnerability and capacity measurement
Mark Fenton, Sheridan Coakes and Nadine Marshall

Introduction
Social impact assessment (SIA) has seen the development of a wide range of techniques, methods and procedures for the assessment of social and community impacts. The techniques themselves are dispersed along a qualitative–quantitative continuum, and rely on participatory or desktop procedures, using either primary or secondary data sources. Calls for multiple methods and the need to triangulate using different assessment techniques, while furthering the methodological rigour within the field, contribute to an ever-increasing emphasis on method and technique within SIA research. It is argued that, although many of these techniques certainly make a significant contribution to SIA research and practice, there is nevertheless a critical need to develop broader theoretical and conceptual frameworks within SIA that would guide the implementation and use of these techniques. This is not an argument for an omnipotent theory of SIA, or an argument for a singular methodological approach. However, it is argued that we should begin to deal with the clutter of techniques, methods and procedures that occupy the conceptual space of SIA. What is needed is conceptual frameworks which assist in organizing and providing direction for both theoretical and methodological inquiry and development. As Rapoport (1985: 256) has indicated, 'conceptual frameworks are neither models nor theories . . . models describe how things work, whereas theories explain phenomena. Conceptual frameworks do neither, rather they help us to think about phenomena, to order material, revealing patterns'.

Within both SIA and environmental impact assessment (EIA), procedural frameworks exist for ordering the sequence of tasks to be undertaken. Most procedural frameworks are initiated through the identification of specific assessment objectives, the scoping of issues, through an assessment phase and completed through both monitoring and auditing tasks. For instance, within SIA, a common procedural framework is to include the four stages of assessment, prediction, mitigation and monitoring, with the assessment stage including the two substages of scoping and profiling. The four stages certainly provide a generic framework for ordering the sequence or procedural steps involved in impact assessment. However, outside of this simple procedural framework, and with the exception of work by Slootweg *et al.* (2001) (see also Chapter 5), there are few generic frameworks to guide the substantive content of SIA.

This chapter provides a description of a conceptual framework, known as town resource cluster analysis (TRC-Analysis) which has been developed in Australia for undertaking SIA within a natural resource management (NRM) and planning context. While the approach has been applied on a regional planning scale and specifically in a number of NRM contexts including fisheries, forestry, mining and water resources, the framework is sufficiently broad for opportunities to exist for it to be applied within other NRM contexts and possibly within a more urban planning context.

As initially described by Hall and Fagen (1956) and further developed in the context of environmental planning and management (Conacher and Conacher, 2000), we conceptualize two systems as being critical components of any approach to SIA within NRM and planning. First are embedded resource systems, which are defined with reference to satisfying human needs and in terms of their utility value to social systems. Fisheries, water and forest resources are clearly of utilitarian value and define important resource systems for many peoples. However, to use the example of Conacher and Conacher (ibid.: 3), uranium 'is regarded as a resource by many technologically developed societies, but has no significance for a primitive society'. This indicates that natural resources are clearly definable only in terms of the culture and social context in which they are found.

In addition to resource systems, which are essentially culturally and socially defined and are therefore part of a singular environmental system, there are social systems. Social systems may be characterized in terms of a number of underlying qualities, including biophysical, health, cultural, social, political/legal, economic and psychological components (Gramling and Freudenburg, 1992). For NRM purposes, these underlying qualities include 'property rights, land and resource tenure systems, systems of knowledge pertinent to environment and resources and world views and ethics concerning environment and resources' (Berkes and Folke, 2000: 4). As clearly identified by Slootweg *et al.* (2001), within the totality of human–social systems, many of these systems and subsystems interact and are certainly not independent.

Given the existence of both social and resource systems, what becomes critical in terms of SIA, NRM and planning generally is the relationship or nature of the linkage(s) between the two systems. Slootweg *et al.* (2001), using a functional evaluation framework for integrating SIA and EIA, have also emphasized the integration of biophysical and social systems through the functions provided by environmental resources and the valuation of these resources within social systems. However, as Berkes and Folke (2000:

4) have pointed out, 'many previous studies have analysed the impact of human activities on the ecosystem, but few have studied the interdependence of social systems and ecological systems'. Conacher and Conacher (2000) have also emphasized the importance of understanding the nature of linkages between resource systems and environments generally. Their description of the important elements in these linkages may be understood in terms of the relationship between social and resource systems. Questions posed by Conacher and Conacher (2000) assist in this understanding:

1. Direction of the linkage: to what extent do changes in the resource system affect social systems? Conversely, to what extent do changes in social systems affect resource systems?
2. Direct or indirect linkage: do changes in the resource system directly affect the social system, or are these effects mediated by other systems and elements?
3. Strength of the linkage: what are the links between the resource system and the social system? How can they be identified, described and measured? How strong or weak are they?
4. Positive or negative effects of the interaction: are the effects of these interactions on the other system positive or negative? The impact of changes in the resource system on the social system is a fundamental question for SIA. On the other hand, identifying and assessing human impacts on resource systems is the fundamental question of EIA.
5. Duration of the linkage: how has the nature of the linkages between social and resource systems changed over time?

Defining social systems
One of the critical questions that confront any SIA process concerns the unit or units of analysis that are to be used in undertaking the assessment. Depending on the context and the objectives of the SIA process, it may be appropriate to undertake the assessment at different institutional levels, such as that of family, industry, stakeholder interest groups, or through groupings of specific types of resource users. Indeed, within any one SIA process, the unit of analysis – whether it focuses on communities of interest or communities of place – may vary, depending on the specific research objectives that are being addressed.

When undertaking large-scale regional SIA processes in the context of NRM, questions about the unit of analysis within social systems often centre upon the spatial location and scale of community. In such regional SIAs, the focus, at least initially, is on communities of place in which there may well be many communities of interest embedded. Berkes and Folke (2000: 16–17) have argued that, when investigating social–ecosystem linkages, 'the level of analysis is not the individual or the household but the social group, which could be a small community, a district, a tribal group or a regional population . . . the description of the social system starts with the people organised as user communities'.

While they may appear simple, questions of defining the social group, or what constitutes community, are complex questions that researchers have been attempting to address for some time. In the context of a regional SIA, should community be defined in terms of a single town, hamlet or regional area? Where there may be changes in the use of natural resources, the linkage from resource to a specific town may be direct, but there may also be indirect or flow-on impacts on a number of additional towns in the region. The question then arises, should 'community' be defined as a collection of interdependent towns within a region? If so, how do we define the boundaries of community, which distinguish one community, or collection of towns or communities, from others? This issue is one of the more basic questions underlying SIA in NRM and planning and again focuses on what the appropriate 'unit of analysis' is in the SIA process. As an aside, this issue also permeates much of the broader applied social science research, particularly within human and regional geography, where a long-standing question has been one of identifying and defining the spatial units that define the parameters or boundaries of studies in this area (Murphy, 1991).

One of the primary objectives of TRC-Analysis is to define meaningful spatial units on which to base later SIA processes. Such locationally and geographically distinct social units are referred to as 'town resource clusters' (TRCs). While many of the units used by NRM agencies are clearly defined on the basis of specific ecological and NRM characteristics, there is no corresponding unit associated with the social environment. Clearly, without a locationally and spatially distinct unit that defines the social environment, any attempt to understand social and community processes and changes, particularly in the context of NRM, will be fragmented and disparate.

The spatial unitization, extent and characteristic spatial interdependencies of social systems are some of the core issues that must be addressed in any definition of community. However, an interrelated issue is that of concurrently defining communities in terms of their dependencies on natural resources. In the first instance, conceptual and methodological issues that are associated with the definition of community in the context of resource dependency continue to be problematic. Depending on the research context – and often issues of data availability – 'community' has been defined in various ways, including town, county, local government area and regions (Machlis and Force, 1988; Machlis *et al.*, 1990). More meaningful boundary definitions are required in relation to community. Most importantly, such definitions of community should be meaningful in relation to prevailing social structures, levels of community organization and interdependence. They should not be defined purely on the basis of convenient administration boundaries or data availability.

Machlis and Force (1988) and Beckley (1998) have suggested that, within the context of better understanding resource dependent communities, community may need to be considered as a hierarchical or nested concept. Such an approach is not too dissimilar to that considered in central place theory (Christaller, 1933), where in a regional context a network of central places or towns exists in relation to specific trade areas and the supply and consumption of goods and services. Cramer *et al.* (1993: 477) have emphasized that, in the context of timber production and natural resource dependency generally, changes in resource availability often lead to chain reactions 'affecting not only loggers and mill workers, but businesses, social services and people not generally involved in timber production'. Such broader indirect effects not only occur in the town in which primary production and resource processing occurs, they may also occur in many adjacent townships and communities located in the same trade areas and areas of social service provision.

Recognition of the 'mutual interdependence' of communities and townships in a regional resource planning and management context is given in Mayfield's (1996) study on the relationship between small farms and the location from which farm goods and services were purchased. This research suggested there was significant microeconomic and financial interdependence amongst farming communities in a regional context. Changes in the operation of farms would have an impact on many smaller adjacent rural communities. It is argued that, through better understanding the interdependencies amongst communities, clusters of mutually interdependent townships (TRCs) can be identified. This would provide a more appropriate theoretical and conceptual rationale for defining community.

Using this approach to defining community is essentially defining what is also commonly referred to as 'social catchments'. These consist of mutually interdependent towns and communities dispersed throughout a region. They may also be hierarchically arranged, as described in central place theory. Using previous research in several NRM contexts (Fenton, 1998a, 1998b, 1999a, 1999b, 2000a), the interdependencies amongst towns may be defined using single or multiple measures of inter-town dependency. Measures of inter-town dependency have included the following:

1. Business expenditure: for those businesses directly involved in resource production, the town locations of business purchases and the magnitude of expenditures (often defined in terms of the percentage of total

business expenditure in specific towns rather than actual dollar amount);

2. Employee expenditure: for those business employees directly involved in resource production, the town locations of purchases of household goods and services and the magnitude of expenditures (often defined in terms of the percentage of total household expenditure in specific towns rather than actual dollar amount);

3. Employee residential locations: for those business employees directly involved in resource production, their residential town location. This is usually expressed as a percentage of employees resident within each town;

4. Social infrastructure services and facilities: for those business employees directly involved in resource production, the town locations in which social infrastructure services and facilities are accessed. This generally includes schools, medical and health services and the use of sporting facilities. It is usually expressed as the percentage of employees using services and facilities in each town;

5. Social networks: for those business employees directly involved in resource production, the residential locations of close personal contacts, including friends and relatives. This again is usually expressed as the percentage of employees with close contacts in specific locations.

Through the use of structured interviews or survey research with business owners and employees directly involved in resource production (that is, fishermen, timber workers, logging contractors, irrigation farmers), information on the level of inter-town dependency is relatively easily acquired. The data are used as a basis for identifying mutually interdependent clusters of towns and communities, which are referred to as Town Resource Clusters (TRCs).

An example is drawn from the social assessment of the Queensland commercial fishing industry in Australia (Fenton and Marshall, 2000). Here, TRCs were identified using locational information drawn from survey data collected from telephone interviews with commercial fishermen. The number of fishing businesses located in each town on the Queensland coast was identified. In addition, linkages and interdependencies amongst towns were identified using information on the location of (a) business expenditure, (b) employee expenditure, (c) employee residential locations, and (d) social infrastructure services and facilities.

The majority of fishing businesses were located in major regional centres. Locational expenditure, employee residential locations, service use and existing social networks generally occurred within the regional centres. However, several cases existed where there were significant 'hinterlands' or

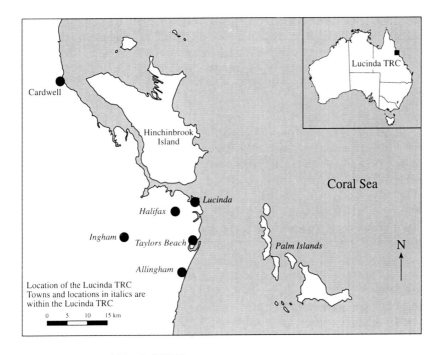

Source: Fenton and Marshall (2000).

Figure 14.1 Lucinda Town Resource Cluster

catchments of surrounding townships and communities that were highly interdependent, and dependent on the regional centres. Figure 14.1 demonstrates this with the Lucinda TRC, located in the region of Ingham, North Queensland. Lucinda was observed to have a hinterland of many smaller towns and communities which are the home towns of fishermen, the location of fishing businesses, and sites of business and employee expenditure or service use.

Table 14.1 shows measures of town interdependency for fishing businesses within the Lucinda TRC, with each measure expressed as a percentage. The first column (Business location) indicates that two-thirds of fishing businesses are located in the town of Lucinda. Some 44 per cent of business expenditure and 85 per cent of employee household expenditure occurs within the town of Ingham. The average dependency score shows that, while the majority of businesses are located in Lucinda, there is considerable dependency on the regional centre of Ingham. The hierarchical nature of TRCs is also shown in Table 14.1. Townsville (a major regional

Table 14.1   An example of inter-town dependency measures

Town	Business location	Business expenditure	Employee location	Household expenditure	Service use	Average dependency
Lucinda	66.6	10.3	40.0	3.2	31.6	30.3
Halifax	13.9	0.0	20.0	3.6	14.6	10.4
Ingham	13.9	44.3	40.0	85.4	34.1	43.5
Dungeness	5.6	3.2	0.0	0.0	0.0	1.8
Townsville	0.0	24.2	0.0	2.5	7.3	6.8
Cairns	0.0	7.6	0.0	0.0	4.9	2.5
Bundaberg	0.0	7.4	0.0	0.0	2.5	2.0
Brisbane	0.0	1.5	0.0	0.0	2.5	0.8
Innisfail	0.0	1.5	0.0	5.3	2.5	1.9
	100.0	100.0	100.0	100.0	100.0	

Note: Table values are column percentages.

centre in close proximity south of Lucinda), has an average dependency score of 6.8 and attracts 24 per cent of all business expenditure. Cairns (a major regional centre further to the north) has an average dependency score of 2.5 and attracts 8 per cent of business expenditure.

Table 14.1 suggests that any change which may impact on the operation and viability of fishing businesses in Lucinda, Halifax, Ingham or Dungeness will have flow-on, or indirect impacts, on other towns within the TRC. In particular, Ingham will be impacted through changes in business and employee expenditure and through changes in service use, while Lucinda is more likely to be impacted primarily through changes in service use. Table 14.1 also shows there are likely to be further flow-on impacts on the higher-order TRCs of Townsville and, to a lesser extent, Cairns.

While Figure 14.1 and Table 14.1 illustrate the definition and extent of a single TRC within the context of a regional social assessment of the Queensland commercial fishing industry, in this same study 22 TRCs were identified (Fenton and Marshall, 2000). Although too large to be presented in full, Table 14.2 shows part of the connectivity matrix for the 22 TRCs that have been defined in this context. Each value in the matrix represents an average score across a number of dependency measures computed for each of the 22 TRCs. The bold diagonal entry within the matrix indicates that much of the inter-town dependency occurs within the defined TRCs, suggesting that any changes to the operation and viability of fishing businesses located within the TRC are likely to impact primarily on towns and communities located within the same TRC. The higher-order TRCs of

Table 14.2 An example of a TRC connectivity matrix

TRCs	Karumba	Weipa	Thursday Is.	Cooktown	Port Douglas	Cairns	Innisfail	Lucinda	Townsville	Ayr	Bowen
Karumba	65.6	0.0	0.0	0.0	1.1	0.2	0.1	0.0	0.2	0.0	0.0
Weipa	1.0	77.3	0.0	0.0	1.4	0.4	0.0	0.0	0.0	0.0	0.0
Thursday Is.	0.0	0.0	79.2	0.0	0.0	0.0	0.0	0.0	0.0	0.0	0.0
Cooktown	0.0	0.0	0.0	71.7	0.5	0.2	0.1	0.0	0.2	0.0	0.0
Port Douglas	0.0	0.0	0.0	0.0	71.0	0.3	0.0	0.0	0.0	0.0	0.0
Cairns	18.7	22.7	19.8	21.5	20.4	94.3	16.5	2.5	7.1	0.0	1.5
Innisfail	0.0	0.0	0.0	0.0	0.0	0.1	77.2	2.3	0.3	0.0	0.7
Lucinda	0.0	0.0	0.0	0.0	0.4	0.0	1.0	77.1	0.0	0.0	0.0
Townsville	8.2	0.0	0.0	2.3	0.0	0.6	0.9	11.3	85.5	11.2	3.4
Ayr	0.0	0.0	0.0	0.0	0.0	0.0	0.0	0.0	0.1	83.5	0.2
Bowen	0.0	0.0	0.0	0.0	0.0	0.0	0.0	0.0	0.6	0.0	87.4

Note: Values in the matrix are average town dependency scores.

Cairns and Townsville are also identifiable in Table 14.2. This shows which lower-order TRCs are nested within these higher-order TRCs. For instance, TRCs from Karumba in the Gulf of Carpentaria, to Innisfail to the south, appear to be dependent upon and nested within the higher-order TRC of Cairns, while the TRCs of Lucinda and Ayr appear to be also dependent upon and nested within the Townsville TRC.

Through the use of information as presented in Tables 14.1 and 14.2, the locational impacts associated with changes in the operation of resource business can begin to be identified at both the local level of the TRC and across TRCs in a broader regional context. While the current example examines inter-town dependencies using expenditure and service use information, other more detailed measures could also be included, among them social networks and place meanings.

Although the TRCs have been defined on the basis of survey data collected directly from resource users, it should also be noted that it may be possible to apply a traditional gravity model approach (Carrothers, 1956) to the definition of boundaries or social catchments surrounding the major regional centres. In this case, the spatial boundary between regional centres becomes a function of the distance between the two centres and some measure of the size of each regional centre (Fenton, 1999c; 2000a). Of course, such an approach does not make use of primary data and the definition of appropriate spatial boundaries is independent of the activities of resource-based industries and employees. Certainly, further research needs to examine whether the desktop gravity modelling approach may provide sufficient approximation to TRC boundaries based on primary data.

Although the previous discussion has used the commercial fishing industry as an example of the way TRCs are defined, it should be emphasized that the same general approach has also been used in other very different NRM and planning contexts, including forestry (Fenton, 1998a; 1998b; 1999a), water resources (Fenton, 1999c; 2000a), mining (Fenton, 1999b) and agriculture (Fenton, 1999d).

Defining the natural resource

Previous research has focussed on the resource-dependent community and issues related to the resource itself have often been left to the research periphery. The resource itself is often merely defined in terms of a simple resource typology, to the effect that communities are dependent upon fishing, native timber harvesting, mining or agriculture. What is needed is to recognize that, while resource-dependent social systems can be defined and described, what is also required is concurrent consideration given to defining and describing resource systems on which communities are dependent. The concurrent consideration of social and resource systems is certainly an important area of research inquiry requiring considerable integration of conceptual and theoretical approaches between the social and natural sciences. Typical of such an approach is current research on social and ecological resilience (Adger, 2000). There consideration is given, not only to defining resilience within social and resource systems, but also to the way changes in the resilience of either system may affect the other.

While questions emerge in defining a resource-dependent community, and in particular its spatial and geographic context, similar questions also arise in relation to defining the resource on which communities may be dependent. This is particularly the case in such resource contexts as fishing, forestry and water resource use, where the resource itself may be dispersed throughout an area.

It is usually the case in the management of natural resources that geographic areas are delineated. For instance, in the management of water resources, specific water or river catchments are often geographically defined. In the management of forest resources, management agencies often define areas of forest on the basis of forest management areas, timber supply zones, forest coupes or other resource-based units. Marine resources on the Great Barrier Reef are delineated in terms of a zoning system, which specifies the permitted use of reef resources. Similarly, several states in Australia manage their natural resources on the basis of spatially defined biogeographic regions, which encompass the entire state.

Given that the spatial and geographic extent of specific social systems (TRCs) have been defined, the question that emerges is: 'What is the spatial extent and location of resource use by resource businesses located within the TRC?' We know the interdependencies amongst towns and communities within a TRC in relation to resource businesses and employees of these businesses. Further, if some understanding is obtained of the location of resource use by businesses, a basic framework can be established for understanding the locational impacts of changes in NRM and use. Such a framework would allow the identification of towns or TRCs potentially impacted by, for example, seasonal closures in specific areas of fisheries resource use, changes in forest tenure from state forest to national parks, or changes in water allocation and use within specific water catchments.

In many cases, the location and often the volume or magnitude of resource use by businesses is available as secondary data from NRM agencies. In some instances, structured interviews and survey research will be required with resource businesses in order to identify the location of resource use. For instance, the location of timber resource use amongst timber mills located in towns within specific TRCs was found to be directly related to specific forest management areas (FMAs) in Victoria. Given knowledge of this relationship, some understanding could be gained of the

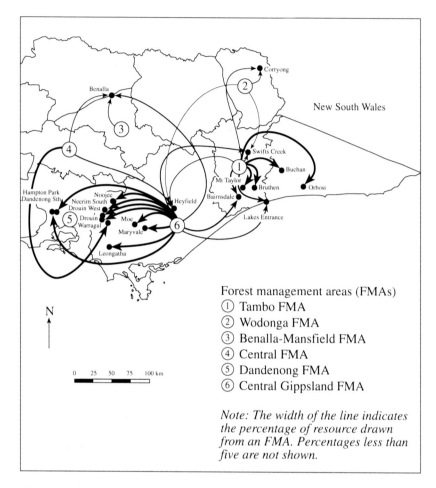

Figure 14.2   Location of timber resource towns in Gippsland, Victoria

locational impacts of changes in timber use and production within specific FMAs. For instance, Figure 14.2 shows six FMAs in Victoria and the location of towns in which timber mills are located that extract timber resources from these areas. It is evident from the figure that there is a relationship between FMAs and clusters of specific towns. Timber resources from the Tambo FMA flow to a cluster of towns in the north east of Gippsland including Orbost, Buchan, Bruthen, Lakes Entrance, Mt Taylor, Swifts Creek and Bairnsdale. The towns themselves were found to be highly interdependent and comprised a single TRC, identified as the Bairnsdale TRC. Again what this relationship suggests is that any change in forest management and, in particular, the use of timber resources within the Tambo FMA is likely to have an impact on several communities within the Bairnsdale TRC.

Identifying relationships between pre-existing resource planning or management units and TRCs is often the most ideal approach to use, as this is the resource planning unit for which environmental and NRM plans are being developed. The location of associated social impacts of these changes can be clearly identified. In addition, there is often considerable ecological, environmental and resource information available for such resource planning units which can be used concurrently with social, demographic and financial information for the TRC in order to better plan and manage resource use and identify the social impacts associated with changes in resource use and management.

In some instances, there may be no appropriate pre-existing NRM units that can be used or that are appropriate. In these cases, structured interviews and survey research must be undertaken with resource users in order to identify the location of resource use. In a social assessment study of Queensland's commercial fishing industry (Fenton and Marshall, 2000), there were no regional classifications of marine coastal areas in Queensland which might have assisted in defining the spatial extent of resource use by fishing business located within specific TRCs. Rather, the spatial extent and location of marine resource use by commercial fishing businesses was defined through interviews with commercial fishermen. The location of resource use was recorded using a 15-minute grid overlay (15 nautical mile grid squares) of marine coastal areas in Queensland. Each 15-minute grid provided information on the number of commercial fishing businesses using the marine resource.

Analysis of marine resource use amongst fishermen from each of the 22 TRCs (as partially identified in Table 14.2) provided consistently meaningful spatial patterns of resource use associated with each TRC. In all cases, and on the basis of count of fishing businesses using an area, it was possible to identify resource areas of high, moderate and low use. As shown in Figure 14.3, 15-minute grids with high use (primary resource catchments) were spatially proximate and adjacent, as were grids associated with moderate use (secondary resource catchments).

What is also evident in the examples of fisheries resource catchments shown in Figure 14.3 is that the primary resource catchment for each TRC is often located immediately adjacent to the TRC in which the fishing businesses are located. The secondary resource catchments are often adjacent to the TRC, but are dispersed over a wider area than the primary resource catchment. In this example, and the earlier examples drawn from the forestry context, the TRC framework allows the identification of resource

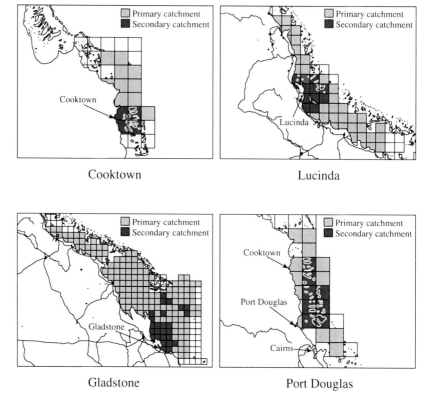

Figure 14.3   Location of fisheries resource catchments for four TRCs in Queensland

catchments and related social catchments (TRCs). The location of social impacts associated with changes in resource use and management can then be clearly identified.

Identifying the social impacts of changes in resource use illustrates one direction (Conacher and Conacher, 2000) of the link between resource and social systems. Having established a framework for linking both systems, it is also possible to examine the link between these systems in the alternate direction; that is, between social system (or the TRC) and the resource system. If the linkage is examined in this direction, the focus is essentially twofold: (a) on the environmental and ecological impacts of resource use by the population from within specific social systems or TRCs; and (b) how the characteristics and behaviours of individuals and organizations within a TRC affect the ecology of the resource catchment. Much of the research focus on the adoption of new or sustainable farming practices (Beal, 1997; Gould *et al.*, 1989; Rogers, 1962) is also of particular relevance in this context. One of its objectives is the identification of demographic, social and psychological characteristics of resource users as important predictors of behaviour change in relation to resource use.

Resource dependency and associations

Resource dependency indicates that a relationship exists between social systems on the one hand and resource systems on the other, to the extent that the maintenance of social systems is in some way reliant on one or more resource systems. In general, much previous research undertaken in the context of resource-dependent communities (for example, Randall and Ironside, 1996) has adopted a similar definition of resource dependency. However, resource dependency continues to be defined in terms of simple one-dimensional economic measures, based usually on the level of employment in the resource sector. For instance, Randall and Ironside (ibid.: 24), in a recent study of resource-dependent communities throughout Canada, identified a community as resource-dependent 'if either (1) employment in the resource sector with the greatest number of employees exceeded employment in any other two-digit standard industrial sector or (2) employment in a combination of all the resource sectors exceeded employment in the combination of health and education services'. Several researchers have argued for a broader, multidimensional definition of resource dependency (Machlis and Force, 1988; Overdevest and Green, 1995; Beckley, 1998; Adger, 2000) in addition to simple economic or financial measures, and which includes the concepts of community stability or resilience to change.

The ability to define the geographic and spatial extent of social systems and resource systems through the framework of TRC-Analysis provides an important basis for developing more conceptually and methodologically rigorous measures or indicators of resource dependency and the extent to which changes in the status of the resource may impact on resource-dependent communities. However, it should be recognized that resource dependency is only one component of the relationship between social systems and broader environmental systems in which resource systems are embedded.

Resource dependency – including extractive uses (such as fishing, hunting and mining) and non-extractive uses (such as leisure, tourism and recreation) of the resource – describes only one type of relationship or linkage between social and broader environmental systems. In addition, the relationship between social and environmental systems may be defined in terms of the associations people have with the environment, which may include a range of symbolic and place meanings as well as specific environmental values. While the research focus to date within TRC-Analysis has been on extractive resource use, the same framework may also be extended to non-extractive resource use and to include broader human associations with the environment. Recent research on the mapping and identification of regionally significant places indicates that place meanings are more commonly reported for locations in close proximity to places of residence (Coakes, Fenton and Gabriel, 1999; Commonwealth of Australia, 1998; 1999; 2000). This suggests the existence of a familiar 'home-range' with associated meanings and values surrounding specific towns, communities or TRCs. A more complete assessment of the social impacts associated with changes in NRM and planning would benefit from a more integrated approach. Within the TRC framework, such an integrated approach would give concurrent consideration to both the spatial and the geographic extent of resource use and broader environmental associations, including specific place meanings and values.

Describing town resource clusters
Defining a TRC and its associated resource catchments is important in providing the basic framework in which further SIA procedures may be embedded. For instance, in understanding and managing the relationship between communities and areas of resource use, the development of community involvement programmes can be more effectively directed at those communities where a known relationship exists between the area of resource use and the community. Community involvement programmes can be focused on specific towns and communities, but also the specific content of the techniques used can be more directed and focused if the relationship between community and resource is known. Knowing the interrelationships that exist amongst a cluster of townships or communities, and their relationship to specific resource catchments, provides an important basis for the development of community involvement programmes. This provides an important basis for co-management or community-based management of natural resources (see Chapter 4). As is evident in Figure 14.3, and in the context of the use of fisheries resources, each of the 22 TRCs identified along the Queensland coast has specific and identifiable resource catchments associated with it. This information clearly identifies those core communities that should be included in community involvement or management programmes associated with management and planning within these resource catchments.

TRCs can be described using traditional quantitative psychosocial, economic and demographic indicators to illustrate the biophysical, health, cultural, social, political/legal, economic and psychological components (Gramling and Freudenburg, 1992). Specifically for the purposes of NRM, the tenure and knowledge systems, world views and ethics governing the use of environment and resources can be measured (Berkes and Folke, 2000). The resource dependency of TRCs may also be assessed through the use of specific social and economic indicators based on employment in the resource sector, levels of resource production, occupational and industrial specialization or through other non-economic indices (Machlis and Force, 1988).

In the same way as the resource condition can be described using ecological indicators, TRCs can be described using a range of social indicators. Their selection and use would be dependent upon the objectives of the social assessment or impact assessment being undertaken. Of particular importance are indicators which provide information on community stability (Waggener, 1977; Machlis and Force, 1988), social resilience (Adger, 2000; Berkes and Folke, 2000), sensitivity to change (Fenton, 1999c, 2000a; 2000b), community wellbeing (Overdevest and Green, 1995) and social capital (Flora, 1998). There is continuing debate as to what the most appropriate indicators of these concepts are, and to what extent the underlying concepts are related. Nevertheless, the ability to make some assessment of the social resilience of TRCs and the ecological resilience of resource catchments on which TRCs are dependent has significant implications for the way natural resources are managed. More specifically, such an approach allows equal and concurrent consideration of both social and ecological criteria in NRM and planning in order that social and ecological systems can be maintained in a sustainable manner.

Figure 14.4 shows the interrelationship between ecological systems (natural resource areas or catchments) on the one hand and social systems (TRCs) on the other. Working in a clockwise direction from the natural resource, changes in the management of the natural resource may have corresponding social impacts on dependent social systems or TRCs. Given that these impacts may occur, the management of change and the development of mitigation strategies can be directed specifically at the associated TRCs. On the other hand, given information on the social and economic characteristics of TRCs, and specifically information on the social resilience, stability or wellbeing of populations within the TRC, this information can be used concurrently with ecological criteria in the management of natural resources. For example, the establishment and location of marine protected areas, national parks or state forests would be based not only on core ecological criteria in terms of ecosystems biodiversity and resilience, but also the social resilience and stability of dependent social systems which may be affected by changes in the status of the natural resource.

The importance of integrating social and ecological assessments in NRM is evident in the recent national policy of the Australian Seafood Industry

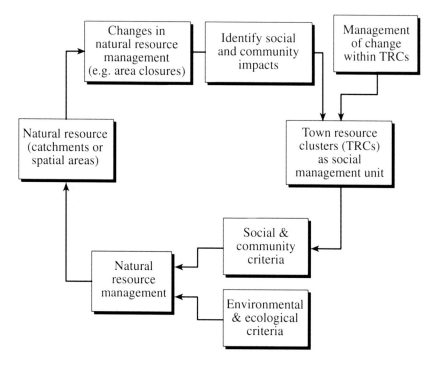

Figure 14.4   A model for the integration of social and ecological systems

Council (2000: 11). This policy was developed in relation to the establishment of marine protected areas (MPAs) in Australia. Recommendation four of this policy states:

> Assessment of the potential economic and social impacts (including flow on effects) of modifying the fishing industry's access to fisheries resources must be undertaken and considered during the planning process of MPAs. ESD [ecologically sustainable development] requires consideration of economic and social, as well as ecological factors. However, consideration and implementation of MPAs to date have been done with scant analysis, or vague recognition, of the social or economic impacts of the establishment of MPAs. MPA agencies seem to be failing to learn the lessons of the forestry debate which resulted in a level of conflict unprecedented in this country before serious action was commenced to integrate data on the social and economic impact of reserve systems into the decision making process.

Conclusion

TRC-Analysis provides an important conceptual framework on which to base social assessments generally. It also assists specifically in the assessment of social impacts arising from changes in the management, use or condition of natural resources. Through the concurrent examination of attributes of resource and social systems, particularly within the spatial context as described through TRC-Analysis, some understanding can be gained of the way changes in resource systems impact on social systems and, conversely, how changes in social systems may impact on resource systems. The range of quantitative psychosocial, economic and demographic methods that are used in the context of social assessment can now be embedded within a framework which integrates both social and resource systems. Furthermore, community involvement programmes and their associated participatory and consultative techniques and procedures may also be usefully integrated within the TRC framework with the added knowledge of the link between social and resource systems and which communities are most likely to be impacted by changes in resource conditions.

References

Adger, W.N. 2000. 'Social and ecological resilience: Are they related?', *Progress in Human Geography*, 24(3): 347–64.

Australian Seafood Industry Council 2000. 'Australian fishing industry develops policy on marine protected areas', *The Queensland Fisherman*, August, 10–13.

Beal, D.J. 1997. 'Economic incentives for farm level resource conservation', *Australian Journal of Environmental Management*, 4(4): 211–23.

Beckley, T.M. 1998. 'The nestedness of forest dependence: A conceptual framework and empirical exploration', *Society and Natural Resources*, 11(2): 101–20.

Berkes, F. and Folke, C. 2000. 'Linking social and ecological systems for resilience and sustainability', in F. Berkes and C. Folke (eds), *Linking Social and Ecological Systems: Management Practices and Social Mechanisms for Building Resilience*, Cambridge: Cambridge University Press, 1–25.

Carrothers, G. 1956. 'An Historical Review of the Gravity and Potential Concepts of Human Interaction', *Journal of American Institute of Planners*, 22(2): 94–102.

Christaller, W. 1933. *Central Places in Southern Germany* (trans. C.W. Baskin, 1966), Englewood Cliffs: Prentice-Hall.

Coakes, S., Fenton D.M. and Gabriel, M. 1999. 'The Application of Repertory Grid Analysis in Assessing Community Sensitivity to Change in the Forest Sector', *Impact Assessment and Project Appraisal*, 17(3): 193–202.

Commonwealth of Australia 1998. 'Social Assessment Report: North East Victoria', Commonwealth and Victorian Regional Forest Agreement (RFA) Steering Committee, Department of Natural Resources and Environment, Melbourne, Victoria.

Commonwealth of Australia 1999. 'Social Assessment Report: West Victoria', Commonwealth and Victorian Regional Forest Agreement (RFA) Steering Committee, Department of Natural Resources and Environment, Melbourne, Victoria.

Commonwealth of Australia 2000. 'Social Assessment Report: Gippsland Victoria', Commonwealth and Victorian Regional Forest Agreement (RFA) Steering Committee, Department of Natural Resources and Environment, Melbourne, Victoria.

Conacher, A. and Conacher, J. 2000. *Environmental Planning and Management in Australia*, Melbourne: Oxford University Press.

Cramer, L.A., Kennedy, J.J., Krannich, R.S. and Quigley, T.M. 1993. 'Changing forest values and their implications for land management decisions affecting resource-dependent communities', *Rural Sociology*, 58(3): 475–91.

Fenton, D.M. 1998a. 'West Australian RFA: Forest industry expenditure, catchment analysis and employee profiles', report prepared for the Department of Primary Industries and Energy (Canberra).

Fenton, D.M. 1998b. 'Resource, forest industry and employee catchment analysis for the South East Queensland RFA Region', report prepared for the Department of Primary Industries and Energy (Canberra).

Fenton, D.M. 1999a. 'Forest industry activity and linkages for the Gippsland CRA Region, Victoria', report for the Social Assessment Unit, Agriculture Forestry Fisheries Australia, Canberra.

Fenton, D.M. 1999b. 'Profiles of the mining industry and employees in Muswellbrook, New South Wales', report prepared for Coal Operations Australia Pty Ltd.

Fenton. D.M. 1999c. 'TRC-Analysis for the Barron water allocation and management plan (WAMP)', report prepared for the Department of Natural Resources, Brisbane, Queensland.

Fenton, D.M. 1999d. 'The social impacts of dairy industry deregulation and water reform on dairy farmers and communities in the Bega Valley', report prepared for the Bega Valley Water Management Committee, Bega, New South Wales.

Fenton. D.M. 2000a. 'TRC-Analysis for the Burnett water allocation and management plan (WAMP)', report prepared for the Department of Natural Resources, Brisbane, Queensland.

Fenton, D.M. 2000b. *Social catchments and socio-demographic profiles for the South Brigalow CRA/RFA Region (NSW)*, report prepared for the Department of Urban Affairs and Planning, Sydney, New South Wales.

Fenton, D.M. and Marshall, N.A. 2000. 'A guide to the fishers of Queensland: TRC-Analysis and social profiles of Queensland's commercial fishing industry (Part A)', report prepared for the CRC Reef Research, Townsville, Queensland.

Flora, J.L. 1998. 'Social capital and communities of place', *Rural Sociology*, 63(4): 481–506.

Gould, W., William, E. and Richard, M. 1989. 'Conservation tillage: The role of farm and operator characteristics and perception of soil erosion', *Land Economics*, 65(2): 167–81.

Gramling, R. and Freudenburg, W.R. 1992. 'Opportunity-threat, development, and adaptation: Toward a comprehensive framework for social impact assessment', *Rural Sociology*, 57(2): 216–34.

Hall, A.D. and Fagen, R.E. 1956. 'Definition of System', *General Systems: The Yearbook of the Society for the Advancement of General Systems Theory*, 1: 18–28.

Machlis, G.E. and Force, J.E. 1988. 'Community stability and timber-dependent communities', *Rural Sociology*, 53(2): 220–34.

Machlis, G.E., Force, J.E. and Burch, W.R. 1990. 'Timber, minerals and social change: An exploratory test of two resource dependent communities', *Rural Sociology*, 55(4): 411–24.

Mayfield, L.H. 1996. 'The local economic impact of small farms', *Tijdschrift voor Economische en Sociale Geografie*, 87(5): 387–98.

Murphy, A.B. 1991. 'Regions as social constructs', *Progress in Human Geography*, 15(1): 22–35.

Overdevest, C. and Green, G.P. 1995. 'Forest dependence and community well-being', *Society and Natural Resources*, 8(2): 111–31.

Randall, J.E. and Ironside, R.G. 1996. 'Communities on the edge: An economic geography of resource-dependent communities in Canada', *The Canadian Geographer*, 40(1): 17–35.

Rapoport, A. 1985. 'Thinking about home environments', in I. Altman and C.M. Werner (eds), *Home Environments*, New York: Plenum, 255–86.

Rogers, E. 1962. *Diffusion of innovations*, New York: The Free Press.

Slootweg, R., Vanclay, F. and van Schooten, M. 2001. 'Functional evaluation as a framework for the integration of social and environmental impact assessment', *Impact Assessment and Project Appraisal*, 19(1): 19–28.

Waggener, T.R. 1977. 'Community stability as a forest management objective', *Journal of Forestry*, 75: 710–14.

15 Citizen values assessment
Annelies Stolp

Introduction

Expert opinions of environmental values and impacts – including those of SIA practitioners – can differ from the way citizens feel about the state of their living environment (that is, where they live, work and play) and how intended activities may impact on the various attributes of that environment. Therefore, in environmental impact assessment (EIA), social impact assessment (SIA) and other planning procedures, it is necessary to investigate the way people judge their living environment, and how they think a planned project may affect its qualities. This may provide additional relevant information to decision makers. SIA practitioners are important gatekeepers in gaining access to local knowledge and making it available to others (see Chapter 3). Unfortunately, consideration of citizens' value judgments is not routinely undertaken in EIA or SIA. Both EIA and SIA tend to remain technocratic in orientation, avoiding any detailed consideration of the ways people are affected (Burningham, 1995; Dale and Lane, 1994, 1995; Gagnon et al., 1993; Ortolano and Shepherd, 1995).

Despite awareness within SIA of differences in perceptions between social groups, and between experts and the affected communities, the SIA literature has very little specification of the actual methods used to determine citizen values. In fact, SIA does not have many specified techniques, despite endorsement of a general procedure in the Interorganizational Committee's Guidelines and Principles for Social Impact Assessment (ICGP, 1994) and despite the outlines provided by Freudenburg (1986), Taylor et al. (1995), Burdge and Vanclay (1995), Burdge (1998) and Vanclay (1999). Although SIA is said to be a fully recognized component of EIA (Burdge and Vanclay, 1995), social impacts are rarely included in EIA studies.

The need to consider differences between citizens and experts in the perceived qualities of the environment, together with the lack of specified techniques, led to the development of citizen values assessment (CVA). Central to CVA is the difference that an intended activity will make to the living environment of people potentially affected by a project, and that this must be described from the perspective of those people in any EIA. CVA is thus primarily an instrument to incorporate within an EIA the importance people attach to particular environmental attributes. The term, 'citizen values', is interpreted here to mean the value judgments of individuals about the quality of their living environment and its various attributes. The living environment comprises the area in which people live, work and play. By 'citizens', we mean all residents and other users of an area potentially affected by an intended activity. The word 'citizen' was chosen because it reinforces the notion that the level of analysis is the individual, and it does not refer to citizenship or nationality.

Quick overview of CVA
CVA provides an inventory of the values people in affected communities assign to their living environment through in-depth interviews with individual citizens. This is later validated by a quantitative survey of a representative sample of the population. Selected key values are presented in a citizen values profile (CVP), which forms the basis of assessment by which project alternatives are evaluated. The CVP is translated into evaluation criteria that are subsequently operationalized by qualitative and quantitative variables.

CVA thus combines a 'normative approach' using subjective value judgments of individual citizens and the meanings they attach to the qualities of the living environment with a 'technocratic approach' using scientifically rigorous and technically sound data. By providing systematic and 'neutral' information, CVA provides a rational basis for decision making. This information is complementary to expert judgments and can be added to the analysis of impacts in environmental impact statements (EIS) and other policy evaluation reports.

CVA does not measure attitudes, nor is it an instrument to investigate citizens' preferences or opinions about alternative plans or projects. The method does not measure community views about the future impacts of projects, nor does it evaluate the extent of acceptance of, or resistance to, intended activities. Instead, it is an EIA instrument that measures citizens' judgments about the qualities of the living environment, and provides a framework for analysis by which the possible impacts of project alternatives on those environmental attributes can be evaluated. Therefore CVA does not provide an overview of the full range of possible social impacts of a given project. It only applies to those social impacts associated with perceived environmental values, and not to other dimensions of social impact such as health and social wellbeing, economic impacts and material wellbeing, cultural impacts, family and community impacts, gender impacts and so on. Furthermore, CVA is not designed to understand why people behave in relation to their living environment. Nor does it predict how they will respond to possible changes in the living environment as a result of a proposed development.

A crucial difference between CVA and public involvement is that CVA is a structured study providing an overview of citizen values and how a project may affect those values. Public involvement, on the other hand, is a process intended to build legitimacy for a project and the assessment process by discussing alternatives directly with representatives of community groups and other interested or affected parties. By identifying the key values of the living environment rather than opinions about alternatives, CVA is not influenced by fears, public resistance, the positions of interest groups or exaggerated NIMBY (not in my backyard) responses.

CVA was founded on three premises. First, decisions about what matters in the environment, and what is studied as part of an EIA, should be based on value orientations that are explicit. They should not come exclusively from technical experts. Local communities have important knowledge to share, which is based on their use and experience of the local environment and their observations of the operations of facilities and infrastructure (see Chapter 3). Their lived rationalities should not only be incorporated by means of public involvement during project planning and the EIA process, but they should also be incorporated as separate criteria in the final document that describes, evaluates and compares alternatives.

Second, the explicit inclusion of citizen values in the EIA process increases the quality of the EIS, providing a broader and more complete overview of the positive and negative impacts of intended activities. Adding CVA to EIA improves the rational basis for decision making because it provides additional information on environmental values, project and mitigation design, impacts and comparison of alternatives. Moreover, CVA puts citizen values on an equal footing with scientific and technical information. This increases the legitimacy of the document from the perspective of the public (van Vliet, 1996).

Third, citizen values are best reflected if the research approach used provides a detailed understanding of the meaning of the living environment to citizens themselves. This requires a research approach that respects citizens' experiences of their living environment in the process of collecting and analysing data.

The Dutch context
CVA was conceived and developed within the Netherlands Ministry of Transport, Public Works and Water Management (Rijkswaterstaat) for the Dutch EIA context. The Dutch EIA system – regarded as one of the most comprehensive and effective in Europe (Arts, 1998; Sadler, 1996; Wood, 1995) – developed because the country is densely populated, has a strong tradition of land-use planning, and has a high and long-standing level of public interest in environmental issues (Arts, 1998). The formal regulatory processes, however, do not prescribe the inclusion of a social dimension in

EIA. As a result of this limited SIA tradition in Dutch EIA, there is little expertise available in the field of applied social sciences or SIA attuned to the Dutch EIA context.

Rijkswaterstaat is the proponent of many projects requiring EIA. In the past decade, these projects have included the construction of high-speed railways, highways, facilities for storing contaminated sediment (massive sludge ponds), land reclamation and dyke-strengthening projects. Because The Netherlands is a small, densely populated country, these projects directly or indirectly affect millions of people and therefore generate considerable public discussion. In the 1990s, public criticism of Rijkswaterstaat focused on several issues. Rijkswaterstaat was considered to overemphasize technical concerns in planning and design. It was perceived as communicating poorly: there was lack of information exchange between project planners and EIA experts on the one hand, and the public and interest groups on the other. The input of citizens through participation procedures appeared to have limited influence on project planning and decision making. Finally, there was a perception that Rijkswaterstaat had conflicting roles, being both the proponent and the regulatory authority.

Dyke reinforcement (see Box 15.1) was one of the issues in the early 1990s which made clear that political acceptability of environmental decision-making required not only EIA, but also participatory approaches to project planning. These new approaches highlighted crucial differences in perception between various groups, notably engineering experts, long-term residents, newcomers, environmental organizations and other interest groups.

Over the past decade, Rijkswaterstaat developed a more open attitude towards the public, and a variety of participatory approaches for policy development and project planning arose. In the same period, EIA processes were being better integrated into planning. Since EIA developed as an instrument to evaluate and compare alternatives, rather than to design

---

BOX 15.1   FROM TECHNOCRATIC TO PARTICIPATORY APPROACHES IN PROJECT PLANNING: DYKE REINFORCEMENT IN THE NETHERLANDS

In the early 1990s, a discussion took place in The Netherlands about the role of environmental values in decision making. It focused on the differences between experts and the public, between experts, and between different groups within the community, in relation to perceptions about the need for, and design of, dyke reinforcement for flood prevention. EIA was not obligatory for dyke reinforcement projects. Project development had been dominated by technical assumptions and requirements, and little consideration was given to ecological or social issues. Technical experts tried to fast-track project planning, emphasizing the urgent need to reinforce river dykes because of flood risk.

Previous dyke reinforcement projects had serious impacts on historical, cultural, landscape and nature values, leading to strong public criticism and negative publicity. There was also discussion between engineers and EIA experts about the way environmental values should be considered. Perceptions of flood risk varied considerably between different groups in the communities.

Many dyke reinforcement projects were delayed by legal action. The issue reached the national political agenda and an evaluation committee was established by the Minister of Transport, Public Works and Water Management to investigate planning processes in relation to dyke reinforcement. One recommendation of the committee was that EIA should become compulsory for dyke reinforcement. Shortly after this recommendation had been implemented, severe flooding occurred, in December 1993, with more in February 1995. The 1995 flood was so severe that 250 000 people and over a million cattle were evacuated.

As a consequence of these floods, the need for EIA was off the political agenda and public opposition evaporated, although nature organizations continued their criticism and arguably delayed projects. An emergency law, 'Deltaplan Large Rivers', was enacted to accelerate dyke reinforcement. Its aim was to make The Netherlands 'waterproof' by the year 2000. It provided for rapid procedures, but mandated the involvement of interest group representatives. Despite initial scepticism, after the first planning procedures had commenced it became clear that the recent flood experience had convinced all actors that a cooperative, interactive approach would be the most efficient way to develop broadly supported plans in the shortest possible time. This positive experience with participatory processes sent a strong signal to Rijkswaterstaat, and to other government agencies and the corporate sector, that participatory processes were useful. This led to much willingness to experiment further with them.

plans, EIA does not necessarily guarantee the development of environmentally sound projects. More emphasis on integration of EIA in project planning provided opportunities for the development of better projects. The changing culture in Rijkswaterstaat – notably the tendency to use less technocratic and more participatory approaches – combined with the limited experience of SIA in Dutch EIA, provided a context which was receptive to the development of a new instrument for impact assessment from the perspective of citizens.

SIA, EIA and CVA

Recent SIA literature argues that SIA should be fully integrated in the planning and decision-making process, and not limited to being merely a tool to predict the likely impacts of intended projects (see, inter alia, Craig, 1990; Dale and Lane, 1994, 1995; Burdge and Vanclay, 1995; ICGP, 1994; Taylor *et al.*, 1995; Vanclay, 2002). This implies that SIA practitioners should exert influence from the very beginning of project development until after project completion. However, there are few examples where this has occurred. In most cases, SIA is used only for the prediction of impacts, and the influence of SIA practitioners has been limited. Project planning and decision making have been in the hands of others, mostly technical experts and politicians.

Instead of being integrated, SIA and EIA have emerged as different disciplines, each with its own paradigm and discourse. EIA generally focuses on biophysical impacts, whereas SIA focuses on sociocultural impacts. Where SIA has been used in EIA, it was mainly as a tool to examine the 'technical' impacts on humans. There was a tendency to avoid any detailed consideration of the ways in which people were affected (Burningham, 1995; Dale and Lane, 1995; Ortolano and Shepherd, 1995).

One advantage of EIA is that it is embedded in legal frameworks, which guarantees its application in certain situations. Because these legal frameworks exist in many countries, the embedding of SIA within EIA potentially provides a sound basis for improved consideration of social issues. Because CVA is directly linked to the EIA process, it provides a mechanism to integrate SIA with EIA, thus establishing a legal mandate for SIA. CVA is an SIA instrument because it is an impact study from the perspective of citizens. At the same time, CVA is an EIA instrument because (a) it addresses the qualities of the environment, and the way these may be affected by planned activities, and (b) because its purpose is to incorporate social considerations within EIA.

Burningham (1995) observed that attempts to incorporate the perceptions of local people in EIA have typically been through some form of attitude or opinion research. Such approaches have limited potential, because residents are likely to engage in a variety of strategies in response to the proposed development and may present a distorted view in order to advance their position (Burningham, 1995; Vanclay, 1999). Because CVA concentrates on environmental values rather than opinions about a project, the bias associated with the opinion research approach to assessment is overcome.

A barrier to integrating SIA in EIA is the lack of SIA procedures attuned to EIA practice. Despite repeated advocacy for the development of procedures and participatory approaches integrated with planning processes (Craig, 1990; Dale and Lane, 1994), in SIA research methods and techniques tend to be implicit. In case studies and SIA reports, there is a lack of adequate reporting of the methods and techniques used. In fact, in the SIA discipline as a whole, very few techniques are specified. The general procedures described in the Interorganizational Committee's Guidelines and Principles for Social Impact Assessment (ICGP, 1994) and other key references, such as Freudenburg (1986), Taylor *et al.* (1995), Burdge and Vanclay (1995), Burdge (1998) and Vanclay (1999), are broad overviews rather than specific procedures.

CVA is a clearly specified method for incorporating citizen values into EIA and planning processes. CVA has been developed as a component of EIA. It follows EIA methodology, including scoping, profiling, describing the existing situation, identifying potential impacts, selecting variables to measure impacts, and assessing and comparing alternatives. Various components of EIA describe environmental impacts from different scientific perspectives, for example the loss of habitat, the threat to biodiversity or to endangered species, the loss of recreational possibilities, and so on. CVA facilitates identification of potential corresponding impacts from the perspective of users of an affected area. By utilizing CVA, expert and lay public perspectives are considered conjointly.

CVA focuses on only a segment of the possible range of social impacts, specifically on the qualities of the living environment that are considered relevant by citizens. It is not a method to provide an overview of the full range of possible social impacts of a given development. Neither is it designed to understand the reasons why, or predict how, people respond to possible changes in the living environment as a result of a proposed development. CVA is limited in that it lacks systematic attention to (a) the full range of potential social impacts that are typically identified by SIA experts. For example, of the six categories of impacts identified in Chapter 6, emphasis is placed on only one, the quality of the living environment; (b) indirect effects, and the upstream and downstream effects; (c) impacts at meso and macro levels; and (d) impacts in the long term, the impacts of long-term developments and the interests of future generations.

For a complete overview of relevant social impacts, an expert SIA is required. However, CVA can be a valuable input in such an expert SIA. The citizen values profile can be used as the basis upon which the SIA practitioner predicts all likely impacts of a project. CVA can thus be characterized as a methodology to provide information useful in several steps of an SIA: specifically, profiling, scoping, impact prediction and projection of estimated impacts (see ICGP, 1994).

Detailed outline of citizen values assessment
CVA consists of four phases and a follow-up step related to integration of the outcomes of CVA in the EIS or other policy evaluation document. Phase 1 consists of problem definition, delineation and identification of interest groups, and the collection of background information. Phase 2 is a preliminary qualitative study to provide in-depth understanding of local people's connections to the area affected by the project. Semi-structured interviews are conducted with people from all relevant interested and affected parties, including residents, commuters, workers, day-trippers and tourists. The outcome is a listing of the selected key values of the affected community (a preliminary profile). In phase 3, a quantitative survey is conducted to validate the key values identified in phase 2, to determine the relative importance of those key values, and how respondents feel about their present living environment in respect of these key values. The outcome is an assessment matrix or citizen values profile (CVP). In phase 4, the CVP is translated into evaluation criteria. Qualitative or quantitative variables are identified for each of the assessment criteria. Impacts are determined and alternatives are compared.

After the CVA study is completed, the results should be integrated in the EIA or other policy evaluation document. A possible way to integrate CVA outcomes in an EIS is the development of a citizen values scenario complementary to other scenarios such as an economic scenario or a nature scenario.

Phase 1: basic groundwork
Phase 1 is a brief investigation to identify the likely area of impact, the geographical area in which impacts may occur (that is, the study area), and the groups of citizens that are potentially affected. It provides insight into land-use patterns, relevant groups of land users and the organizations representing them. Relationships between interests, and between interests and the proposed development, are analysed. The study area may differ from that considered by the various experts, depending on how alternatives are defined, and how the zone of impact is determined. In CVA, the study area is usually defined as the area where impacts can be experienced by the sensory perception of those who live there and/or who use it.

A preparatory study starts with an analysis of relevant documents – maps, photographs, municipal guides, reports, newspapers and other sources of information – in order to identify land-use patterns and relevant interest groups. An interest group is considered relevant when the interest(s) it represents are likely to be affected by the proposed development. Such groups include small local interest groups representing specific activities or neighbourhoods, as well as large, professional, national (and potentially international) organizations, such as nature conservation associations. These organizations provide information for understanding the study area through interviews with key informants, often the representatives of these interest groups. Note that these representatives are *not* specifically involved as respondents in phase 2, as they represent specific interest groups. Telephone interviews are conducted with key informants, liaison contacts for relevant groups and other knowledgable local individuals. The preparatory study results in a research plan, defines categories of respondents and identifies a process for selecting representatives of the various groups. Respondent groupings are typically based on factors such as geographic distribution, land-use patterns and specific activities.

Phase 2: identifying key values
The primary objectives of phase 2 are (a) to investigate the baseline conditions of the study area; (b) to collect data illustrating the location-specific relationships of citizens with their living environment; and (3) to identify the environmental values which are considered relevant by citizens. This information becomes the basis for the development of a preliminary profile. The identification of the key values is the core of a CVA study. Data are collected by means of face-to-face interviews with citizens. The interviews provide detailed understanding about what the environment means to citizens. The interviews are semi-structured, with the course of the conversation led by the interviewer following strategically arranged discussion themes (see Box 15.2). Respondents are invited to discuss these themes in their own way, using their own words, and from their own perspective. Interviews last approximately one hour.

Interviews are conducted with representatives of relevant groups such as residents, commuters, workers, day-trippers and tourists. For accuracy, CVA requires skilled professional interviewers committed to its premises. They should be able to approach respondents in an unbiased way and respect differing perceptions of reality. Interviews are tape-recorded and transcribed for qualitative data analysis.

The large quantity of information collected is organized into a coherent picture by a process of 'open coding' and 'analytical memo writing'

BOX 15.2   DISCUSSION THEMES IN A CVA
INTERVIEW WITH RESIDENTS
(PHASE 2)

Perceptions of environmental qualities. Why did the resident choose to live here? What is the specific connection with this living environment? What makes the person feel 'rooted' in the area? What is special about this living environment? What factors cause nuisance? How does the resident make use of the area?

Observed and expected changes in environmental qualities. What changes has the resident recently observed? Are these changes positive or negative? Why? What changes does the resident antic-ipate will occur in the near future? Are these changes positive or negative, and why?

The problem underlying the proposed project. Does the resident know about the underlying issue? Does the resident acknowledge the problem? Does the resident agree that the problem should be tackled in the way intended by the proponent? What is the resi-dent's opinion of the proposed project?

Opinion towards proposed project. [Note – this information is used to increase understanding of residents' value judgments about environmental qualities and impacts on environmental qualities; this information is not meant to investigate the extent of public acceptance or resistance.] What is the opinion of the resident about the project and the alternatives that are relevant to them? [maps, drawings and/or artist impressions of alternatives are shown to the resident to provide background.]

Perceptions of possible impacts. The interviewee is asked which environmental qualities may be affected by the proposed alterna-tives. [As before, maps, drawings and/or artist impressions may be shown.]

Issues relevant for design. What measures should be taken to minimize those possible impacts that are relevant to the resident? What other measures could the resident think of to compensate for those impacts that cannot be avoided?

(Neuman, 1996). Each transcript is examined for mention of elements of the living environment, and for specific meanings associated with those ele-ments. This results in a listing of 'element–meaning pairs' – elements of the environment together with the meanings ascribed to those elements by interviewees. Then follows a process of sorting (interview themes), categorizing (types of values) and synthesizing a listing of key values underlying the perceived attributes of the living environment. This phase requires social researchers adequately skilled in qualitative analysis.

The results of this phase are presented in a separate report structured along the interview themes. One intention of CVA is to allow citizens to recognize themselves in the outcomes, showing them that they have been heard and listened to, and reinforcing the legitimacy of citizens' values and rationality in the EIA process. To achieve this, many quotations are used to illustrate and justify the descriptions of what the living environment means to citizens. The outcome of phase 2 is a listing of the key values. The report, or at least a summary, from this phase should be sent to all respondents. This is an important step to check whether the analysis is perceived to be adequate. Ideally, the outcomes of this phase are discussed with community representatives. The report, and preliminary drafts of the report, should be distributed to the proponent's project team, so that the information can be used as an input for project mitigation and design and as feedback on the impact of the communication strategies of the proponent. If CVA is initiated early enough, the (preliminary) outcomes can be used to profile the content of the EIA study. The use of these preliminary results is a substantial part of the total contribution of CVA to the EIA process.

Phase 3: constructing a citizen values profile
In phase 3, the preliminary profile is transformed into a final assessment matrix, or citizen values profile (CVP). The CVP represents the importance of the environmental values from the perspective of citizens. Data are collected by a quantitative survey, normally a mail survey of a random sample of the potentially affected population. This is done to validate the preliminary profile. Data are collected to confirm whether the set of key values is comprehensive and that each is actually relevant. It also serves to determine the importance of each of the key values by asking respondents to prioritize them. Potentially, this can be done in three ways: (a) scoring each of the key values on a scale, say, from 1 to 10, or 1 to 100; (b) rating each value on a Likert scale; (3) ranking them. Ranking is not usually practical since the large number of values makes it too taxing on respondents. Statistically, it is preferable for Likert scales to contain more categories (that is, 5 or 7) to provide greater differentiation, but respondents generally prefer fewer categories. The aggregated scores across all respondents provide the basis for determining the weighting to be assigned to each key value.

Finally, the survey is undertaken in order to be able to score the present living environment in respect of the key values, and to collect information to assist in developing mitigation measures and/or for the consideration of compensation.

The questionnaire consists of four sections (see Box 15.3). To avoid large non-response bias, it is very important that the questionnaire and accompanying letter are 'citizen-friendly' (no jargon, no official language). They must clearly describe the status of CVA within the EIA process to prevent inflated expectations of what will be done with the outcomes of the CVA. Where the proposed project has alternative locations, separate samples are required. In this situation, the key values may differ between locations, requiring different questionnaires. To ensure validity and reliability of the results, the sampling procedures need to be justified explicitly, and the way in which key values are translated into questions needs to be transparent.

The results of this phase are presented in a separate report in which the final CVP is presented. The CVP may consist of a number of different sub-profiles for different locations and/or different alternatives. Each subprofile lists the key values in order of importance.

BOX 15.3   OUTLINE OF A CVA QUESTIONNAIRE (PHASE 3)

Introduction. Description of the objective of the study and a brief description of the proposed project and the underlying problem.

Part 1: evaluation of the present living environment. For each selected key value in phase 2, respondents are asked to consider (1) whether or not they consider the key value relevant in terms of their living environment, and (2) how they judge the quality of their current living environment in relation to this key value. Space exists for respondents to nominate new key values under an 'other' heading. Any additional value must be scored in the same way.

Part 2: the relative importance of the key values. Respondents are asked to judge the key values (which may include the values added by the respondent), by scoring each key value on a scale from 1 to 10 (or 100), or to rate them on a Likert scale.

Part 3: mitigation and compensation measures. Different questions are formulated depending on the type of project and the project environment. Questions may relate to impacts such as noise nuisance or loss of visual amenity, or to design and siting issues such as road layout, location of facilities or land reclamation.

Part 4: general demographic and socioeconomic characteristics of the respondents.

Phase 4: determining impacts of project alternatives
In phase 4, the CVA researcher translates the key values into evaluation criteria. The outcome is an overview, from the perspective of citizens, of the
potential impacts of alternatives on the living environment. This phase
starts after the design of alternatives has been finalized. It consists of the
following steps: (a) translation of key values into evaluation criteria; (b)
operationalization of evaluation criteria by identification of quantitative or
qualitative variables, and identification of data sources; (c) determining
importance of impacts for each criterion; and (d) recommendations for
mitigation and/or compensation.

The crucial step in this phase is how the CVP is transformed into evaluation criteria. This involves selection and judgment of the available information by the CVA researcher. Transparency and justification are essential.
There should be no doubt about how the criteria were operationalized.

The first step is the selection of those key values that discriminate
between alternatives. For example, concern about safety in a residential
area may be relevant for assessing impacts of an infrastructure project
when the factors that make people feel unsafe are related to traffic (for
example, short cuts through residential areas). However, safety concerns
may not be relevant to the CVA when such concern is caused by anti-social
behaviour unrelated to the proposed project. In the second step, each dis-
criminating key value is translated into an evaluation criterion. For each
criterion, the underlying meanings, how operationalized, whether by means
of qualitative or quantitative variables, and what data sources exist, need
to be explained on the basis of the outcomes of phase 2.

The primary and most appropriate data sources are the various impact
studies (expert studies) carried out by the EIA team. For example, a criterion 'quiet, green living environment' may be operationalized by utilizing
expert studies on noise nuisance, traffic patterns and visual amenity. The
importance of probable impacts can either be determined directly from the
empirical results of the expert studies or it can be derived from interpretations of these studies made by the CVA researcher. However, the information needed for the determination of impacts considered relevant by
citizens will not always be available in the expert studies. When a criterion
cannot, or can only partly, be linked with the expert judgments, additional
variables have to be conceived. For example, in the case of a proposed
highway, the evaluation criterion 'preservation of outlook or vista' (referring to the scenic or aesthetic qualities of the residential area) might be connected with the variable, 'road surface height' in terms of height above (or
below) ground level. If so, this may provide an indication of the extent to
which the road embankments will block the view of citizens.

In some cases, situations may arise where the majority of required data is not available in the expert studies. To overcome this, workshops to derive impact measures could be held with a selection of experts, representatives of interest groups and knowledgable citizens. A Delphi technique could be applied, with participants coming to consensus on the weightings (Taylor *et al.*, 1995).

Ultimately, each alternative requires a score for each evaluation criteria. This can be done with a five point scale (such as $++$, $+$, 0, $-$, $--$). Another option is to rank the alternatives for each criterion. An overall assessment is conducted by considering all scores of each alternative, together with the weighting for each criterion. This can be done by qualitative analysis, resulting in an overview of positive and negative aspects of each alternative. Such an analysis can be summarized in a final score based on an average appreciation of an average user of a local area. The weights can be used in an analysis of the essential differences between alternatives. Such an analysis should focus on those criteria that have relatively high weights, and/or those criteria for which the impacts score relatively high. Alternatively, multi-criteria analysis (MCA) can be employed, using various weighting techniques (such as using a five-point scale, $++$, $+$, 0, $-$, $--$, rankings, or quantitative techniques) (see de Vries, 1999). Where alternatives are located in different sub-areas, CVA may result in different criteria and/or varying weights. In these cases, criteria need to be clustered into coherent themes at a higher abstraction level, before MCA is applied. In any case, simple forms of CVA are preferable. A complicated MCA procedure implies a degree of quantitative precision and does not reflect the character of CVA, which is primarily a qualitative instrument.

The outcome of phase 4 is the final (and full) CVA report in which the whole process is described, the outcomes of each phase are summarized, the impacts of alternatives are presented and alternatives are compared.

There are several problems that can be encountered in phase 4. The CVA researcher plays an important role in interpreting data and drawing conclusions, which means that it is very important that this input be validated. Transparency and justification of interpretations are an important basis for quality control, but they cannot prevent all bias. Ideally, verification is achieved through short workshops, in which representatives of project planners, experts involved in impact assessment, and community and other interest groups discuss the operationalizations proposed by the researcher. This, however, is labour-intensive. Preferably, verification is integrated in the concurrent communication process, for instance through discussion in existing advisory groups in which community groups and other interested parties are represented. To be able to make optimal use of the impact studies conducted in the EIA process, specific periods of information exchange between the CVA study and the expert studies should be planned.

Thus CVA should start in the very early stages of project design (and the EIA process) so that its preliminary results can be used as input for scoping.

Working with the outcomes of the various studies used as part of the EIA has revealed that there is considerable variation in the scales used to score impacts. This makes results hard to compare. Further, it is clear that, in many EIA subreports, interpretations are often implicit. When justification is lacking, a secondary analysis of these data is difficult for the CVA researcher. Some harmonization between CVA, SIA and EIA is required, and greater recognition of the role of CVA (and SIA) in EIA is desirable.

Follow-up phase: integrating CVA in the EIS
The results of a CVA need to be integrated into the final EIS. This is crucial for the potential role of CVA in decision making. The more explicit and elaborate the CVA outcomes presented in the EIS, the greater the chance that they will influence decision making. Furthermore, the more explicitly they are presented, the more recognizable citizens' value orientations will be to the citizens who read the EIS. This will potentially increase the legitimacy of the EIS in their eyes.

There are four ways in which CVA outcomes can be incorporated in the EIS. Presenting the outcomes of a full CVA independently gives the strongest statement of commitment that citizens' values will be respected. This option emphasizes the different nature of the information CVA presents, being based on citizens' perspectives rather than those of experts. It allows for the development of a 'most citizen-friendly' alternative as a counterpart to the 'most environment-friendly' alternative often defined in EIA studies.

A second way of presenting CVA outcomes is as one of the subcomponents of the topic, 'living environment'. This places them alongside the expert impact studies on other subcomponents such as noise nuisance and emissions. However, this option not only reduces the prominence of the CVA outcomes within the overall EIA, it neglects the distinct character of data provided by CVA. This option can also lead to confusion because some aspects, like landscape or recreation, may be presented twice in the final table (under technical sections as well as in the CVA).

Third, a citizen values scenario can be developed. Here the outcomes of the CVA study are used as input for an MCA applied to the main themes in the overall assessment matrix. The citizen values scenario can be compared with other scenarios, such as a nature scenario or an economic scenario. The CVP is used to assign weights to these aspects or themes in the overall assessment matrix. Two approaches are possible in developing the scenario. In one approach, the CVA assessment matrix is matched with the expert assessment matrix. All variables in the expert assessment matrix which are not mentioned by citizens are deleted. The weights for the remaining variables are calculated by translating weights from the CVA into weights in the expert evaluation matrix. Alternatively, weights can be assigned only to the main categories (aggregates of variables) in the assessment matrix. In both procedures, a ranking of alternatives is constructed by means of MCA. The development of a citizen scenario may be used as the sole outcome of a CVA study, in which case phase 4 of the CVA method can be omitted. However, this reduces the potential value of the data collected earlier.

The final option, and weakest form of applying CVA, is to use the information from the citizen values profile to comment on any list of impacts provided by other sources. For example, a CVA/SIA practitioner may be asked by an EIA team to comment on the impacts of alternatives. Here information about the community could be used by the CVA practitioner to assign weights on behalf of the community. This option is relatively cheap and can be undertaken in a shorter timeframe (because phase 4 is not required), but it seriously reduces the potential of the method.

The contribution of CVA: a question of rationality

In conventional EIA, the views, statements and results emanating from the 'experts' are generally regarded as being objective, verifiable (that is, valid and reliable) and rational. Social considerations, on the other hand, are deemed to be emotional and/or irrational and therefore are not seen as appropriate input for a scientifically rigorous EIA. Although there is now widespread consensus that social impacts should be considered as part of the environment, there are still (technical) EIA experts who believe that social considerations have no role in EIA. Burdge and Vanclay (1995) refer to the 'asocietal mentality' and technical discourse that dominates EIA procedures affecting public officials, politicians at all levels of government, physical scientists, engineers and even economists and planners. The technocratic approaches of many scientists and engineers involved in EIA – the so-called 'hard scientists' – are a major barrier to the utilization of SIA in EIA (Burdge, 1998; Denq and Altenhofel, 1997; Burdge and Vanclay, 1995). Despite the fact that involvement of local people and the use of local knowledge are becoming generally accepted, the technocratic culture of planning agencies tends to focus on whatever is quantifiable and technocratic (Dale and Lane, 1995). This creates what Firth (1998: 329) refers to as a spiral of distrust:

> The missing link is at the point where public agencies exclude the emotional/irrational 'stuff' the public offers, seeing it as non-data. Agencies may even take specific measures to avoid the 'non-data' . . . while their public is deciding to oppose projects based on that 'non-data'. In a deepening spiral of distrust, the agency's disregard of the public's emotional 'non-data' leads to the public viewing the agency's 'rational' data as irrational.

The question is: how far does the rationality of scientists and engineers extend? Within EIA, expert judgments are inherently based on the specific value orientations of the individual expert, even if those orientations are shared with other members of the profession or discipline. For example, there are obvious differences between ecologists and hydraulic engineers in relation to dyke reinforcement. In the case of Bomendijk, near Deventer in The Netherlands, there is a unique forest growing on the dyke bank. While engineers argue that the trees should be removed because the roots destabilize the dyke, ecologists want to preserve the ecological values of this unique phenomenon. Others consider Bomendijk to be of cultural and historical value.

Disciplinary value orientations are not the only source of bias within EIA. Although expert judgments are often presented as value-free, the EIA process involves interpretations, uncertainties, information gaps, normative elements and value orientations (Mostert, 1996). Numerous subjective judgments lie behind the choices experts make regarding those aspects of the environment that will be investigated, which key variables will be used, how data will be collected and interpreted, and how the results will be presented. Premises may be false, and the evidence supporting expert judgments may be flawed or inadequate. How often are subjective value orientations invisibly hidden in statistics and other so-called 'hard' data? Ortolano and Shepherd (1995: 7) conclude that this happens frequently:

> Surveys of the methods used to predict impacts in EIA . . . find that technical specialists often rely heavily on professional judgement to forecast environmental impacts, and predictions are often so vague they cannot be validated. Mathematical models are also used in making predictions; this practice is sometimes criticised because models are presented as 'black boxes', and the bases for predictions are not made clear. Indeed, because EIAs generally contain so little information about models and their assumptions, 'errors that are inherent in this approach are not readily traceable, and the results are not subject to scrutiny' (Leon, 1993: 657).

Obviously, EIA should be based on as much empirical data as possible. Technocrats believe that, because EIA should provide a rational basis for decision making, it therefore should only consist of data based on technical considerations. The view that social issues, especially when investigated by means of qualitative research methods, are too subjective and therefore not appropriate for EIA is wrong. All assessments are subjective, and any assessment, including those focusing on social considerations, can be done rigorously, that is, in a methodologically and scientifically sound manner. There is no basis for the assumption that social sciences, using qualitative or quantitative research methods, cannot be applied in EIA. EIA is a decision-making arena where political, public and scientific rationalities interact, and where different value orientations are juxtaposed. The only legitimate considerations that determine whether data are relevant for EIA are the following:

1. Do they provide information on the relevancy and acceptability of a project?
2. Do they provide relevant information for the design of alternatives?
3. Do they have the potential to discriminate between alternative plans?
4. Do they have relevance to determining compensation and/or developing mitigation measures?

According to these considerations, the use of social data is as legitimate (or even more so) than other types of data.

The question, therefore, is not *whether or not* to address social considerations in EIA, but *how* to do it. The increasing level of public involvement in EIA worldwide illustrates that increasing effort is put into the inclusion of the norms, values and interests of communities in planning and policy development (Roberts, 1995). But public involvement does not necessarily systematically represent the community (Burdge and Vanclay 1995, Vanclay 1999). Those individuals involved in participation processes are often more highly educated, better informed and have a higher level of interest in the project. Participation processes are generally not designed to obtain a systematic representative overview of what the environment means to all potentially affected citizens. In many cases, people are not knowledgable about EIA, its role in decision making, the accessibility of EIS documents and their right to comment on them. Public participation processes, no matter how carefully designed and conducted, and no matter how satisfactory they are to the public, cannot prevent a project from having sometimes major environmental and social impacts. Therefore, it is important to investigate these impacts.

The ultimate rationale for obtaining information about the way local people perceive their living environment is that an analysis which fails to incorporate these value judgments is not only incomplete, but is likely to be (partly) incorrect. CVA recognizes the legitimacy of citizen values as a contribution to the decision-making process, and as a counterpart to expert judgments. Because these citizen values are based on rationalities other than those of the experts, it is vital that they be explicitly considered in the description of impacts and the comparison of alternatives in an EIS.

The contribution of CVA in practice

CVA is not a goal in itself. The task is not to provide a nice CVA impacts table, but to add relevant information to the quality of an EIS so as to broaden the rational basis of decision making, and/or to contribute to informed decision making (with a view to achieving better decisions). Three major types of contributions of CVA to EIA and other planning processes can be distinguished.

1. CVA broadens the scope of the impact assessment process
In EIA, impacts on 'the residential and living environment' are often dealt with by investigating a limited number of quantitatively measurable variables like the increase in decibels. CVA provides insight into all environmental values considered relevant by citizens and how these environmental values relate to one another. CVA adds information, or provides more differentiated information, but can also provide totally new understandings (eye-openers).

In the Rotterdam highway example described in Box 15.4, the expectations of the project team were that noise nuisance would be the major factor affecting the quality of the living environment. Furthermore, it was anticipated that the limited possibilities of crossing the highway (with the highway acting as a dividing barrier) would be a serious issue. However, the interviews in the residential areas surrounding these highways revealed quite different information. Most of the residential areas surrounding the highways were perceived as comfortable, green, quiet living environments, away from the hectic and overcrowded city centre, close to the countryside and multifunctional recreational areas, yet easily accessible from the centre. Many respondents said things like 'this neighbourhood is nice and quiet'; 'we live just outside the city centre, yet it feels as if we live in a village'; 'the mentality is different, people know each other'; and 'this is an oasis of peace in the middle of the hectic city'.

Obviously, noise nuisance was mentioned as an issue, but not with as much emphasis as had been expected by the project team. The other unexpected outcome of this study was that the highways were not considered to be a constraining barrier. Apparently, the residential areas on either side of the highway developed independently over the years and people had adapted to the limited number of access points.

This example illustrates how much nuisance perception is context-dependent and how important it is to provide location-specific information to assess impacts on the living environment. In Table 15.1, the citizen values profile for this CVA is presented. The CVP shows that noise nuisance is ranked eighth for area 1, and ranked sixth for areas 2 and 3. Accessibility of the city centre was ranked third and fourth and was judged – contrary to the professionals' expectations – positively.

Environmental values therefore can be included in an EIA through the means of CVA. In the 'Bomendijk' example (described earlier), the CVA

BOX 15.4   ROTTERDAM HIGHWAY CONGESTION

Highway A20 is a component of the transport network of The Netherlands built specifically to allow access to Rotterdam City (a city of some 600000 inhabitants) and its harbour (arguably the world's largest port). The A20 links them to the Amsterdam Schiphol airport (a major airfreight centre) and to other major Dutch cities (Amsterdam, The Hague, Utrecht) and ultimately to Germany, Belgium, France and England. A bottleneck occurs with north–south traffic – travelling along the two major highways, A16 and A13 – being forced to traverse a seven-kilometre section of the A20. Here the chance of congestion (that is, the probability of being in a traffic jam on a specific highway section over a 24-hour period) was above 20 per cent in 1995. This is much higher than the accepted national standards of 2 per cent for international access highways (A20 and A16) and 5 per cent for other national highways (A13). It was considered that, if no action was taken, the chance of congestion would increase to over 35 per cent by 2010.

The consequences of this increasing congestion include declining accessibility and longer journey times, as well as severe negative effects on residential areas, particularly declining quality of the living environment and safety. With only small distances between the roadway and buildings, noise nuisance and air pollution are considerable. Traffic jams also occur on the feeder roads. Nuisance is caused by cars traversing residential areas, often at high speed, in an attempt to avoid traffic jams. An English translation of the Dutch word for this phenomenon, *sluipverkeer*, is 'sneaky traffic'.

Two main alternatives were identified for addressing the problems. One involved the reconstruction and upgrading of the existing highway A20 (with a further option relating to the construction of an additional local road). The other alternative was the construction of an alternative route, or deviation, between the A16 and A13, thus bypassing the inner city area. An EIA procedure started in 1996 in which CVA was an integral part. The study area was divided into three subareas. Fifty in-depth interviews were conducted with representatives across four user groups.

Table 15.1   Citizen values profile

Area 1: bypass construction (ranking)	Key value	Areas 2 & 3: A20 reconstruction (ranking)
1	Quiet living environment	1
2	Facilities in the neighbourhood	2
3	Accessibility to centre of Rotterdam	4
4	Recreational facilities	5
5	Different species of plants and animals	7
6	Large nature area	9
7	Cycling possibilities	8
8	Noise nuisance of highway	6
9	Accessibility of recreational areas	17
10	Traffic exhaust	3
11	Heavy traffic on local roads	11
12	Diversity of recreational facilities	15
13	Rural character of the living environment	10
14	Traffic jams on highways	12
15	Noise nuisance of local roads	14
16	'Sneaky traffic'	13
17	View of/over highway	16
18	Accessibility of aquatic areas	18

concluded that some of the specific values of the area were emotional and inspirational values for artists and nature lovers. These values may be hard to quantify, but they can be analysed and operationalized into qualitative criteria for the evaluations of plans.

2. CVA provides input in developing and designing plans and policy measures

Location-specific information that is provided by CVA can be used in design and local spatial integration, and in the development of compensation and mitigation measures. For example, useful information for harbour design could include desires of local residents about the integration of the harbour in the local landscape; desires of locals about recreational facilities such as a walking path with benches; and the ideas of barge captains about harbour layout. CVA studies on highways have provided useful information about 'sneaky routes' or short cuts (see Box 15.4) and the degree of nuisance these cause. Furthermore, CVA may provide useful information about perceived unsafe locations, the use of tunnels and viaducts, noise nuisance, recreational activities and other specific aspects of residential and rural areas.

An EIA was conducted for the upgrading of the highway bypass (ring road) around the city of Eindhoven in the south of The Netherlands. The upgrading was intended to solve traffic jams on major connecting highways. The identification of key values through CVA, which was conducted as part of that EIA, provided useful location-specific information on the recreational use of the areas surrounding the highways, as well as on traffic nuisance. This included information on the following topics: horses crossing the highways being blinded by car lights (the area is known for equestrian activities); the importance of the openness of the landscape (even a green noise barrier would impact on the aesthetics of the landscape); a perceived increase of noise nuisance in other locations even after noise reduction measures; the nature of the traffic nuisance (local traffic versus highway traffic); and nuisance caused by through traffic in local streets.

The CVA study for the Lake IJmeer sediment storage (see Box 15.5) revealed, amongst other things, that (despite communication efforts) the intended project was largely unknown to the potentially affected communities. Furthermore, people were shocked at the idea of bringing heavily contaminated sediment into such a relatively undisturbed area which had so many environmental and recreational values. Many of the respondents questioned why Lake IJmeer had been selected at all as a potential location for this type of intervention in the first place, and suggested other locations. Although this issue was incorporated in the CVA report, the information was excluded from the EIA because it was outside the stated Terms of Reference. The selection of Lake IJmeer was the negotiated outcome of discussions amongst politicians at the provincial level. The completed EIS identified the preferred location within the Lake IJmeer district, and a formal rezoning procedure was commenced to enable the development to proceed. However, the issue did not disappear from the agenda of local interest groups. One of these groups successfully lobbied members of the national Parliament and generated much publicity. As a result, national politicians overruled provincial politicians and forced them to find another location for the facility. The EIS was left unread.

An example where CVA could have made a difference, had it been utilized, is the Amsterdam–Brussels high-speed railway line, which commenced construction in 2000. The previously conducted EIA study and project planning procedure considered a number of proposed routes. Noise nuisance was one of the issues that was extensively discussed and studied. The Minister promised the Dutch Parliament that the maximum noise level from the railway once operational would be no more than 57 decibels at each house along the route. Where higher noise levels occurred, they would be mitigated by the most practical and efficient measures. As a consequence, noise barriers were planned along many sections of the railway. In

BOX 15.5   STORAGE OF CONTAMINATED SEDIMENTS

In the mid-1990s, The Netherlands faced a planning problem related to the establishment of several large depots for the storage of heavily contaminated sediments from Rhine Delta waterways. Pollutants have entered the Rhine along its whole course from its source in Switzerland and Germany, and have become deposited in the Rhine Delta in The Netherlands. Over time, the accumulated sediments in most canals, lakes and other waters of the Delta have become seriously contaminated with a wide range of toxic substances. For environmental reasons, the government decided to dredge the sediment in a number of locations where pollution posed a continuing threat. The sludge would be sorted and the most heavily polluted sludge, which was unable to be converted into new products, would be stored in specially constructed sludge ponds. These sludge ponds would be massive facilities for retaining and isolating the contaminated sediments. An EIA study was commissioned for each area where a sludge pond was planned.

One proposed location for a sludge pond was Lake IJmeer. An EIA and CVA were conducted to identify the preferable location. Lake IJmeer, near the city of Amsterdam, has now – since its separation from the North Sea with the completion of the Afsluitdyke in 1932 – become a shallow freshwater lake. Its historical coastline has been registered as an international wetland under the Ramsar Convention. It is an area known for its magnificent scenic beauty. Along the coast of Lake IJmeer are many historic fishing villages, such as Muiden and its 13th-century castle, 'Muiderslot'. The views over the lake from the shore are magnificent, making living in these old villages very special. The whole IJmeer area is a recreational site for day-trippers, watersports, cyclists and fishers, and the traditional fishing villages, especially Volendam and Marken, attract tourists from all over the world. Along the eastern coast of Lake IJmeer is the Flevoland polder, consisting of some fast-growing cities and large-scale agriculture.

Rotterdam, some citizens have organized themselves to prevent noise screens being built. They prefer the noise of the trains to the visual impacts caused by the large noise barriers. Furthermore, they are concerned that the construction of the noise barriers will require the removal of much vegetation. They appealed to the Council of State (the highest advisory council of the Dutch government) against the decision to build noise barriers in an attempt to preserve their vistas and the green elements in their immediate neighbourhood. Had a CVA been undertaken, these concerns would have been identified earlier.

The CVA for the Eindhoven highway project revealed that noise barriers (screens) and grassed embankments would affect the openness of the landscape and were considered undesirable. While the existence of local protest movements may indicate an awareness of concern in the community, the advantage of the use of CVA is that it involves a representative sample of the population, and not only those motivated to join the action group – who may very well have different views to the other residents. In Rotterdam, the citizens forming the action group tended to be well-established residents, who did not necessarily represent the views of all sections of the community, the area being home to many migrants. CVA could have brought information for the development of mitigation measures based on a representative picture of citizen values.

3. CVA provides input for project communication
In another highway study, the CVA revealed that one of the alternatives was considered by the community to be unrealistic in solving existing traffic congestion problems. As a result of this information, the project team was able to reconsider the information being provided about that alternative. The team then made changes to it to correct the potential miscommunication. The CVA also revealed that certain local groups had not been involved in the participatory process to date. As a result, they were directly approached by the project manager.

CVA can support dialogue with local communities in various ways. CVA can be communicated as a serious attempt to include the perceived quality of the living environment in the impact study. Although it does not guarantee that major impacts can be prevented, the very fact that a CVA study is carried out is likely to be judged positively by the community. An evaluation of EIA studies in The Netherlands, both with and without CVA, revealed that, as perceived by citizens, CVA contributed to the quality of EIS (Rodenhuis, 2001). Quotations collected by Rodenhuis (2001) in the evaluation illustrate this (translated from Dutch): for example, from persons involved in participatory processes:

'The study made very clear where the interests of this village lie; what people in this village consider valuable.'

'If no CVA had been conducted, we would not have known about its potential. Now that it has been conducted, it is very clear that it improved the quality of the EIS.'

From persons involved in an EIA without CVA, we have the following:

'They count the numbers of deaths. But where can I find something about how I feel; about how the people who actually live here experience traffic nuisance? And there is a lot of information about populations of species, but what about us? Don't we need to be protected?'

'Sometimes I think I would be better off if I was a rare reptile or a dead Roman in the old castle. Fair enough that rare species and historic monuments can't speak for themselves and need to be protected – but, even though we can speak for ourselves and argue as much as we can, we still end up somewhere in a marginal section of the report.'

In large national or regional projects, CVA can locally verify and specify the outcomes of negotiation processes. CVA contributes to the effectiveness of project communication and assists project teams in presenting information and standpoints, to facilitating optimal project designs and to the avoidance of conflict. A CVA can be used as the basis for a participatory process. By providing information on the outcomes of the various steps, individual citizens and interest groups are stimulated to react and interact with project development.

Conclusion
CVA is a useful instrument for integrating citizen values into EIA. But CVA has the potential to be applied in a much wider context than just within EIA. 'Livability', or 'quality of the living environment', is becoming a major factor in many decision-making arenas. CVA has the potential to contribute to decision making relating to spatial development, public safety, especially in terms of risk perception, and environmental and nature management.

Successful application of CVA requires the commitment of the project team. Many scientists and engineers still need to be convinced that social considerations should be part of EIA. When members of the project team are sceptical about the added value of CVA, its contribution will be limited. Another factor affecting the successful integration of CVA in EIA is quality control. Social impact practitioners with relevant expertise need to be involved to guarantee high-quality results. Ideally, feedback with representatives of the community should take place at each phase.

What is even more important than the application of the CVA instrument itself is the explicit recognition by politicians of the relevance of systematic information about citizen values as a data source in decision-making. This requires a change in attitude in relation to expert judgments: expert judgments should be considered an appropriate but not exclusive information source.

CVA has limitations. What citizens observe and expect does not necessarily include all aspects relevant to them, neither will citizens' judgments be based on a clear picture of the situation at the time the project is intended to be implemented, which may involve long time spans. However, the value of including citizen values explicitly in the EIA process is that they become a serious component of what is considered the rational basis for decision making. An EIS that puts citizen values on an equal footing with scientific and technical information provides a broader overview of positive and negative aspects of alternatives than does a conventional EIA. Combining public rationalities and scientific rationalities in an EIS is more likely to make the document legitimate from the public point of view.

Acknowledgments

I thank all current and former CVA team members for their enthusiasm and great efforts to make CVA work in practice. Wim Groen and Jacqueline van Vliet, especially, made essential contributions to the development of CVA. I also thank Frank Vanclay for his methodological advice and stimulating discussions on the scientific robustness of CVA. This chapter draws on material previously published as A. Stolp *et al.* (2002), 'Citizen values assessment: incorporating citizens' value judgements in environmental impact assessment', *Impact Assessment and Project Appraisal*, 20(1): 11–23.

References

Arts, J. 1998. *EIA Follow-up: On the role of Ex-Post Evaluation in Environmental Impact Assessment*, Groningen: Geopress.

Burdge, R. (ed.) 1998. *A Conceptual Approach to Social Impact Assessment* (rev. edn), Middleton (WI): Social Ecology Press.

Burdge, R. and Vanclay, F. 1995. 'Social impact assessment', in F. Vanclay and D. Bronstein (eds), *Environmental and Social Impact Assessment*, Chichester: Wiley, 31–65.

Burningham, K. 1995. 'Attitudes, accounts and impact assessment', *The Sociological Review*, 43(1): 100–22.

Craig, D. 1990. 'Social impact assessment: politically oriented approaches and applications', *Environmental Impact Assessment Review*, 10(1/2): 37–54.

Dale, A. and Lane, M. 1994. 'Strategic perspectives analysis: a procedure for participatory and political social impact assessment', *Society and Natural Resources*, 7(3): 253–68.

Dale, A. and Lane, M. 1995. 'Queensland's Social Impact Assessment Unit: Its origins and prospects', *Queensland Planner*, 35(3): 5–10.

Denq, F. and Altenhofel, J. 1997. 'Social impact assessments conducted by federal agencies'. *Impact Assessment*, 15(3): 209–31.

Firth, L. 1998. 'Role of values in public decision-making', *Impact Assessment and Project Appraisal*, 16(4): 325–9.

Freudenburg, W. 1986. 'Social Impact Assessment', *Annual Review of Sociology*, 12: 451–78.

Gagnon, C., Hirsch, P. and Howitt, R. 1993. 'Can SIA empower communities?', *Environmental Impact Assessment Review*, 13(4): 229–53.

Interorganizational Committee on Guidelines and Principles 1994. 'Guidelines and principles for social impact assessment', *Impact Assessment*, 12(2): 107–52.

Leon, B.F. 1993. 'Survey of analyses in environmental impact statements', in S.G. Hildebrand and J.B. Cannon (eds), *Environmental Analysis: The NEPA Experience*, Boca Raton: Lewis, 653–9.

Mostert, E. 1996. 'Subjective environmental impact assessment: causes, problems and solutions', *Impact Assessment*, 14(2): 191–213.

Neuman, W. 1996. *Social Research Methods: Qualitative and Quantitative Approaches*, Boston: Allan and Bacon.

Ortolano, L. and Shepherd, A. 1995. 'Environmental impact assessment', in F. Vanclay and D. Bronstein (eds), *Environmental and Social Impact Assessment*, Chichester: Wiley, 3–30.

Roberts, R. 1995. 'Public Involvement: From Consultation to Participation', in F. Vanclay and D. Bronstein (eds), *Environmental and Social Impact Assessment*, Chichester: Wiley, 221–46.

Rodenhuis, R. 2001. 'Kwaliteit van milieu-effectrapportage door de bril van de burger' (Quality of environmental impact assessment from the perspective of citizens), Directorate General of Public Works and Water Management, Civil Engineering Division, Utrecht.

Sadler, B. 1996. *Environmental assessment in a changing world: evaluating practice to improve performance*, Final report of the International Study of the Effectiveness of Environmental Assessment, Ottawa: Ministry of Supply and Services.

Stolp, A., Groen, W., van Vliet, J. and Vanclay, F. 2002. 'Citizen values assessment: incorporating citizens' value judgements in environmental impact assessment', *Impact Assessment and Project Appraisal*, 20(1): 11–23.

Taylor, C., Bryan, C. and Goodrich, C. 1995. *Social Assessment: theory, process and techniques* (2nd edn), Ricarton (NZ): Taylor Baines & Associates.

Vanclay, F. 1999. 'Social impact assessment', in J. Petts (ed.), *Handbook of Environmental Impact Assessment* (vol. 1), Oxford: Blackwell, 301–26.

Vanclay, F. 2002. 'Social impact assessment', in M. Tolba (ed.), *Responding to Global Environmental Change* (vol. 4 of *Encyclopedia of Global Environmental Change*, series ed.: Ted Munn), Chichester: Wiley, 387–93.

van Vliet, J. 1996. 'M.e.(e)r. Waarde Belevingsonderzoek' (The added value of Citizen Values profiling in EIA), Directorate General of Public Works and Water Management, Civil Engineering Division, Utrecht.

de Vries, M.S. 1999. *Calculated Choices in Policy-Making: Theory and practice of impact assessment*, Houndmills: Palgrave.

Wood, C. 1995. *Environmental Impact Assessment: a Comparative Review*, Harlow: Longman.

16 Involving the public
Richard Roberts

Introduction

The current practice of public involvement is, in many ways, the by-product of a cross-fertilization of populist ideas, the information revolution and widespread disenchantment with a society where neither industry nor elected officials appear to act 'in the public interest'. Although it is very difficult to ascertain a definite beginning, some analysts believe that the current form of public participation began at a 'grassroots' level and that community development and participation 'just happened', with the initiative coming from the people (Roberts, 1995).

The last two to three decades have seen the development and implementation of environmental impact assessment (EIA), social impact assessment (SIA) and public involvement (PI) in many developed and developing countries around the world. The process, approach and ultimate form have varied greatly in different countries. Similarly, the legal framework for these activities ranges from very formal, legislated requirements to much less formal policy or regulated approaches. In 1993, the World Bank set a precedent by requiring public consultation in EIAs for all projects which they are funding. The World Bank requires consultation with affected groups in the very early stages of project design and planning and again when the draft EIA is prepared. The major change is that public participation is required for projects that affect cultural and indigenous people, that involve involuntary resettlement (for example, associated with dams) or that depend on local responsibility for their success. As this is seen as a minimum requirement, many organizations are developing ways to involve the public. Many other countries and international development organizations are following the World Bank's lead, including the United Nations Environment Programme (UNEP) and United Nations Development Programme (UNDP). The overall trend is towards more consultation, with 'participation' increasingly becoming mandatory.

An earlier publication of this author (Roberts, 1995) ended with the challenge of public involvement:

> As societies and peoples become more informed about their environments and organize into more complex structures, the current demand by the public to be involved in decision making will continue to increase. People expect and demand to be more involved. They live with the consequences of decisions and expect to

share and be responsible for making them. To be successful in meeting these demands, organizations will need to be more proactive, less reactive. They will need to meet the public in communities and on the street. They will need to find a common language, to learn to listen, and to consider and incorporate what is being said. But most of all, they will need to learn that if it is well organized, open and honest, public involvement can be more than just a means to an end. It can be an end in itself, a permanent dialogue that will benefit the organization for many years.

This chapter takes up the above challenge and describes two approaches to public involvement in a project setting. The first approach is somewhat linear, and many practitioners will see it as a traditional consultative model. It suggests a level of involvement already commonly exceeded by project proponents (who may be either government or industry) and regulators, particularly in developed countries and where World Bank or equivalent guidelines have influenced a project. However, in many jurisdictions, including some in developed countries, the requirements of this consultative model have yet to be achieved. While this model meets the basic requirements of consultation with the public, it falls short of providing participation of the public or of all stakeholders in the project decision-making process.

The second approach is more innovative, allowing both stakeholders and the public to participate in the project decision-making process much more directly. This approach meets the needs of the many proponents who believe in true public 'participation' and its value in the impact assessment, mitigation and decision-making processes. It also meets or exceeds the requirements as identified by the World Bank in terms of 'participation'. The foundation for this proposed approach was developed by the author and a number of team members on several EIA projects undertaken in the tar sands region of north central Alberta (Suncor Oilsands Limited).

Before discussing these two models in detail, it may be useful to discuss the issue of who is the public? The terms 'public involvement', 'public consultation' and 'public participation' are used interchangeably by many people with no recognition of the subtle and not-so-subtle differences between them. In the author's view, the term 'public involvement' is the over-arching concept: public involvement is a process for involving the public in the decision-making process of an organization. Such involvement can be brought about through a spectrum of activities ranging from consultation to participation, the key difference being the degree to which those involved in the process are able to influence, share or control the decision-making. While 'consultation' includes education, information sharing and negotiation – the goal being better decision making by the organization consulting the public – 'participation' actually brings the public into the decision-making process. Typically, public involvement has focused primarily on consulting the public, with no options for greater participation. Arnstein (1969) was one of the first to identify the 'ladder of citizen participation', which ranged from persuasion at the one end of the spectrum to self-determination at the other end. This is the strongest form of public participation where the process is directly undertaken by the public with the proponent accepting the outcome. Programmes often rely heavily on education and information sharing and, at best, consultation. However, a growing number of organizations have begun experimenting with greater degrees of public participation in the form of joint planning and delegated authority, where the public actually controls and directs the process and the ultimate results.

Two models — consultative or participatory?

What is referred to as the consultative model lies at the persuasion end of the public involvement spectrum, along with public information or education. The public and stakeholders may be consulted at various points throughout a public process, such as during the scoping process or by reviewing the draft EIA, but are not involved directly in developing the material or assessing the effects, or in project decision making. Participants may merely be receivers and reviewers of information developed by the project proponent. If this is the case, the final EIA will be largely a corporate (or proponent-controlled) document describing and supporting a corporate position. This corporate position can be that of a company or government agency; the issue is that, in either case, the organization is presenting their internal, corporately-approved position on the project for comment and review.

The participatory model lies nearer the other end of the public involvement spectrum. In this model, proponents will offer the public and the stakeholders an opportunity to participate more directly in decision making, building a feeling of ownership among participants, while creating non-confrontational communications and involvement that can provide a mitigating influence when project issues are being debated.

Both the consultative and the participatory models are feasible, doable and appropriate in various project situations. Choosing the best model depends to a large extent on the degree of involvement in decision making desired by the proponent, the regulator and the public. The outcome is usually somewhere between consultation and participation. Herein lies the delicate balance: towards which end of the spectrum does the proponent move? Prior to adopting either model, the proponent must assess its own internal commitment to involving the public and stakeholders. The proponent also needs to determine how to use the information received from the public throughout the process. The worst possible situation is to involve the public and then not use their input if the proponent does not like what it is hearing. Factors such as previous community experiences, the volatility of the community, the extent of controversy, the levels of potential impacts and the cost of delay, among others, need to be assessed in making this decision.

It is essential for senior managers and the executive of the organization to sit down at the beginning of the project and assess the risks and opportunities, make their decisions early and stick to them through the duration of the project. This is not to say that the proponent cannot be flexible. Flexibility will be essential on any project and especially where the public and stakeholders are involved in a participatory manner. This approach can save the proponent a significant amount of internal and external grief, debate, time and resources.

Assumptions and requirements for both models
No matter which model is chosen, certain essential steps need to be taken by the proponent in the early stages. Three are identified, as follows. First, *provide accurate and comprehensive information on the project:* the proponent should provide the public and stakeholders with information on the project(s), the regulatory requirements and the approval process in order for participants to be meaningfully involved.

Second, *provide a clearing house for public information:* the proponent should have an easily accessible location (or locations) where participants can obtain project information and, where appropriate, discuss the project with the proponent's staff. At a minimum, local libraries, community centres or a proponent shop-front office can be used. Opening a shop-front office staffed with community relations staff with senior management personnel available or on-call may be very effective. If a number of communities are potentially affected, the proponent can establish a rotating presence, moving its materials and presentations to each of the communities at differing stages of the process. It can also use new technologies such as web-based Internet sites to make available information and solicit feedback through Internet response forms, questionnaires or comment sheets.

Third, *develop a coordinated, integrated management team and organizational structure:* it is essential for the proponent to have a reporting structure 'on the ground' that can respond quickly and efficiently when immediate decisions are required and that supports 'getting the message to the top'. To achieve this, and to obtain public support and credibility, it may be necessary for the proponent to restructure itself so that the technical staff and the technical departments are much more integrated with the people side of project activities.

Often a proponent must develop a management team for all public, governmental and stakeholder activities. This team must have good internal coordination among the team members and with internal departments so that there is consistent and continuing contact with the public, from initial planning to construction and operations.

The consultative model

The final EIA is a statement, controlled by the proponent, with input and advice from the public and stakeholders. Model aspects are the following:

- more advisory,
- more static,
- more controlled,
- more prescriptive,
- more orchestrated,
- more directive,
- more fixed or rigid,
- more company accountability,
- more methodological,
- more linear.

Figure 16.1 illustrates a typical, linear consultative approach associated with an EIA and a regulatory review. The EIA process and the public involvement process are generally separate, but linked at critical junctures or review points. The process usually begins with an initial public announcement or press release, continuing through to the regulatory hearing. In addition, although often forgotten, the consultation process must continue through construction and ongoing operations, if approval is received. In the process outlined, the proponent may involve the public in general or may create a multi-stakeholder advisory committee to provide more coordinated input and discussion over the duration of the process.

Stage one: preliminary planning and issue scoping
The proponent may canvass stakeholders and key publics on their issues, the information they require, and how they would like to be involved in reviewing the Terms of Reference, table of contents, any primary or secondary research that is undertaken, the EIA draft document and the regulatory application for the project. The general public and stakeholder representatives are usually invited to review draft EIA or SIA components of the project. These specific stakeholder representatives may form a stakeholder advisory committee to review the various components of the EIA or SIA.

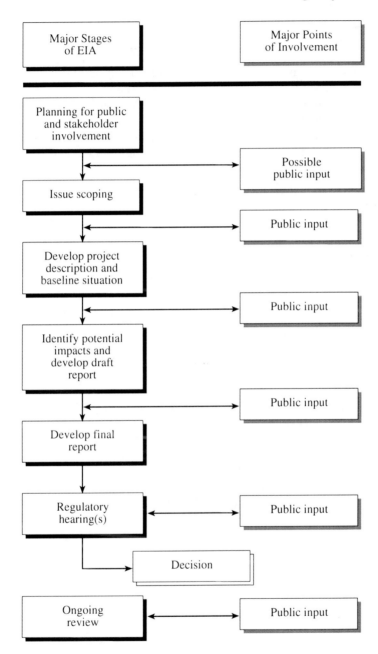

Figure 16.1   EIA process and points of public involvement in the consultative model

Depending on the situation, the stakeholder committee can include the following:

- representatives from municipal and regional government, local business, social and health services and educational institutions;
- representatives from First Nations and Aboriginal organizations;
- individuals directly affected by a project;
- representatives from environmental and economic interest groups;
- representatives from industry, labour unions and potential contractors; and
- the general public.

In Canada, the provincial and federal governments, through independent government agencies, are usually the regulators or reviewers of these projects. Usually, they cannot be directly involved in such working groups or the process itself. However, there are a number of opportunities where they can participate as observers or resource people to the process and the committee.

The general public and stakeholders may make recommendations or suggestions regarding the range of public activities or events, which may occur throughout the process, such as public meetings, open houses, workshops and other activities. However, it will be up to the proponent as to which of the recommendations they accept, reject or modify.

Stage two: development of baseline information and impact identification
The public or a stakeholder committee, if formed, meets with the proponent to receive progress reports and to identify what they, the stakeholders, believe are the major issues. They can review the major components of the EIA and SIA and other studies that are produced by the proponent. During these meetings, the proponent brings in staff or consultants to assist in the discussion. In all cases, the resulting products, at each stage, may go forward for broader public review, as discussed previously.

Stage three: development of draft EIA
The public or stakeholder committee continues to contribute to and review portions of the draft EIA and the Application, suggesting changes and discussing issues pertaining to their concerns. They review the final supporting documents and the actual Application. These documents may or may not go out for broader public review prior to being submitted to the regulatory review process.

Stage four: completion of the EIA and regulatory review
The proponent finalizes the EIA document and submits it for regulatory review. The regulator determines the need for a public review and/or the need for public hearings and these are carried out, as required. Following the hearing, a decision is made and the proponent acts on that decision. If a stakeholder committee was created, it may be dissolved at the time of the hearings. However, in some cases, the proponent has kept the stakeholder committee in place to consult during the ongoing stages of the process, if approval is granted.

Stage five: ongoing review of construction and operations
Depending on the decision, there may or may not be any follow-up activity. In the case of 'an approval' or 'approval with conditions', there will need to be some form of ongoing review mechanism that involves both the stakeholders and the public.

The participatory model
The final EIA is a public statement agreed on by most, if not all, participants in the process, including both the public and stakeholders. Model aspects are as follows:

- more non-directive,
- more enpowering,
- more uncertain,
- more evolving,
- more innovative,
- more shared,
- more dynamic,
- more mutual accountability,
- more flexible,
- more spontaneous,
- more creative,
- more participatory.

While many people, organizations and governments aspire to a more participatory approach to project reviews, few actually manage to achieve this goal. The reason is that it is an evolving art. Participation means that many people and organizations with many differing views and values must be brought to the table. This is difficult, at best, to achieve.

The World Bank is one example of an organization that is attempting to move towards such a participatory model. However, it takes more than a new range of techniques and methods; it requires a shift in values, which allows for a more open, honest and transparent relationship to develop among all parties, and a shift in the way power is shared. Above all, it takes time, resources and commitment by all parties including the public and stakeholders.

So why should we try to achieve this? For a myriad of reasons. Notably, because the public is becoming more aware and educated in the way they can use power to oppose, delay and stop not only projects, but policies, regulations and legislation over which they have significant concerns. The general public increasingly distrusts politicians, governments, businesses and other power-wielding organizations, as has been seen with the discussion of free trade and globalization in recent years.

As a result, it is becoming harder and harder to obtain project or policy approval using the traditional models. It is time to rethink the approaches and look for ways to bring the public and community on board and to develop greater buy-in for projects or policies being proposed by a variety of proponents. This requires a newthink. The participatory model described in the following is but one attempt to move towards such a newthink.

This participatory model integrates the technical and engineering development, the EIA regulatory review process and the public involvement process. It can fast-track these processes by having them occur simultaneously. It can also reduce and refine the number of issues brought to a regulatory review or a hearing, through negotiations to reach consensus prior to any public hearings. In the best case scenario, the regulator may decide that there is no need to proceed with a hearing at all, as all the project issues have been dealt with in a manner agreed to with the public. This has happened recently in Alberta, Canada, where the Alberta Energy and Utilities Board and Alberta Environmental Protection scheduled hearings on four major oil sands projects (the Suncor Steepbank Oilsands project, the Syncrude Millennium Oilsands development, the Shell Muskeg Oilsands project and Petro-Canada's MacKay River project), but few, if any, intervenors/objectors (those contesting a regulatory approval) came forward. As a result, the hearings were cancelled or reduced to a single day and the projects approved with minimal additional conditions. It should be recognized that each of these projects represented a multi-billion dollar investment. In several cases, this was due to the work the company or companies did to develop agreements with the major stakeholder groups, including First Nations and regional environmental organizations (ENGOs), so that all groups were happy with the agreement and chose not to intervene. Not only are all parties satisfied, but the costs both to the government and to the companies were reduced. Hearings and the hearing process itself are not inexpensive.

The participatory model is based on an interactive and involving approach to the planning, engineering and EIA process. In this model, the proponent's staff and consultants form a series of working groups reflecting major areas of study in the EIA. In addition to the proponent's staff and consultants, these teams include members of the public and stakeholder groups and others who identify with a specific team. An important element of this model is that each team works together to determine its own terms of reference and then sets out to complete the actual work required to deliver its product. In preparing for this process, the proponent must undertake the steps previously discussed. Following this, a series of steps or stages may be completed.

Stage one: identifying participants
The proponent initially identifies which publics may be involved in the EIA process. This can be based on previous information and working relationships, interviews and discussions with the local and regionally-based organizations, government, other companies, environmental organizations and local landowners. Within this universe of potential participants, involvement levels will differ dramatically. At one end of this spectrum are those individuals or groups who only want information related to the project in order to monitor the progress of the EIA and the public involvement process. At the other end of the spectrum are those who immediately know that they want to be, need to be or must be involved extensively and intensively in the process, as they have specific interests or concerns, or perceive themselves to be directly affected by the project. Between these two extremes are those who may want some involvement in the process, but are not sure how much, or when, they want involvement. They will want to be informed about activities so they can assess progress from their perspective and may step into or out of the process as they determine their level of interest or concern. This may result in a frequent change of players over the duration of a process. Such an eventuality can be accommodated in this model.

On the basis of this initial input, the proponent organizes and identifies the major environmental and socioeconomic issues likely to face the project. One way of organizing this information is to use a 'menu approach', similar to the way in which a computer displays various possible actions or activities. These menus represent the major technical and environmental components and issues related to the project. A description of each menu item acts as a terms of reference for that particular aspect of the work. A menu approach allows people to select areas of concern to them, and to focus on specific issues if they do not want to be involved in all project aspects. Given the public involvement burn-out currently taking its toll, any method that allows the public and stake-holder organizations to focus on the aspects or issues critical to them is extremely helpful. Those who want to be involved in all issues have some decisions to make. For organizations, the easiest approach is to assign different people to different working groups, thus distributing the work-load. Each individual, however, will have to set priorities and choose the working group(s) they believe will be the most effective for their purposes. Typical, major menu items are illustrated in Figure 16.2.

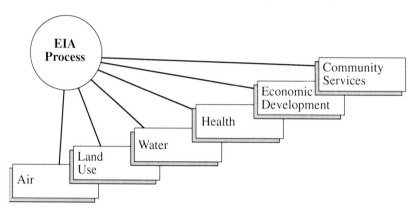

Figure 16.2   Examples of menu items

In addition to making materials available in traditional locations, such as community centres, or through traditional means, such as an initial mailing list, the information can now be made remotely accessible to indi-viduals and stakeholders through an on-line computer system, Website, Homepage or e-mail.

The roles of the various levels of government must be determined at the beginning of the process. Discussions should occur between the proponent and the government representatives to determine if and how they want to be involved. They may want to be totally at arm's length, to act as a resource in selected areas or to selected working groups. Alternatively, they may prefer to sit directly with a working group through the process – this may be especially true of agencies that do not have any regulatory role at this stage of the process. Given the reduced resources available at all levels of government today, it is increasingly likely that they will only want to be observers to the process, and only when required. Direct contact should be made by the proponent to avoid any false assumptions about the informa-tion and the resources that these levels of government may be able to bring to the process.

Stage two: public scoping session(s)

Public scoping to determine overall issues is not new. It has been used successfully for a number of years. The difference in this situation is that the output of the scoping process forms the major menu items for the ongoing process. The proponent may use such techniques as media advertisements, newspaper inserts, the Internet, public service announcements and verbal contact to announce the process, provide initial information and invite stakeholders and the public into the scoping process. It is usual to start with an open house, a workshop or some other public activity. The advertisement can also serve as a mail-out to those people and organizations on the proponent's own mailing list.

Public materials may include a response card on which participants can indicate their issues and concerns, a fax-back request form, an on-line Web survey or response form and a toll-free telephone number for information.

At the scoping meeting(s), the proponent presents the project description, describes the various components and asks participants to identify their key issues and concerns in addition to those that the proponent may have identified. An open discussion is an effective way to raise issues. These issues are then incorporated into the overall menu items.

Stage three: forming working groups

The results of the scoping session(s) are organized and reported back to the scoping session(s) participants in an expanded menu format. These results are sent to all those on an updated mailing list, including all those who attended the scoping meeting(s). This document invites people to participate in the working groups based on the menu items: working groups generally follow the menu items, but are not limited to them. Recipients are asked to provide a response indicating which groups (or menu items) interest them. Some respondents may ask to participate in the process; others may simply want to be informed of the progress of a working group.

In some cases, a community or organization potentially affected by the project may be interested in most of the menu items and so, in order to study them all, it could become a working group itself to represent the views and concerns of that community. New issues and working groups may be identified and developed later as the process moves forward.

There are a number of issues facing the formation and operation of each working group:

- There may be too few or too many participants interested in a particular working group. A workable size can vary from 5 up to 25; however, the optimal size is around 15 directly involved participants.
- In all cases, the sessions of each working group should be facilitated,

summarized and a record sent to all participants in a timely manner. A set of operating guidelines or ground rules should be established and agreed on by all members of the working group. In fact, this is a good way to achieve a first small consensus by the group and may help them in later stages.

- Decision making should be by consensus. When this does not occur, it should be recorded that a number of participants dissented. These issues may have to be negotiated by more senior individuals in the organization. If agreement still cannot be reached, this issue needs to be forwarded with the eventual report(s) to the regulator.
- If the working group achieves consensus, the report or document should go forward as agreed upon. As this is a public, transparent process, if changes are subsequently made, this fact will be visible to both the participants and the regulators.
- The length of the process will depend upon the scale, profile and scope of the project, the complexity of the issues and the ability to work them through to completion. The working group process could take from as little as two months to as long as 18 months, depending on the scale, complexity and issues that are related to the project. Members need to be made aware that such is possible and be prepared for such a commitment.
- Media involvement is always a question in an open, public process. Decisions as to how the media should be involved should be part of the development of the working groups' operating guidelines.

Figure 16.3 illustrates four typical working groups: air quality, employment, land use and health/safety. Other groups, such as engineering, socioeconomic or other environmental aspects of the project, are not shown in this example. A management or staff member leads and/or supports each working group. The management or staff member may sit on one or several working groups, depending on the requirements.

Of key importance will be the engineering, environmental and socioeconomic staff and/or consultants who support each of these working groups. A technical expert, consultant or internal person may not be familiar with this type of working relationship. They must work with a team composed not only of specific experts, but also of those who may not have a specific expertise in an area, rather a concern or issue. Municipal, provincial or federal government representatives may act as advisers, or resource people, to the working groups on a regular or as-needed basis.

Figure 16.4 presents the membership of a typical working group, in this case a Health and Safety Working Group. The proponent or management person(s) responsible for the working group should contact the potential

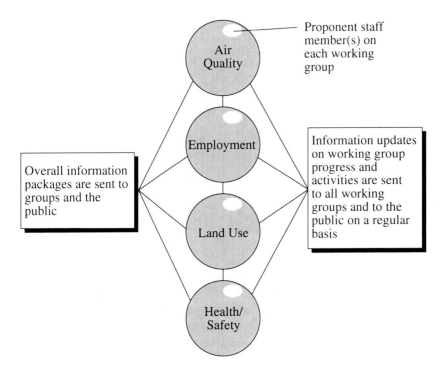

Figure 16.3   Working group structure

members of the group and call a first meeting. The purpose of the first meeting or two should be to select a chairperson or a facilitator and a recorder, develop the working group's terms of reference and develop operating guidelines.

Stage four: coordinating committee and working groups
Continuing problems when a series of committees or working groups are proceeding independently include coordination between the groups and access to decision-making authority within the organization. There may be need for a coordinating committee, with senior management on the committee or with direct access by committee members to senior management. This committee must oversee the process, coordinate and distribute updates, resolve issues between working groups, and monitor and negotiate issues and disputes. The committee should have no more than six to eight members and should comprise a range of participants, such as the following:

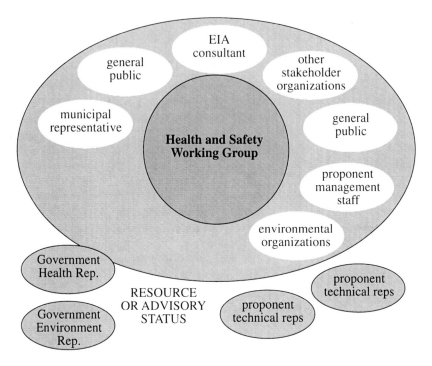

Figure 16.4   Working group composition

- proponent manager with immediate decision-making ability;
- head or designate from each working group;
- selected working group representatives from a spectrum of public and stakeholder groups, including Aboriginal members, where appropriate;
- head of the EIA internal or external (consultant) team; and
- municipal or regional government representatives.

This committee assists in integrating and coordinating the work of the groups and acts on any special requirements, decisions and policy implications forwarded from any working group. It is anticipated that the committee might meet quarterly, or as needed to deal with specific issues. Figure 16.5 presents the overall participation process, starting with the first information session and ending with the hearing itself. It should be noted that these groups could carry on after the hearing, depending on the outcome and need for ongoing input or involvement.

Working groups require resources. Facilitators and recorders will be

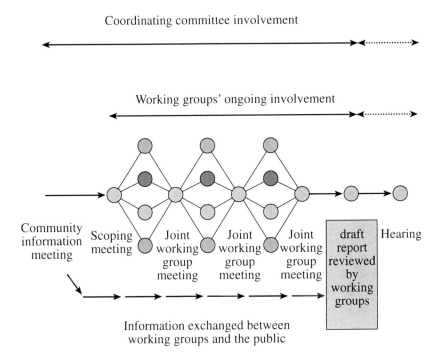

Coordinating committee involvement

Working groups' ongoing involvement

Community
information
meeting

Scoping
meeting

Joint
working
group
meeting

Joint
working
group
meeting

Joint
working
group
meeting

draft
report
reviewed
by
working
groups

Hearing

Information exchanged between
working groups and the public

Figure 16.5   Participatory process diagram

needed by most working groups. It is not recommended that group participants to undertake these roles as participants are there to contribute ideas.
Some groups may require access to teleconferencing facilities or computer
communications services if members live in remote or diverse locations.
While many new forms of technology are making their presence known, a
cardinal rule must be to use the level of technology that works for the
group. The proponent must be prepared to meet the needs of the working
groups, wherever possible.

Along with the more traditional EIA study components that will be
required for the regulatory review, the working groups may find that additional special studies are needed. The working group develops the terms of
reference for any and all studies required for their group, and the studies
are carried out either by the in-house proponent staff or external consultants, under the review and vetting of the working group. If the skills or
experience for doing this are not available within the group, the working
group should request that the coordinating committee contract out the
required studies. The working group monitors and evaluates the work and

approves the final product before it is incorporated into the overall EIA. When all working group studies or EIA report sections are complete, vetted and approved by the respective working group, all the sections are integrated by the proponent and reviewed by the coordinating committee. If there are changes to any working group report as a result, any such changes will need to be vetted by the responsible working group. Any disagreement will have to come forward to the coordinating committee for resolution.

The working groups need to meet jointly on a periodic basis to share findings and report on progress. This can be achieved through a series of workshops or mini-conferences which might occur three or four times during the overall EIA process, depending on the scale and intensity of the issues being reviewed. A final workshop would integrate the products of all the working groups into a draft EIA. The draft EIA should be reviewed by each working group individually, as well as in one large final joint workshop of all groups which would finalize any changes before submitting the EIA to the regulatory body.

Some working groups may complete their tasks earlier than others and disband, leaving their final reports with the coordinating committee. Some members of the public monitoring the project's process may decide to become involved in one or another of the working groups well into the process. Either situation should not adversely affect a working group. Groups can have alternates assigned to the working group, use summaries or minutes from meetings and develop short fact sheets and other tools for keeping records of their meetings, activities and ongoing progress. This material can be used by new participants in the process to become informed quickly and easily.

Stage five: the hearing and beyond
Each working group must sign off its report or reports. Most of these reports will become chapters or sections in the draft and final EIA. The reports must make it clear in which areas group members agreed and in which they disagreed – and the reasons for any disagreement. This becomes part of the public record for the final hearing. If intervenors/objectors criticize any portion of the work, it is the working group coordinator, the proponent's technical representative, or the external consultant attached to that working group, who should be able to speak at the hearing for the entire working group, explaining the decisions of the working group and the process that led to the decisions.

The working group members could remain in place following the regulatory decision to 'proceed' or 'proceed with conditions'. The purpose would be to monitor the implementation process. However, this is asking for a significant commitment from these members. In such an event, the working group may develop a transitional strategy from planning to construction. This will save time as the working group members are familiar with the issues and can quickly move forward with specific aspects of the project. The coordinating committee may also remain in place. If the project is 'not approved' there will be no need for the working groups unless a reapplication is being considered. However, the coordinating committee should develop a strategy in either case so that the public is informed of the decision, its implications and any anticipated next steps. This should be done for the 'no-go' decision, as the public is often left with no knowledge or understanding of what really happened. The proponent should make this clear and outline what the future might hold in relation to the project. This will be very helpful, especially if the proponent later decides to reactivate the project in the same or another form.

Involving non-resident stakeholders and the public
Non-resident interested stakeholders and members of the public should be given an opportunity to participate in the working groups wherever possible. Such parties might include regional or national environmental organizations and other public interest groups. They should receive all of the information local residents and participants receive, including the invitation to participate in the working groups. The proponent may have to provide some travel or computer and telecommunications resources to allow more distant members to participate. Another option is that the proponent could form a working group (or working groups) outside the project region in an area where a number of potential participants reside.

Funding participation in the process
Probably one of the most difficult decisions the proponent will have to make in any development process is whether to provide funding to enable stakeholder participation in 'front-end' planning and EIA development. The moment one individual or group receives funding, others will request it. The first step is to establish whether the proponent will fund any individual or group for such participation. If the decision is made to fund some level of participation, the next questions are who will receive funding, for which activities, for how much, and for how long? In some jurisdictions, there are regulatory requirements for funding of participants, although this can be relatively limited, and is often just for the regulatory review stages. The question is, 'What will the proponent do in advance of the regulatory process to support organizations in need of resources?'

If the proponent decides to provide funding, criteria for receiving funding should be developed and published for all participants to review. The criteria should (at a minimum) address whether the proponent will fund (a) participants' out-of-pocket travel, accommodation and communications costs; (b) participants' time in the form of a per diem or honorarium for attending meetings; (c) participants' time in the form of a per diem or honorarium for any EIA-related work; (d) technical support to carry out a research project that will benefit the EIA; and (e) technical support to undertake activities such as water or air quality monitoring under the auspices of some of the consulting firms contracted to the project.

The proponent may want advice on funding pre-hearing activities from other proponents, government agencies and regulators with jurisdiction in the region. The answers can be used to develop a consistent policy and criteria for all participants.

Conclusion

Merging the public involvement process directly with the development and production of an EIA in the manner described in the participatory model provides for a better process and will contribute to greater buy-in of local and regional stakeholders and the public. Since stakeholders become directly involved in designing, planning and implementing the various studies, they will better understand the results of the EIA, the potential and real impacts of the project and any recommendations for mitigation. This should provide greater comfort, to the regulators and government agencies involved in the approvals and follow-up, that the work is acceptable to the stakeholders and the public, and that there will not be a sudden adverse reaction on a project's approval.

Compared to the consultative model, the participatory model requires more direct involvement by members of the public, stakeholders, the proponent's technical, environmental and socioeconomic staff and consultants, and senior management. The proponent must place more trust in such a process and relinquish some control.

Governments, stakeholders, Aboriginal groups and the public may see this model as proactive, progressive and more participatory in nature. Trust is fostered among parties and good will is generated from the outset. In the end, this may save months of time and prohibitive costs due to drawn-out hearing processes, disallowing of the project by the regulator or prohibitive regulatory conditions from the proponent's view if the project is approved at all. True participation from the earliest stages may prove to be the only effective option if a project, policy or legislation is to be approved and supported at the end of the day.

References

Arnstein, S.R. 1969. 'A ladder of citizen participation', *American Institute of Planning Journal*, 35(4): 216–24.

Burdge, R.J. 1990. 'The benefits of social impact assessment in third world development', *Environmental Impact Assessment Review*, 10(1/2): 123–34.

Burdge, R.J. 1990. 'Social impact assessment and the public involvement process', *Environmental Impact Assessment Review*, 10(1/2): 81–90.

Canadian Petroleum Association 1989. *Public Guidelines for the Canadian Petroleum Industry*, Calgary: Canadian Petroleum Association.

Creighton, J.L. 1980. *Public Involvement Manual: Involving the Public in Water and Power Resources Decisions*, Washington, DC: US Department of the Interior, Water and Power Resources Service.

Creighton, J.L. 1984. *Public Participation: A Manual for EEI Member Companies*, Saratoga, CA: Edison Electrical Institute.

Environment Canada 1992. *Consultations and Partnerships: Working Together with Canadians*, Ottawa: Environment Canada, Transition Team Steering Committee on Consultations and Partnerships.

Roberts, R. 1995. 'Public Involvement: From Consultation to Participation', in F. Vanclay and D.A. Bronstein (eds), *Environmental and Social Impact Assessment*, Chichester: Wiley, 221–46.

Suncor Oilsands Limited 1998. 'Steepbank Mine Environmental Impact Assessment', unpublished report.

World Bank Environment Department 1993. *Public Involvement in Environmental Assessment: Requirements, Opportunities and Issues*, Environmental Assessment Sourcebook Update, Washington, DC: World Bank.

17 Handling complex societal problems
Dorien DeTombe

What are complex societal problems?

There are many problems that can be categorized as 'complex societal problems'. These are problems where the 'solution' is to be found at the societal level. Complex societal problems are real-life problems reflecting much uncertainty and are therefore hard to deal with. Complex societal problems are often unique in the course of their progress, although they may have occurred many times before. This means that there is no routine way of solving them. Complex societal problems are often ill-defined, multifaceted, as well as hard to analyse, to structure and to change. Knowledge and data are missing and/or contradictory. The causes of the problem are vague or ambiguous. It is difficult to see where, when and by whom the problem was started, who is involved in the problem and who is not, and who is affected by the problem. Although many phenomena, actors (private and governmental) and people are involved, it is seldom clear beforehand which are involved. There may be a changing group of actors. Each actor has their own views about the problem, their own goals, power and emotion.

Complex societal problems are unstructured and dynamic. They have a considerable impact on society at the macro, meso and the micro levels. Sometimes they are local problems, although mostly they are region-wide or even worldwide. They can be found in all countries of the world. It is often uncertain what impact the problem has on society, what the goals and interests of the actors are and what will be the outcome of the problem. There are no easy, simple answers for these problems. Solutions, if there are any, can only be found with great effort and are often only temporary.

Complex societal problems are interdisciplinary, in that they include aspects that are the subject of study in several scientific disciplines. Handling societal problems involves knowledge, power and emotion. The knowledge for handling complex societal problems comes from a variety of scientific disciplines. Two kinds of knowledge are needed for handling these problems: content knowledge, which means knowledge about the subject of the problem, and knowledge about problem handling. The content knowledge comes from content experts; for example, in a health issue, it might be a doctor, hospital manager or other actor. The process knowledge comes from facilitators working in the field of complex societal problems. Facilitators may have backgrounds in different scientific disciplines, but use methods derived from their original field combined with methods specially created for handling societal problems. Methods and insights used derive from a wide range of fields, including law, economics, social sciences, mathematics, computer sciences, technology, engineering sciences, chaos theory and operational research (DeTombe, 1999).

Power also plays an important role in handling complex societal problems. Power in a democracy is divided among the problem owner and other actors. Together they must find mutually acceptable solutions or compromises. Further, in all phases of the problem-managing process, emotions also play a role, including emotions about the problem and emotions about the desired goal, as well as emotions between the groups and actors, and between the people who handle the problem.

> Something is called a problem when there is a discrepancy between the actual or (near) future situation and the desired future situation and/or there is a lack of knowledge and/or a lack of knowhow, and/or a lack of relevant data; as for complex interdisciplinary societal problems, the problem is often undefined and the desired situation is not always clear. (DeTombe, 1994: 58)

Problem handling of complex societal handling can be defined as

> the process of analyzing, structuring and guiding a problem in order to gain more insight into the problem, whether or not this leads to influencing the problem in order to reach the desired situation. This process can take place actively or passively, consciously or unconsciously, routinely or once only, whether it is by circumventing or by forgetting the problem, by shifting the problem to another party or by (partly) changing the problem, whether through thinking, applying tools and/or methods. (Ibid.)

'Handling problems' is preferred to 'problem solving' because solving refers to a certain desired goal and, as the desired goal potentially differs from actor to actor, the end of one problem process might mean a solved problem for one actor, and a new problem for another actor.

Examples of complex societal problems from agroindustry are the pollution of land and watertable by manure (Glasbergen, 1989; DeTombe, 1993), foot and mouth disease and mad-cow disease (bovine spongiform encephalopathy, BSE). Examples from industry include pollution by emissions, chemical contamination, noise and odour. Societal problems include issues of hunger, unemployment and poverty. Healthcare examples include HIV/AIDS and malaria. Problems related with the Internet, stock market and urban planning can also be considered and treated as complex societal problems (DeTombe, 2000b).

Although complex societal problems are diverse and may appear to be unrelated, they have in common that their causes and solutions often exceed the available knowledge in the relevant disciplines. 'Solutions' will only be found in a combination of changes in different areas. For example, the hunger problem in developing countries is often due to local wars. Fighting prevents local people taking care of their agriculture and their families. Often these wars are caused by political differences created in the colonial past (NRC, 2000b). Intervention in the hunger problem primarily requires a political solution, typically the creation of a stable democratic political situation. Despite their differences, all complex societal problems can be managed in a similar way.

Causes of complex societal problems
People are the cause of most complex societal problems. To complex societal problems like wars, pollution and building new infrastructure, the role of human intervention is obvious. However, humans, with the help of nature, even cause natural disasters such as avalanches and floods. Humans build houses in vulnerable areas on mountains or in the floodplains of the rivers. People live in areas of known high risk of hurricanes. Even in the case of rare events, there is a human contribution to the extent of the disaster. For example, following a rare ice storm in Montreal, Canada in January 1998, a large area of Montreal was without electricity (used for heating, cooking and lighting) for three weeks in the middle of the winter, with temperatures far below zero. The ice storm destroyed the above-ground electricity cables, a situation that would not have occurred if the cables had been underground (Abley, 1999).

Another example relates to flooding. The frequent flood disasters – in China the Yangtze River, in Canada the St Lawrence River and in The Netherlands the rivers Rhine and Maas – are often caused by too much manipulation of the curves of the river or by building houses in floodplains.

Complex societal problems are not handled optimally
Complex societal problems are usually not handled optimally or efficiently, leading to a waste of taxpayers' money. The reasons why these problems are handled inadequately include the following:

- economic limitations: there may not be enough money to handle the problem in a certain department, or at all;
- political reasons: politicians may have hidden agendas to benefit certain groups. The manure problem in The Netherlands, for example, was inadequately handled during the period 1950–97 because of electoral benefits to the political party (the conservative religious party) that was in power at the time (Glasbergen, 1989; DeTombe, 1993). Politicians prefer easy, quick, short-term solutions to finding

difficult but more sustainable long-term solutions which may take more time;

- psychological reasons: people tend to jump to conclusions instead of taking the time and effort to study the problem fully before discussing solutions;
- methodological reasons and the nature of the problem itself: complex societal problems are often too complex and too dynamic to control. The complexity of the problem itself, the many fields, actors and phenomena that are involved, and the interactions between them, make the problem hard to analyse, to guide and to control;
- the problem owner: the problem owner is often not fully aware of the complexity of the problem, and may prefer to have a simple solution rather than a more realistic, but complicated answer. Problem owners are usually not aware of the more effective methods for handling these problems, and/or are not willing or able to use these methods. There may not be adequate skills available in complex problem solving (DeTombe, 2000c).

The role of science
There is no doubt that the new century will confront society with problems that are very difficult to handle. There is a growing gap between the complexity of the problems faced by society and human capacity to deal with them. More knowledge and imagination, better methods and more tools are needed for society to survive amidst these problems. New approaches are needed for handling societal problems in an interdisciplinary manner. However, scientists are confronted by difficulties when trying to combine their efforts to meet this challenge. In order to combine their knowledge, scientists should deviate from their standard practice. The time has come to broaden the scope. When it is accepted that complex social phenomena have their own rules and laws, why not combine the knowledge, skills and methods drawn from the technical and natural sciences with the social sciences? Structuring and guiding the process more efficiently can save time, money and effort. This can increase the quality of the outcome in terms of a more sustainable agreement, a more transparent and better 'solution'. Relatively little attention has been given to these problems until now. The field of handling complex societal problems is relatively new.

The subdiscipline of complex societal problems started looking at knowledge developed in other fields that could be applied to this issue (DeTombe, 1999). The field of methodology provides an adequate domain to discuss such a combination of scientific knowledge. Taking logic as a starting point, the question to consider is, 'How can valid scientific knowledge about handling complex societal problems be found?' In combining the ideas and methods developed in the area of the natural, technical and social sciences, new ideas and methods can be developed and some of the already existing ideas and methods can be integrated. A key issue is how to combine useful knowledge derived from several disciplines in order to enhance the handling of complex societal problems.

The field demands a multidisciplinary approach in order to combine the existing methods and tools and to develop new approaches. Theoretical scientists, applied scientists and practitioners can combine their methodological knowledge in a way that allows existing methods and tools to be applied. New methods and tools can be developed, using an optimal combination of qualitative and quantitative methods. Fruitful use of existing methodologies has been drawn from (cognitive) psychology, sociology, computer science, artificial intelligence, methodology, mathematics, engineering, system theory, chaos theory, philosophy, sociocybernetics (Geyer and van der Zouwen, 1986) and operational research (DeTombe, 1999). Most of the scientific support for complex societal problems comes from specific methods and tools such as scenario making, multiple criteria analysis, operational research, group decision support systems (DeTombe, 1997), decision support systems and simulation (Forrester, 1987).

Sometimes only some aspects of a field can be used to support handling complex societal problems. In social science, especially in the field of cognitive psychology and learning theory, there is much expertise on problem solving. However, examination of the research in this area reveals that the problems discussed differ on essential points from complex societal problems. The field of cognitive psychology and learning theory focuses on how a person handles a problem, rather than how a problem is solved. The problems these fields focus on are well structured, static, relatively easy to solve and comprise problems to which an answer is already known (cf. Newell and Simon, 1972). The knowledge and the methodology of this field can therefore be applied only in part to the field of complex societal problems.

The field of management also considers complex problems, at least management problems in organizations (Mintzberg, 1983). The problems management theories focus on sometimes resemble complex societal problems. Complex organizational problems, for instance with respect to international organizations, can be considered as complex societal problems. However, many publications in this field are of a popular genre and not necessarily scientifically reliable. These books often simplify a complex issue for commercial appeal, and most do not offer a scientifically reliable base to found a method.

Table 17.1　Knowledge phases in the problem-handling process

Subcycle 1: defining the problem
Phase 1.1　becoming aware of the problem and forming a (vague) mental idea
Phase 1.2　extending the mental idea by reflection and research
Phase 1.3　putting the problem on the agenda and deciding to handle the problem
Phase 1.4　forming a problem-handling team and starting to analyse the problem
Phase 1.5　gathering data, exchanging knowledge and forming hypotheses
Phase 1.6　formulating the conceptual model of the problem

Subcycle 2: changing the problem
Phase 2.1　constructing an empirical model and establishing the desired goal
Phase 2.2　defining the handling space
Phase 2.3　constructing and evaluating scenarios
Phase 2.4　suggesting interventions
Phase 2.5　implementing interventions
Phase 2.6　evaluating interventions

Phases in the problem-handling process
The problem-handling process comprises several phases. By identifying phases, it is possible to recognize the phase the problem handling process is in, what to do and what action to take (see Table 17.1). The scientific support given to complex societal problems mostly focuses on only two phases in the problem-handling process: the phase of constructing and evaluating scenarios, and the phase suggesting interventions (Table 17.1). These scientific activities are related to those moments in the problem-handling process where the problem owner wants support in making decisions and in selecting alternatives. However, these two phases are only a part of the whole problem handling process. Skipping (or only facile performance of) the first phases can lead to a less creative or fruitful solution, or, in the worst case, it can even lead to handling the wrong problem.

Awareness of the problem and putting it on the agenda
Before a societal problem can be managed, there must be an awareness of the problem at the societal level. Awareness of a problem depends on the cultural circumstances. Many issues now considered in a modern democracy as a social problem were often accepted historically as 'the way things were' and they were not considered as a problem. The awareness of a problem is influenced by the amount of power an affected group has. This can be real power (or powerlessness) or imaginary power (or powerlessness). A significant example is the position of women in the world. The

limited influence women have on politics is in contradiction to the huge amount of work they perform. The political influence women have is reflected in their own view of their value and social worth. Because of this self-perception, it took ages before women became aware of their own value and, correspondingly, of their shocking position in society. Gender inequality, now rightfully considered a major issue, for a very long time was not considered a complex societal problem.

The second phase in the problem-handling process is extending the concept by reflecting and researching: by hearing, thinking, reading, discussing, talking and asking questions about the problem. This is often done by those people who are affected by the problem. Discussion groups form and may become action groups in order to create power. Examples of action groups include the feminist action groups of the 1970s and 1980s, homosexual emancipation groups and environmental awareness groups. These action groups attempt to gain the attention of the people that eventually have to handle the problem. They do this by emphasizing the problem with demonstrations and other direct action in order to get the attention of the media and, through doing this, to put pressure on the political process. The step from awareness of a societal problem by a special group to putting it on the political agenda can be a long and hard struggle, and a critical mass is often needed before political action will follow.

It took a long struggle to create a critical mass to put the gender inequality problem on the political agenda. Although there have been some positive changes in the position of women, especially in western countries, money and (public and private) power are still almost completely in the control and possession of men. Only gradually has the subordinate position of women come to be seen as a problem which must be solved as a societal problem rather than being a private problem of women. Abortion is an example of the low position of women in society. For a long time, the need for abortion was considered a private problem of 'fallen women', rather than a societal issue to be put on the political agenda and handled as a societal problem with a solution to be found at the societal level.

Another example of the long time it takes before people become aware of a complex societal problem is the flood problem in The Netherlands. The Netherlands contains the deltas of the rivers Rhine and Maas. These two large rivers have much higher flow rates in early springtime, when there is much rain and snowmelt, than in the rest of the year. Sometimes the volume of water is so great that there is widespread flooding. In the past, these large floods were considered as the punishment of God. In the 17th century, the Dutch government wanted to control this flood problem. It sent civil servants to the local authorities to convince them to take action. Only after much effort, which took decades, could the civil servants convince the local people that the floods were not the punishment of God, but should be considered as a societal problem that could and should be managed (Lintsen, 1980). More recently, Dutch engineers argued that river dykes were not strong enough and that there needed to be a national dyke-strengthening programme. There was considerable public opposition to this, but floods in 1993 and 1995 led to a diminishing of this opposition (see Chapter 15).

The HIV/AIDS issue is a similar example. In the early 1980s, HIV/AIDS was considered a homosexual matter. Many people, especially in the USA, saw it as a punishment of God. This meant that, in the beginning at least, the heterosexual majority was not willing to consider this problem fully (Shilts, 1986).

Some societal problems, however, do receive easier and quicker attention. Societal problems that threaten the wealth or power of the ruling class get direct and full attention. Recent examples of complex societal problems which have been a threat to the ruling class include the Vietnam war, the so-called 'Cold War', North Atlantic Treaty Organization (NATO) intervention in Kosovo in 1999 and the September 11 (2001) terrorist attack on the World Trade Center in New York. These actions cost extremely large amounts of money and they ruin and destroy land, houses, goods and life. Afterwards they leave chaos, sometimes for generations. Considering the amount of resources governments provide for military purposes in comparison to social goals, such as education, healthcare, providing for elderly people or single mothers, demonstrates the importance military intervention arguably has in protecting the power and economic benefits of those who are in charge.

Knowledge, power and emotion
There are three basic elements in the management of complex societal problems: knowledge, power and emotion. Knowledge includes having information about the problem. This information is often missing crucial elements; the data needed are often missing or have internal contradictions. It is virtually impossible to have all the knowledge needed to manage complex societal problems properly, because of their complexity and dynamic character. There will always be 'white spots' and 'blind spots'. White spots are the areas of knowledge where it is known that information is lacking, and that it takes time and money to obtain it. Blind spots are areas where the lack of information is unacknowledged.

The management of complex societal problems involves different actors in the process. In these group processes, all forms of power play a role, especially in reaching an agreement on the definition of the problem and on selecting interventions. There is official (formal) power and unofficial (informal) power, legal power and illegal power, institutionalized power and non-institutionalized power.

The third basic element in the problem-handling process is the often underestimated influence of emotion in the process. Emotions can stimulate or obstruct cooperation between individuals and between groups. Emotions include anxiety, fear, joy, sympathy and hate. There can be emotions based on prejudice or discrimination. Emotions can be rational or irrational. Emotions appear when one's interests are threatened, for example when the goal of the management process or the problem itself is undesired.

Supporting problem handling

Societal problems need to be supported more adequately to enhance the quality and the effect of the process, and to ensure that time and money are not wasted. This can be achieved by using various techniques and tools. The COMPRAM method (Complex Problem Handling method), as developed by DeTombe (1994; 1996; 2001), is an example of such a method. It is based on the need for an adequate, transparent and well-structured method for the problem-handling process of large societal problems. COMPRAM, as distinct from most other methods, supports many phases of the problem-handling process. It guides the problem handling after the problem is put and accepted on the political agenda.

COMPRAM is based on theoretical scientific notions from cognitive psychology, sociology, computer science and theories about group processes, as well as sociocybernetics, chaos theory and systems theory. COMPRAM is interdisciplinary in two ways. First, the types of problems concern many fields, phenomena and actors. Second, the method requires input from several scientific disciplines. The COMPRAM method is efficient, transparent and democratic in the way complex societal problems are analysed, decisions are taken, policy is made and interventions are implemented and evaluated. The method was developed in the period from 1990 to 1994 by DeTombe (1994) and elaborated from 1994 to 2001 (DeTombe, 2001).

The different disciplines associated with a problem, the impact on society of these problems, and the many actors involved in the process, dictate that the problem-handing process is a group process. COMPRAM starts when the legitimate problem owner, perhaps supported by one or more content experts, together with a facilitator, invites participants to address the problem by forming problem-handling teams. Two kinds of problem-handing teams are involved. One team consists of 'neutral' content experts with knowledge in one of the areas identified with the problem. The content experts are more or less neutral towards a certain outcome of the problem-handling process. The other team consists of actors that are a party to the process. They have a direct interest in a certain outcome of the problem.

The legitimate problem owner
The term 'problem owner' implicitly means a legitimate problem owner. 'Legitimate' means that the problem owner has by law, habit or convention the legitimate task, right or duty to handle the problem. It is very important to have a problem owner who has the right (and responsibility) to manage the problem. This increases the chances that the teams invited to discuss the problem (experts and other actors) are willing to participate. Even more important, the outcome of the problem-handling process has a greater chance of being accepted and implemented. With an illegitimate problem owner, the risk is high that the main actors will not want to participate. It also reduces the likelihood that the interventions will be implemented or appropriate. A legitimate problem owner can be a group or institution, as well as an individual. Sometimes a group of problem owners can be formed, who together have the responsibility, and gain the authority of the other actors, to handle the problem.

The experts
The process of cooperative problem handling begins with the selecting a team of 'neutral' experts by the facilitator, in cooperation with the problem owner. The selection of experts depends on the major fields, phenomena, actors and other groups that are involved in the problem. At the start of the process, it may not be clear which fields, phenomena, actors and groups are involved. In that case, the facilitator undertakes in-depth interviews with the experts and actors that are known, in order to gain more information about the elements that ought to be involved.

The actors and groups
Actors have a direct interest in the goals and outcomes of the problem handling process. The process affects them directly. Two kinds of actors can be distinguished: well-organized groups and unorganized groups, the latter being often forgotten. Both groups, however, are affected by the problem-handling process. The well-organized actors coordinate their interests, and try to influence the process. Unorganized and less organized groups, like the elderly, the handicapped and children, have an interest in the outcome of the problem, but they do not have a particular defender of their interests. In theory, policy makers should take care of the interests of both the well-organized and the less organized groups. In practice, however, it is exceptional for the interests of the unorganized groups to be taken just as seriously as those of the well-organized groups. The actors involved in the problem-handling process each have their own view on the problem, their own definition of the problem and their own goals. Often actors have hidden agendas. In COMPRAM, both the actors and the unorganized

groups are invited to join the problem-handling process at an early stage (DeTombe, 2000a). The problem owner and the major actors must agree on the way the problem-handling process is guided. The method must have credibility (DeTombe, 2000c). Before starting the problem-handling process, the problem owner and the actors should be introduced to the way the problem will be guided.

The six steps of COMPRAM
COMPRAM distinguishes six steps. These are not to be confused with phases in the problem-handling process (see Table 17.2). In the first step, the problem is analysed and described by a team of neutral content experts. In the second step, the different actors analyse and define the problem. The third step is where the experts and actors try to find interventions that are mutually acceptable. In the fourth step, the societal reactions of the selected interventions are anticipated. In the fifth step, the interventions are implemented. And finally, the changes are evaluated from both the original perspective and the perspective of the problem as it changed during the process.

Table 17.2   The six steps of COMPRAM

Step 1	analysis and description of the problem by a team of neutral content experts
Step 2	analysis and description of the problem by different teams of actors
Step 3	identification of interventions by experts and actors
Step 4	anticipation of the societal reactions
Step 5	implementation of the interventions
Step 6	evaluation of the changes

COMPRAM is a framework method. This means that the method provides an overall approach by which to handle the problem, rather than a detailed step-by-step specification. Different data-analysing tools and knowledge-elicitation tools, such as brainstorming and interview tools, are used to elicit and analyse the data. There are methods and tools for selecting participants, for data retrieval, data manipulation and simulation, as well as for reflecting on the results. Games, for example, can be fruitful instruments for reflecting on the consequences of an intervention. Some tools, for example the seven-layer model (DeTombe, 1994), are developed specially to support the knowledge exchange and communication between the members of the interdisciplinary teams.

Depending on the specific problem, the problem-handling team, the moment in the problem-handling phase and the time and money available, the facilitator must decide, in addition to following the prescribed steps of the framework method, which methods and tools can support the problem handling-process. This demands that the facilitator has knowledge of a variety of methods and tools that can be applied. Next to methodological expertise, computer knowledge is required. Knowledge on guiding group processes and using tools is also required. The facilitator should also be able to guide group processes, be aware of knowledge confusion, power differences and emotions, and issues such as hidden agendas, envy and groupthink. Groupthink in decision making, which is by definition negative, occurs when the individual critical thinking of individuals is surrendered to conform to a mutual decision. In large problem-handling processes, facilitators do not have to know how to use all the support methods and tools personally. They may be assisted by other specialized facilitators, who guide the teams with the support of a specific method or tool.

An example of a complex societal problem: HIV/AIDS in South Africa

For too long, HIV/AIDS was regarded solely as a medical issue, with solutions being considered only from a medical perspective. However, from the early 1990s, it was already clear that the medical world did not foresee an adequate answer to this issue within the next decade. The strong emphasis on a medical solution prevented fruitful non-medical interventions from being accepted and supported. This gave the problem the chance to assume enormous proportions, especially in some African countries. Fortunately, over the last few years, the problem owners, such as the United Nations Programme on HIV/AIDS (UNAIDS) and the World Health Organization (WHO), have become aware that HIV/AIDS was a societal issue, albeit with medical aspects, and should be approached as a complex societal problem (DeTombe, 1994) making it amenable to being handled with COMPRAM.

Over 90 per cent of HIV-infected people live in developing countries. Many have no access to the medical advances available in the industrialized world. Considering the percentage of people infected by HIV and the way this epidemic affects society, the HIV/AIDS epidemic is a major threat for the developing countries. In Africa, the HIV/AIDS epidemic primarily affects the sub-Saharan countries. HIV prevalence in South Africa is 22 per cent of the adult population (NRC, 2000a). Some 300 000 people have already died of AIDS.

Acquired immune deficiency syndrome (AIDS) is caused by the human immunodeficiency virus (HIV). Although transmitted also by infected needles and blood transfusions, in Africa HIV is spread primarily by heterosexual contact. The fast spread of the virus is due to the frequent promiscuous behaviour of men and women. However, the fact that in Africa HIV/AIDS is mainly regarded as a heterosexual disease does not mean that homosexual men are not infected, rather that rates of transmission are greater in the heterosexual population. AIDS is a disease that cannot be cured, for which there is no vaccination, and for which there is not sufficient medical treatment. The treatment that is available – to fight the symptoms and postpone death – is too expensive for most people in South Africa, even with reduced prices (NRC, 2001).

HIV/AIDS is the cause of much suffering for the men, women and children that are infected. The disease also influences the family and friends of the patients, who see their family members and friends suffering and dying. There is a loss of family income and family care. Men and women are left without a partner after that partner's long period of increasing illness, and children become deprived of parental care.

The majority of the infected people in South Africa are black. As a result of HIV, it is anticipated that the average life expectancy at birth of black people in South Africa will drop from 62 to 35 years (UNAIDS, 2000a, 2000b; African Development Forum, 2000, 2000). A large percentage of the working population will be too weak to work, and will die before reaching 50. The society will be left without a large group of healthy young adults, who normally form the basis of the economy and have responsibility for raising the next generation. Because of its large impact, the disease is a threat to the whole society (World Bank, 1999).

The high proportion of pregnant women who are HIV-infected (in one study in Durban, it was 33 per cent) means that around 11 per cent (one-third of 33 per cent) of the newborn babies will also be HIV-infected. They will develop AIDS, and die within 7 to 9 years (UNAIDS, 2000a, 2000b; African Development Forum, 2000, 2000). The HIV-negative children of the HIV-positive mothers will, within a few years, have a terminally ill mother. As the period between HIV infection and death is 7 to 9 years, the majority of these children will be without a mother before they reach the age of 10. Many mothers raise their children without, or with only limited support from, a man. This means that a large group of children will be without parental care at an early age. Although some family care may be assumed by grandmothers, their potential as carers is limited. Moreover, within 20 years, there will also be a shortage of grandmothers to look after the orphaned infants.

There are several reasons why attempts to reduce the rate of infection have not been successful.

● Taboo on discussing sex: although promiscuous behaviour is regarded as normal, especially in the black community, discussing sexual behaviour is taboo. This social taboo makes awareness of, and talking about, prevention difficult.

- Crime: the poor living conditions in homelands, townships and squatter areas lead to high rates of criminal behaviour, including rape of young women and sexual abuse of children.
- Culture and religion: the power of the traditional organized religions in South African society prevents discussion of the real sexual behaviour of men and women, and prevents discussion of the ways the HIV virus spreads among the population and the ways people can protect themselves. Some of the methods of protection (such as use of condoms) are not acceptable to some of the churches in South Africa.
- HIV/AIDS patients are stigmatized: because, in most parts of South Africa, sexual activities, sexually transmitted diseases in general and HIV/AIDS in particular, are not to be discussed and are taboo, people who are HIV-infected are socially blamed, stigmatized and left alone in their suffering. This means that those who are HIV-infected are not willing to disclose this fact to their family and friends, and, more seriously, to their sexual partners. This contributes to the further spread of the disease. Because of the taboo, people ignore the illness until it is no longer possible not to seek medical intervention. Culturally, most black people prefer help from a traditional healer rather than western doctors.
- Lack of awareness of the problem: because awareness of the problem is not high and there is an avoidance of the subject, the chances are low that people will take the necessary, but not popular, precautions. The future consequences of a society with a high rate of HIV infection and transmission are not considered.
- Using a condom is not popular: the use of condoms is not popular with those who lead a promiscuous sex life. It is not regarded as necessary to protect oneself against sexually transmitted diseases, and the use of a condom is considered to be not macho. Black women lack the power to insist on the use of condoms.
- Poverty and prostitution: the high degree of poverty and other aspects of South African society mean that there is a high degree of prostitution. Prostitutes are used by men, and many women are forced into prostitution.
- Unorthodox views and the role of government: the Department of Health in South Africa is not very effective in handling the HIV/AIDS epidemic. There is an acceptance by some individuals in government (including the current President, Thabo Mbeki) of unorthodox views about the relationship between HIV and AIDS –

specifically of the Duisenberg view that AIDS is not caused by HIV but by a range of other factors including drug overload. Mbeki promotes the idea that AIDS is not caused by the HIV virus, but by poverty.

● Lack of a realistic prevention programme: at present, the official HIV/AIDS promotion policy is 'Abstention, Be faithful, use Condom and take care of the Disease' (ABCD). The policy has not been very successful and it fails to appreciate the realities of sexual activity in South Africa.

Nevertheless, many interesting interventions to prevent the spread of HIV have been undertaken in the last five years in South Africa. These include the distribution of free condoms in bars, hotels and cafes; television advertisements emphasizing the danger of promiscuous and unprotected sexual contact; and popular performers increasing awareness of the issue. People with AIDS are treated in the state hospitals, although resources are limited. The interventions taken up to now, although done with the best of intentions, have not been sufficiently effective. In order to develop a more effective intervention strategy, a thorough analysis of the problem has to be made, with exchange of knowledge between the many experts and actors.

A hypothetical application of the COMPRAM method in handling the HIV/AIDS issue

HIV/AIDS is a complex societal problem that would benefit from the application of the COMPRAM method. Below, a hypothetical application of COMPRAM to this issue is described, outlining the six steps in the problem-handling process (see Table 17.2).

Step 1 involves developing knowledge about the issue. Experts in all subject areas associated with HIV/AIDS discuss the topic and develop a description of the overall problem in order (1) to see how relevant factors are interconnected; (2) to see which actors, organized and unorganized groups, and which government agencies and NGOs are involved; (3) to consider what the possibilities for intervention are; (4) to see what the causes and effects of the problem are; and (5) to analyse the past and present situation and possible futures. A facilitator promotes interdisciplinary knowledge exchange. Relevant fields include healthcare, education, economics, law, psychology, sex work, mining, religion, local, provincial and central government, as well as others. In the discussion, the experts are prompted to describe the problem in a creative way as completely as possible, covering all aspects of the problem. This step would take a total elapsed time of about two months, representing 16 work days for the facilitator, and about 8 days for each expert. The output of this step is a report comprising an overview of main aspects, and their interrelationships, of the HIV/AIDS issue in South Africa.

Step 2 relates to understanding the influence of power and how this power affects the problem. In this step, the problem definition of each of the actors is constructed. The process continues by inviting all the main actors concerning HIV/AIDS to participate. Actors include the insurance companies, the local, provincial and national government, industry, farmers, miners, sex workers, representatives of different religions, traditional healers, freight transporters and others. These groups are invited by the facilitator to discuss the problem among themselves, to give their own view of the problem, and to indicate what kind of interventions they will support or oppose. This step would also take a total elapsed time of about two months, representing an additional 16 work days for the facilitator, and about 2 days for each actor. The output of this step is a report containing an overview of the main views of the different actors, including a statement of their power and emotional attachment to the issue.

Step 3 is about identifying interventions that would be mutually acceptable. The experts and the representatives of actors discuss the combined possible interventions on all the aspects of the problem. This leads to a combined and mutually structured integral intervention in the problem. Elapsed time of two months is estimated, with 16 work days for the facilitator and 8 days for each expert and actor. The output is a report with an overview of main interventions in the HIV/AIDS problem in South Africa, and their correlations. The interventions could range from school and city education to better living conditions, family reunions, orphanages, medical treatment for the infected persons and facilities for disposal of the dead.

Step 4 is the process of reflecting on the societal effects of the interventions. Before implementing the interventions, there must be reflection to see what the societal reactions to the interventions are likely to be. This way, the interventions can be changed, if necessary, before they are implemented. The elapsed time for this step would be a further two months (16 facilitator days) and 4 days for each participant. The output is a report providing an overview of the extent of likely cooperation (complicity) and resistance to the planned interventions.

Step 5 relates to implementing the interventions. The interventions are implemented according to the implementation strategy devised by the problem-handling teams. Implementation time will vary, depending on the devised interventions, but it could be of the order of 12 months or more. Since most of the implementation responsibility relates to the actors, the number of facilitator days will be low (allow for 20 work days in a 12-month period of implementation). The output at this stage is the actual implementation of the planned interventions.

Step 6 is an evaluation step, taking an elapsed period of two months and involving 16 facilitator days. There would be a report detailing (1) the success or otherwise of the planned interventions in terms of reducing the HIV/AIDS problem in South Africa, (2) how well the interventions were implemented, and (3) how effective the problem-handling process was.

It is important to appreciate that, going through this process, even when doing so is efficient and effective, does not mean that the HIV/AIDS problem will be solved within two years. However, the use of this approach could be the start of some fundamental changes in relation to HIV/AIDS, and is likely to lead to a reduction in the transmission rate, and to better care of those directly and indirectly affected by HIV/AIDS.

Conclusion

The COMPRAM approach is a structured problem-handling approach based on research from many disciplines. The method includes the three basic components of the problem-handling process: knowledge, power and emotion. COMPRAM uses a six-step approach to guide the problem-handling process. Teams of experts and actors guided by a facilitator participate in the process. The method can be used for all kinds of complex societal problems. This coherent, mutually-integrated approach increases the effectiveness of the interventions, and leads to more sustainable solutions for lower cost. COMPRAM provides a better opportunity to involve all affected groups and to consider all possible interventions. However, in order to handle a societal problem fruitfully, the problem must be recognized as a societal problem that needs intervention at the society level, as well as recognition that the problem can usefully and desirably be handled with the COMPRAM procedure.

References

Abley, M. (ed.) 1999. *Stories from the Ice Storm*, Toronto: Canadian Publishers.
African Development Forum 2000, 2000. *AIDS in Africa*, Geneva: UNAIDS.
DeTombe, D.J. 1993. 'An interdisciplinary process of problem handling for policy making on environmental problems', in E. Stuhler and M. O'Súilleabháin (eds), *Enhancing Human Capacity to solve Ecological and Socio-economic Problems* (vol. 2), Mering: Hampp Verlag, 30–46.
DeTombe, D.J. 1994. *Defining Complex Interdisciplinary Societal Problems: A theoretical study for constructing a co-operative problem analyzing method*, Amsterdam: Thesis Publishers.
DeTombe, D.J. 1996. 'COMPRAM: a method for analysing complex interdisciplinary societal problems', in D.J. DeTombe and C. van Dijkum (eds), *Analyzing Societal Problems*, Mering: Hampp Verlag, 7–29.
DeTombe, D.J. 1997. 'Experiments with groupware for analyzing complex technical environmental policy problems', in M. Vezjak, E. Stuhler and M. Mulej (eds), *Environmental Problem Solving: From Cases and Experiments to Concepts, Knowledge, Tools and Motivation* (Proceedings of the 12th International Conference on Case Method and Research and Case Method Application), Munich/Mering: Rainer Hampp Verlag, 36–43.
DeTombe, D.J. 1999. 'Facilitating complex technical policy problems', in E. Stuhler and D.J.

DeTombe (eds), *Cognitive Psychological Issues and Environment Policy Application*, Munich/Mering: Hampp Verlag, 119–28.

DeTombe, D.J. 2000a. 'Anticipating and avoiding opposition in large technological projects', *International Journal of Technology Management*, 19(3/4/5): 301–12.

DeTombe, D.J. 2000b. 'A new method for handling complex spatial problems', in A. Reggiani (ed.), *Spatial Economic Science: New Frontiers in Theory and Methodology*, Berlin: Springer Verlag, 212–40.

DeTombe, D.J. 2000c. 'Testing methods for complex real life problems', in J. Blasius *et al.* (eds), *Social Science Methodology in the New Millennium: Proceedings of the Fifth International Conference on Logic and Methodology*, Cologne: T-T Publikaties, 1–14.

DeTombe, D.J. 2001. 'COMPRAM, a method for handling complex societal problems', *European Journal of Operational Research*, 128(1): 266–82.

Forrester, J.W. 1987. 'Lessons from system dynamics modeling', *System Dynamics Review*, 3(2): 136–49.

Geyer, R.F. and van der Zouwen, J. (eds) 1986. *Sociocybernetic Paradoxes. Observation, Control and Evolution of Self-Steering Systems*, London: Sage.

Glasbergen, P. 1989. 'Beleidsnetwerken rond milieuproblemen: Een beschouwing over de relevantie van het denken in termen van beleidsnetwerken voor het analyseren en oplossen van milieuproblemen', Verenigde Uitgeverijen Gemeente Administratie, 's-Gravenhage.

Lintsen, H.W. 1980. *Ingenieurs in Nederland in de negentiende eeuw*, Delft: Uitgever eigen beheer.

Mintzberg, H. 1983. *Power in and around Organizations*, Englewood Cliffs: Prentice-Hall.

Newell, A. and Simon, H.A. 1972. *Human Problem Solving*, Englewood Cliffs: Prentice-Hall.

NRC 2000a. 'AIDS in Zuid Afrika', *NRC Handelsblad*, 9 March, p.3.

NRC 2000b. 'Oorlogen in Africa', *NRC Handelsblad*, 18 May, p.5.

NRC 2001. 'Pharmaceutische industrie verlaagd prijs AIDS medicijnen in Africa', *NRC Handelsblad*, 14 March, p.3.

Shilts, R. 1986. *And the Band played on: Politics, People, and the AIDS Epidemic*, New York: St Martin's Press.

UNAIDS 2000a. *Enhancing the greater involvement of people living with or affected by HIV/AIDS in Sub-Saharan Africa*, Geneva: UNAIDS.

UNAIDS 2000b. *The International Partnership against AIDS in Africa*, Geneva: UNAIDS.

World Bank 1999. *Confronting AIDS: Public Priorities in a Global Epidemic* (rev. edn), New York: Oxford University Press.

18 Environmental mediation
Helen Ross

Introduction

The term 'environmental mediation' is used very broadly in the literature to encompass all forms of environmental dispute settlement other than litigation (Crowfoot and Wondolleck, 1990; Bingham, 1986; Sandford, 1990). It is similar to the use of the term 'alternative dispute resolution' (ADR). In environmental contexts, the term 'mediation' is often used synonymously with 'negotiation', but may be used to refer specifically to negotiations or other joint problem-solving forms which are facilitated by a third party whose main role is to help the participants to communicate and reach agreement (Bingham, 1986: 5). Negotiation is 'a voluntary, collaborative process of problem-solving in which parties to a dispute try to reach a mutually acceptable, workable solution to their differences through direct, face-to-face dialogue' (Sadler, 1987: 76). Some accept 'shuttle diplomacy', in which a mediator liaises between the parties before, or instead of, bringing them face to face, as a form of environmental mediation.

'Environmental mediation' generally refers to attempts to resolve specific disputes or episodes of conflict (Crowfoot and Wondolleck, 1990). However, a number of the published examples could also be described as joint decision making as understood in the environmental impact assessment (EIA) public participation literature. For instance, Bingham (1986) includes consensus building and policy dialogue among approaches to environmental dispute resolution. If one looks beyond specific disputes to the resolution of longer-term issues, collaborative planning (Gray, 1989; Healey, 1997; Ingram, 1998) and other cooperative stakeholder planning or decision-making processes can also be considered among uses of environmental mediation. This chapter provides a general introduction to environmental mediation, and discusses its relationships with social impact assessment (SIA) and public participation.

Common forms of environmental mediation

Negotiation and mediation concerning environmental issues take place in a wide variety of ways. Typically, these involve more than two parties, and complex sets of 'stakeholders' – referring to all those who affect, or are affected by, a particular issue (Susskind and Secunda, 1998: 27–8). The set of issues may also be complex, with different stakeholders focusing on different issues within the set. Three of the common forms are listed here.

296

Out-of-court settlements

Mediation may be used to solve environmental disputes which might otherwise go to court, for instance challenges brought by environmental or community groups against particular developments or acts of pollution. Bingham (1986) and Susskind and Secunda (1998) give many examples, including the origination of the field of environmental mediation through the settlement in 1973 of a long-standing dispute over a proposed flood control dam on the Snoqualmie River, Washington State, USA. Many of these disputes could be termed 'commercial industrial disputes' (Napier, 1998) in which issues tend to revolve around the costs of regulatory compliance, remediation of contaminated land, compensation for harm to the environment, and liability issues.

Designing new environmental management procedures

Several US federal and state government departments have adopted mediation processes to bring key stakeholders together with their own technical staff to design new environmental management standards or regulations, under the term 'negotiated rule making' (Schneider and Tohn, 1985; Susskind and Secunda, 1998). For example, the US Environmental Protection Agency (EPA), weary of its draft regulations being challenged in court, convened a group of representatives of stakeholders to work with its technical staff to design a new set of standards which were acceptable to all present (Schneider and Tohn, 1985). The EPA engineers found that the standards produced were technically better than they would have produced alone, as well as less likely to be challenged.

Another early example was designed to reduce planning challenges. Hundreds of similar development applications in Florida, usually for housing, were processed each year, inviting separate objections to each. The US Army Corps of Engineers decided to simplify and take the heat out of this situation, by inviting stakeholders (developers, regular objectors such as environmental groups, and the approval body) to design a common basis on which individual applications would be approved or rejected. This simplified the appraisal processes and reduced the number of objections drastically (Delli Priscoli, 1987).

Planning and co-management

Collaborative planning (Healey, 1997; Gray, 1989; Moore, 1996) involves planning in which stakeholders collaborate (possibly using negotiation) in order to form plans. Collaborative planning can be regarded both as a form of mediation, especially when facilitated, and as a strong form of public participation. It is closely related to 'cooperative management' (see Pinkerton, 1989; 1992), in which government and non-government parties negotiate and implement arrangements to manage a resource together. An example of co-management stemming from environmental mediation is the Timber–Fish–Wildlife Agreement (TFW) (Pinkerton, 1992; Ross, 1999; see case study below), which was negotiated in Washington State USA between the operators of privately owned timber land, Native American Tribal governments, state government departments and environmental groups. Its purpose was to settle disputes over forest practices which were damaging salmon habitat. In choosing to negotiate, the tribal governments recognized that they were winning most of their court cases, but not meeting their underlying need to save fish. The agreement gives all of the parties roles in policy, procedural and actual field decisions over logging practices, and has remained viable for well over a decade.

Environmental disputes are distinguished from commercial and industrial disputes by, in most cases, greater complexity of both issues and parties. Key characteristics of environmental mediations are summarized in Box 18.1.

Case study: negotiation of the Timber-Fish-Wildlife agreement

The TFW (Pinkerton, 1992; Ross, 1999) was mediated to settle years of legal disputes between Native Americans of Washington State, USA, and the commercial timber industry throughout that state, environmentalists and the state government regulatory authority for forestry practices. The disputes centred upon protection of salmon habitat, which was easily damaged by forestry practices. Seminal court cases in 1974 and 1980 had confirmed Native Americans' treaty rights to fish, and extended these to an obligation on the state to protect salmon habitat (Ross, 1999).

A group of industry people connected with water resources began meeting to explore whether there were alternatives to continued litigation. They hired a mediator as consultant to explore the feasibility of alternative dispute resolution (ADR). At much the same time, the Native Americans realized that, although they were winning the vast majority of their legal cases, this was not saving any salmon. A 1985 conference on the links between timber and fisheries, jointly convened by a non-government research body with strong links to the stakeholders and the University of Washington, proved a catalyst for negotiations. Much of the information presented came from private industry and the Indian tribes, as well as from university researchers. Many of the 400 participants left feeling that the problems were more soluble than they had thought (Waldo, 1988: 15).

The parties decided to try negotiation in 1986. The negotiations commenced with a three-day exploratory meeting, to which each party sent their best political, technical and managerial experts. This meeting agreed on a broad basis on which to proceed. All parties had to commit themselves to achieving all of the goals, and to making all decisions by consensus. The

BOX 18.1   FEATURES OF ENVIRONMENTAL MEDIATION

Parties. Frequently more than two parties. Large and complex parties (stakeholder groups), involving issues of representation and communication between those participating directly and their constituencies. Environmental groups are not as cohesive as labour unions, and may fragment over a proposed agreement (Susskind and Secunda, 1998: 28). Interorganizational as well as interpersonal relationships, often influenced by past interactions as well as differing interests and philosophies, affect the process. Issues of power relationships among the parties, an 'uneven field' for negotiation, and how to compensate for these. These include keeping the balance of information power, and recognizing that dispute resolution is a mutual learning process which requires time (Harashina, 1995).

Issues. Usually numerous and complex. May be viewed differently by the parties. May involve intense value contrasts and moral judgments. Technical complexity, disputed scientific arguments. May involve fundamental or irreversible impacts on environment or human health.

Alternatives to negotiation. The same issues could be contested in court, or advantage sought through political lobbying.

Timing. Issues need to be 'ripe' for negotiation, and the parties willing to try negotiation. This is often quite late in a dispute, when other avenues have been tried unsuccessfully. Consensus-building approaches, like the public participation approaches advocated in the impact assessment field, are not restricted to 'ripeness'; indeed, they may be more effective when used early in the development of issues.

Whether or not to use mediators (facilitators). Direct negotiations and use of mediators are both common. Some of the literature recommends a facilitation team, which includes members able to understand and help explain the scientific issues, as well as those skilled in the interactive processes involved in mediation (Boer *et al.*, 1990: 96).

Negotiation philosophy. Usually 'win–win' (principled negotiation) (after Fisher and Ury, 1981).

Signed or unsigned agreements?. Both signed and unsigned ('handshake') agreements are possible, with signed ones possibly more common.

Factors influencing success. Mediators analysing the conflict beforehand, helping the parties to decide whether mediation is appropriate. Establishing 'ground rules'. Parties need an incentive to negotiate a fair and stable agreement. The way the process is conducted. Direct involvement of decision makers and implementers (including government agencies). The likelihood of success does not appear to be influenced by the number of parties, the issues or having a deadline (Bingham, 1986). Most environmental mediation literature is produced from the perspective of the mediators. Moore (1996) argues that one needs to look at the success from the standpoints of the participants. She identifies a number of forms of success: product (an agreement), politically oriented (general acceptance), interest-oriented (parties protected their interests), responsibility-oriented (ownership of the outcome) and relationship-oriented (resulting relationships within and between the parties).

Implementation of agreements. It is difficult to 'bound' environmental agreements in terms of time horizons and spillover effects to other geographical areas (Susskind and Secunda, 1998). Implementation has been more successful in site-specific cases than with policy disputes (Bingham, 1986: 77). In complex cases such as policy issues and environmental management practices, the implementation phase appears as important as the original negotiation, and the maintenance of relationships among the participating parties remains necessary (Ross, 1999). Agreements may contain clauses concerning implementation and review.

Efficiency of mediation. The claim that environmental mediation is cheaper and faster than litigation is difficult to test because of problems in finding comparable samples (Bingham, 1986). The cost of preparing for negotiation and convening the process may be high, although 'per day' costs for mediators are lower than legal costs. Sipe and Stiftel (1995) identified substantial savings per party in their set of Florida case studies.

Sources: Bingham (1986), Crowfoot and Wondolleck (1990), Boer *et al.* (1990), Ross (1999).

negotiations were mediated by a team of four facilitators. The parties were Native Americans, the timber industry peak body, the state government and environmentalists represented through a peak body. The process started with the negotiation of ground rules, including one which indicated the severity of the conflict: 'leave your guns at the door'. Over 40 negotiation meetings were held over the following six months. Little is documented about what went on at the table. Although the atmosphere was very tense at times, the participants built strong and lasting relationships, both among individuals and as groups. The parties developed a process of 'caucusing', whereby the meeting would break for periods to allow each party to confer separately, then to rejoin the table. Each party had a negotiation team, whose members took turns to sit at the table or observe. A pivotal insight enabling successful negotiation – and the agreement to endure – was the parties' ability to develop a shared set of goals. These included the viability of the timber industry, since the Native Americans recognized that the alternative to commercial forestry, should the industry fail, was land clearing. This would be far worse for salmon habitat. Local government was added as a fifth party after the initial agreement was reached.

After six months, an agreement was reached which produced guidelines for future forest practices with less impact on salmon and wildlife habitat, and laid out a continuing process solving the underlying issues of the dispute. The result was a cooperative management arrangement with structures and processes to confer on policy issues, research and on-ground logging decisions (see Ross, 1999). It includes an annual review process. The agreement has now endured for 15 years and has expanded to incorporate new issues and parties. It has come close to breaking up at some of its annual reviews, but each time the parties have decided that they had more to lose than to gain by leaving the agreement.

While the agreement has been relatively successful in improving conditions for salmon, the wildlife issues included in the agreement proved far less soluble. The parties went on, with some additional parties, to attempt two other major negotiations over similar issues to TFW. One, over water resources throughout the state, endured four years before breaking up, though two regional pilot studies continued, despite being hampered by lack of resources for implementation. Another, attempting to address the wildlife issues which had proved intractable under TFW, came close to agreement after a year of negotiation, but failed in its last weeks (see Ross, 1999, for details).

How environmental mediation is related to SIA
Both environmental mediation and SIA usually deal with multiple stakeholders and their interests and issues. If the number of stakeholders is few,

the issues may also be too simple to require a full SIA. They may also be negotiated directly as a 'business' negotiation between a proponent and an interest group affected by its proposal, rather than as an environmental negotiation. The distinction here is slim. A number of instances in which Indigenous Australians have sought to optimize financial benefits and minimize particular risks associated with mining proposals have been negotiated directly between the parties (Craig & Ehrlich Ltd *et al.*, 1996; O'Faircheallaigh, 1995). These issues are simultaneously 'business' and environmental, but are handled like a business negotiation.

Negotiation may be used very effectively to solve potential social and environmental impacts that have already been documented through EIA and SIA. In the final stages of two relatively standard EISs conducted on proposed mines by Australia's Commonwealth Environmental Protection Agency (EPA), since renamed Environment Australia, the proponent and Indigenous parties came together to solve their outstanding issues by negotiation (Craig & Ehrlich Ltd *et al.*, 1996; O'Faircheallaigh, 1995). This was just before the EPA was required to write its 'Assessment Report' which normally would have highlighted such outstanding issues and recommended procedures to solve them as conditions of project approval. Since solutions were already agreed by the other interested parties, the Assessment Report only needed to record and support these solutions. This procedure, while creative on the part of the participants, does leave open the possibility that the parties may agree to actions which the EPA might prefer not to endorse. If, for instance, the Indigenous parties (perhaps lured by financial benefits) agree to environmental standards which the EPA would have queried or rejected, the EPA could come under political pressure for withholding approval against the wishes of the participants or for compromising environmental standards.

SIA may be very valuable to inform negotiations (O'Faircheallaigh, 1999). For instance, the Indigenous community at Uluru-Kata Tjuta National Park owns the land outright (although it is compulsorily leased back to the national government for 99 years) and has a joint management (co-management) agreement with Australia's National Park Authority for its management. When the management plan was due for five-yearly renegotiation, the Indigenous community commissioned an SIA on the cultural, social and economic impacts of joint management (Holden, 1998). The recommendations were to contribute to the new plan by offering strategies to minimize negative impacts on the Indigenous Traditional Owners and to optimize potential benefits to them of the Park's operation. It also provided a baseline for future monitoring. The SIA also empowered them by articulating, in writing, long-standing concerns that had not been voiced successfully by Traditional Owners (or heard properly by Park management and government staff), not even through the board of management mechanism (Holden, personal communication, June 2001).

In West Papua (formerly Irian Jaya), a social impact monitoring programme at the Freeport Indonesia copper and gold mine (Banks, 2000) was followed by, and incorporated into, a series of negotiations between the mining company and affected local people. There had been no SIA prior to the mine being established in the late 1960s, and there was a background of severe corporate and military conflict with local communities. The negotiations sought, in part, to address some of the social impact matters raised in the SIA. This process has been complicated by the role of a third party, the Indonesian military, in causing or exacerbating some of the impacts. The mining company has little influence over the actions of the military, and it is not considered appropriate for the military to be party to these negotiations (Glenn Banks, personal communication, July 1999, June 2000).

Manring *et al.* (1990), in an examination of the potential for integration of SIA with environmental conflict management in the USA, identified potential for SIA to predict conflicts, thence avert and manage conflicts, and to provide data for environmental mediation.

How environmental mediation is related to public participation

The relationship between environmental mediation and public participation needs to be considered with respect to the relationship between SIA and public participation (see, for example, Roberts, 1995; Burdge and Vanclay, 1995; Taylor *et al.*, 1995). This has not always been well articulated, and opinions on the nature of the relationship differ. Some people confuse public participation with SIA, since members of the public do report impacts from their own perspectives, and timely public participation makes an important contribution to averting and solving potential impacts.

SIA carries an important analytical role, of making a dispassionate investigation into the potential impacts (or actual impacts, in the case of monitoring current or past impacts). This may or may not accord closely with the public's assessments of the impacts. Public participation means involving sections of the public in decisions which affect them. It includes informing them so they better understand what is proposed, enabling them to articulate their views, and, it is hoped, to engage them in decision making about the ways the proposal, or alternatives, should proceed.

It is difficult to conceive of carrying out an SIA without interviewing or consulting members of the public, unless perhaps by examining historical records or demographic statistics (Becker, 1997). Information brought forward by members of the public (such as local knowledge, scientific information gathered by local people and observational knowledge) and the public's anticipations of the impacts of a given project (knowing their own values and lifestyles) are central aspects of SIA. Further, many practition-ers advocate participatory approaches to carrying out SIA (and planning): for example, Ross (1990), Dale and Lane (1994), Taylor *et al.* (1995). While there is overlap between the SIA and public participation roles in environ-mental impact assessment, especially in the realm of information, the roles are nevertheless distinguished by slightly different purposes. SIA is primar-ily to *assess* impacts, while public participation is primarily to *consult* about impacts. Both have roles in suggesting solutions to impacts.

There is a strong institutionalized link between mediation processes and impact assessment in the USA – the statutory scoping procedures under regulations associated with the National Environmental Policy Act 1969. Under these procedures, key parties affected by a development proposal are brought together to decide the scope of the environmental impact assess-ment, by identifying which potential impacts are sufficiently important to warrant study (Branch and Ross, 2000). Canadian scoping procedures also incorporate mediation (Mulvihill and Jacobs, 1998).

Mediation can be placed among the strongest forms of public participa-tion on 'ladders' of public participation (Arnstein, 1969; Wandersman, 1979; Parenteau, 1988). It equates with joint decision making, in which former power holders (usually government) and new participants decide matters on an equal basis. In the environmental management literature, 'cooperative management' (Pinkerton, 1992; Osherenko, 1988) and its close relation 'joint management' (Woenne-Green *et al.*, 1994; de Lacy, 1994) are good examples of this. Modavi (1996), however, cautions against a depic-tion of mediation as empowering the 'grass-roots', arguing that mediation channels activism against development projects away from confrontation and publicly visible tactics, and narrows the demands and concerns. In Hawai'i, it has helped to reduce business uncertainty (ibid.: 313).

It is always recommended that public participation start early, and con-tinue throughout a decision-making process. Commencing public partici-pation late can be quite damaging to the effectiveness of the participation, and to trust among the parties. Mediation is somewhat different: it can well be used in the final stages of a decision-making process, whether or not pro-ductive relationships have been built up beforehand through effective public participation processes. If the issues are considered 'ripe' for negoti-ation, even when the parties are highly polarized but need to find solutions, it can work. Indeed, the parties are most often motivated to negotiate when alternative avenues of problem solving have been exhausted. Here the task of the mediators, to encourage productive communication and progress towards solutions, is particularly demanding. The parties have to have a desire to negotiate: one can compel people to negotiate under certain legis-lative scenarios, but they cannot be compelled to negotiate productively. If they are not willing to negotiate in good faith, the opportunity is gone, so it would be unwise to rely on late-stage negotiation as a form of public participation.

On the other hand, it is interesting to speculate whether common forms of negotiation work as well as other forms of public participation early in a proposal, when issues are yet to be clarified. It may be too early to negotiate the issues, but good timing to negotiate a protocol for a process, including 'ground rules' for the research and discussion to follow (Ross, 1999). It may be useful for setting parameters, for instance by sometimes demonstrating that a proposed project will never, under any circumstances, be acceptable to members of the public, such as with value conflicts (O'Leary, 1997). Developments on Indigenous sacred sites, or highly sensitive environmental areas, are further examples (Lane *et al.*, 1997; Hawke and Gallagher, 1989). Or there may be 'no go' areas which must be avoided within, or among, the areas with potential for development. An excellent example of this is the Pitjantjatjara model of sacred site protection (Toyne and Vachon, 1987), which the Australian Pitjantjatjara people negotiated with several mining companies to produce a 'win–win' variation on legislated procedures to protect sacred sites. Instead of carrying out intensive anthropological surveys, and needing these scrutinized, to demonstrate which areas were too sacred to allow mining, the new procedure involved company representatives and Traditional Owners (both parties empowered to make decisions on the spot) travelling the land together to identify areas which were both free of sacred sites and prospective for minerals. This was faster, cheaper, and created far better relationships.

My own opinion is that, in the early stages of project development and public participation, negotiation *procedures* are more fruitful, embedded in processes such as collaborative planning and joint decision making, than treating the interactions as a full-on negotiation in its own right (which implies a responsibility to solve the issues conclusively and expeditiously). The label 'negotiation' is often perceived as bringing pressure on some, or all, parties to compromise. Public participation is more open-ended, seldom binding on the parties (although proponents or other parties may give undertakings) and seldom requires the parties to enter any formal agreements. The relationships between mediation, SIA and public participation and their respective roles are expressed in Figure 18.1.

Features of mediation in impact assessment

So far, the synergies, overlaps and subtle differences among SIA, public participation and environmental mediation have been discussed and illustrated. Mediation methods are already enriching environmental management. Negotiation and impact assessment procedures are combined in a

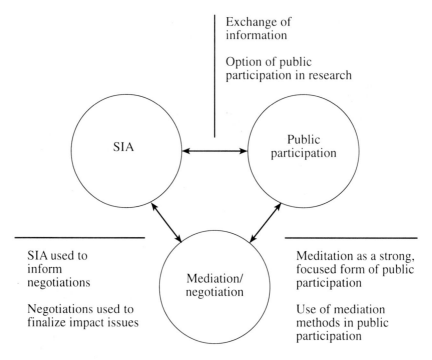

Figure 18.1   Relationships between SIA, public participation and mediation

number of environmental management procedures, such as collaborative planning and co-management. The know-how developed in environmental mediation, the negotiation literature and public participation is mutually enriching.

These hybrid forms of impact assessment and management (including the positive impacts of securing benefits), through forms of negotiation, share the features of environmental mediation itself. As emphasized earlier, there are multiple stakeholders and multiple issues at stake. This implies probable differences in power relations, access to information and therefore trust in one another's information.

What are suitable techniques for using mediation or negotiation procedures in environmental management? It is appropriate to consider all forms of environmental management here, as there is no reason to restrict this discussion to SIA. The forms of environmental management which use negotiation are all ways of averting negative social and environmental impacts, or of taking them into account among other factors.

Stakeholder analysis

Stakeholder analysis – a method for identifying those in a position to affect, or who are affected by, an issue – is used in SIA, public participation and, often, in mediation. The categories of stakeholder are often specified according to interests, such as 'neighbours of the development', and are not restricted to actual organizations. They may include abstract categories such as 'future generations'. Participation methods can be tailored more easily to the needs of the participants and the specific issue. Negotiation is unwieldy when carried out among many parties, especially when those parties need several people 'at the table'. This is related to the effective size of groups, a phenomenon well known in psychology and sociology. It is further complicated if some of the parties (such as tourists) are loosely organized or not associated with one another at all. A common strategy is to try to group stakeholder interests, having one party at the table to represent several similar interests, for instance one conservation group to speak formally for several.

Negotiation philosophy

The literature on environmental mediation is based on negotiation methods developed originally for a limited numbers of parties, and often individuals rather than organizations. This is elaborated by publication of the experiences of mediators, through case studies. 'Win–win' philosophies such as principled negotiation (Fisher and Ury, 1981) are intuitively appealing, but we need research into the real effectiveness of mediation methods developed in and for business, domestic and neighbourhood disputes in dealing with environmental issues. Are additional principles or different methods necessary to cater for disputes or aspirations based on intense differences in values? How should one cater for the nature of the parties, cross-cultural differences (see Ross, 1995) and the structures of environmental groups and public interest groups?

Timing and presentation

Among the stronger forms of public participation, that is, Arnstein's (1969) 'joint decision-making', the distinctions between negotiation and public participation are subtle. The key differences are that negotiation generally requires a more tightly defined set of participating stakeholders than public participation, and usually implies an attempt to reach a formal agreement. In public participation associated with development, often only the proponent needs to make commitments, either voluntarily, as an act of good faith within the participation process, or as a condition of attaining government approval. While the processes are similar, there are likely to be advantages in casting a process as 'public participation' or 'negotiation' in different

conditions, particularly related to timing within the evolution of a proposal, policy or plan, and depending on the nature of the parties and the
issues.

Participants' organizational structures and ways of communicating
Public participation methods have a particular advantage over negotiation,
in that there are methods for use on any scale, and an effective public participation programme can combine a variety of activities to engage different parties. Negotiation is usually intense and sustained. The process
requires clear limits to the numbers of individuals participating directly,
and is also simplest if the number of parties (organizations or otherwise)
are also limited.

Trying to restrict the numbers participating 'at the table' in a negotiation
brings in questions of representation. Even for formally constituted organizations, the choice of representatives to participate in the proceedings can
make a great difference to progress at the table, and to constituency support
for whatever is agreed. For many stakeholder categories, there is no formal
organization available or capable of speaking for those concerned. Common
strategies here are to facilitate those affected to meet and decide their mode
of representation, perhaps by designating some of their number to participate and report back to others; or for the convenors of the process to 'hand-
pick' individuals known to belong to, or have affinity with, that stakeholder
group. This applies more often in public participation than in negotiation,
since the parties to a negotiation have to have authority to decide a matter.
A clever solution to this was tried in two negotiations in Washington State,
USA, subsequent to the negotiation of the Timber–Fish–Wildlife Agreement. The negotiation processes alternated with large conferences, which
many members of the negotiating parties could attend, with focused discussions through working groups designated to discuss detail and bring options
back to the parties (Ross, 1999).

Preparation
In the environmental mediation literature, little attention has been paid to
the value of preparing the participants. One could be forgiven for thinking
many negotiations included only one day's training for participants, and
negotiation of ground rules. The relatively successful Timber–Fish–Wildlife
Agreement was preceded by about three years' relationship building among
the parties, before they felt ready to negotiate. Negotiations then took six
months and over 40 meetings (Ross, 1999).

There is general agreement that deciding ground rules at the start of the
process, sometimes combined with briefing or training for the participants
in the philosophy of negotiation, is valuable. Wondolleck *et al.* (1996) advo-

cate that citizens' groups prepare themselves for a mediation process by paying attention to representation, agenda setting, ground rules, the process, clarifying procedures, data gathering and how final agreements will be reached. They must then deal with differences in skills and understanding among those involved, maximize their power and influence, and manage their constituencies and coalitions.

Information

Just as it is accepted that *informed* public participation is important, information has an important role in successful mediation (Manring *et al.*, 1990). Harashina (1995) points out that both values and 'facts' are at stake, and suggests that joint fact finding by the parties helps to build a common basis of information among them. This supports a learning process among the participants, and helps to redress issues of power (through unequal access to information). While technical information can contribute to allaying misperceptions and fears, there are often debates over the validity and relevance of technical data, creating a demand for 'data mediation' (Manring *et al.*, 1990: 260). Strategies such as the parties agreeing to share all information used to support their arguments, or to base their models and predictions on a common pool of data, can help (ibid.).

Advantages of mediators

The role of mediators is to facilitate the negotiation process, both in the sense of convening the process and facilitating the discussions, and of making it progress more smoothly through additional contributions such as analysis of the conflicts. It is generally expected that their role will be a neutral one among the parties' perspectives, and that it will concentrate on helping the parties communicate effectively. This can include helping to manage power imbalances among the parties, helping all to be heard. Some studies advocate a mediation team, in which some members have expertise to help communication about technical issues. Many environmental negotiations have succeeded without facilitators, however.

Maintaining agreement

Since much of the literature has been written by mediators rather than those in a position to observe later stages, we also hear relatively little about the challenges of implementing an agreement and maintaining cooperation among the parties in doing so. Maintaining fruitful working relationships, and implementing whatever has been decided during negotiations, can be difficult. Like a marriage, an environmental negotiation can be the start of a long relationship, not concluded the day of the main event.

Contending with cross-cultural issues

The negotiation literature used to inform environmental mediation has been developed in western countries, particularly in North America. Different societies have had their own protocols for decision making and conflict resolution, often quite different to those used in contemporary negotiation (for example, Behrendt, 1995). Imposition of western communication styles can add to the many other ways in which power relationships can be unbalanced in negotiations (Ross, 1995). The same applies in public participation, and in SIA methods (O'Faircheallaigh, 1999). Further research and development would be useful to explore methods of both mediation and public participation which could suit cross-cultural situations better.

Ways mediation can be used in and with SIA and planning

Mediation is a potentially useful complement to SIA, and negotiation techniques can be used fruitfully in environmental assessment processes. For instance, Boer *et al.* (1990), in an analysis of the potential for mediation and negotiation to contribute to an Australian government inquiry process (the now defunct Resource Assessment Commission), argued that mediation techniques would be a desirable extension to its existing consultation and public participation procedures. Rather than three commissioners reaching conclusions from evidence put to them, mediation would allow the parties contesting a resource issue to interact directly and contribute to reaching solutions to the environmental conflicts. Using mediation selectively within an impact assessment process could take SIA from being largely reactive (anticipating positive and negative impacts, and reporting these to decision makers who, it is hoped, take account of problems) to being proactive. When conditions are promising for successful negotiation, those affected could join in evaluating the extent of impacts – hopefully using SIA research as an information base – and finding mutually acceptable solutions.

Creating joint visions

Stakeholder participation processes have been used as a basis for land-use planning, for instance in bringing parties together to define a common vision for a future (Helling, 1998). Where environmental mediation commonly focuses on settling disputes, planning techniques such as visioning, when combined with stakeholder analysis and public participation or mediation, can help parties to focus on what they have in common and to create a desired future they can share. For example, in Cape York Peninsula, northern Australia, Indigenous Australians, pastoralists and conservation groups met to discuss ways in which they could cooperate in promoting land-uses for the Cape. The result was the Cape York Land Use Heads of

Agreement (1996), a set of principles and an action plan which accommodated the parties' mutual interests. This was a landmark in cooperation among these formerly conflicting groups. State government was not invited to be a party to the initial agreement, and had difficulty with a number of the proposals. This led to a lack of support for their implementation.

Strategic perspectives analysis
Dale and Lane (1994) describe the strategic perspectives analysis (SPA) method, intended for use in planning, and to proceed to negotiation. In SPA, interviews or workshops are held with members of each stakeholder group, to identify and compare each party's goals, and perceived opportunities and constraints with regard to achieving those goals. This has much in common with dispute analysis and 'conflict mapping' (Cornelius and Faire, 1989). The steps in conflict mapping are to frame the issue(s) in a clear statement, identify the parties involved in that issue, and then describe the needs and fears of each of those parties. The emphasis on needs, rather than positions, highlights Fisher and Ury's (1981) recommendation to focus on underlying needs, not stated positions, in negotiation.

Conclusion
For practitioners of EIA and SIA, environmental mediation can be viewed as a useful part of the repertoire of public participation techniques, and as an opportunity to link processes so that SIA is used to inform negotiations (O'Faircheallaigh, 1999). The research base on environmental mediation can enhance that on public participation methods, and vice versa. Mediation could be used to enhance methods in SIA, by tightening public participation in the analytical SIA process, and by moving from stand-alone assessment of impacts to incorporate equitable processes towards deciding solutions to the impacts. Even where there is substantial overlap between public participation and mediation methods, as in the stronger forms of public participation, conscious choices should be made as to the labelling of the process. Negotiations can appear to be favouring some parties, and excluding others. It can also carry connotations of needing to reach closure on a matter, and perhaps to compromise, which are less likely to apply in public participation.

As in the choices between mediation and litigation, there are circumstances where mediation is usefully associated with impact assessment, and circumstances where it will not be the optimum approach. Other forms of public participation remain available, and impact assessment can be conducted without any mediated elements. Where the parties have opposing values which do not lend themselves to any compromise, let alone 'win–win' solutions, they may prefer a statutory decision maker to decide (especially if they feel their views have at least been heeded in a process they consider legitimate). The timing of the process and maturation of the conflicts makes a difference. Where the issues may not be 'ripe' for negotiation, the timing may be better for a more open-ended participatory approach. Where the relationships among key parties may be too polarized to make negotiation in good faith feasible, other participatory processes can be designed to put less pressure on the relationships, or even to avoid the need for the parties to interact directly. Regardless of the choices for any occasion, awareness of the experience from environmental mediation can enrich our practice of impact assessment and public participation in it.

References

Arnstein, S.R. 1969. 'A Ladder of Citizen Participation', *Journal of the American Institute of Planners*, 35(4): 216–24.

Banks, G. 2000. 'Social impact assessment monitoring and household surveys', in L.R. Goldman (ed.), *Social Impact Analysis: An Applied Anthropology Manual*, Oxford: Berg, 297–343.

Becker, H. 1997. *Social Impact Assessment: method and experience in Europe, North America and the Developing World*, London: UCL Press.

Behrendt, L. 1995. *Aboriginal dispute resolution*, Sydney: The Federation Press.

Bingham, G. 1986. *Resolving environmental disputes: a decade of experience*, Washington, DC: The Conservation Foundation.

Boer, B., Craig, D., Handmer, J. and Ross, H. 1990. *The use of mediation in the Resource Assessment Commission Inquiry process*, Resource Assessment Commission, Canberra: Australian Government Publishing Service.

Branch, K. and Ross, H. 2000. 'Scoping for Social Impact Assessment', in L.R. Goldman (ed.), *Social Impact Analysis: An Applied Anthropology Manual*, Oxford: Berg, 93–126.

Burdge, R.J. and Vanclay, F. 1995. 'Social Impact Assessment', in F. Vanclay and D. Bronstein (eds), *Environmental and Social Impact Assessment*, Chichester: Wiley, 31–66.

Cornelius, H. and Faire, S. 1989. *Everyone can win: how to resolve conflict*, Sydney: Simon and Schuster.

Craig & Ehrlich Ltd, Ross, H., Lane M. and Northern Land Council 1996. *Indigenous participation in environmental impact assessment*, Agency Review of Commonwealth Environmental Impact Assessment report series, Canberra: Commonwealth Environment Protection Agency.

Crowfoot, J.E. and Wondolleck, J.M. 1990. *Environmental disputes: community involvement in conflict resolution*, Washington, DC: Island Press.

Dale, A.P. and Lane, M.B. 1994. 'Strategic perspectives analysis: a procedure for participatory and political SIA', *Society and Natural Resources*, 7(3): 253–67.

De Lacy, T. 1994. 'The Uluru/Kakadu Model – Anangu Tjukurrpa: 50,000 years of Aboriginal law and land management changing the concept of national parks in Australia', *Society and Natural Resources*, 7(5): 479–98.

Delli Priscoli, J. 1987. 'Conflict Resolution for Water Resource Projects: Using Facilitation and Mediation to Write Section 404 General Permits', *Environmental Impact Assessment Review*, 7(4): 313–26.

Fisher, R. and Ury, W. 1981. *Getting to Yes: Negotiating agreement without giving in*, Boston: Houghton Mifflin.

Gray, B. 1989. *Collaborating: Finding Common Ground for Multiparty Problems*, San Francisco: Jossey-Bass.

Harashina, S. 1995. 'Environmental dispute resolution process and information exchange', *Environmental Impact Assessment Review*, 15(1): 69–80.

Hawke, S. and Gallagher, M. 1989. *Noonkanbah: Whose Land, Whose Law?*, Freemantle: Freemantle Arts Centre Press.

Healey, P. 1997. *Collaborative Planning: shaping places in fragmented societies*, Basingstoke: Macmillan.

Helling, A. 1998. 'Collaborative visioning: Proceed with caution!: Results from evaluating Atlanta's Vision 2020 project', *Journal of the American Planning Association*, 64(3): 335–49.

Holden, A. 1998. 'Cultural and Social Impact Assessment of Joint Management at Uluru-Kata Tjuta National Park', Office for Joint Management, Mutitjulu Community, Mutitjulu, Northern Territory, Australia.

Ingram, H. 1998. 'Environmental consensus-building and conflict resolution in the UK', in C. Napier (ed.), *Environmental conflict resolution*, London: Cameron May, 112–57.

Lane, M., Ross, H. and Dale, A. 1997. 'Social impact research: integrating the technical, political and planning paradigms', *Human Organization*, 56(3): 302–10.

Manring, N., West, P.C. and Bidol, P. 1990. 'Social impact assessment and environmental conflict management', *Environmental Impact Assessment Review*, 10(2/3): 253–65.

Modavi, N. 1996. 'Mediation of environmental conflicts in Hawaii', *Sociological Perspectives*, 39(2): 301–16.

Moore, S.A. 1996. 'Defining "successful" environmental dispute resolution', *Environmental Impact Assessment Review*, 16(3): 151–69.

Mulvihill, P.R. and Jacobs, P. 1998. 'Using scoping as a design process', *Environmental Impact Assessment Review*, 18(4): 351–69.

Napier, C. 1998. 'The practice of mediation in commercial environmental disputes', in C. Napier (ed.), *Environmental conflict resolution*, London: Cameron May, 198–208.

O'Faircheallaigh, C. 1995. 'Negotiations between mining companies and Aboriginal communities: process and structure' (discussion paper no. 86), Centre for Aboriginal Economic Policy Research, Australian National University, Canberra.

O'Faircheallaigh, C. 1999. 'Making social impact assessment count: a negotiation-based approach for Indigenous peoples', *Society and Natural Resources*, 12(1): 63–80.

O'Leary, R. 1997. 'Environmental mediation and public managers: what do we know and how do we know it?' (Indiana Conflict Resolution Institute Research Paper), University of Indiana, Bloomington.

Osherenko, G. 1988. 'Sharing the power with native users: co-management regimes for Arctic wildlife' (Canadian Arctic Policy Paper no 5), Canadian Arctic Resources Committee, Ottawa.

Parenteau, R. 1988. *Public Participation in Environmental Decision-making*, Ottawa: Federal Environmental Assessment Review Office.

Pinkerton, E. (ed.) 1989. *Cooperative Management of Local Fisheries*, University of British Columbia Press, Vancouver.

Pinkerton, E. 1992. 'Translating legal rights into management practice', *Human Organization*, 51(4): 330–41.

Roberts, R. 1995. 'Public involvement: from consultation to participation', in F. Vanclay and D.A. Bronstein (eds), *Environmental and Social Impact Assessment*, Chichester: Wiley, 221–46.

Ross, H. 1990. 'Community Social Impact Assessment: a framework for Indigenous peoples', *Environmental Impact Assessment Review*, 10(1/2): 185–93.

Ross, H. 1995. 'Aboriginal Australians' cultural norms for negotiating natural resources', *Cultural Survival Quarterly*, 19(3): 33–8.

Ross, H. 1999. 'New ethos, new solutions: lessons from Washington's co-operative environmental management agreements', *Australian Indigenous Law Reporter*, 4(2): 1–28.

Sadler, B. 1987. 'Building mediation into the Federal Environmental Assessment and Review Process', in B. Sadler and A. Armour (eds), *The place of negotiation in environmental assessment*, Hull: Canadian Environmental Assessment Research Council, 75–83.

Sandford, R. 1990. 'Environmental dispute resolution in Tasmania', *Environmental and Planning Law Journal*, 19(1): 19–29.

Schneider, P. and Tohn, E. 1985. 'Success in negotiating environmental regulations', *Environmental Impact Assessment Review*, 5(1): 67–77.

Sipe, N. and Stiftel, B. 1995. 'Mediating environmental enforcement disputes: how well does it work?', *Environmental Impact Assessment Review*, 15(2): 139–56.

Susskind, L. and Secunda, J. 1998. 'Environmental conflict resolution: the American experience', in C. Napier (ed.), *Environmental conflict resolution*, London: Cameron May, 16–55.

Taylor, C.N., Bryan, C.H. and Goodrich, C.G. 1995. *Social assessment: theory, process and techniques* (2nd edn), Christchurch, New Zealand: Taylor Baines and Associates.

Toyne, P. and Vachon, D. 1987. *Growing up the country: the Pitjantjatjara struggle for their land*, Melbourne: McPhee Gribble and Penguin.

Waldo, J. 1988. 'Redefining winning: the TFW process', *Forest Planning Canada*, 4(3): 14–19.

Wandersman, A. 1979. 'User participation in planning environments: a conceptual framework', *Environment and Behaviour*, 11(4): 465–82.

Woenne-Green, S., Johnston, R., Sultan, R. and Wallis, A. 1994. *Competing interests: Aboriginal participation in national parks and conservation reserves in Australia*, Melbourne: Australian Conservation Foundation.

Wondolleck, J.M., Manring N.J. and Crowfoot, J.E. 1996. 'Teetering at the top of the ladder: the experience of citizen's group participants in alternative dispute resolution processes', *Sociological Perspectives*, 39(2): 249–62.

Index